Morality without Foundations

Morality without Foundations

A Defense of Ethical Contextualism

Mark Timmons

New York   Oxford
Oxford University Press
1999

Oxford University Press

Oxford   New York
Athens   Auckland   Bangkok   Bogota   Buenos Aires   Calcutta
Cape Town   Chennai   Dar es Salaam   Delhi   Florence   Hong Kong   Istanbul
Karachi   Kuala Lumpur   Madrid   Melbourne   Mexico City   Mumbai
Nairobi   Paris   São Paulo   Singapore   Taipei   Tokyo   Toronto   Warsaw

and associated companies in
Berlin   Ibadan

Library of Congress Cataloging-in-Publication Data
Timmons, Mark, 1951–
Morality without foundations :
a defense of ethical contextualism
/Mark Timmons.
p.   cm.
Includes bibliographical references and index.
ISBN 0-19-511731-X (cloth)
1. Ethics.   2. Naturalism.   I. Title.
BJ37.T55   1998
170'.42 — dc21   97-26312

1 3 5 7 9 8 6 4 2

Printed in the United States of America
on acid-free paper

To my parents, Jean and Marilyn,
who provided a foundation,

and to Betsy,
for her love and support.

Preface

My main purpose in writing this book was to gain a better understanding of philosophical issues and questions about the status of morality. I am as much interested in questions of philosophical methodology as I am in the substantive philosophical positions that philosophers articulate and defend. I have thus tried to produce a book that is clearly written and methodologically self-conscious. I have also tried to stake out a metaethical position that is not obviously on the menu of standard metaethical options (though its similarity in many respects to the views of certain other metaethical irrealists will be apparent). Since I wanted the book to be relatively short, I have zeroed in on opposing views and arguments that strike me as providing the clearest and stiffest challenges to the sort of irrealist metaethical view I defend in the pages to follow. My hope is that I have managed to get to the heart of things in making a case for the sort of metaethical view that I favor. I will let the reader judge whether and to what extent I have succeeded in doing these things.

In the recent years that I have been working out the ideas contained in this book, I have benefited from comments and criticisms on part or all of this book from Robert Audi, John Bickle, William Frankena, Michael Gorr, Mitchell Haney, R. M. Hare, William Connolly, Stephan Sencerz, William Throop, and William Tolhurst. I have also benefited greatly from discussions with and written comments from my colleagues David Henderson and John Tienson. The written comments I received from Michael DePaul and Walter Sinnott-Armstrong were very useful in helping me to improve the clarity and content of this work.

I owe my greatest debt to friend and colleague Terry Horgan, who not only coauthored with me a number of articles whose contents have found their way into this book but with whom I have had many useful and illuminating philosophical discussions about ideas, themes, and arguments contained in the chapters to follow. In particular, much of chapter 4, in which I set out an irrealist moral semantics, derives from a paper, "Taking a Moral Stance," that I coauthored with Terry and which we presented at a conference in honor of the retirement of

R. M. Hare from the University of Florida ("Hare's Heritage: The Impact of R. M. Hare on Contemporary Philosophy," March 1994).

I mentioned that my metaethical position bears some resemblance to the views of other irrealists. The view about moral semantics that I defend is quite similar in some respects to the views of R. M. Hare and Simon Blackburn. Terry and I worked out various details of the semantic view with an eye on Hare's work, particularly his 1952 book *The Language of Morals*. I later discovered just how similar some aspects of the view are to some of the details of Blackburn's so-called quasi-realist treatment of moral discourse (which is particularly evident in his 1996 work "Securing the Nots: Moral Epistemology for the Quasi-Realist"). However, there are some important differences between the Horgan and Timmons semantic view and the views of Hare and Blackburn, some of them indicated in the text.

Some of the material in various chapters is taken from the following articles: "Troubles on Moral Twin Earth: Moral Queerness Revived" (with Terry Horgan), *Synthese* 92 (1992); pp. 221–60; "New Wave Moral Realism Meets Moral Twin Earth" (with Terry Horgan), *Journal of Philosophical Research* 16 (1991), pp. 447–65, reprinted in *Rationality, Morality, and Self-Interest*, J. Heil (ed.), Rowman & Littlefield, 1993; "Troubles for New Wave Moral Semantics: The 'Open Question Argument' Revived" (with Terry Horgan), *Philosophical Papers* 21 (1993), pp. 153–75; "Irrealism and Error in Ethics," *Philosophia* 22 (1992), pp. 373–406; "Outline of a Contextualist Moral Epistemology," in W. Sinnott-Armstrong and M. Timmons (eds.), *Moral Knowledge? New Readings in Moral Epistemology*, Oxford: Oxford University Press, 1996; "Moral Justification in Context," *The Monist* 76 (1993), pp. 360–78. I wish to thank the various editors for permission to use material from these publications.

Finally, I wish to thank Robert Milks, production editor at Oxford University Press, for his help in guiding this book to press. And I wish to thank Linda Sadler, production editor for the *Southern Journal of Philosophy*, for her generous help in preparing the manuscript for publication.

Contents

Morality without Foundations

Introduction

This book addresses fundamental metaphysical, semantic, and epistemological questions about moral discourse and practice—so-called *metaethical questions*. In recent years, there has been a rebirth of interest in metaethical issues after a couple of decades of relative inactivity, and metaethical inquiry is again in full swing. If we compare recent metaethical inquiry with metaethical inquiry as it was practiced during the bygone era of analytic philosophy, we notice a change in how metaethics is conceived and practiced.

From around the turn of this century, beginning with the work of G. E. Moore and into the 1950s, metaethics was primarily focused on the analysis of moral language. Metaethical inquiry during this period was preoccupied with questions about whether or not moral terms, and sentences containing such terms, could be reductively analyzed into terms and sentences of some other sort and, if so, what sort. Philosophers divided on these questions, some arguing that moral terms and sentences could not be reductively analyzed, others arguing that they could. The predictable result was an outpouring of competing metaethical views ranging from the non-naturalism of Moore, W. D. Ross, and A. C. Ewing, to the brands of non-descriptivism defended by A. J. Ayer, C. L. Stevenson, and R. M. Hare. However, despite these metaethical disagreements, the work of philosophers at this time was guided by general views about semantic analysis and about proper philosophical methodology. In short, semantic analysis was understood to involve investigation into analytic meaning connections—an investigation that was supposed to yield necessary truths about what our terms mean. Consequently, proper philosophical methodology was thought to differ markedly from the empirical methods of the sciences; philosophical investigation was essentially a priori. These guiding philosophical assumptions about the proper content and methodology of philosophy put severe limits on all philosophical inquiry, including, of course, metaethical inquiry. But times have changed.

By around the mid-1950s, the various recognized metaethical options had been more or less played out, and increasingly, philosophers began to see metaethics as a rather dull and sterile exercise having little bearing on more substantive moral issues. Moreover, at the same time, philosophers were beginning to question some of the deeply embedded assumptions of analytic philosophy, assumptions about semantic analysis and about proper philosophical methodology. To question the tenability of the guiding assumptions of analytic philosophy was, of course, to question the tenability of those metaethical theories resting on those assumptions. The metaethical theories from the analytic period seemed to rest on shaky ground. Nevertheless, during this same time of philosophical uncertainty and changing climate, developments in such areas of philosophy as metaphysics, the philosophy of language, the philosophy of mind, and epistemology emerged. These developments helped create a new philosophical climate that allowed metaethical questions to be reexamined in a new philosophical light. Of particular importance here is the fact that constraints on proper philosophical methodology were considerably loosened, philosophical inquiry was coming to be viewed as continuous with scientific investigation, and thus projects in metaphysics, semantics, and epistemology were no longer viewed in quite so narrow a manner as was characteristic of analytic philosophy.

The effects of these changes in philosophical climate are particularly evident in connection with a philosophical program associated with philosophical naturalism. To put it roughly, philosophical naturalism is the view that all that exists — including any particulars, events, facts, properties, and so on — is part of the natural, material world that science investigates. This general philosophical outlook generates a philosophical program, namely, the program of accommodating all sorts of phenomena — for example, mental phenomena, moral phenomena, aesthetic phenomena — in terms of this metaphysical stance. In the former days of analytic philosophy, this project of *naturalistic accommodation* was severely constrained by the generally accepted views about proper content and methodology of philosophy. So, for instance, in order to naturalistically accommodate moral properties and facts, it was believed that one must be able to provide analytic definitions of key moral terms and expressions — a project that seemed to most philosophers quite implausible.

We now find ourselves in what may fairly be called a post-analytic era in which, as I have said, constraints on proper content and methodology have been considerably loosened. Narrowly conceived reductive programs have given way to programs with relaxed, more reasonable standards of naturalistic accommodation. So, for example, it is no longer believed that naturalistic accommodation of moral phenomena requires reductive analytic definitions of moral terms and expressions; the road to naturalistic accommodation is not so hard. In these kinder, gentler philosophical times, we find the emergence of new metaethical theories and, in particular, metaethical theories that tackle the project of naturalistically accommodating moral phenomena freed from older, implausibly narrow constraints on carrying out this project. This book, which takes seriously the project of naturalistically accommodating moral discourse and practice, is meant to contribute usefully to the current philosophical dialogue over the nature and status of morality in these post-analytic times.

In *Morality without Foundations*, my central aim is to articulate and defend a metaethical theory that I will call *ethical contextualism*. My work engages the recent metaethical debate between moral realists on the one hand, who defend the idea that morality is objective (in a fairly strong sense of that term), and moral irrealists on the other who argue that morality is not objective, at least not in the way the realist thinks. I side with the irrealists.

To give the reader an idea of what is contained in the chapters to follow, here is a brief overview, chapter by chapter.

First, in chapter 1, I explain the methodological assumptions that constrain metaethical theorizing. Put most generally, metaethical inquiry is engaged in the dual project of accommodating both the deeply embedded commonsense presumptions of moral discourse and practice, as well as any well-supported general assumptions, theories, and views from other areas of inquiry. Given the plausibility of a naturalistic worldview, I construe the project of accommodation as being constrained by the general metaphysical and epistemological commitments of naturalism. So my investigation of metaethical questions is guided by the project of naturalistically accommodating moral discourse and practice.

Second, having placed my methodological cards on the table, I focus on a recent version of moral realism engaged in the project of naturalistic accommodation, namely, the version defended by, for example, David Brink, Richard Boyd, and Nicholas Sturgeon. These philosophers have ably marshaled various resources mined from recent work in metaphysics, philosophy of language, philosophy of mind, and epistemology, in the articulation and defense of a new strain of moral realism that is apparently immune from problems besetting older, more traditional versions of this view. This "new wave" version of moral realism is arguably the most plausible current version of moral realism. However, despite the ingenuity of its advocates in defending this view, new wave moral realism has an Achilles' heel. I argue that (1) in order to fully discharge its accommodation obligations, and thus avoid J. L. Mackie–style queerness objections, these realists seemingly must rely on the sort of causal moral semantics that we find in Boyd, but that (2) causal moral semantics is implausible.

Finally, if moral realism is rejected, what are the prospects for defending a plausible version of moral irrealism? Realists have convincingly argued that standard versions of moral irrealism that would attempt to 'reduce' moral and evaluative notions to non-moral and non-evaluative notions cannot accommodate some of the most deeply embedded commonsense presumptions of moral discourse and practice. The most powerful such criticism (I contend) is the *argument from moral error*, according to which irrealism is not able to accommodate the presumption that error in moral judgment is always, in principle, possible. In chapter 3, I argue that standard, reductive versions of moral irrealism cannot fully answer this objection, and so the irrealist should explore the possibility of developing a non-reductive version of her view. The rest of the book is an elaboration and defense of irrealism that avoids the reductive pretensions of more traditional irrealist views in metaethics.

In chapter 4, I begin my defense of ethical contextualism — a version of non-reductive moral irrealism that incorporates a *contextualist moral semantics* and associated *contextualist moral epistemology*. Contextualist moral semantics exploits a quite general semantic view — contextual semantics — which construes semantic notions as normative and context-sensitive. On the general view, the truth of a moral claim is a matter of its *correct assertibility* (where the notion of correct assertibility, though normative, is not an epistemic notion and so is not equivalent to warranted assertibility). Furthermore, norms for the correct assertibility of moral claims are not monolithic; indeed, they vary from one context to another depending on which norms for semantic evaluation are being invoked in the context. For ordinary descriptive discourse that purports to represent some sort of objective reality, the contextualist holds that the truth of a sentence is a matter of the semantic norms (governing the correct use of the terms and expressions the sentence contains) conspiring with the world to yield determinate correct assertibility of the sentence in the context. However, my critique of moral realism and certain brands of irrealism, especially versions of moral relativism, shows that moral discourse is not primarily descriptive discourse. And so we face the question of how to understand, in terms of the general contextualist semantic picture, this sort of non-descriptive discourse.

Contextualist moral semantics, then, attempts to spell out a plausible (and appropriately non-reductive) semantic story for moral discourse. Some of the main ideas of the story I end up telling include the following claims: (1) Moral discourse is fundamentally non-descriptive discourse; its primary function is not to represent some objective reality, but rather to guide personal choice and be used for guiding the behavior of others. (2) However, although moral language is non-descriptive, moral sentences are typically used to make genuine assertions. They possess genuine assertoric content, and hence are truth-apt. (3) This means that we should reject a deeply embedded assumption operating in traditional metaethical thought, namely, that all genuinely assertoric discourse is descriptive discourse. (4) I advocate rejecting this assumption and consequently admitting that, in addition to there being discourses that have genuine descriptive assertoric content, there are discourses (like moral discourse) that have genuine *evaluative assertoric content*—moral sentences are used (primarily) to make genuine evaluative assertions. (5) In elaborating a semantical story about moral discourse that recognizes evaluative assertoric content, I recommend that we (a) focus on the primary point or purpose of the discourse to gain illumination of its semantical workings and (b) that in making sense of how the truth predicate operates in this kind of discourse we exploit some of the so-called minimalist themes in recent philosophy of language that we find in such writers as Paul Horwich and Crispin Wright.

The semantic package represented by contextualist moral semantics is very much in the spirit of the views of traditional non-descriptivists (particularly the early views of Hare), but in important ways parts company with the traditionalists. The overall result, I argue, is a metaethical view about the metaphysics and associated semantics of moral discourse that is quite plausible when evaluated in terms of the dual accommodation aims that guide metaethical inquiry generally.

In chapter 5, I complete my account by defending a contextualist version of moral justification. Epistemological contextualism, which concerns the justification of moral belief (i.e., so-called doxastic justification), is an alternative to more traditional foundationalist and coherentist views. About moral justification, the contextualist agrees with the foundationalist in maintaining that there are moral beliefs that are epistemically basic in providing the grounds for the justification of other, non-basic moral beliefs, but also agrees with the coherentist in maintaining that there are no intrinsically justified beliefs that can serve as a monolithic foundation for a system of moral knowledge. The ethical contextualist holds that there are *contextually basic moral beliefs* that can serve as an adequate basis for coming to have all sorts of non-basic moral convictions and beliefs. Contextually basic beliefs are often moral generalizations like 'Lying is prima facie wrong,' 'Intentionally harming others is prima facie wrong,' and so forth, that play the following epistemic role in our lives: (1) In an engaged context of moral thought and deliberation, these general moral beliefs do not need justification, although they serve (in the context) as the ultimate basis of justified moral belief. (2) Moral beliefs that are contextually basic in the sense just described can be called into question in other, less morally engaged contexts as, for example, when philosophers and social critics question ordinary moral convictions. I argue that this sort of view can accommodate (unlike its competitors) the commonsense presumption that many ordinary adults are fully justified in a good many of their moral beliefs.

In the end, I argue that the overall metaethical package I offer can satisfy both accommodation aims reasonably well: first, the view fits nicely with a naturalistic worldview, and second, it can accommodate the commonsense presumptions of moral thought and practice. I thus argue that my version of ethical contextualism represents a plausible metaethical view without needing to look for a metaphysical foundation in some realm of moral facts and without needing to find some unshakable epistemological foundation upon which to rest our justified moral beliefs. In short, we get a philosophical account of morality *without foundations*.

1

Metaethics and Methodology

In this chapter, my central aim is to clarify the sorts of second-order, metaethical issues and arguments that this book is about. In the past decade or so, significant changes have taken place in just how metaethics is conceived and practiced. These changes in conceptions of the content and method of metaethical inquiry are important for reasons that will become apparent as we proceed. So it will be useful to spend part of this chapter going over some metaethical history and explaining, in broad outline, the methodological approach to be followed in this book.

I begin in §I by contrasting metaethics with normative ethics, and then move on in §II to describe the most fundamental aims of metaethical inquiry. In §III, I consider the project of philosophical naturalism, a project that has dominated much philosophical inquiry in recent years, and that will guide the inquiry of this book. In §IV, I provide a characterization of *analytic metaethics*—representing a conception of metaethics that more or less dominated thinking in this area from about 1900 to the mid-1970s. Since the narrowly conceived subject matter and methodology of analytic metaethics has all but disappeared from the philosophical scene, in §V, I briefly describe the motivation for rejecting analytic metaethics and how metaethical inquiry is conceived in these post-analytic times. Having thus set forth the methodological constraints that will guide our inquiry, we will be ready for the chapters to come.

I. Normative Ethics and Metaethics

Used as a term for a particular discipline, 'ethics' refers to that area of philosophy that inquires into morality. It is standard to distinguish two general sorts of philosophical question one might raise regarding morality: first-order moral questions and second-order questions about morality. Let us briefly consider each in turn.

First-order moral questions are about the moral status of persons, actions, institutions, practices, and the like. Providing answers to such questions is to engage in what is called *normative ethics*. Within normative ethics, it is standard to distinguish between questions of theory and questions about specific moral issues. Normative ethical theory attempts to provide answers to very general normative questions — questions like:

> What features of actions make them either morally right or morally wrong?
> What characteristics of persons make them morally good or bad?
> What features of things, events, and states of affairs make them good or bad?

Usually, philosophers attempt to answer such questions by formulating principles of right conduct and principles of value or goodness that purport to state the most general conditions under which actions are to be judged right or wrong, persons are to be judged as having or lacking moral worth, and states of affairs are to be properly classified as being intrinsically good or bad. Mill's principle of utility, according to which, in his own words, "actions are right in proportion as they tend to promote happiness, wrong as they tend to produce the reverse of happiness" (Mill, 1861: 10), is one well-known principle of right conduct. Kant's categorical imperative, which states, "We must be able to will that a maxim of our actions should become a universal law" (Kant, 1785: 91), is another. Again, the principle of hedonism claims that only states of pleasure are intrinsically good and only states of pain are intrinsically bad. Such principles or generalizations are taken to provide one with a normative theory about right and wrong action, intrinsic value, and so forth.

Investigation of such theoretical first-order questions is supposedly important for providing clear and well-supported answers to moral questions about specific actions, persons, and states of affairs. Of particular interest are those moral quandaries concerning such activities as abortion, euthanasia, preferential hiring, capital punishment, treatment of animals, and a host of other perplexing moral issues that seem to resist any easy resolution. According to a standard textbook view of the matter, a quite ordinary source of interest in moral reflection results from interpersonal or perhaps intrapersonal conflict of belief or conviction in connection with difficult moral issues. Confronted with such conflict, the reflective person is led to ask moral questions of a more general sort — the sort of questions normative moral theory attempts to answer. So a very common order of inquiry (guided by practical interests to resolve conflicts of moral belief and conviction) leads from specific moral issues to normative theory. The hope is that by providing answers to first-order theoretical questions — questions about the basis of right and wrong, good and bad — one can use the results (typically expressed as moral principles) and descend from the level of theory to resolve specific moral problems.

But, of course, there turn out to be competing normative moral theories, and so the reflective person will be led to ask which (if any) of the competing theories is correct. That is, one is naturally led to raise questions about theory acceptance in ethics. And questions about theory acceptance move one from asking first-order questions to asking non-moral questions about competing moral theories. Of particular concern are questions about the nature and possibility of justifying or validating moral statements. Given the fundamental role of moral principles in justifying specific moral statements, the focus thus tends to be on the nature and possibility of justifying or validating moral principles, of adjudicating from among competing normative moral theories. Questions about adjudicating among competing normative theories are second-order questions — questions about first-order moral discourse and practice that are studied by those engaged in metaethical reflection. Metaethical questions include the following:

> How (if at all) can moral judgments be rationally supported or justified?
> Are there moral facts and properties that moral discourse is about?
> If so, what sorts of facts and properties are they — psychological? sociological? biological? a combination of these? Or are they facts and properties of a non-scientific kind?
> Are moral judgments true or false in the way in which ordinary judgments about objects and events are true or false?
> What do moral judgments mean as ordinarily used?

In what follows, I want to consider the questions and methods of metaethics in a bit more detail, beginning with some general remarks about the aims of metaethical inquiry.

II. Metaethics and Accommodation Projects

I begin with an unvarnished statement of the central aims guiding metaethical inquiry. My formulation of these aims, and the associated accommodation projects they involve, will be refined as we proceed.

A philosophical interpretation of moral discourse and practice that purports to answer metaethical questions about that discourse is usually guided by one or both of the following desiderata. First, one may be guided in one's metaethical investigation into moral discourse by various assumptions deeply embedded in people's ordinary use of that discourse. The idea is to interpret the discourse in a manner that comports with so-called commonsense assumptions of that discourse; in other words, one wants to be able to *accommodate* those commonsense assumptions. So there are features of ordinary moral discourse — for example, it is (or appears to be) fact-stating; we take there to be right answers to many moral questions; and so forth — that should (if possible) be accommodated by a plausible story about such discourse.

One may also approach the discourse in question from some philosophical perspective that involves very general metaphysical and epistemological commitments. The general commitments guide inquiry into the discourse, and so the aim is to *accommodate* the discourse in question to those commitments reflecting one's philosophical worldview. In other words, the aim is to construe the metaphysical and epistemological commitments of the discourse in a way that comports with one's general philosophical view. One dominant brand of accommodation project (which guides my own metaethical inquiry) involves commitment to philosophical naturalism. (I say more about the particular accommodation project associated with philosophical naturalism in later sections.)

Since the first sort of project involves looking to linguistic and non-linguistic phenomena internal to moral discourse and practice, I call the first project one of *internal accommodation*. Since the second project looks to assumptions and theories outside of moral discourse and practice, I refer to it as the project of *external accommodation*. So, speaking very generally, metaethical theorizing is typically taken to be constrained by these two (roughly formulated) desiderata:

> D1 A plausible metaethical view should comport with deeply embedded presumptions of ordinary moral discourse and practice. This guides the project of internal accommodation.

> D2 A plausible metaethical view should comport with plausible general views and assumptions from other relevant areas of inquiry. This guides the project of external accommodation.[1]

Although some philosophers have only concerned themselves with one or the other of these accommodation projects, ideally one should work toward satisfying the desiderata associated with both projects. Granted, there is no guarantee that one's efforts at accommodation will satisfy both of these aims; in some cases, success with one accommodation project can only be purchased at the expense of the other. However, in judging competing attempts at accommodation, any view that does a better job than its rivals at both accommodation projects is the more adequate metaethical view.

Of course, talk of one view *comporting* with another or, equivalently, of the *accommodation* of one view by another, is quite vague and intended to capture a certain pre-theoretic idea or intuition. Just what counts as one view comporting with another is something that is up for discussion and clarification, though certainly those engaged in accommodation projects in metaethics have generally sought to *explain* either the commonsense assumptions of moral discourse or the metaphysical and epistemological commitments of such discourse, or both. Again, the operative notion of explanation needs to be clarified, and over the course of twentieth-century metaethics, constraints on what counts as acceptable explanation and hence accommodation, particularly in connection with D2, have altered along with changes in the general philosophical climate. Before recounting these changes, let us consider the specific accommodation program — the program of external accommodation — associated with D2 that guides my inquiry in this book.

III. Philosophical Naturalism

I take the naturalist outlook in philosophy to be, at bottom, a metaphysical or, more precisely, an ontological view about the nature of what exists. The vague, pre-theoretic idea that the philosophical naturalist tries to articulate and defend is that everything — including any particulars, events, facts, properties, and so on — is part of the natural, physical world that science investigates. Although I take philosophical naturalism for granted in this book, this outlook should not be viewed as a mere assumption or brute article of faith.[2] The undeniable attraction

---

1. For a particularly nice illustration of the project of external accommodation, see Benacerraf's discussion of mathematical truth. Part of his concern is with "how to fit mathematical knowledge into an over-all epistemology" (1973: 669).
2. For more on the contingent status of metaphysical naturalism, see Kornblith, 1994.

of this outlook in contemporary philosophy no doubt stems from the rise of modern science and the belief that science is our best avenue for discovering the nature of reality. Summing up the reasons for taking the current scientific view of the nature of reality as our best guide to what there is, Brian Ellis writes:

> [T]here is no other body of knowledge which is as well supported or attested, as thoroughly checked, as precise and detailed in its predictions, as comprehensive and systematic in its explanations, or as satisfying intellectually. Moreover, the practice of science, and the body of knowledge it has yielded, are the products of a long history of inquiry by many thousands of dedicated men and women, operating with a code of honesty and objectivity, or reporting designed precisely to yield objective knowledge of the world, i.e. knowledge which is independent of creed, political interest and authority. One would have to have very good reasons indeed, or be very arrogant, not to accept the scientific viewpoint on questions of ontology as the best there is. (Ellis, 1990: 19)

When we add to this the fact that science seems to provide strong evidence for supposing that we live in a thoroughly natural universe, we can summarize the attraction of philosophical naturalism by saying, quoting Hilary Putnam, that this outlook purports to be "metaphysics within the bounds of science" (Putnam, 1983a: 210).[3]

The naturalist begins with an ontological presumption about what sorts of particulars, entities, and so forth are fundamental, which can be roughly captured in the following *thesis of ontic primacy*:

> N1   The ontologically primary or fundamental entities (properties, facts, etc.) in the world are all part of the subject matter of science.[4]

Although N1, as expressed, does not commit one to a naturalist metaphysical view (since, after all, it could turn out that our world is inhabited by, say, non-physical Cartesian egos that science would need to recognize), this thesis is taken to exclude supernatural, occult entities, facts, and events, as well as the instantiation of any

---

3. Wilfrid Sellars expressed the idea when he wrote that "science is the measure of all things, of what is that it is, and of what is not that it is not" (1963: 173).

4. Two comments are in order. First, I have stated the thesis of ontic primacy without supposing that naturalism is committed to what some philosophers call 'physicalism'—the view that all that exists is restricted to the entities, properties, and events that are the subject matter of physics. The thesis is meant to allow the entities, properties, and events studied in chemistry, biology, geology, and other sciences to have ontological recognition, though most contemporary naturalists characterize naturalism as involving a certain ontological hierarchy according to which microphysical entities are most fundamental, and phenomena studied by the other sciences bear a certain relationship (e.g., identity, constitution, or realization) to the phenomena at the microphysical level. (See, for example, Tye, 1995: 38–43 for more on this feature of contemporary naturalism.) The second, related point I wish to make is that I have formulated N1 in a manner that is officially neutral with regard to the so-called *unity of science* thesis, i.e., the thesis that all of the 'special sciences' ultimately reduce (in some sense or other) to physics. (For a discussion on this, see Oppenheim and Putnam, 1958, and Fodor, 1974.) In this book, my interest is in ethical naturalism, and so even if the unity of science thesis is false because, say, the sciences dealing with organic things are not reducible to those sciences dealing with inorganic matter, still, if moral properties (assuming there are any) are reducible to, for instance, biological

supernatural, occult properties. In what follows, I shall understand philosophical naturalism accordingly.[5]

This broad metaphysical outlook generates a particular external accommodation project—the project of *naturalistic accommodation*. The idea is that non-scientific discourse concerning all sorts of phenomena—that is, moral discourse, aesthetic discourse, semantic discourse—makes sense, and much of it appears to be true or correct. The naturalistic accommodation project involves making sense of non-scientific discourse within the naturalist's general perspective. Prima facie, there would appear to be two ways in which some mode of discourse might be naturalistically accommodated. First, for any mode of discourse that does involve commitment to entities, properties, or facts, those entities, properties, or facts would need somehow to be accounted for or explained (and hence, accommodated) within the naturalist's metaphysical picture. If, for example, moral discourse were best interpreted as involving commitment to moral properties and facts, one might attempt to accommodate these sorts of items by arguing that they are identical to some more fundamental scientific properties and facts. However, it may be that some mode of discourse is not plausibly interpreted as involving commitment to a realm of entities, properties, or what have you. In connection with any such mode of discourse, accommodation would require that one make sense of that discourse from within the naturalist's perspective. For example, if one were to construe moral discourse as not purporting to be about any sort of moral properties or facts, one would still need to make sense of such discourse, accounting for its role in the lives of naturally evolved human beings. So the project of naturalistic accommodation that the metaphysical picture of the naturalist generates can be expressed as a *thesis of metaphysical accommodation*:

> N2   All non-scientific discourse must be accommodated from within the scientific (naturalistic) picture of the world.

Additionally, the metaphysical viewpoint and associated program embodied in N1 and N2 has typically been accompanied by a non-skeptical outlook in epistemology, according to which we have access to, and possible knowledge of, the phenomena that constitute the natural order. So, as an epistemological adjunct of the naturalist's metaphysical outlook, we should add the *thesis of epistemological accommodation*:

> N3   All knowledge (and justification) associated with non-scientific discourse must comport with the sort of naturalistic explanation we use to explain our access to, and knowledge of (and justified beliefs about), the natural, physical world generally.[6]

---

properties, then (a realist version of) ethical naturalism would have been vindicated. That is, moral properties would have been integrated into the natural world that science investigates.

5. There is a good deal more that would have to be said in order to clarify these admittedly vague remarks about philosophical naturalism, but saying this much is enough to get us started. I will refine this characterization somewhat in ch. 2.

6. In Quinean spirit, I take philosophical inquiry to differ from scientific inquiry mainly in degree of generality and abstraction, and so I construe N1–N3 as broadly empirical theses. Thus, knowledge of

So, for instance, any view that would acknowledge a mode of non-sensuous, intellectual intuition through which we are supposed to come into contact with Platonic forms, would not, according to N3, comport with philosophical naturalism.

Admittedly, these tenets of philosophical naturalism are quite vague, but they serve to convey some of the basic ideas guiding one dominant sort of accommodation program in philosophy. To clarify things, we need to know just what is involved in metaphysical and epistemological accommodation. And here we find that in the course of twentieth-century metaethical inquiry, views about acceptable naturalistic accommodation have altered as a result of changes in how philosophers have conceived of the proper content and methodology of philosophical inquiry. For purposes of clarifying the methodological assumptions of this book, it will be useful if we consider in broad outline the project of accommodation as it has evolved in this century, particularly in the field of metaethics.

IV. Analytic Metaethics

Upon examining almost a full century of metaethical inquiry, we do find that although the central questions and guiding aims of metaethical inquiry have remained more or less constant, there have been significant changes both in how the major questions are approached and in our understanding of what counts as successfully satisfying the guiding aims. Moreover, there has been an expansion of the available metaethical options. In order to conveniently call attention to some of these changes, I distinguish between what I call *analytic metaethics* and *post-analytic metaethics*. Analytic metaethics runs roughly from the work of G. E. Moore from the beginning of this century into the 1950s, though its dominance extended well into the 1970s. I date the post-analytic period beginning in the late 1970s, when, after a couple of decades of relative inactivity, metaethical inquiry once again began to flourish.

In this section, what I am interested in are the underlying assumptions about the nature of metaethical problems, methods, and doctrines distinctive of the analytic period. More precisely, I am interested in the common assumptions about metaethical problems and methodology that more or less dominated philosophical thinking during the period from around 1930 into the 1970s, when the so-called linguistic turn was in full swing.[7] Of particular interest is how the dominant assumptions of metaethical inquiry at this time constrained the project of naturalistic accommodation.

---

such theses (if they are true) will, according to my philosophical naturalism, conform to N3. That this conception of philosophical inquiry and, in particular, epistemological inquiry, though a posteriori as opposed to a priori in method, is nevertheless not committed to any objectionable form of scientism, is well argued by Haack, 1993: ch. 6.

7. Although Moore and other pre-1930s philosophers were not officially part of the linguistic turn, nevertheless their influence was strongly felt by those who took the turn. See L. J. Cohen, 1986: ch. 1.

Here is an example of a standard textbook description of what I'm calling analytic metaethics, taken from William Frankena:

> As usually conceived, meta-ethics asks the following questions. (1) What is the meaning or definition of ethical terms or concepts like "right," "wrong," "good," "bad"? Or, what is the nature, meaning, or function of judgments in which these and similar terms or concepts occur? Or, what are the rules for the use of such terms and sentences? (2) How are moral uses of such terms to be distinguished from non-moral ones? What is the meaning of "moral" as contrasted with "non-moral"? (3) What is the analysis or meaning of related terms or concepts like "action," "conscience," "free will," "intention," "promising," "excusing," "motive," "responsibility," "reason," "voluntary"? (4) Can ethical and value judgments be proved, justified, or shown valid? If so, how and in what sense? Or, what is the logic of moral reasoning and of reasoning about value? (Frankena, 1963: 78–79)[8]

The first set of three questions concerns meaning; the fourth set is about justification. Frankena goes on to make the following two points: first, questions included under 1 and 4 represent the central problems of metaethics, and second, although 4 is of primary interest, we should begin with 1, since what moral terms and sentences mean will help determine how, if at all, moral claims might be proved, justified, or validated. Thus, analytic metaethics can be characterized as involving these two tenets:

> A1   There are two central questions raised in metaethical inquiry: (1) questions about the justification of moral judgments and (2) questions about the meaning of moral discourse.

> A2   Metaethical questions about meaning are methodologically prior to questions about justification.

But there is more to analytic metaethics than what is expressed in these two tenets. In the first place, there is no mention of distinctively metaphysical and, in particular, ontological issues — issues regarding the existence and nature of moral properties, relations, and facts — though certainly the metaethical positions characteristic of the analytic period involved ontological claims. According to *moral realists* (or *objectivists*, as they were called), there are moral properties and moral facts whose existence and nature is independent of our moral beliefs, our attitudes, our conventions, and the like. *Moral irrealists* (or *subjectivists*)[9] deny such claims, holding either that there are no moral facts, or that moral facts are dependent upon human beliefs, attitudes, or conventions. No doubt, the dominance of matters linguistic and, in particular, the idea that metaphysical issues are best approached through linguistic analysis probably explains why such issues aren't mentioned by Frankena. (I come back to this point in the next section.)

---

8. See Hancock, 1974: ch. 1, for a similar characterization.

9. An unhappy label, since 'subjectivism' was and is still used to denote a particular irrealist metaethical view.

Another addition I should make to this characterization concerns the fact that underlying these tenets about subject matter and methodology are assumptions about semantic analysis and proper philosophical methodology that were deeply embedded in philosophical thought during the analytic era: assumptions about meaning and semantic analysis, and about the proper starting place for approaching philosophical problems. So to complete our characterization of analytic metaethics, we need to bring these assumptions to the surface. Let us first consider just how questions about the meaning of moral discourse were generally understood during the heyday of analytic metaethics.

Although it would be incorrect to claim that during the first half of this century those engaged in metaethics accepted one theory of meaning,[10] there does seem to have been a certain conception of semantic analysis and associated notion of meaning commonly shared by proponents of different theories of meaning. This conception of semantic analysis—what I call the *classical conception*—involved (at least in connection with metaethics) two components: one about meaning itself; the other about the nature of semantic analysis.

First, the meaning component. According to the classical conception of semantic analysis, to analyze the meaning of a term or expression involved associating with that term or expression some other term or expression that was *synonymous* with the analysandum term or expression. Sentences expressing synonymy relations thus represented a class of sentences—*analytic sentences*—whose truth was solely a matter of the meanings of the constituent terms. Analyzing the meaning of a term or expression, then, was supposed to yield an *analytic definition* of the term or expression. But not just any analytically true sentence expressing a synonymy relation between a moral term or expression and some other term or expression would count as an *analysis* of the analysandum term or expression. After all, moral terms like 'right,' 'wrong,' 'obligatory,' and 'forbidden' are interdefinable. For example, 'right,' as applied to actions, can be defined as the 'not wrong.' Finding synonyms for moral terms is easy if one picks from among the moral vocabulary.

The aim of semantic analysis as practiced by analytic metaethicists was to find (if possible) synonymy relations between moral terms and expressions on the one hand, and non-moral terms and expressions on the other, that would prove philosophically illuminating. This search for illuminating analytic definitions was presumably guided by the following considerations. First, moral terms and expressions were taken to be comparatively problematic, relative to certain other non-moral terms and expressions. Most obviously, questions about the justification of moral sentences seemed impossible to answer unless such sentences could be paraphrased into language that would allow one to raise epistemological questions that we know how to answer. Furthermore, it seemed that only those paraphrases that

---

10. For a concise survey of various conceptions of meaning prevalent at the time (e.g., referential, psychological, behavioristic), see Alston, 1963. See also Hudson, 1970: chs. 1 and 2, for a discussion of the influence of such theories of meaning on metaethical inquiry.

reflected genuine relations of synonymy would do since, after all, one would otherwise be changing the subject. To paraphrase moral sentences in this way—that
is, to 'reduce' ordinary moral discourse to some other presumably more perspic-
uous discourse—was to engage in *reductive semantics*.

So the second component of the classical approach (at least as practiced in
metaethical inquiry) involved the search for *reductive analytic definitions* of moral
language. Moreover, it is worth adding that philosophers engaged in the project
of finding reductive analytic definitions were seeking relatively compact analyses
of important philosophical and, in particular, moral terms—analyses that mentioned a relatively small set of defining conditions. And, because they were looking
for definitions of key terms and expressions, the aim was to produce analyses that
were counterexample-proof: analyses that completely specified those individually
necessary and jointly sufficient conditions for possession of the property or whatever being defined. Thus, what was being sought in reductive analytic definitions
were *illuminating*, *compact*, and *complete* analyses of terms (and the concepts they
express).

We should incorporate this classical conception of semantic analysis into our
characterization of analytic metaethics with this addition:

> A3 Semantic analysis of moral discourse involves providing (if possible) reduc-
> tive analytic definitions of moral terms and expressions.

Turning from assumptions about semantic analysis to associated assumptions
about proper philosophical methodology, the preoccupation with moral semantics
was based on the widely shared methodological assumption—reflected in A2—
that semantic analysis was a propaedeutic for dealing with philosophical problems.[11] The methodological primacy attributed to semantic issues stemmed largely
from the conviction that progress on philosophical questions (stressed early on in
ethics by Moore)[12] required that these questions be suitably clarified and, further,
that clarifying the meanings of troublesome terms and expressions would provide
both the needed clarity and a common philosophical starting point from which
philosophers might hope to reach consensus on philosophical issues.[13]

Of particular interest for the saga of analytic metaethics is that an a priori
methodology accompanied the focus on semantic issues. After all, semantic inquiry involved in large part the search for analytic truths—statements whose truth
is independent of how things are in the empirical world and hence are true 'come

---

11. See L. J. Cohen for a general discussion of the so-called linguistic thesis about the nature of analytic
philosophy, viz., the thesis that the distinctive feature of analytic philosophy "consists in its adherence
to the methodological principle that philosophical problems are best approached as, or reduced to,
problems about the linguistic expression of thought" (1986: 8). Interestingly, Cohen rejects the linguistic thesis. But see Dummett, who argues that "analytical philosophy was born when the 'linguistic
turn' was taken" (1993: 5). See also Burge, 1992: 4–29, for a discussion of the role of philosophy of
language in twentieth-century Anglo-American philosophy.

12. See especially Moore, 1903: ch 1.

13. For illuminating discussions of philosophical methodology prevalent during this period, see Rorty,
1967; L. J. Cohen, 1986: ch.1; and Burge, 1992.

what may.' This sort of inquiry, then, was generally taken to be an armchair exercise that philosophers presumably were especially good at. Thus, many analytic philosophers believed there was a sharp methodological discontinuity between philosophy and science: the former relied mainly on a priori procedures of inquiry, while the latter relied mainly on a posteriori empirical procedures. So associated with the methodological maxim represented by A2 was a generally accepted conception of the philosophical enterprise that we can express this way:

A4   Proper philosophical methodology, involving semantic analysis, proceeds by way of a priori inquiry into the meanings of terms and expressions.[14]

This conception of semantic analysis and associated methodology, encapsulated in A3 and A4, led to a certain understanding of standard semantic views about moral discourse. Let us consider a sampling of those views.

There are two general semantic views about moral discourse: descriptivism (or what is often referred to as cognitivism) and non-descriptivism (or what is often called non-cognitivism).[15] According to descriptivism, moral sentences (at least in their primary usage) purport to describe or represent moral reality. There are two closely related claims that characterize descriptivism: (1) Moral terms purport to denote or pick out moral properties and relations that actions, practices, persons, institutions, and so forth may or may not possess, and moral sentences purport to describe or report moral facts—facts about which actions, persons, practices, institutions, and so forth do (and do not) possess certain moral properties. (2) Consequently, moral sentences containing such terms and expressions have genuine assertoric content—they are used to make assertions about what is true (or false) and so have truth values.

Non-descriptivism, by contrast, is the view that moral sentences do not purport to describe or represent a moral reality. Non-descriptivists, then, deny the first claim of the descriptivists, claiming instead that moral terms do not purport to denote or

---

14. This methodological assumption squares with the rationalism of Moore and his followers and with the empiricism of the positivists. Moorean semantics involved direct intuitive insight into necessary connections among Platonic meaning entities supposedly yielding a priori knowledge. Positivist semantics, too, involved analytic meaning connections that were supposedly knowable a priori, an artifact of linguistic convention.

15. There are at least three good reasons for preferring descriptivist/non-descriptivist terminology over the cognitivist/non-cognitivist terminology. First, there are a good many ways in which language has been divided into the cognitive versus the non-cognitive. Frankena (1965) discusses nine different divisions this pair of terms has been used to mark. An advantage of the descriptivist/non-descriptivist terminology, then, is that because it is less commonly used, it does not suffer from such ambiguity. Second, the former is primarily a distinction having to do with matters linguistic, while the latter (given its etymology) has primarily to do with belief and knowledge. (Of course, given certain conceptual connections between, e.g., assertion and truth on the one hand and belief on the other, both sets of terms can appropriately be used to refer to the set of views that characterize the two major metaethical orientations being discussed here.) Third, it is possible, as I shall argue later in ch. 4, to break apart the packages that make up traditional descriptivist and non-descriptivist views. My own view is non-descriptivist, though I allow for genuine moral belief and so I can fairly be called a cognitivist. (See Hare, 1985, who also insists on keeping these sets of distinctions straight.)

pick out moral properties and relations and that moral sentences and expressions do not purport to describe or report moral facts. On this view, moral sentences perform some non-fact-stating linguistic function.[16] And so, the non-descriptivist (typically) goes on to deny the second claim of the descriptivists: moral sentences, despite their grammatical form, do not have assertoric content—they are not used to make assertions and so are not candidates for being either true or false.[17]

From the perspective of classical semantic analysis, specific versions of these two general types of semantic view were cast in terms of moral sentences (and the moral terms they contain) that were, or failed to be, reducible via synonymy to other, non-moral sentences. So, for example, within the ranks of the descriptivists, there was disagreement over the question of whether moral terms could be analytically defined by non-moral terms and expressions. The most prominent brand of analytic reductionism was *semantic naturalism*, according to which moral sentences are synonymous with sentences, all of whose terms refer to natural entities, events, properties, and relations of the sort subject to ordinary empirical investigation. Thus, terms like 'good' (in its moral sense) were thought to be analytically reducible to psychological, sociological, or perhaps biological terms. For example, the semantic views of many of the late nineteenth- and early twentieth-century evolutionists represented a version of semantic naturalism. Typical of such views was the claim that moral sentences of the form 'X is good' are (roughly) synonymous with sentences of the form 'X is conducive to the survival of the human species,' and so the term 'good' (when used for moral evaluation) can be analytically defined in terms of what is conducive to the survival of the species.[18] Because the sorts of natural entities, properties, and so forth that the evolutionists appealed to in their reductions were mind-independent, objective entities, properties, and so on, their brand of semantic naturalism was typically referred to as a species of *objective naturalism*. Alternatively, according to (semantic) *subjective naturalism*, moral terms and expressions are definable by psychological terms and expressions, so that, for instance, 'X is good' means (when thought or uttered by me) 'X is an object of my approval.'[19]

---

16. The contrast I'm describing here between descriptivist and non-descriptivist treatments of moral language is between 'pure' forms of these views. More complex versions, e.g., 'mixed' semantic accounts of moral language that would, for example, hold that moral terms and expressions have the dual function of stating facts and expressing attitudes or whatever, were defended by such philosophers as Stevenson (1944), Hare (1952), Edwards (1955), and Nowell-Smith (1954), who are nevertheless properly classified as non-descriptivists since they took the non-descriptive component to be primary. For present purposes, these details are not important.

17. I am making a point of sorting out two theses that combine to characterize descriptivism, both of which traditional non-descriptivists reject, because I want to defend a metaethical view that rejects the first (and main) thesis of descriptivism yet accepts the second thesis. On the view I plan to defend in ch. 4, moral sentences (in their primary usage) are not in the business of describing or representing anything, but they are used to make real assertions—*evaluative assertions*—that are genuinely truth-apt.

18. One of the evolutionists, Herbert Spencer, wrote: "[T]he conduct to which we apply the name good is the relatively more evolved conduct; and that bad is the name we apply to conduct which is relatively less evolved" (Spencer, 1895, vol. 1: 15).

19. *Semantic supernaturalism* is another view worth mentioning in this context, representing an attempt to analytically reduce moral terms and expressions to terms and expressions about such supernatural

Opposed to any attempt to provide analytic definitions of moral terms were *semantic non-naturalists* (often called 'intuitionists'), who (as descriptivists) agreed with semantic naturalists that moral sentences are fact-stating, but who thought that moral terms could not be analytically defined in non-moral terms. Thus, G. E. Moore, with whom the tale of analytic metaethics usually begins, claimed that all forms of semantic naturalism commit what he called the 'naturalistic fallacy.' This fallacy, as revealed by Moore's famous 'open question argument,' was intended to show that fundamental moral terms and expressions were simply not synonymous with natural terms and expressions (or any other non-moral terms and expressions). (See chap. 2, §I for a discussion of Moore's argument.) So, as a descriptivist, Moore argued that if fundamental moral terms cannot be reductively analyzed—that is, if they are unanalyzable—then terms like 'good' must refer to some sui generis, unanalyzable property, namely, the property goodness.

Non-descriptivists were in agreement with the non-naturalists that moral sentences are not synonymous with non-moral sentences, but were not willing to countenance non-natural, sui generis moral properties to which non-naturalism was committed. Instead, they denied that moral sentences are fact-stating. Their view was that such sentences are synonymous with (or at least significantly analogous to) sentences that perform some non-fact-stating linguistic function.[20] So, for example, *emotivists* held that moral sentences functioned primarily to express the speaker's negative or positive attitudes toward some object of moral evaluation and to influence the attitudes of others. Moral sentences of the form 'X is good' were thus construed as, for example, synonymous with sentences of the form 'X: hurrah!' (A. J. Ayer's own version of emotivism became dubbed the 'Boo—Hurrah theory' of moral discourse.) By contrast, *prescriptivists* like R. M. Hare argued that the primary function of moral discourse was to advise or to tell someone what to do based on reasons. Interjections, prescriptions, commands, and other non-fact-stating sentences were taken to be meaningful, though unlike the fact-stating sentences that possessed *descriptive meaning*, these sentences were said to have (perhaps in addition to descriptive meaning) some other sort of meaning that was primary. Emotivists talked about these sentences having *emotive meaning*, whereas Hare talked about their having *evaluative meaning*.

From the publication in 1903 of Moore's *Principia Ethica* through the 1950s, metaethical debate was primarily concerned with semantic analysis of moral terms. During this time the basic semantic options just described were elaborated at length, resulting in quite sophisticated descriptivist and non-descriptivist semantic stories about moral language. My purpose here is not to recount the detail of this analytic period in metaethics. Rather, the point I am making is that there was a

---

entities and phenomena as God and what God does or does not command or approve. For a discussion, see Frankena, 1973.

20. This characterization of non-descriptivism, though typical, is not quite accurate. Although a good many non-descriptivists attempted to reduce moral sentences to some other type of non-fact-stating sentences, other non-descriptivists like Hare (1952) construed moral sentences as performing a *unique* non-fact-stating function, which, though analogous in important ways to other types of statement (e.g., commands), could not be reduced to them. This point is made in Ewing, 1959: 33–4.

more or less common understanding of semantic analysis as aiming to provide (where possible) reductive analytic definitions of key moral terms.

So during the period of analytic metaethics, we find various metaethical packages, made up of semantic, metaphysical, and epistemological views. The practiced philosophical methodology of the time (tenet A2) was to bracket epistemological questions, focus on the meaning of moral terms and expressions, and then, with some worked-out moral semantics in hand, draw conclusions about what sort of justification (if any) is appropriate in connection with moral discourse.[21] And, as we have seen, the driving force behind all of this was a certain conception of the basic problems and the appropriate methodology, involving reductive semantic analysis.

What I have left out of my characterization of analytic metaethics so far is an explicit indication of how the most general aims of metaethical inquiry, represented by D1 and D2, were operative in the debate over competing semantic views. Here, I am particularly interested in how D1 and D2, interpreted in light of philosophical naturalism, pushed and pulled the major players of the analytic period in various metaethical directions, and how the project of naturalistic accommodation looked at this time.

Ideally, as I have said, one would like to satisfy both desiderata. If we begin with D1—the requirement that a plausible metaethical view should comport with deeply embedded assumptions of ordinary moral discourse—we find that such discourse embeds those features characteristic of typical fact-stating discourse. And so D1 pushed many in the direction of some form of descriptivist treatment of moral discourse that would construe such discourse as being about moral properties and expressing moral facts.

But, of course, for the philosophical naturalist, D2—the requirement that a plausible metaethical view comport with plausible views and assumptions from other areas of inquiry—requires that any metaphysical and associated commitments of moral discourse be naturalistically accommodated. Furthermore, given A2 and A3, accommodation here requires that one find analytic reductive definitions of moral terms by naturalistic terms and expressions. In other words, for the philosophical naturalist who accepts a descriptivist analysis of moral discourse, some version of semantic naturalism must be defended. But in light of Moorean arguments, the prospects for this type of metaethical view looked especially bleak.

In response to this situation, there was a parting of philosophical ways. Many philosophers, including Moore, Ross, and Ewing, placed greater weight on D1 than they did on D2 (naturalistically interpreted). Moreover, they found descriptivism to comport best with commonsense moral discourse and practice, and so were led to conclude that the sorts of moral facts and properties this discourse is

---

21. Descriptivists claimed that since moral sentences have truth value, they admitted of *epistemic justification*—that species of justification that aims at showing or establishing the truth of a claim. However, those non-descriptivists who wanted to distinguish justified from unjustified moral convictions were interested in *non-epistemic justification* having to do with various practical goals like interpersonal coordination.

about must be non-natural in character. This attitude toward the project of naturalistic accommodation was well expressed by the non-naturalist Ewing, commenting on the views of semantic ethical naturalists:

> As a matter of fact the philosophers who give naturalist definitions of ethical terms do not, despite their predilection for empiricism, commend their conclusions as the direct result of a plain empirical investigation of our moral experience, but put these forward on the assumption that if they can find a hypothesis which will rid them of any concept different from those of the natural sciences they ought to accept it whether or not it seems introspectively plausible. This *a priori* assumption I can see no reason to make. (Ewing, 1947: 44)

Other philosophers, the non-descriptivists, who held onto D2 (interpreted naturalistically) went the other route: constrained by D2, they wanted to construe moral discourse, despite outward appearances, as being reducible to, or very much like, certain forms of non-fact-stating discourse. But the non-descriptivists were generally seen as placing too little weight on D1 in not taking seriously enough the common-sense objectivist assumptions of ordinary moral thought. Still another option was taken by the moral skeptic, who, like J. L. Mackie (1946, 1977), agreed with those antireductivist descriptivists that ordinary moral language was best interpreted as purporting to be about some non-natural moral properties and relations, but also agreed with philosophical naturalists that no such properties or relations exist. The result was an 'error theory' about ordinary moral thought: such thought presupposes the existence of non-natural moral properties and relations, but since there are no such things, (affirmative) ordinary moral statements are all false.

If we view these various metaethical positions from the perspective of the project of naturalistic accommodation and focus in particular on the metaphysical commitments and associated semantic components of these views, we can neatly classify attempts at accommodation along two axes or dimensions, largely orthogonal to each other: ontological and semantic. Along the ontological axis, the metaethical position is either realist or irrealist vis-à-vis moral discourse. Along the semantic axis, a philosophical position can either assert or deny that moral sentences are analytically reducible to, for example, sentences whose content is overtly naturalistic; that is, the position can either be *semantically reductionist* or *semantically non-reductionist* (fig. 1–1).

Analytic ethical naturalists who, like the evolutionists, construed moral discourse as being about objective natural properties fit into cell 1A. For them, accommodation of the ontological commitments of moral discourse required that moral terms and expressions be analytically reduced to naturalistic terms and expressions. Cell 1B represents those non-naturalistic realists (objectivists) who, like Moore, believed in objective moral properties but rejected any sort of reduction of moral discourse to non-moral discourse, and so concluded that moral properties are sui generis, non-natural properties. Cell 2A is occupied primarily by non-descriptivists who took moral sentences to be synonymous with non-moral, non-fact-stating sentences. Finally, cell 2B is occupied by, for example, the sort of error theory espoused by Mackie, who, as just explained, sided with the non-naturalists in rejecting any sort of reduction of the moral to the non-moral, but who also sided with the naturalists in rejecting commitment to any non-natural moral properties or facts.

	Reductionist Semantics	Non-Reductionist Semantics
Realism	1A	1B
Irrealism	2A	2B

FIGURE 1–1 Metaethical positions in relation to the project of accommodation

The point I wish to stress here is that accommodation generally, and naturalist accommodation in particular, was severely constrained during the period of analytic metaethics. To accommodate any metaphysical and associated commitments of moral discourse, or to otherwise philosophically account for the point and purpose of the discourse, involved working within a quite narrowly conceived reductive program in which analytic meaning reductions were the main vehicle of accommodation.

V. Post-Analytic Metaethics

If analytic metaethics is fairly described as being narrowly conservative about proper subject matter and methodology, then the current period of post-analytic metaethics can be called comparatively broad and liberal in its view of the proper subject matter and methodology for metaethics. More specifically, one can point to three features of the current metaethical scene that help set it apart from its analytic phase: (1) the classical conception of semantic analysis has lost its hold in thinking about semantics in general and moral semantics in particular; (2) metaethical inquiry is no longer as dominated by narrow linguistic concerns; and (3) various positive views and theories of recent vintage propounded in such areas as epistemology, philosophy of language, and philosophy of mind (see later in this section for more details) have significantly influenced work in metaethics. The general result has been that new metaethical options not previously on the philosophical landscape have been recognized and developed. Of particular interest here is that in the gradual transition from the analytic to the post-analytic periods, we find that the requirements for acceptable naturalistic accommodation have been considerably loosened, resulting in new and improved versions of metaethical naturalism.[22]

22. For a more wide-ranging discussion of the move from analytic to post-analytic metaethics, see Darwall, Gibbard, and Railton (1992), who call the period of transition, beginning in the 1950s, the period of Great Expansion in ethics. See pp. 121–24.

In this section, I plan to briefly elaborate features 1–3 just mentioned. My discussion is not meant to be a thorough treatment of what surely is a complicated story about changes in Anglo-American philosophy beginning around 1950. Furthermore, given our interest in the project of naturalistic accommodation, my discussion will be quite selective.

As early as 1951, we find Rawls ("Outline of a Decision Procedure in Ethics") approaching questions about justification in ethics without first tackling semantic issues. A particularly clear rejection of both classical semantic analysis represented by A3 and the 'semantics first' methodology of analytic metaethics expressed in A2 is provided by Morton White:

> But they [proponents of analytic metaethics] suppose that to discover how we know that a given action ought to be done we must give an analysis of what it means to say that an action ought to be done. In my view, however, this is an unwarranted supposition. It seems to me possible to say something illuminating about the justification of ethical beliefs without venturing into the semantics of ethical language or the analysis of ethical concepts. In fact, I believe that it is necessary to bypass the murky notion of synonymy and the equally murky notions that we employ when we speak of the analysis of ethical attributes or concepts. (White, 1981: 5–6)[23]

The source of White's rejection of A2 is his rejection of the classical conception of semantic analysis, resting as it does on the analytic/synthetic distinction and associated notions like synonymy. Of course, the locus classicus of the attack on the analytic/synthetic distinction is Quine's 1951 "Two Dogmas of Empiricism." Quine, along with Goodman (1949) and White (1950), argued that semantic notions like analyticity and synonymy are obscure and hence not able to bear the explanatory burden of accounting for the alleged difference between sentences whose truth is solely a matter of meaning and sentences whose truth depends on meaning plus extralinguistic fact. If such notions as analyticity and synonymy cannot be usefully clarified, so much for classical semantic analysis and the investigation into reductive analytic definitions of moral terms and expressions (so much for A3). Moreover, Quine's attack on analyticity was part of a general indictment of a priori methodology.[24] Against the logical positivists, Quine's attack on analyticity undermined the attempt to ground philosophical inquiry on principles like the verificationist criterion of meaning that were supposed to enjoy an a priori status and thus be immune from revision in light of experience.[25] But the implication of Quine's indictment was quite general: essentially, any sentence, even

---

23. White's move from rejecting synonymy and analysis to rejecting semantics clearly indicates that he was thinking of semantics in the classical way.

24. On this point, see Putnam, 1981: 82–84 and Putnam, 1983b.

25. As Burge writes:

> There was something more general than empiricism at stake in the dispute over analyticity. The positivists hoped "first principles," the boundaries of rational discussion, could be established as vacuously true and not subject to philosophical questions about legitimation. . . . If these principles were themselves analytic, they could be exempted from the traditional metaphysical and epistemological questions. (Burge, 1992: 8)

(See also Putnam, 1981: 109–10.)

one of mathematics or logic, is in principle revisable in light of experience. Thus, the idea of a priori starting points in philosophical inquiry goes by the boards; A4 goes by the boards.

In place of a priori methodology, Quine advocated a thoroughgoing epistemological holism: in science at least, we test whole systems of belief against experience. Revisions we make as a result of experience may be made anywhere within the system (no belief is immune from possible revision); our aim is to maximize the overall coherence of the system. But further, Quine's attack on a priori methodology meant that philosophical and scientific inquiry were continuous; both areas of inquiry are guided by the ideal of maximizing the coherence of our total system of beliefs.[26] This, of course, contrasts sharply with the older analytic view that philosophy and science are methodologically discontinuous.[27] For metaethics in particular, this shift in thinking about methodology resulted in metaethical inquiry being more self-conscious in its appeal to empirical work, particularly work in the social sciences.[28]

In addition to the reasons just mentioned for the classical conception of semantic analysis losing its hold in philosophy is the fact that philosophers simply failed to come up with illuminating, compact, and complete analyses of concepts that were of philosophical interest. Perhaps the most dramatic of such failures, sparked by Gettier's famous 1963 article, was the attempt by many philosophers to provide an analysis of knowledge. With this failure and others, it began to dawn on philosophers that perhaps providing analyses of concepts like knowledge, free will, mentality, and so on, simply couldn't be done. In recent years, this suspicion has been bolstered by the work of cognitive psychologists working on conceptualization. Their work strongly suggests that concepts simply do not have the sorts of necessary and sufficient conditions that the classical conception supposes them to have and that it tries to articulate in providing a semantic analysis of the terms that express such concepts. (For more discussion of the impact of empirical work on philosophy of language, see ch. 3, §XII.) So, as a result of the impact of the work of Quine and others on semantic notions like meaning and analyticity, the history of failure by those attempting semantic analyses, and the questioning of the classical conception of concepts coming from empirical research, philosophers these days have largely given up the project of classically conceived semantic analysis.[29]

---

26. As we shall see below, this means that what counts as a *relevant* area of inquiry in D2 will have to be suitably broadened.

27. The influence of this methodological outlook is perhaps most prominent in epistemology, where *naturalized epistemology*—the view that sound epistemological theorizing should be informed by empirical work, particularly in psychology—has taken firm hold. See Kornblith, 1980; Kim, 1988; and Kitcher, 1992, for discussions of this trend.

28. See for example, Brandt's (1979) use of results from psychology, Wong's (1984) appeal to work in comparative anthropology, and the recent work in metaethics appealing to the work of such cognitive psychologists as Kohlberg (1981, 1984), and Gilligan (1982, 1988). Flanagan (1991) provides a useful overview and discussion of recent work in moral psychology as it bears on issues in ethical theory.

29. See Stich, 1992, and Tye, 1992, for discussions of how giving up this conception of semantic analysis affects the project of naturalism in connection with the mental.

Related to the general rejection of classical semantic analysis and the move away from the 'semantics first' methodology of analytic metaethics was the increasing recognition of epistemological and metaphysical issues as distinct from related semantic issues. We see this in the quote from White, who proposes to set aside questions about moral semantics and tackle epistemological questions concerning moral discourse head-on. This mood of separation is particularly clear in the case of metaphysical questions.[30] In the last section, I noted that in Frankena's characterization of the main questions of metaethics, no mention is made of metaphysical and, in particular, ontological questions in ethics—questions about the existence and nature of moral properties and facts. Of course, the metaethical views characteristic of the analytic period did incorporate ontological stances toward moral properties and their nature. Many descriptivists took moral terms to (successfully) refer to moral properties and moral sentences to be fact-stating, and thus embraced moral realism. Non-descriptivists denied the existence of any such putative properties and facts and thus were committed to moral irrealism. But an operative assumption regarding matters ontological was that they were to be handled linguistically—that questions about whether there are moral properties and facts and, if so, whether they are identical to non-moral properties and facts were to be answered by settling questions about the meanings of moral terms and expressions.[31] Thus, the preoccupation with semantic analysis.

One clear manifestation of this preoccupation was the widespread acceptance of a synonymy criterion of property identity.[32] According to this criterion, the putative referent of a moral term or expression is identical to the referent of some non-moral term or expression if, and only if, the relevant terms and expressions are synonymous. If one accepts this criterion, then, of course, ontological questions about the nature of moral properties (whether or not they are reducible to non-moral properties) can be settled linguistically.

The complaint that Mackie lodges against analytic metaethics is that this kind of fixation on linguistic inquiry tends to obscure ontological questions about the existence and nature of value and obligation, and tempts one to make inferences about ontological matters based solely on semantic analysis:

> Those [second order questions] most often mentioned are questions about the meaning and use of ethical terms, or the analysis of ethical concepts. . . . But there are also ontological, as contrasted with linguistic or conceptual, questions about the nature and status of goodness or rightness or whatever it is that first order moral statements are distinctively about. These are questions of factual rather than conceptual analysis: the problem of what goodness is cannot be settled

---

30. For a particularly forceful statement of the claim that semantic and metaphysical questions and issues should be kept distinct, see Devitt, 1984: introduction. An especially useful discussion of these matters is to be found in Tienson, 1989.

31. This is not to say that this assumption was shared by all participants in the story of analytic metaethics; some non-descriptivists, for example, began metaethical inquiry with a certain ontological outlook that excluded non-natural properties and facts. Nevertheless, this assumption was sufficiently widespread for Mackie (see later in this section) to make explicit his rejection of it.

32. For a discussion of the basis of this criterion, see Putnam, 1970 and 1981: 84–85.

conclusively or exhaustively by finding out what the word 'good' means, or what it is conventionally used to say or to do. (Mackie, 1977: 19)

Here, Mackie appeals to the seeming obviousness of the distinction between semantic and ontological issues. But also philosophical theses, like the synonymy criterion of property identity that would tie ontological issues to semantic issues, were increasingly rejected by philosophers in light of numerous alleged counterexamples. For instance, the (sortal) property *being water* is identical with the property *being composed of H₂O molecules*; heat is identical with molecular motion; temperature is identical with mean molecular kinetic energy; and so on. But being water and being composed of H_2O molecules are not synonymous, and the same holds for the terms and expressions involved in the other scientific identities. We thus need to insist on separating metaphysical/ontological issues and questions from linguistic issues and questions, since failure to do so tends to obscure certain metaethical options. For example, Mackie's own skeptical view in metaethics, as we have seen, involves accepting a certain descriptivist account of the meanings of moral terms and expressions, according to which ordinary moral statements purport to be about objective moral properties and facts, but then denying that there are any such properties or facts. If one fails to clearly distinguish semantic questions about moral discourse from ontological questions (recall the quote from Frankena), Mackie's skeptical position tends to be hidden from view.

Again, the move away from the narrow methodological outlook of analytic philosophy helped create a philosophical environment in which new philosophical views were articulated and defended. Of particular interest to this discussion are some of the developments in the 1960s and 1970s in philosophy of language and philosophy of mind. (Here I shall just mention these developments; in the next chapter they are treated in more detail in connection with moral realism.)

In the philosophy of language, the work of S. Kripke (1972) and Putnam (1975b) on the semantics of names and natural kind terms is significant. Older, traditional semantic views about names and general terms held that the meanings of such terms were given by a set of descriptions that were analytically related to the term in question. Thus, for example, the meaning of the natural kind term 'gold' was specified in terms of certain descriptive features such as *being a metal* and *being yellow in color*. Thus, it is analytically true that gold is a yellow metal. The term 'gold,' then, refers to something just in case that thing possesses the constellation of descriptive features analytically associated with this term. Kripke and Putnam criticized such 'description' views of names and natural kind terms, and in their place, proposed a causal semantic story about names and natural kind terms. According to such stories, the reference of a name or general term is not determined by descriptions analytically associated with the name or term; rather, reference is understood as involving causal chains that connect our use of a name or general term with its referent. One important result of this development in philosophy of language was the coming to be of expanded semantic options available for general philosophical exploitation. And, as we shall see in the next chapter, the causal story has been applied to moral terms and serves an important underpinning role in the recent revival of naturalistic moral realism.

Developments in the philosophy of mind during this time contributed significantly to changes in our understanding of constraints on an acceptable version of philosophical naturalism. In short, those interested in naturalistically accommodating the mental came to recognize that reduction of the mental to the physical via analytic definitions of mental terms was unnecessary. Moreover, many came to realize that reductively identifying mental properties with physical properties was unnecessary in order to naturalistically accommodate the mental. Instead, it was plausibly argued that instantiations of mental phenomena by human beings were 'nothing over and above' complex configurations of physical phenomena in the sense that mental phenomena 'supervene' on, without being identical with, physical phenomena. Again, this theme in philosophy of mind is explained more fully in the next chapter, where we consider a version of naturalistic moral realism that emerged in the past decade, largely as a result of these changes and developments. For present purposes, it is sufficient to note that the project of naturalistically accommodating mental discourse was not taken to require any sort of analytic meaning reductions; the prospects for such accommodation were considerably broadened.

To summarize: the key assumptions, A1–A4, that held sway in the era of analytic metaethics have gradually given way, and we find ourselves in a period of expanded metaethical options, including, especially, expanded options for naturalistic accommodation. More specifically, if we take A1–A4 one at a time, the basic points to be noted are these. (1) A1, as stated, is too narrow for adequately specifying the central questions of metaethical inquiry. There is no mention of metaphysical and specifically ontological questions associated with moral discourse and practice. Moreover, it should not be assumed that such questions just are, or are reducible to, semantic questions. (2) The semantics-first methodology of A2 — indeed, philosophy of language — is no longer so dominant in recent philosophical inquiry.[33] However, the fact that semantic inquiry does not dominate philosophical inquiry does not mean that it is no longer important. Quite the contrary. As we shall see, even if philosophical issues are no longer thought to be just reducible to, or best approached by semantic analysis, considerations of moral semantics have a pivotal role to play in defending a metaethical view. (3) The narrowly conceived view of semantic analysis represented by A3 has by and large been given up in light of suspicions about analyticity, and in light of newly propounded semantic views like those of Kripke and Putnam. Finally, (4) the a priori methodology recommended by A4 has also been eclipsed. Instead, philosophical inquiry generally, and metaethical inquiry in particular, is taken to be a matter of maximizing coherence of our philosophical views with views and assumptions from other areas of inquiry, including the sciences. This means that what counts as a *relevant* area of inquiry in D2 — the desideratum that says that a plausible metaethical view should comport with plausible views and assumptions from various relevant areas of inquiry — includes both general views and assumptions from other areas of philosophy *and* from other disciplines. That is, we could reformulate D2, as it has come to be understood, as follows:

---

33. See Burge, 1992: 28–29, for some reasons why philosophy of language lost its status as first philosophy in the late 1970s.

D2*   A plausible metaethical view should comport with plausible views and assumptions from other areas of philosophy, as well as with plausible views and
assumptions from other disciplines.

(For convenience, I will continue to refer to D2.)

However, despite these changes, metaethical inquiry today is still guided by
the dual aim of making sense of commonsense moral discourse and practice, and
interpreting the ontological, semantic, and epistemological commitments of such
discourse and practice in light of some general worldview. As I have said, I am
specifically interested in making sense of morality from within a naturalistic
worldview, and so the project of naturalistic accommodation is central to my inquiry.

VI. A Glance Ahead

In the chapters to follow, then, I will be exploring various metaethical options that
presuppose philosophical naturalism and are engaged in the project of naturalistic
accommodation. In the next chapter, I shall examine the attempt to defend a
realist metaethical position. Although I focus attention on but one version of naturalistic moral realism—namely, the view recently developed by David Brink,
Richard Boyd, and Nicholas Sturgeon—this version attempts to ride the new wave
of philosophical developments I've mentioned and represents the most plausible
and certainly most developed version of the general view. I argue that this new
wave version of moral realism rests on a questionable view about the semantics of
moral terms that results in a dilemma for the view: the view cannot simultaneously
satisfy both D1 and D2. I then go on to examine the prospects for developing a
plausible naturalistic version of moral irrealism.

One major obstacle for any moral irrealist is to satisfy D1 and plausibly accommodate those 'objective pretensions' of moral discourse and practice. The most
forceful of such challenges to the moral irrealist (so it seems to me) is the argument
from moral error that charges that the irrealist is not able to make sense of, and
hence plausibly accommodate, the idea that error in moral judgment is ubiquitously possible. In chapter 3, I tackle this challenge, arguing that it is quite forceful
against standard 'reductive' versions of moral irrealism, and so the irrealist is best
advised to explore the possibility of defending a non-reductive version of her view.
Chapters 4 and 5 take up this project. Specifically, in chapter 4, I articulate and
defend a contextualist moral semantics that avoids reducing or analyzing away
moral or other evaluative notions. I then defend the semantic view by arguing that
it fairly satisfies the dual accommodation aims by which we evaluate metaethical
theories, and seems to do a better job of it than competing metaethical views. In
chapter 5, I turn to moral epistemology and defend a contextualist account of
moral justification. I argue that this view, unlike its rivals, avoids skepticism by
being able to nicely accommodate the commonsense assumption that many people are justified in holding many of the moral beliefs they do hold.

What I argue, then, is that my version of moral irrealism does a reasonably
good job at accommodating common sense, as well as comporting with philo-

sophical naturalism, and moreover that it does a better job than its realist rivals and its irrealist allies in satisfying D_1 and D_2 (naturalistically interpreted). In the end, I won't be able to claim that I have completely defended my brand of irrealism, but I do hope to have made a strong presumptive case in favor of my brand of ethical contextualism.

2

New Wave Moral Realism

I will be defending a version of moral irrealism that I claim represents an overall plausible metaethical position. Since judging the overall adequacy of any philosophical position is a comparative matter, part of my defense of moral irrealism must involve the claim that other views are not (overall) as plausible as the one I will defend. However, I will not undertake to present and raise objections to every currently defended metaethical view opposed to my own; I must be selective. As explained in the last chapter, I am, for the purposes of this book, committed to philosophical naturalism (broadly understood), which imposes constraints on what is going to count as a plausible metaethical view. So I will not be discussing any metaethical views (except indirectly) that would involve metaphysical or epistemological commitments that obviously do not comport with philosophical naturalism. Readers who do not feel constrained in their metaethical thinking by naturalism, and readers who are antecedently sympathetic with metaethical views that do not comport with philosophical naturalism, will probably be unhappy with my limited menu. But in light of serious and well-known problems with any metaethical view that would, for instance, countenance non-natural moral properties that we are supposed to be able to detect in some special manner, I maintain that we ought to explore various metaethical options within the naturalistic picture. A naturalistic metaethical view that would construe the metaphysical and epistemological commitments of moral discourse as no more puzzling than the corresponding commitments of commonsense object discourse and scientific discourse would certainly be worth the effort required to develop it.

One major competitor to my view is, of course, moral realism. But I cannot hope to survey all of the species of this general metaethical orientation; again, I must be selective. However, as I noted in the last chapter, a version of naturalistic moral realism has quite recently been elaborated and defended by David Brink (1984, 1989), Richard Boyd (1988), and Nicholas Sturgeon (1984, 1986). This new wave moral realism is not the only realist view in ethics defended in recent years, but there are a number of reasons for focusing on this particular version. For one thing, the new wavers are clear in their commitment to philosophical naturalism and the associated project of accommodation, and so they fall within the scope of my study. Second, one finds, particularly in Brink's work, a detailed working out of the various metaphysical and epistemological commitments of the view, rather than something highly programmatic with details to be provided later. Finally, I suspect that other versions of moral realism that differ significantly from the new wave version either do not comport with philosophical naturalism or succumb to the sorts of objections I will raise against the new wavers.[1]

In the first part of this chapter (§§I–V), I set out the doctrines distinctive of moral realism; elaborate the naturalistic accommodation project that I began describing in chapter 1; consider two types of accommodation strategies realists have tried; clarify the position of the ethical naturalist; and then present some of the most important challenges that naturalistic realists must overcome in fully carrying out the accommodation project. We will then be ready to appreciate the doctrines and strategy of the new wave moral realists that will be elaborated at some length in §§VI–VIII, involving, in particular, close consideration of the metaphysical and semantic commitments of this version of moral realism. Having set forth the new wave position, in §IX I raise what I take to be the central problem for this position. In rough outline my argument the following: (1) In order to fully discharge the metaphysical (and epistemological) accommodation burdens that come with naturalistic moral realism, the new wavers need some sort of semantic account of key moral terms like 'good' and 'right.'[2] (2) Moreover, the writings of Brink and Boyd strongly suggest a causal construal, in particular, a *causal-functional* construal of key moral terms that, if correct, would allow them to discharge their accommodation burdens. (3) However, a particular thought experiment relevant for evaluating causal construals of terms—a Twin Earth thought experiment—provides strong evidence that the particular version of causal moral semantics under con-

1. Peter Railton's version of moral realism is a near cousin of the views of Brink, Boyd, and Sturgeon that will be under discussion here. I do touch on Railton's view (in §IX, n. 34), but for brevity's sake I have chosen not to discuss the view at length. Also, by not discussing the views of such realists as McDowell (1979, 1985) and Platts (1979, 1980, 1991), I do not mean to be dismissive of the metaethical views of these philosophers. Rather, in the case of these writers, it is not clear to me that they are interested in the project of naturalistic accommodation—it may not bother them that their versions of moral realism might force one to embrace a non-naturalist moral metaphysics. Moreover, it isn't clear to me what sort of semantic view is needed to undergird the sort of realist views being advocated by McDowell and Platts. In connection with Platts's view, for example, Wong (1984: 103) suggests that perhaps what Platts may need in telling a semantic story about moral concepts (at least one that would allow that human beings can have access to, and thus come to have knowledge of, moral facts and properties) is some causal semantic story. I suspect that Wong is right about this, and if so, then the objections I am going to raise against what I'm calling new wave moral realism will also be telling against Platts. And, given the similarity of McDowell's view to Platts's, the same goes for McDowell's view.

2. As I explain in the next section, moral realism does involve commitment to certain semantic claims including the claim that moral sentences are to be construed as fact-stating (i.e., descriptivism) and the correspondence theory of truth. My claim here is that the realist needs, in addition, some semantic story about the reference and meaning of key moral terms and the concepts they express.

sideration is false and, indeed, that any other kindred semantic construal of moral terms is false. And so, (4) lacking the relevant sort of moral semantics means that the moral realist is not able to naturalistically accommodate the various meta-physical and epistemological commitments of his view after all. I discuss the main lesson that I think is to be gleaned from the Moral Twin Earth thought experiment in §X.

Furthermore, as I explain in §XI, reflection on this thought experiment reveals an apparent dilemma for this view. On the one hand, a causal moral semantics (or something like it) is needed in order to fully discharge the external accom-modation burdens and thereby satisfy D2—the requirement that a plausible meta-ethical view should comport with views and assumptions from other areas of in-quiry, including general views and assumptions of metaphysics and epistemology. However, in light of the Twin Earth thought experiment, the causal view seems quite implausible. On the other hand, if the new wavers attempt to turn aside the thought experiment and propose the causal account as a revision of ordinary moral semantics, then they will fail to fully satisfy D1. That is, their view will then fail to accommodate some important commonsense presumptions of moral discourse, and so they will have failed at the project of internal accommodation. Quite simply, they can't have it both ways; they can satisfy one of the basic desiderata constraining metaethical inquiry only at the expense of violating the other.

Let me mention before going on that part of my aim in §§I–V is to set up my presentation and critique of new wave moral realism by providing some back-ground in the areas of metaphysics, philosophy of mind, and philosophy of lan-guage that have been exploited in the development of this metaethical view. Doing so helps one appreciate (I think) the initial plausibility of the view. Those who are familiar with this background can zip ahead to §VI.

I. Moral Realism and Naturalistic Accommodation

In the last chapter I touched on the doctrine of moral realism and the metaethical project of accommodating moral discourse from the perspective of philosophical naturalism. Before examining new wave moral realism, I need to say a bit more about moral realism and about the naturalistic accommodation project.

Moral Realism

I take realism of any sort to be a metaphysical—and, in particular, an ontological—thesis about the existence and nature of some realm of (putative) entities, prop-erties, or relations, although typical versions of realism, including moral realism, involve a semantic component as well. Furthermore, most realists want to claim that we have, or can have, justified belief about, if not knowledge of, the realm of entities or whatever in question. So versions of realism in philosophy often involve a combination of metaphysical, semantic, and epistemological views. For present purposes, let us put the non-skeptical epistemology often associated with realism to one side and take up the metaphysical and semantic components, in that order.

A rough, general characterization of (metaphysical) realism is the following: with regard to some realm of discourse (commonsense, scientific, moral, religious, etc.) that involves reference to (putative) entities, properties, or relations (or is taken to involve such reference), realism is the view that such entities, properties, or relations have objective existence.[3] Realism thus makes two basic claims: (1) such and such entities or whatever exist, and (2) their existence has objective status. (I will comment on what is meant by 'objective existence' in a moment.) So commonsense realism — realism associated with discourse about ordinary external objects — is the view that such objects have objective existence. What is called scientific realism is the view that the sorts of unobservable theoretical entities that scientists posit do exist, and objectively so. Moral realism, then, is the view that there are moral facts — facts concerning goodness and rightness — and that they exist objectively.

Discussion of objective existence is often characterized in terms of 'mind-independence,' though such talk is vague. I am not aware of any definition or partial characterization of mind-independence that could be used to distinguish all forms of realist doctrine (no matter what the area of discourse) from all associated irrealist doctrines (see Sober, 1982). But since we are interested in moral realism, all we really need is a characterization, even if rough and partial, that will serve to distinguish views standardly taken to be realist from those standardly taken to be irrealist. In connection with commonsense object discourse, the relevant notion of mind-independence is typically explained as the idea that there do exist things like chairs, trees, dogs, and so forth, and their existence does not depend, either conceptually or metaphysically, on what we think or believe about those things. The rough idea is that the existence and nature of those things is independent of our systems of concepts, of our beliefs, and of our theories about them. Moral realists, likewise, hold that moral properties and facts exist and that their existence and nature are conceptually and metaphysically independent of our moral beliefs and theories, including our warranted or even ideally warranted moral beliefs and theories. They typically also hold that these properties and facts are independent of our other attitudes, particularly our desires. So, for example, the view that the value or goodness of something depends on that thing's being the object of someone's desire is not, on this construal of realism, a realist view since, on such a view, value or goodness is not a property that a thing has independently of the mental attitudes of people.

The semantic component typical of realist views is about the relevant discourse. This component construes such discourse as (1) fact-stating, that is, com-

---

3. My characterization of the metaphysical thesis of realism is, of course, imprecise in various ways. For one thing, there is a conception of property that identifies properties with concepts, and there is a conception of fact that identifies facts with propositions. Understood in these ways, of course there are moral properties and facts. So to be more precise, I should say that the dispute is over whether moral properties are ever instantiated and whether any (affirmative) moral propositions are true. There are other ways in which one might want to make the realist thesis more precise. However, such refinements will not affect my discussion of the debate between moral realists and their irrealist opponents; we need not bother with them. (See Devitt, 1984: 16–17, for some discussion of such matters.)

prising statements purporting to refer to and truly describe things, and in which (2) the truth or falsity of those statements is a matter of correspondence to what objectively exists. Statements constituting the discourse are then understood to be true if and only if the relevant portion of objectively existing reality is the way the statement says it is. This, of course, amounts to a *correspondence theory of truth* and is typically expressed by saying that a statement is true if and only if it corresponds to the 'facts'; otherwise it is false. This correspondence account is often called *semantic realism*. In ethics, moral realists (at least those I shall discuss) accept both the metaphysical and associated semantic tenets of realism. So, in addition to the two claims about the existence and nature of moral properties and facts, there is the semantic view that the claims that constitute moral discourse are (or purport to be) fact-stating (this, of course, is the semantic thesis of descriptivism discussed in the last chapter) and so are true if and only if they correspond to objective moral facts; otherwise they are false. Moral realists, then, are committed to these claims:

M₁   There are (instantiated) moral properties and facts.

M₂   Such properties and facts are objective.

S₁   Moral discourse is fact-stating.

S₂   The statements constituting the discourse are either true or false (depending on whether or not they correspond to objectively existing moral facts).

M₁ and M₂, then, are the central metaphysical components of the view, whereas S₁ (or descriptivism) and S₂ are the central semantic components.

Moral irrealists also hold some combination of metaphysical and semantic views in opposition to some of the metaphysical and semantic tenets of moral realism, depending on the version of irrealism. The typical non-descriptivist, for instance, who denies S₁ and S₂, takes typical moral sentences to perform some non-fact-stating linguistic function. Presumably one reason for thinking that these sentences are not fact-stating (despite what the surface grammar of many of them suggest) is commitment to moral nihilism—the view that denies there are any moral facts (denies M₁). As we will see in the next chapter, other versions of moral irrealism accept some but not all of the claims characteristic of moral realism.

Hopefully, my characterization of the metaphysical and associated semantic theses of moral realism is clear enough for our purposes. Let us turn now to the accommodation project.

Naturalistic Accommodation

My characterization of moral realism is neutral with regard to the question of what sort of property or fact a moral property or fact is. Realists who are committed to philosophical naturalism take moral properties and facts to be identical with, or at least realized by, natural properties and facts. Realists like G. E. Moore were non-naturalists about objective moral properties and facts. Our interest is in naturalistic moral realism, and here I want to elaborate some of the remarks I made in the previous chapter about the project of naturalistic accommodation as it concerns the moral realist.

Recall from chapter 1 that in describing philosophical naturalism and the philosophical program it generates, I began with what I take to be the fundamental claim of this view, namely, the *thesis of ontic primacy*, according to which the ontologically primary or fundamental entities (properties, facts, etc.) in the world are all part of the subject matter of science. I interpret this claim, in the usual way, as committing one to a broadly naturalistic conception of the world — ruling out, at a minimum, anything supernatural. This outlook generates a philosophical program, that is, to accommodate or explain all sorts of non-scientific discourse, especially those modes of non-scientific discourse that seem to make genuine assertions about the world. Furthermore, this accommodation project has both an ontological and an epistemological component, which I expressed by the *thesis of metaphysical accommodation* (N2) and the *thesis of epistemological accommodation* (N3), respectively. If we reformulate those theses as they concern moral discourse (as the moral realist interprets that discourse) we have:

N2* All moral properties and facts must be accommodated from within the scientific (naturalistic) perspective of the world.

N3* Our access to moral properties and facts and (possible) moral knowledge (justification) must comport with the sort of naturalistic explanation we use to explain our access to, knowledge of, and justified beliefs about the natural, physical world generally.

As I said in the last chapter, naturalistic accommodation involves explaining the ontological and epistemological commitments of some mode of discourse in naturalistically acceptable terms. For the moral realist, putative objective moral facts are somehow to be explained on the basis of ontologically more basic facts, and associated moral knowledge is to be explained according to epistemic principles involved in our knowledge of the natural world generally. Again, one can understand the explainability requirement in various ways. As we saw in the last chapter, during the course of this century, views about constraints on an acceptable naturalistic explanation of the metaphysical and epistemological commitments of some mode of discourse have changed. Let us consider these matters a bit further as they relate to moral realism.

II. Accommodation via Narrow Reduction

Older versions of philosophical naturalism that were defended in the days of analytic metaethics involved a quite narrow conception of the accommodation project — a narrowly reductivist conception. In these post-analytic days, the project of naturalistic accommodation involves a quite broadly conceived reductionist view. Here, my use of the term 'reductionist' and its cognates requires some comment.

For purposes of carving up the metaethical landscape, it will be useful to classify all versions of naturalistic moral realism as essentially reductivist views. When it comes to the realist's treatment of the semantics of moral terms, such terms and expressions are taken to be in some sense definable by naturalistic terms and expressions. As I am about to explain, post-analytic versions of naturalistic moral realism differ markedly from analytic versions in the kind of definition of moral terms and expressions being suggested. Nevertheless, both older and newer versions accept the idea that moral terms and expressions can be systematically re-expressed in naturalistic terms. When it comes to the ontological component of the naturalistic moral realist's view, again, I call all such views ontologically re-ductive since, after all, according to this view, moral facts and properties are just (in some sense) natural facts and properties. Granted, there are important differ-ences between older versions of naturalistic moral realism and newer versions. To mark these semantic and ontological differences, I shall distinguish between nar-row and broad reductive semantics. Likewise, I plan to differentiate narrow and broad reductive realism, depending on what sorts of natural properties and facts the realist identifies as moral properties and facts. Thus, referring to my chart in chapter 1 (fig.1-1), versions of naturalistic moral realism all fit within cell 1A (the cell representing the combination of realism and semantic reductionism), though to maintain important distinctions among various versions of naturalistic moral realism, we will need to subdivide that cell. (These distinctions are explained below.) Let us now consider the sort of narrowly reductive accommodation project typical of analytic metaethics.

If, as the moral realist claims, there are objective moral properties and facts, then, according to N2*, they must be accommodated, that is, somehow explained on the basis of more basic properties and facts. For convenience, we can talk of 'higher level' discourse, properties, and facts as referring to the discourse, proper-ties, and facts to be accommodated, and we can talk of 'lower level' discourse, properties, and facts as referring to the discourse, properties, and facts to which the accommodation is to be made. So, one way to effect an explanation would be to reduce, in the sense of identifying, higher level properties and facts to more basic, lower level properties and facts, and thus identify moral properties and facts with properties and facts on some lower level, such as sociological, psychological, or biological properties and facts. Moreover, at least from the perspective of ana-lytic metaethics, it seemed that about the only way to show that properties and facts associated with one mode of discourse are identical to properties and facts associated with some other mode of discourse was to show that terms and expres-sions of the first sort mean the same as, in the sense of being synonymous with, terms and expressions for properties and facts of the second sort. In other words, a synonymy criterion of property identity was commonly taken for granted by those doing analytic metaethics.

The particular reductivist program, applied to moral phenomena, meant that moral properties and facts were to be reductively identified with more basic prop-erties and facts. Moreover, the reduction was to proceed by way of reductive an-alytic definitions intended to express meaning connections between moral and other naturalistic terms. Let us call this view *analytic semantic naturalism*, which can be expressed as follows:

ASN   Fundamental moral terms like 'good' have analytically true naturalistic definitions.

Regardless, appealing to ASN was the vehicle of naturalistic accommodation for the moral realist during the days of analytic metaethics, as we saw in the last chapter (§IV). Certainly, providing acceptable analytic definitions, and hence reducing moral properties and facts to other natural properties and facts would meet requirement N2*. Moreover, if one could provide analytic definitions of moral terms, one would be able to meet the epistemological requirement expressed in N3*: our access to, and possible knowledge of, objective moral facts would be no more or less problematic than our access to and (possible) knowledge of whatever natural properties and facts with which moral properties and facts are identical. We may call any such view undertaking this program *analytic ethical naturalism*.

Moore took all versions of ethical naturalism to commit what he called the *naturalistic fallacy*. In order to expose this fallacy, Moore proposed an *open question argument*, designed to show that any analytic definition of a moral term must be mistaken—that ASN is false. His refutation of ASN turned on what he took to be a crucial test of any specific proposal for an analytic definition of a moral term, a test involving consideration of whether a certain form of question is open. A question is open if, and only if, it is possible for someone to completely understand the question yet not know its answer; otherwise it is closed. The rationale behind this test is clear. If ASN is true, then certain statements of the form 'Anything that has natural property N is good' are analytically true. And any competent speaker (i.e., anyone who understands the statement, including, of course, the meanings of the terms it contains) will know, upon mere reflection on the terms contained in the statement, that it is true. In other words, for a fully competent speaker, the statement will be knowable a priori. But if statements of the above form are a priori, then surely questions of the form

Q1   Entity E has natural property N, but is it good?

Q2   Entity E is good, but does it have natural property N?

will be closed; any competent speaker will know, upon contemplating the meaning of Q1, that if entity E does indeed have N, then the question's answer is affirmative (similarly for Q2). Of course, if Q1 and Q2 are open, the hypothesis about the meaning of 'good' expressed in ASN is false. Moore claimed, with a great deal of plausibility, that if Q1 were closed, then it should strike us intuitively as being on a par with the question 'Entity E has natural property N, but is it N?' (again, similarly for Q2). But while this question is utterly trivial and its answer obvious, the same is not true of questions having the form of Q1. As Moore remarked in connection with the suggestion that 'good' just means 'pleasure': "[W]hoever will attentively consider with himself what is actually before his mind when he asks the question 'Is pleasure (or whatever it may be) after all good?' can easily satisfy himself that he is not merely wondering whether pleasure is pleasant" (1903: 16).

Moore's argument, while not absolutely decisive, did hold many philosophers in its sway.[4] In any case, ASN certainly seemed false in light of the open question argument, and this led many to suppose that ethical naturalism was doomed. One

---

4. See Brandt, 1959: 163–66, for a response to Moore's open question test.

could express the predicament of the analytic ethical naturalist in terms of a dilemma: in light of Moore's criticism, either (1) one is left with no means of naturalistically accommodating moral properties and facts, and so the die-hard moral realist seems forced to opt for a non-naturalist moral metaphysics, or (2) one can give up the realism and be an irrealist instead. These two options fairly well sum up the main lines of response by those who were persuaded by Moore's criticism. Moore (1903), Ross (1930), Broad (1930), and Ewing (1947) all went the non-naturalist route, while Ayer (1946), Stevenson (1944), and Hare (1952) opted for a non-descriptivist treatment of moral discourse and irrealist moral metaphysics.

III. Accommodation via Broad Reduction

As long as naturalistic moral realism was wedded to the reductive semantics of ASN, things looked bleak for that view. However, developments in the philosophy of language and the philosophy of mind that began to take hold in the 1960s and 1970s held out new hope for the moral realist. First of all, as mentioned in the last chapter, there has been widespread rejection of the synonymy criterion of property identity in light of numerous counterexamples. For instance, the sortal property *being water* is identical with the property *being composed of H_2O molecules*; heat is identical with molecular motion; temperature is identical with mean molecular kinetic energy; and so on. But these identities don't require what is pretty obviously false, namely that being water is synonymous with being composed of H_2O molecules, or that temperature is synonymous with mean molecular kinetic energy, and so forth for other scientific identities.[5] The upshot is that if one wants to reduce, in the sense of identifying, moral properties and facts to properties and facts of, say, psychology or biology, one need not be a semantic reductionist who endorses ASN.

A second important development in the philosophy of language has resulted from the pioneering work of Kripke (1972) and Putnam (1975b). Ever since their work, there has been widespread acceptance of the idea that names and natural kind terms are *rigid designators*; that is, such expressions designate the same entity with respect to every possible world in which that entity exists. Two important consequences result: (1) identity statements involving rigid designators flanking the identity sign, as in 'Water = H_2O' are necessarily true without being analytic, and (2) such statements constitute *definitions* — not the kind that express analytic meaning connections, but rather *synthetic definitions* that give the real essence of the entity, property, or kind designated by a certain term. Thus, if true, 'Water = H_2O' is a non-analytic necessary truth that expresses the real, underlying essence of water and thus provides a synthetically true definition of 'water.'

A third recent development is the widespread acceptance of so-called causal theories of reference for names and natural kind terms. In the simplest versions,

---

5. Nor are there one-way meaning implications between, e.g., 'mean molecular kinetic energy' on the one hand and 'temperature' on the other.

such theories assert that the semantic property of reference is to be understood as essentially involving appropriate causal connections between speakers' uses of a term and the thing to which the term refers. Such theories propose to explain (1) how the reference of a term is originally determined (e.g., there being some sort of baptism or dubbing ceremony through which speakers in causal contact with an item acquire the ability to refer to that item through the use of some expression used in the ceremony) and (2) how the capacity to refer is spread throughout a linguistic community (again, by speakers causally interacting with one another and with the item). Of course, this rather simple sketch can be elaborated in a number of ways, but the basic idea is clear: for some terms at least, reference is 'grounded' by relevant causal hookups between speakers and the world.

These developments provide the basis for a semantic treatment of many terms (quite different from older, analytically reductive treatments) that, as we shall see, is pressed into service by new wave moral realists in their attempt to apply causal accounts of reference to moral terms like 'good' and 'right,' and consequently treat them as having synthetic definitions. But new wavers have also sought to exploit developments in the philosophy of mind. And so, to fully appreciate their view, it will be useful to digress in order to briefly recount some of these developments.

In the philosophy of mind, defenders of so-called materialist theories of the mind or the mental have been engaged in the sort of naturalistic accommodation program we have been considering in connection with moral discourse. Such theories about mental phenomena accept that there are mental properties and facts, and, given a commitment to philosophical naturalism, take up the task of naturalistically accommodating the mental. Of present interest is the fact that these views have evolved in a certain direction, thus changing how the accommodation project has been conceived in the philosophy of mind.

Consider first the *identity theory* of the mental, according to which, each mental property (state, process) *type* is identical to some *type* of physical property of the brain or central nervous system. This view yields a form of ontological reduction: mental property types are reduced to (in the sense of being identical with) physical property types. As identity theorists recognized, it would be patently implausible to attempt any sort of narrow semantic reduction (via synonymy) of mental terms to physical terms in parallel fashion to the way in which analytic ethical naturalists attempted to secure the identity of moral properties and facts with natural properties and facts. But, of course, identity theorists also recognized that mental-term/physical-term semantic reduction was not required for ontological identities; the counterexamples mentioned above are evidence of that. Rather, the identity theorists of the late 1950s and 1960s sought to exploit the strategy of successful *intertheoretic reductions* in the sciences.[6]

Science has plausibly identified such phenomena as light with electromagnetic waves, temperature with mean molecular kinetic energy, sound with trails of compression waves in the air, and so on. Cases of successful intertheoretic reduction fol-

6. See Nagel, 1961: ch. 11, for a classic discussion of intertheoretic reduction.

lowed a typical pattern: new and explanatorily powerful theories (e.g., statistical mechanics) involving theoretical terms purporting to refer to real phenomena (e.g., mean molecular kinetic energy) also involve or entail a set of propositions and principles that mirror the propositions and principles of some other theory (e.g., thermodynamics) or some commonsense framework involving reference to various entities and properties (e.g., temperature). If the new theory performs well (and other conditions are met),[7] we are justified in positing what are called 'bridge laws,' linking higher level phenomena with lower level phenomena.[8] The bridge laws, in turn, are the basis for identifying the entity, property, or whatever that is the referent of the higher level term mentioned in the law with the entity, property, or whatever that is the referent of the lower level term mentioned in the law.

Identity theorists hoped to reductively identify mental properties with physical properties on the model of intertheoretic reduction in science, that is, by positing mental-physical bridge laws connecting mental properties and states with physico-chemical properties and states. If successful, the result would be a version of naturalism about the mental that is ontologically reductive without requiring analytically true meaning reductions of mental terms and expressions to physical terms and expressions. These theorists' attempt to defend this position made clear that naturalistic accommodation does not require analytic semantic reduction. However, the next phase in the philosophy of mind loosened the requirements for successful naturalistic accommodation even more.

Largely because of *functionalist* theories in the philosophy of mind, philosophers have increasingly rejected the idea that naturalistic accommodation expressed in N2 must be understood as requiring that the entities (properties, facts) of higher level forms of discourse be *identical* to entities (properties, facts) posited by more fundamental, lower level scientific discourse. According to functionalism, mental-state types (properties), except perhaps phenomenal properties ('qualia'), are functional properties—that is, their essence consists not in any intrinsic features, but in a certain syndrome of typical causal relations (1) to environmental effects on the body, (2) to other state types (in particular, to sensory states and other mental states that are themselves also functionally characterized), and (3) to bodily behavior. The basic idea, then, is that mental states are characterized in terms of their causal role. Thus, for example, pain is characterized as that state of the organism that typically results from some form of bodily tissue damage, typically causes distress and annoyance, and also typically causes flinching, removing oneself from the external source causing the pain, and so forth. Understood as identical to functional properties, mental properties are potentially 'physically realizable' quite differently from one occasion of instantiation to another—depending, perhaps, upon the specific physical composition of the subject in which they

---

7. Nagel (1961: ch. 11) mentions both formal and informal conditions on successful intertheoretic reduction in the sciences.

8. Here, I am using talk of higher and lower levels to refer respectively to the properties, laws, and theories to be reduced, and the properties, laws, and theories to which the reduction is made.

are instantiated.[9] This fact points to perhaps the most important consideration that led many materialists about the mental to favor functionalism over the identity theory, namely, that it is plausible to suppose that creatures whose physical constitution is quite different from ours might correctly be said to experience pain, dread, and joy, and have desires, beliefs, and so forth—a possibility ruled out by the identity theory, but not by functionalism.

Again, for our purposes, the important point is that functionalism in the philosophy of mind yields a more relaxed, California-style attitude toward the project of philosophical naturalism, an attitude that counts certain higher order, multiply realizable properties as natural properties—functional properties being the paradigm case. Although functional properties are not identical to any of the types of lower level property that realize them, their naturalness consists in the fact that (1) they supervene on lower level properties (in the sense that the lower level properties necessitate the higher order, functional properties) and (2) the essence of mental properties can be described in non-mental, naturalistic terms.[10]

Of particular significance for our purposes is the coming together of functionalism in the philosophy of mind with causal semantic theories from the philosophy of language to yield a species of functionalism, namely, *psychofunctionalism*. According to this view, mental properties are multiply realizable functional properties whose relational essences are fully capturable by the generalizations of the (ideally complete) empirical psychological theory T that happens to be true of humans. Mental terms on this view refer rigidly to these properties; and this rigid reference underwrites certain synthetic definitions of mental properties—whereby the definitive causal role of each property is specified by means of the empirical theory T. The reason why our mental terms refer to these properties in particular is that there are suitable reference-subserving causal relations linking instantiations of these specific functional properties to people's uses of mental terms and concepts. (As we shall see later in this chapter (§§VI–VII), new wave moral realists have used psychofunctionalism in the philosophy of mind as a model for the sort of realist view of morals they defend.)

To represent the various options for naturalistic accommodation that I have been describing, let us return to the two-by-two chart from chapter 1 (fig. 1-1) and make some modifications. That chart, you will recall, was used to represent the main metaethical options during the era of analytic metaethics, though it could also be used to represent the basic options in the philosophy of mind from that same era. Let us focus on cell 1A—the cell that represents the intersection of realism (about some area of discourse) and semantic reductionism

9. Notice that functionalism in the philosophy of mind does involve an identity between mental properties and functional properties, the latter, of course, being realizable by a variety of lower level, more narrowly natural properties.

10. Although functionalists characterize individual mental properties and states partly in terms of other mental states, functionalists like Armstrong, Lewis, and Putnam have thought that the nature or essence of such properties and states can be described non-mentally. Lewis (1972), for instance, employs the device of Ramsey sentences in defining mentalistic vocabulary that has the effect of specifying mental properties and states in non-mental terms. For an overview of this matter, see Block, 1980.

(about that area of discourse). From the perspective of the project of naturalistic accommodation, we can subdivide cell 1A in order to reflect the sorts of options now open to the realist in the philosophy of mind. First, we need to make some distinctions.

As I mentioned above, I plan to use the term 'reduction' and its cognates in a fairly broad sense. And so, in general, let us take any semantic view that in some way defines (or otherwise characterizes) the terms of some higher order discourse by terms from some lower order discourse as a reductive semantic view. Then we can distinguish narrowly reductive semantic views from more broadly reductive semantic views. According to the former sort of view, the terms of the relevant higher order discourse can be given analytic reductive definitions by means of terms from the relevant lower level discourse. According to the latter sort of view, no such analytic reductive definitions are available. However, the relevant higher level discourse can be defined by terms from the relevant lower level discourse, the sorts of synthetic definitions mentioned earlier (e.g., 'Water = H_2O') being prime examples.

Again, from the perspective of philosophical naturalism, if we are talking about the entities, properties, facts, or what have you, posited by some higher order discourse, then to be a realist about those entities, and so on, is to embrace a reductivist position. Here we can distinguish between narrow and broad versions of the ontological thesis of realism with regard to the entities posited by some higher order discourse. We shall call those properties, states, events, facts, or whatever, posited by the relevant lower level discourse *narrowly natural*, and we shall call those properties, states, and so forth, that are not directly characterized or defined in narrowly natural terms—but that are nevertheless realized or constituted by the more narrowly natural properties—*broadly natural*. In the context of the philosophy of mind, the properties and events posited by neuroscience are narrowly physical, while more abstractly characterized functional properties are broadly natural.

With these distinctions in hand, we can subdivide cell 1A in order to represent some expanded realist options in the philosophy of mind (fig. 2–1).[11]

---

11. Those familiar with work from the philosophy of mind and metaphysics generally will note that I use the term 'reduction' (as applied to semantic and ontological views) more broadly than it is often used in the philosophy of mind and metaphysics. My usage here is guided by the vague, pretheoretic idea behind talk of reduction involving, in particular, the idea of systematic explanation of one form of discourse (or type of entity, property, fact) in terms of some other form of discourse (or type of entity, property, fact). Unfortunately (in my opinion) talk of reduction is often used in connection with specific reductive programs. So, for instance, in the philosophy of mind, although both the identity theory and functionalism count for me as reductionist views, it is common for functionalists to distance themselves from the identity theory by pointing out that functionalism rejects the specific sort of reduction advocated by the identity theory, viz., the reduction of mental property types to human types of human brain states. Functionalism is thus often called a version of the non-reductive materialist view of the mental. I plan to stick with the more generic, pretheoretic idea associated with talk of reduction.

	Narrow Semantic Reductionism	Broad Semantic Reductionism
Narrow Ontic Reductionism	I Ai	I Aii
Broad Ontic Reductionism	I Aiii	I Aiv

FIGURE 2–1 Some realist options in the philosophy of mind

    This chart is not intended to neatly represent all of the various types of materialist theories of the mental that have been advanced in recent times; it is not fine-grained enough for that. Nor have I sketched or even mentioned views in the philosophy of mind represented by cell 1Aiii.[12] However, from what I have said, we can see some of the options for the realist that go beyond the narrow forms of semantic and ontological reduction. Cell 1Ai represents any materialist theory of the mental that would attempt to reduce, via analytic definition, the mental directly to the physical. Cell 1Aii represents standard versions of the identity theory that reject any sort of narrow semantic reduction of mental to physical terms but nevertheless attempt to reduce mental properties and states to narrowly natural properties and states. Some versions of functionalism (e.g., psychofunctionalism) belong in cell 1Aiv. These views are broadly reductive in both their semantic and ontological commitments.

    Returning from our brief digression, the implications for the moral realist are clear. Not only can the moral realist reject the semantic reductionism of ASN and still hope to naturalistically accommodate moral properties and facts, but accommodation does not even require any sort of narrow ontological reduction. That is, objective moral properties might be construed as, for instance, functional properties not reducible to more narrowly natural properties, though nevertheless realized by such properties and thus naturalistically respectable. So, even if versions of analytic ethical naturalism, occupying cell 1Ai, are implausible, the moral realist has other broad options.[13] This is not to say that the moral realist can simply and

12. However, typical versions of *commonsense functionalism*, perhaps more appropriately labeled *analytic functionalism* — see Horgan and Timmons, 1992b, for a discussion — would go into this slot. See also Block, 1980: 171–84, for a discussion of this view.

13. I am not aware of any realist metaethical views that are explicitly presented as combining a broadly reductive moral semantics with a narrowly reductive account of moral properties and facts, though, of

without argument go for some broadly reductive view; he needs to make a plausible case for this sort of view. But the important thing is that whereas at earlier times in this century, naturalism in ethics did not appear to be compatible with a realist treatment of moral discourse, the rejection of the idea that naturalism must be underwritten by narrow semantic reduction, or even by narrow ontological reduction, held out some hope for the naturalistically inclined moral realist.

However, given the broadening of options for the naturalist in ethics, the reader may be wondering how to distinguish naturalist from non-naturalist views in ethics. Here is the place to say something brief about the contrast between these views and thus to take up some unfinished business from chapter 1 by giving a fuller characterization of the naturalist project in ethics.

IV. Naturalism and Non-Naturalism in Ethics

In chapter 1, I explained the ontological thesis of naturalism in part as a rejection of the reality of anything supernatural. In ethics, what may be called supernaturalism is the view (roughly) that moral facts and properties are identical with or somehow dependent upon supernatural facts and properties, like the will of God. Of course, in twentieth-century metaethics, Moore's views about moral ontology are taken to represent a clear case of ethical non-naturalism, though, for him, the most fundamental moral property—the property of goodness—is not supernatural. So, there is more to ethical naturalism than a mere rejection of any sort of ethical supernaturalism, and given what I've been saying about contemporary conceptions of naturalism, one might well wonder whether Moore would count these days as a non-naturalist. I think he would; let me explain why.

If there were some clear and widely accepted notion of 'natural' (as applied to properties, states, and entities for philosophical, ontological purposes), then we could perhaps straightforwardly settle whether this or that putative property, state, or entity is natural and, hence, whether some ontological view that countenances such items comports with philosophical naturalism. Unfortunately, 'natural,' 'naturalistic,' and 'naturalism' are used in various ways by philosophers, so the straightforward path is not available to us.[14] In chapter 1, I characterized philosophical naturalism partly in terms of the thesis of ontic primacy, according to which what

---

course, one can see what such a view would be like. If we take the view that a term like 'good' can be analytically defined in regard to experiences or states of pleasure as our paradigm of a 1Ai type metaethical view, then any view that held onto the claim that the property *goodness* was identical to the property *experiencing pleasure*, but rejected the idea of any sort of associated analytic definition linking the two properties, would be an example of a type 1Aii metaethical view. During the 1960s and early 1970s, you may recall, work in metaethics was fairly stagnant, and by the time metaethics was under way again and moral philosophers began to exploit work in such areas as the philosophy of mind, functionalism was already in fashion.

14. In response to some objections of C. D. Broad (1942), Moore himself admitted that his characterization of the distinction between natural and non-natural was "utterly silly and preposterous" (1942: 582), and that he was not able to give a clear characterization of the distinction. For a useful discussion of this distinction, see Tye, 1995: 38–43, and Crisp, 1996.

is ontologically basic are the entities, properties, and facts that are the subject matter of science. However, I did not place any restrictions on what counts as science (since I wanted my characterization to be as uncontroversial as possible). Certainly, physics belongs on the list of sciences whose subject matter includes at least some of the most basic items among the naturalist's ontological inventory, but what about other 'natural' sciences like chemistry, geology, and biology, and what about social sciences like psychology? Instead of trying to give a principled answer to this question, let us instead consider the sorts of naturalizing projects in the philosophy of mind and in ethics. Doing so will, I think, help clarify what is generally taken to count as naturalism in these fields.

From the earlier discussion of developments in the philosophy of mind, particularly in connection with the emergence of functionalism, the following ideas seem most prominent in the project of naturalizing the mental. First, there are features of mental phenomena (most important, the features of intentionality and the qualitative character of the mental) that seem to be relatively problematic from a naturalist worldview, in which the sciences of physics, chemistry, and biology are taken as metaphysically unproblematic. At least in the context of inquiry into ontological questions about mental phenomena, psychology is not going to be understood as among the sciences mentioned in the thesis of ontic primacy. Second, with regard to entities, properties, and facts that are not part of the subject matter of these more basic sciences, some sort of reduction (in the broad sense) of the entities, properties, and facts of the problematic area of inquiry to entities, properties and facts of the non-problematic areas of inquiry is required. Furthermore, successful reduction would seem to require not only specifying how the higher level, problematic items are systematically related to the more basic lower level items (e.g., by the relations of identity, constitution, or realization),[15] but it is also widely held that the nature or essence of the higher order properties (to focus just on properties for the time being) must be describable in (what is taken in the context to be) non-problematic, naturalistic terminology. So, in the philosophy of mind, the thought is that mental properties, if not identical, are realized by more basic physico-chemical properties, *and* that the essence of such states and properties can be described in non-mental vocabulary. Thus, as noted in the last section, functionalists have held that mental states with intentional content, such as beliefs, desires, hopes, and the like, can be characterized in their essence in causal terms—terms that are thought to be naturalistically kosher.

In ethics, the project of naturalizing moral properties and facts displays, I think, the same sort of pattern just described in connection with work in the philosophy of mind. First, the naturalizing project in ethics displays the same sort

---

15. Following Tye (1995, ch 2), we may understand the idea of constitution as a relation between a concrete particular and the sum of its parts (e.g., the Eiffel Tower at time t, while not identical to the sum of its parts at t, is nevertheless constituted by those parts at t). The relation of realization is understood to hold between higher level types and properties and lower level types and properties (e.g., the property of being in pain may be realized by a variety of different types of lower level properties).

of context sensitivity as we saw in connection with the project of naturalizing the mental. That is, in ethics, moral normative notions like oughtness and goodness (and normative notions in general) are thought to be problematic from the perspective of naturalism. The naturalizing project here proceeds against the presumption that the metaphysical status of the entities, properties, and facts of sciences (both natural and social) are unproblematic. And so, in this context, were it possible to reduce moral properties to properties that are the subject matter of any of the sciences, including psychology, it would count as a version of ethical naturalism — even if psychological states and properties were not themselves reducible to, say, biological states and properties. Second, what is sought by the ethical naturalist is some sort of reduction of the moral to the non-moral, which involves (1) explaining how moral properties and facts (if they exist) are systematically related to more basic properties and facts (e.g., by the relation of identity, constitution, or realization) and (2) being able to express the essence or nature of such properties and facts in non-moral and, more generally, non-normative terms.

Returning to Moore, his view does still count as a version of non-naturalism by contemporary standards. Moore thought that goodness supervenes on more basic natural properties of things, but he did not think that one could describe or characterize the property of goodness, without remainder, in non-moral terms. In fact, Moore held that the property of goodness was sui generis, by which he meant that not only is it ontologically simple (not composed of parts), but that its nature cannot be expressed in non-moral terms. So it will be useful for our purposes to characterize ethical naturalism as the ontological thesis that the nature of moral properties like rightness and goodness can be described in non-moral and, in general, non-normative terms. Ethical non-naturalism, then (in the sense in which it contrasts with both naturalism and supernaturalism), is the view that moral properties like rightness and goodness cannot be described in non-moral or non-normative terms.[16] Granted, this local, context-sensitive characterization of the difference between naturalism and non-naturalism (within an area of inquiry) falls short of a global, all-purpose characterization of philosophical naturalism (though we still have the vague guiding idea expressed by the thesis of ontic primacy), but it will have to do. At least this means of characterizing the difference will be useful for our purposes, since new wave moral realists, who attempt to pattern their view after psychofunctionalism in the philosophy of mind, do think that the essence of basic moral properties can be characterized in non-normative and, hence, non-moral terms.[17]

16. This characterization is in the spirit of how philosophers have typically understood the view. See, for instance, Broad, 1945: 194.

17. I am not proposing this way of dividing naturalism from non-naturalism as one that all naturalists would accept. David Chalmers (1996), for instance, does not think it is possible to characterize the essence of qualia in non-mental terms (and so he does not consider himself to be a 'materialist' in the philosophy of mind), but he does think that such mental properties should count as naturalistically kosher. If one expands naturalism to include the sort of moral analog to Chalmers's view in metaethics, then whatever line there is dividing Moore's position from ethical naturalism is very thin indeed.

But before moving on to new wave moral realism, let us consider what would appear to be a serious obstacle to any version of moral realism engaged in the accommodation project I have described.

V. Mackie's Queerness Arguments

Mackie's so-called queerness arguments are intended to block the combination of moral realism with philosophical naturalism. The more basic metaphysical queerness argument and its epistemological adjunct are summarized in this way:

> If there were objective values [properties, facts], then they would be entities or qualities or relations of a very strange sort, utterly different from anything else in the universe. Correspondingly, if we were aware of them, it would have to be by some special faculty of moral perception or intuition, utterly different from our ordinary ways of knowing everything else. (Mackie, 1977: 38)

Relating Mackie's remarks to our characterization of the naturalistic accommodation program, his first remark about objective values implies that the moral realist cannot satisfy N_2^*, while his second remark about our access to putative objective values implies that the moral realist cannot satisfy N_3^*. I take it that an acid test for any realist-naturalist in ethics is overcoming Mackie's charges, and it is against this background that I want to consider new wave moral realism. But first we need to clarify the arguments behind the quoted remarks. After all, why should (putative) objective values and our knowledge of them require ontological and epistemological commitments inconsistent with philosophical naturalism?

Since the metaphysical queerness argument is supposed to be more basic than its epistemological companion, let us focus on it. If we inspect Mackie's reasons for claiming that moral realism involves ontological commitments incompatible with naturalism, we actually find two distinct arguments: one of them (alluded to in the above quote) focuses on those objective moral properties and facts countenanced by the realist, and the other focuses on the sort of relation between natural properties and facts and moral ones. We need to consider both versions, since they may well differ significantly in their force against moral realism.

The first of the queerness arguments involves the premise that were there any objective moral properties or facts, they would be, as Mackie says, *intrinsically prescriptive*—somehow they would be intrinsically motivating in (roughly) the sense that mere recognition of their presence would (independently of any desires) motivate or provide a reason for anyone to act accordingly. Mackie writes:

> Plato's Forms give a dramatic picture of what objective values would have to be. The Form of the Good is such that knowledge of it provides the knower with both a direction and an overriding motive; something's being good both tells the person who knows this to pursue it and makes him pursue it. An objective good would be sought by anyone who was acquainted with it, not because of any contingent fact that this person, or every person, is so constituted that he desires this end, but just because the end has to-be-pursuedness somehow built into it. (Mackie, 1977: 40)

The claim that moral properties and facts are intrinsically prescriptive is supposed to be a conceptual truth about our ordinary moral terms and the concepts they express. So Mackie's first metaphysical queerness argument can be outlined in the following way.

METAPHYSICAL QUEERNESS ARGUMENT 1

1. It is a truth of ordinary moral discourse that our moral terms (and the concepts they express) purport to refer to intrinsically prescriptive properties and facts, so that if there were any moral properties or facts, they would have to be intrinsically prescriptive.
2. But the existence of intrinsically prescriptive properties or facts — properties or facts that would somehow motivate us or provide us with reasons for action independent of our desires and aversions — does not comport with naturalism.

Therefore,

3. If there are any objective moral properties and facts, they would not comport with naturalism; that is, they would be metaphysically queer.

The second premise perhaps requires some comment. In light of the discussion in the previous section, we could express Mackie's idea here by saying that our ordinary concept of a moral property has an ineliminatable normative component, "to-be-pursuedness" or intrinsic prescriptivity, and so whose essence or nature cannot be fully described in non-normative language. Thus, such properties are by nature non-natural, and countenancing their instantiation would not be consistent with philosophical naturalism. Of course, the realist (were he to accept the premises) could simply decide to live with the conclusion and thus reject a thoroughly naturalistic metaphysics. But, as we shall see in a moment, the moral realist need not (it seem) accept these premises.

Mackie's second version of the metaphysical queerness objection is contained in this passage:

> Another way of bringing out this queerness is to ask, about anything that is supposed to have some objective moral quality, how this is linked with its natural features. What is the connection between the natural fact that an action is a piece of deliberate cruelty — say, causing pain just for fun — and the moral fact that it is wrong? It cannot be an entailment, a logical or semantic necessity. Yet it is not merely that the two features occur together. The wrongness must somehow be 'consequential' or 'supervenient'; it is wrong because it is a piece of deliberate cruelty. But just what *in the world* is signified by this 'because'? (Mackie, 1977: 41)

Although the exact argument behind this 'what in the world?' complaint that Mackie had in mind is not made clear by this passage, the basic idea seems to be as follows.[18] We cannot plausibly explain the necessary connection between nat-

---

18. Cf. Mackie, 1982: 118, where he makes clear that the problem with moral supervenience is that "there would be something here in need of explanation."

ural features of a thing and any putative objective moral features of that thing by appeal to the idea that the presence of the natural property or fact entails the presence of the moral property or fact, since this would require some form of narrow semantic reduction. But to invoke supervenience in order to explain the connection involves positing, according to Mackie, a "mysterious consequential link between the two" (1977: 41). Hence, the would-be moral realist-naturalist is stuck. Set out more formally, here is the argument.

METAPHYSICAL QUEERNESS ARGUMENT 2

1. Versions of moral realism that would take (putative) objective moral properties to supervene upon certain lower level properties (biological, psychological, or whatever) posit some objective, in-the-world necessary relation between moral properties and these other, lower level properties—a relation that cannot be explained by appeal to semantic considerations.
2. But without being able to satisfactorily explain this in-the-world necessary connection between moral and natural properties, the realist must admit into his ontology an unexplainable and, hence, metaphysically mysterious relation.

Therefore,

3. If there were moral properties and facts that supervene on other properties and facts, this would involve having to posit a metaphysically mysterious relation—a relation that would not comport with philosophical naturalism.

In connection with both of these arguments, Mackie points out that the moral realist—who would countenance metaphysically queer properties, facts, and relations—must also posit some special faculty through which we have access to these mysterious things. Otherwise, the realist is stuck with skepticism about moral knowledge. If Mackie's queerness arguments are good ones, the moral realist cannot hope to satisfy either $N2^*$ or $N3^*$, and thus cannot hope to naturalistically accommodate the metaphysical and epistemological commitments of his metaethical view.

VI. Enter the New Wave

New wave moral realism exploits developments in philosophy of the 1960s and 1970s (e.g., the philosophy of mind) in order to develop a strain of moral realism that satisfies the desiderata operative in constraining metaethical inquiry and, in particular, answers the sorts of ontological and associated epistemological objections represented by Mackie's queerness arguments. In the following sections, I want to present and then evaluate this view. My presentation of the new wave view relies heavily on the work of David Brink and Richard Boyd, work that is nicely complementary and in which we find a broadly reductivist position occupying, as I said, cell 1Aiv of our chart.

Brink argues that his version of moral realism, unlike competing irrealist views, satisfies our two desiderata, D1 and D2, for judging metaethical views. First he claims that ordinary, commonsense moral discourse and practice presupposes such things as there being objective moral properties and facts. Brink argues that moral realism (but not moral irrealism) can neatly accommodate such presupposed phenomena and then concludes that moral realism satisfies D1 — the requirement that a plausible metaethical view comport with commonsense presumptions embedded in moral discourse and practice. He then goes on to argue that the metaphysical and epistemological commitments of his view comport nicely with philosophical naturalism (thus satisfying N2* and N3*) and that, in general, the view satisfies D2 — the requirement that one's metaethical view comport with various non-moral assumptions and theories. So the 'master' argument of Brink's book is the following: since the new wave brand of moral realism with its various metaphysical and epistemological commitments beats out versions of irrealism when it comes to D1, and since it comports with non-moral views and assumptions at least as well as competing metaethical views, this view is overall more plausible than its competitors.

Beginning in the next chapter, I consider the claim that realism beats out irrealist contenders in better squaring with the ordinary presumptions of commonsense moral thought and practice. Our immediate concern is with the defensive part of Brink's program — his attempt to show that his brand of moral realism squares with philosophical naturalism, that Mackie's queerness worries don't apply.

In Boyd's work, we find semantic views that complement Brink's metaethical views and, indeed, figure importantly in the overall new wavers' program. The resulting Brink-Boyd package involves a good deal of complexity and sophistication. In order to manage my treatment of their view, I have found it convenient to subdivide my presentation as follows. In the next section, I shall focus mainly on the metaphysical commitments of Brink's view, including his replies to Mackie's queerness arguments, and then in the following section, I will take up the complementary semantic views of Boyd.

VII. Moral Metaphysics

The essential ingredients of Brink's moral realism are: (1) an externalist construal of moral discourse, (2) a broadly reductive version of ethical naturalism,[19] and (3) a coherentist moral epistemology (1989: 7). The first two ingredients concern us here, since they represent the basis for the new wavers' responses to Mackie's two metaphysical queerness arguments.[20]

Speaking very generally, ethical internalism represents a view about moral considerations and moral convictions, according to which such considerations (or

19. Following the usage in the philosophy of mind, and thus in order to contrast his view with older, more narrowly reductive versions of ethical naturalism (that would identify moral properties with more narrowly natural properties), Brink calls his view a *non-reductive* version of ethical naturalism.

20. For a critical evaluation of the attempt to combine a coherentist moral epistemology with moral realism, see Timmons, 1990a.

convictions) are essentially practical. This vague thesis requires clarification to be of any philosophical use. It can and has been variously specified, so that in the philosophical literature we find a number of distinct views lumped under the internalist banner.[21] Internalism is, of course, characteristic of non-descriptivist semantic views that maintain that moral language primarily performs some non-fact-stating, practical function. In the days of analytic metaethics, internalism was construed narrowly as the view that the meanings of moral terms and expressions analytically contain this action-guiding practical function. Thus, for example, according to a standard form of internalism, which would construe moral judgments (convictions) as essentially action-guiding, it is an analytic and, hence, necessary truth that anyone who sincerely utters a moral judgment ('X is wrong') is motivated to act accordingly (avoid doing X).

Brink rejects ethical internalism in all of its many varieties. We need not be detained with the many versions and his objections to them. The outcome of his objections to all the various versions of internalism is that they implausibly take the connection between moral language and action to be a conceptual connection: internalism takes the action-guiding function of moral discourse to be a matter of the very meaning of moral terms. According to Brink, internalism thus interprets the connection between morality and action too strongly. One of his typical criticisms, designed to make this point, goes this way. First, consider what Brink calls *appraiser internalism*, according to which anyone who sincerely utters the moral judgment 'X is wrong' must thereby be motivated appropriately in regard to X (i.e., she will typically be averse to performing X, and so on). But this sort of strong conceptual connection between sincere moral judgment and motivation implies that there could not be a genuine *amoralist*—someone who sincerely utters a moral judgment but who is not at all motivated to act accordingly. But surely, as the argument goes, it is conceptually possible for there to be a genuine amoralist; hence, appraiser internalism is false. This and similar arguments lead Brink to conclude that externalism[22]—the view that denies any sort of conceptual connection between morality and practice—is more plausible than any version of internalism:

> This is because externalism, rather than internalism, is the appropriate way to represent the practical or action-guiding character of morality. The rationality and motivational force of moral considerations depend, as the externalist claims, not simply on the concept of morality but (also) on the content of morality, facts about agents, and a substantive theory of reasons for action. Not only can moral realism accommodate the action-guiding character of morality, properly understood; it can do so better than its traditional opponents can. (Brink, 1989: 79–80)

---

21. The fact that are there many varieties of ethical internalism is partly due to the fact that there are differences about the items that constitute the *relata* of this alleged necessary connection. See Brink, 1989: ch. 3, for a detailed discussion of various internalist theses.

22. In ch. 4, as part of my semantic story of moral discourse, I show how one can be an internalist and yet avoid the amoralist objection. So I think Brink moves too hastily from his rejection of standard forms of internalism (that really do overdraw the connection between sincere moral judgment and motivation) to embracing externalism. There is some middle ground not recognized by Brink. For a direct response to Brink's amoralist challenge to internalism, see Michael Smith, 1994: ch. 3.

The rejection of an internalist construal of moral discourse is the basis for a response to Mackie's first metaphysical queerness argument. The first premise of that argument, you may recall, was that moral discourse is practical: if moral terms really did successfully refer to objective moral properties, those properties would have something like "to-be-pursuedness" wired into them, and so they would be metaphysically queer. And as Brink points out, this premise seems to be equivalent to some form or other of ethical internalism. If, following Brink, one argues that internalism overdraws any link there is between moral discourse and action and that, consequently, we should reject the idea that morality is intrinsically prescriptive, then construing moral terms as referring to objective moral properties does not commit one to anything metaphysically queer from the perspective of the philosophical naturalist. Brink's rejection of ethical internalism apparently saves him from Mackie's first queerness argument.

How then should we construe the sorts of properties (and facts) that moral terms (and moral statements) are about? And, furthermore, how are moral properties and facts related to more narrowly natural properties and facts? Brink's answers to these questions involve an account of moral properties modeled on functionalism in the philosophy of mind:

> [T]he moral realist might claim that moral properties are functional properties. He might claim that what is essential to moral properties is the causal role which they play in the characteristic activities of human organisms. In particular, the realist might claim that moral properties are those which bear upon the maintenance and flourishing of human organisms. Maintenance and flourishing presumably consist in necessary conditions for survival, other needs associated with basic well-being, wants of various sorts, and distinctively human capacities. People, actions, policies, states of affairs, etc. will bear good-making moral properties just insofar as they contribute to the satisfaction of these needs, wants, and capacities . . . [and] will bear bad-making moral properties just insofar as they fail to promote or interfere with the satisfaction of these needs, wants, and capacities. The physical states which contribute to or interfere with the satisfaction of these needs, wants, and capacities are the physical states upon which, on this functionalist theory, moral properties ultimately supervene. (Brink, 1984: 121–22)

If, as Brink proposes, moral terms are to be construed as purporting to refer to functional properties that supervene on certain physical states, how are we to characterize the functional essences of properties like rightness and goodness? Brink claims that we discover these essences through moral inquiry:

> The details of the way in which moral properties supervene upon other natural properties are worked out differently by different moral theories. Determination of which account of moral supervenience is best will depend upon determination of which moral theory provides the best account of all our beliefs, both moral and non-moral. (Brink, 1984: 121; see also Brink, 1989: 175)

The result of this functionalist construal of moral properties is a broadly reductivist version of ethical naturalism: moral terms and expressions are construed as purporting to pick out certain functional properties whose essence is revealed by the generalizations of some normative moral theory that best fits with our beliefs, "both moral and non-moral." Moral properties are thus realized by, and hence supervene on, natural properties. Moreover, construing moral properties as supervenient in this way does not automatically force one to abandon one's philosophical naturalism. Granted, supervenience in this case does amount to a necessary connection without there being an entailment relation between the natural and the moral. But this is not enough to show that the relation is somehow metaphysically queer. For one thing, as mentioned earlier in §III, there is wide acceptance of Saul Kripke's views about rigid designation and the consequent idea that some necessary truths are empirical rather than being knowable a priori (Kripke, 1972). So we need not assume that all necessary truths are analytic or reflect entailment relations. Furthermore, as we have already seen in connection with developments in the philosophy of mind, philosophers in the 1960s and 1970s increasingly began to repudiate older, narrowly reductionistic modes of naturalistic accommodation and invoked the notion of supervenience itself in order to articulate a form of philosophical naturalism with only broad reductionist commitments.

So in a philosophical milieu where empirically necessary truths are widely accepted, and where supervenience relations are widely invoked for the purpose of articulating a broadly reductive form of naturalism, it is not surprising that the new wave moral realist would be unimpressed with Mackie's second queerness argument. Thus, a perfectly sensible-looking reply to Mackie is given by Brink:

> There is nothing strange and certainly nothing unique about the supervenience of moral properties on physical properties. Assuming materialism is true, mental states supervene on physical states, yet few think that mental states are metaphysically queer (and those that do do not think that supervenience makes them queer). Social facts such as unemployment, inflation, and exploitation supervene upon physical facts, yet no one supposes that social facts are metaphysically queer. Biological states such as being an organism supervene on physical states, yet no one supposes that organisms are queer entities. Macro-scopic material objects such as tables supervene on micro-scopic physical particles, yet no one supposes that tables are queer entities. In short, it is difficult to see how the realist's use of supervenience in explaining the relationship between moral and physical properties makes his position queer. (Brink, 1984: 120; see also Brink, 1989: 177–80)[23]

This plea of innocence by association draws upon a comparison between (putative) objective moral properties, construed as supervening on natural properties, and supervenient properties and facts, usually taken to be uncontroversial and certainly not incompatible with naturalism. It would appear that there is nothing queer about the supervenience relation itself, and hence that the moral realist, who would invoke this relation in articulating the connection between the moral and the natural, has nothing to fear from Mackie's second metaphysical queerness argument.

---

23. Notice that this argument joins the focal points of Mackie's two queerness arguments by shifting attention away from the supervenience relation itself and onto the various sorts of supervening properties and facts.

In sum, given his rejection of internalism and his innocence-by-association argument, apparently the new wave moral realist can quite easily sidestep Mackie's objections. Certainly, the burden of proof is on the irrealist to show that there is anything about the realist's metaphysical commitments that would block naturalistic accommodation of those commitments.

However, I think problems remain and that Mackie's misgivings can be pressed further. In particular, I think that Mackie's provocative question about what *"in the world"* is signified by the 'because' of moral supervenience is connected to a little appreciated concern about objective supervenience relations generally and how such relations figure into the metaphysical picture of the naturalist. Terry Horgan and I have argued (1) that objective, in-the-world supervenience relations linking higher order properties and facts to lower order properties and facts (whether in ethics or elsewhere) require explanation if they are to comport with naturalism,[24] (2) that such explanations are possible for various sorts of objective supervenience relations, including those linking mental properties and facts to physico-chemical properties and facts, (3) but that such explanations are not available to the moral realist in connection with objective supervenience facts. If we are right about this, then the innocence-by-association argument will not work and the moral realist must, along with Moore and other metaethical non-naturalists, posit brute, unexplainable supervenience facts of a sort not compatible with naturalism.

I do not plan to press this particular queerness worry here (I refer the interested reader to Horgan and Timmons, 1992b; 1991) because for one thing, there is some disagreement over the issue of whether positing sui generis supervenience facts is incompatible with naturalism,[25] but for another, according to Horgan and myself, the hitch in the new wavers' attempt to explain objective moral supervenience relations has to do with the sort of semantic view needed to undergird such explanations. So in order to raise the main problem with new wave moral realism, one can proceed directly to their semantic view without taking a detour through thorny questions about explaining supervenience.

VIII. Moral Semantics

New wave moral semantics is a view that has resulted from the attempt to extend those relatively recent developments in the philosophy of language mentioned earlier in §III to the understanding of moral language. You may recall those developments: (1) rejection of a synonymy criterion of property identity, (2) the view that names and natural kind terms are rigid designators—rigid in the sense that

---

24. That is, they should not be understood as unexplainable sui generis relations, which is how Moore understood them. See Moore, 1903: 143.

25. Among those who think that supervenience relations require explanation (at least from a naturalistic perspective) are Hare (1984), Blackburn (1985b), Schiffer (1987), Kim (1993), and Horgan (1993). However, Zangwill (1997) challenges the thesis that supervenience relations must be naturalistically explained in order to fully comport with philosophical naturalism.

they designate the same entity with respect to every possible world in which they refer at all, and (3) the causal theory of reference for names and natural kind terms. New wave moral semantics has emerged in the context of these developments, and one finds a representative version of this semantic view in the work of Boyd (1988), who puts the view to work in his recent defense of moral realism. All three of the just mentioned ideas are present in Boyd's semantic view about such terms as 'right' and 'good.'

First, he contends that 'good,' like many other terms, has a synthetic, or what he calls 'natural,' definition[26] that reveals the essence of the property that term expresses. And, of course, this claim implies the rejection of the synonymy criterion of property identity: the property goodness is identical with such and such natural property, even though the term 'good' is not synonymous with any naturalistic term or phrase designating the relevant natural property.

Second, the claim that moral terms admit of synthetic definitions requires that such terms are rigid. Like natural terms, moral terms allegedly rigidly designate the properties (natural properties for the ethical naturalist) to which they refer. It is the rigidity of moral terms that underlies the necessity possessed by synthetic definitions.[27]

Third, Boyd maintains that for moral terms, just as for names and natural kind terms, reference is a matter of there being certain causal connections between the use of moral terms and relevant natural properties. According to Boyd's own version of the causal theory of reference, reference is essentially an epistemic notion and so the relevant causal relations constituting reference are just those causal connections involved in knowledge-gathering activities:

> *Roughly*, and for nondegenerate cases, a term *t* refers to a kind (property, relation, etc.) *k* just in case there exist causal mechanisms whose tendency is to bring it about, over time, that what is predicated of the term *t* will be approximately true of *k* (excuse the blurring of the use-mention distinction). Such mechanisms will typically include the existence of procedures which are approximately accurate for recognizing members or instances of *k* (at least for easy cases) and which relevantly govern the use of *t*, the social transmission of certain relevantly approximately true beliefs regarding *k*, formulated as claims about *t* (again excuse the slight to the use-mention distinction), a pattern of deference to experts on *k* with respect to the use of *t*, etc. . . . When relations of this sort obtain, we may think of the properties of *k* as regulating the use of *t* (via such causal relations). (Boyd, 1988: 195)

Extending this version of the causal theory of reference to moral terms, as Boyd proposes to do, commits him to a *causal regulation thesis*:

---

26. See Boyd, 1988: 194–95, 209–12.

27. Admittedly, Boyd is not as explicit as one would like about the rigidity of moral terms. But this view fits well with his claim that moral terms have 'natural' definitions, and also helps fend off a form of relativism that runs counter to the realist form of ethical naturalism Boyd defends. However, as I explain later (see n. 34), even if Boyd does not take moral terms to be rigid, this will not affect in any substantial way the criticism to be offered of the Boydian view.

CRT *Causal regulation thesis*: For each moral term t (e.g., 'good'), there is a natural property N, such that N and N alone causally regulates the use of t by humans.

Furthermore, on Boyd's view, the essence of goodness, rightness, and other moral properties consists primarily in certain *relational* connections they bear to one another and to other properties, actions, institutions, and so forth. So it would seem that, for Boyd, moral properties are *functional* properties whose essential relations and interconnections are captured by some specific normative theory. It is an empirical question, on this view, which particular normative theory has this status. This functionalist construal fits exactly with Brink's functionalist characterization of moral properties and follows the model of psychofunctionalism in the philosophy of mind.

The causal regulation thesis, then, presumably allows one to treat moral terms like 'good' as semantically akin to natural kind terms: they refer rigidly to certain natural properties and hence possess synthetic definitions. So we can summarize what I'm calling new wave moral semantics (as developed by Boyd) as the following thesis:

CSN *Causal semantic naturalism*: Each moral term t rigidly designates the natural property N that uniquely causally regulates the use of t by humans.

A corollary of CSN is that each moral term t has a synthetically true natural definition whose definiens characterizes, in purely natural terms, the unique natural property that supposedly causally regulates the use of t by humans.

Boyd's and Brink's views are compatible and, in fact, nicely complementary. Brink is explicit in claiming that moral properties are functional properties (and Boyd's remarks about goodness strongly suggest a functionalist story) whose essence is captured by a specific normative moral theory, but he says rather little about the semantics of moral terms. Boyd, on the other hand, explicitly claims that moral terms work like natural kind terms in science, and that they designate natural properties, but he says rather little about the nature of these properties. Indeed, if we press the comparison between psychofunctionalism in the philosophy of mind and this version of ethical naturalism, the Brink-Boyd proposal for understanding the semantics of moral terms would include, in addition to CRT and CSN, the following *functional causal regulation thesis*. Terminology: If T is a normative moral theory and t is a putatively property-expressing moral term, let T(t) be the functional property whose relational essence is just the functional role that, according to the generalizations of T, constitutes the t-role.

FCRT *Functional Causal Regulation Thesis*: There is a unique normative moral theory T such that for each moral term t, humankind's uses of t are causally regulated by the functional property T(t).

The theses FCRT plus CRT together entail this corollary:

CSFT *Causal Semantic Functionalism Thesis*: Each moral term t rigidly designates the unique functional property that causally regulates the actual-world uses of t by humans.

This causal-functional construal of the semantics of moral terms would appear to be just what the moral realist, who is interested in the project of naturalistic accommodation, needs. Apparently, Mackie's queerness objections can be turned aside by the new wave moral realist. So the big question is: Is the Brink-Boyd view (or one like it) plausible?

IX. Troubles on Moral Twin Earth

I believe there are reasons for thinking that the causal-functional semantics for moral terms is fundamentally incorrect. On this account, as we have seen, moral terms like 'good' and 'right' function like natural kind terms in the sense that, through their use of them, ordinary competent speakers purport to refer to some single, objective natural property (presumably a functional property) that regulates their use and whose essence is discoverable through moral inquiry. What I want to argue is that there is good reason to suppose that this is false, that it is not part of the semantics of such moral terms (as ordinarily used) that they work in the way the causal-functional theory describes. More precisely, I plan to argue that even if we grant the causal regulation thesis (i.e., CRT and its functionalist correlate, FCRT) — the claim that human uses of key moral terms are by and large causally regulated by some single, objective natural property — still, one may not conclude that causal semantic naturalism in general (i.e., CSN) and causal semantic functionalism in particular (i.e., CSFT) for those moral terms are correct.[28] Thus, despite the fact that new wave moral semantics comports with some features of ordinary moral discourse and practice (e.g., it allows for the possibility of genuine error in moral belief), it does not comport with certain other deep features of the semantics of moral discourse. So, given the importance of new wave semantics to the entire realist project in ethics, the view is not able to discharge the dual metaphysical and epistemological burdens required of the thoroughgoing philosophical naturalist.

How might one go about testing the hypothesis that central moral terms function in the way described by the causal-functional account? The most obvious strategy is to consider how philosophers have argued for causal accounts of natural kind terms generally. And here we find a particular type of thought experiment that looms very large: the Putnam-style Twin Earth scenario. Let us recall how those operate, using Putnam's own water example.

Suppose that someone grants that the use of 'water' by humans is causally regulated by some specific physico-chemical natural kind, but then questions the claim that 'water' rigidly designates the natural kind (viz., H_2O) that happens to fill this role. The skeptic might believe, for instance, that 'water' designates a more general physical natural kind — a genus that has H_2O as only one of its various actual or physically possible species. How could we convince the skeptic that 'water' really does rigidly designate the sortal kind property H_2O? In one of Put-

---

28. Since CSN is the backbone of CSFT, my critical focus will be on this more fundamental thesis.

nam's stories, we are to imagine Twin Earth—a planet much like Earth except that the oceans, lakes, and streams are filled with a liquid whose outward, easily observable properties are just like those of water, but whose underlying physico-chemical nature is not H_2O, but some other molecular structure, abbreviated XYZ. Despite outward similarities and the fact that speakers of twin English apply the word 'water' to this liquid composed of XYZ, reflection on this scenario yields a very strong intuition that Twin Earthlings don't mean by their twin-English term 'water' what we mean by 'water,' and that their term is not translatable by our orthographically identical term. Along with this judgment come two further intuitive judgments: (1) that the English term *rigidly designates* H_2O, whereas the twin-English term rigidly designates XYZ and (2) this fact explains why the terms differ in meaning.

Competent speakers have a strong intuitive mastery of both the syntactic and the semantic norms governing their language. Consequently, the intuitive judgments described concerning the Twin Earth scenario constitute important (though, of course, defeasible) empirical evidence for the hypothesis that 'water' rigidly designates the specific physico-chemical physical kind that happens to causally regulate the use of this term by humans, namely, the kind H_2O. The statement 'Water $= H_2O$,' then, is held to be a synthetic definition that gives the real essence of water, not an analytic definition that gives a synonym of 'water.' Let us call this sort of argument a *semantic competence argument*.[29]

Just as speakers have an intuitive mastery of syntactic and semantic norms governing the proper use of natural kind terms like 'water,' so competent speakers presumably have a comparable intuitive mastery of the semantic working of 'good' and other fundamental moral terms. So if the causal-functional theory is correct, then the scenario should go the same way it went with 'water.' That is, if indeed the term 'good' purports to rigidly designate the unique natural property (if there is one) that causally regulates that use of 'good' by humans in general, then it should be possible to construct a suitable Twin Earth scenario with these features: (1) reflection on this scenario generates intuitive judgments that are comparable to those concerning Putnam's original scenario, and (2) these judgments are accompanied by the more general intuitive judgment that 'good' does work semantically as the causal theory (CSN) says it does. Conversely, if the appropriate Twin Earth scenario does not have these features—in other words, if the semantic intuitions of competent speakers turn out not to be what they should be if CSN is true—then this will be evidence for the conclusion that in all probability CSN is

---

29. Calling such arguments *semantic competence arguments* is intended to suggest a relevant analogy between such arguments and a common form of reasoning within empirical linguistics, namely, the appeal to speakers' intuitions about the grammaticality or syntactic ambiguity of certain sentencelike strings of words, as evidence for or against various empirical hypotheses about natural-language syntax. The latter kind of argument rests on the (empirically plausible) background assumption that syntactic intuitions normally reflect what Noam Chomsky has called speakers' 'linguistic competence.' For an illuminating discussion of how linguistic intuitions are properly construed as constituting *empirical* evidence for semantic hypotheses (as opposed to construing such methodology in the old way as essentially a priori), see Graham and Horgan, 1994.

false (and, consequently, that the functionalist correlate of CSN, namely, CSFT, is false).

So let us begin with the supposition that, as the causal-functional view claims, human uses of 'good' and 'right' are regulated by certain *functional* properties; and that, as a matter of empirical fact, these are the consequentialist properties whose functional essence is captured by some specific consequentialist normative theory. I shall call this theory T^c. Suppose further that the coherentist methodology of reflective equilibrium is effective, and that if it is properly and thoroughly employed, it will lead us to discover this fact about our uses of moral terms.

Now consider Moral Twin Earth, which, as you can guess, is almost exactly like good old Earth: it has the same geography and natural surroundings, people who live in the twin United States by and large speak twin English; and so on. Of particular importance here is the fact that Moral Twin Earthlings have a vocabulary that works much like human moral vocabulary; they use the terms 'good' and 'bad,' 'right' and 'wrong' to evaluate actions, persons, institutions, and so forth. (At least those who speak twin English use these terms, whereas those who speak some other twin language use terms orthographically identical to the terms for good, etc., in the corresponding Earthian dialects.) In fact, were a group of explorers ever to visit Moral Twin Earth, they would be strongly inclined to translate Moral Twin Earth terms 'good,' 'right,' and the rest as identical in meaning to our orthographically identical English terms. After all, the uses of these terms on Moral Twin Earth bear all of the 'formal' marks that we take to characterize moral vocabulary and moral practice. In particular, the terms are used to reason about considerations bearing on Moral Twin Earthlings' well-being (and, perhaps, the well-being of other Twin Earth creatures). Moral Twin Earthlings are normally disposed to act in certain ways corresponding to judgments about what is 'good' and 'right'; they normally take such considerations about what is 'good' and 'right' to be especially important, even of overriding importance in most cases, in deciding what to do, and so on.

Let us now suppose that investigation into twin-English moral discourse and associated practice reveals that their uses of twin-moral terms are causally regulated by certain natural properties distinct from those that regulate English moral discourse. The properties tracked by twin-English moral terms are also functional properties, whose essence is functionally characterizable by means of a normative moral theory. But these are *non-consequentialist* moral properties, whose functional essence is captured by some specific deontological theory. Let us call this theory T^d. These functional properties are similar enough to those characterizable via T^c to account for the fact that twin-moral discourse operates in Twin Earth society and culture in much the same manner that moral discourse operates on Earth. (It has already been noted that if explorers ever visit Moral Twin Earth, they will be inclined, at least initially, to construe Moral Twin Earthlings as having beliefs about good and right, and to translate twin English uses of these terms into our orthographically identical terms.) The differences in causal regulation, we may suppose, are due at least in part to certain species-wide differences in psychological temperament that distinguish Twin Earthlings from Earthlings. For instance, perhaps Twin Earthlings tend to experience the sentiment of guilt more readily and more intensively, and tend to experience sympathy less readily and less intensively, than do Earthlings. Let us further suppose that if Twin Earthlings were to employ reflective equilibrium in a proper and thorough manner, it would lead them to discover that their own uses of moral terms are causally regulated by functional properties whose essence is captured by the deontological theory T^d.

Given all of these assumptions and stipulations about Moral Twin Earth,[30] what is the appropriate way to describe the differences between moral and twin-moral uses of 'good' and 'right'? Two hermeneutical options are available. On the one hand, we could say that the differences are analogous to those between Earth and Twin Earth in Putnam's original example, to wit: the moral terms used by Earthlings rigidly designate the natural properties that causally regulate their use on Earth; hence, moral and twin-moral terms *differ in meaning* and are not inter-translatable. On the other hand, we could say that moral and twin-moral terms do not differ in meaning and reference and, hence, that any apparent moral dis-agreements that might arise between Earthlings and Twin Earthlings would be *genuine disagreements*—that is, *disagreements in moral belief and in normative theory*, rather than disagreements in meaning.[31]

I submit that by far the more natural mode of description, when one considers the Moral Twin Earth scenario, is the second. Reflection on the scenario does not generate hermeneutical pressure to construe Moral Twin Earthling uses of 'good' and 'right' as not translatable by our orthographically identical terms. But if CSN were true, and the moral terms in question rigidly designated those natural prop-erties that causally regulate their use, then reflection on this scenario ought to generate intuitions analogous to those generated in Putnam's original Twin Earth story. That is, it should seem intuitively natural to say that there is a difference in meaning and that twin-English 'moral' terms are not translatable by English moral terms. But when it comes to characterizing the differences between Earthlings and Twin Earthlings on this matter, the natural-seeming thing to say is that the differ-ences involve belief and theory, not meaning.

One's intuitions work the same way if, instead of considering the Moral Twin Earth scenario from the outside looking in, one considers how things would strike Earthlings and Twin Earthlings who have encountered each other. Suppose that Earthlings visit Twin Earth (or vice versa), and both groups come to realize that different natural properties causally regulate their respective uses of 'good,' 'right,'

---

30. Granted, the description of Moral Twin Earth involves more complexity than Putnam's description of Twin Earth, but I don't see how this affects the thought experiment or its being a genuine test of the semantic hypothesis under consideration.

31. It should be stressed that differences in normative moral theory, between Earthlings and Twin Earthlings, do not constitute different claims about which property is identical to goodness, or to rightness, etc. For, normative theories do not make such property-identity claims. Rather, they make claims, for instance, about which natural property is the fundamental good-making property, which property is the fundamental right-making property, etc. Normative theories per se are neutral between metaethical claims (1) that moral properties are identical with these natural properties; (2) that moral properties are non-natural properties that supervene upon the natural ones without being identical to or realized by them; or (3) that moral properties do not exist at all.

and other moral terms. If CSN were true, then recognition of these differences ought to result in its seeming rather silly, to members of each group, to engage in intergroup debate about goodness—about whether it conforms to normative theory T^c or to T^d. Compare Putnam's original scenario and how things would strike the two groups: when those groups learn that their respective uses of 'water' are causally regulated by different physical kind properties, it would be silly for them to think that they have differing views about the real nature of water. But such intergroup debate in the Moral Twin Earth story would surely strike both groups not as silly, but as quite appropriate, because they would regard one another as differing in moral belief and moral theory, not in meaning.

Since semantic norms are tapped by human linguistic competence, and since the relevant linguistic competence is presumably reflected in one's intuitive judgments concerning the Twin Earth scenarios, the outcome in the Moral Twin Earth scenario constitutes strong empirical evidence against CSN (and consequently against its functionalist correlate, CSFT).

You may recall from the outset of this section that my strategy was to show that even if we grant CRT (the causal regulation thesis), which is an empirical assumption built into the Moral Twin Earth scenario, the causal semantic theory of Boyd (CSN) is not correct. I have not focused on CRT, which is obviously contentious.[32] Indeed, one can easily bring Moral Twin Earth down to Earth by noting that the intuitive ease with which we imagine Twin Earthlings tracking a different natural property corresponding to their use of, say, 'good,' simply indicates that it is plausible to suppose that here on Earth, different groups whose moral beliefs do consistently track some natural properties, track *different* natural properties. Of course, this issue is an empirical one and engages the debate between metaethical camps about the depth and extent of disagreement in moral belief. I do believe there is some evidence to suppose that, here on Earth, there are deep differences in moral belief that reflect differences in the non-moral, natural features of things that different groups and individuals take to be morally relevant. (See, for instance, Wong, 1984: chs. 8–11.) I shall not enter into this debate here; I only want to register pessimism about an empirical assumption embedded in Boyd's moral semantics.

But even if, to my surprise, CRT did turn out to be true, this would not affect the central criticism provided in this section, namely, that even if human uses of moral terms like 'good' are causally regulated by some single, objective natural property, reflection on relevant Twin Earth scenarios reveals that CSN, and hence CSFT, are false.

Let us return for a moment to Mackie's queerness objections to moral realism. In order to overcome those objections, the moral realist needs to be able to tell a naturalistically kosher story both about the nature of objective moral properties and about matters semantic. The Brink-Boyd story would satisfy this demand were it plausible. But its plausibility is thrown into doubt by the Moral Twin Earth

---

32. I note that the audience reaction to Boydian semantics at philosophical conferences where I have presented his view is very unsympathetic to his causal regulation thesis. I think this reaction is justified.

story. So, without a plausible metaphysical and semantic story about morality, Mackie's queerness objections have not been answered.

In order to further reinforce this pessimistic conclusion about naturalistic moral realism, I want to make clear that the Moral Twin Earth argument, which I have aimed at the specific causal-functionalist construal of moral terms under consideration, is really more than a specific thought experiment directed at the specific semantic theses of CSN and CSFT. That is, notice, first of all, that CSN is really a species of the following more general semantic thesis:

> SSN   *Synthetic semantic naturalism*: Fundamental moral terms like 'good' have synthetic natural definitions.

It might be thought that even if CSN is not tenable because of Moral Twin Earth, there remains a serious possibility that some other species of SSN might still be tenable — perhaps a version of SSN that nobody has yet articulated. But Moral Twin Earth, in addition to being a specific thought experiment aimed at the specific version of SSN under consideration, is a *recipe* for thought experiments. For any potential version of SSN that might be proposed, according to which (1) moral terms bear some relation R to certain natural properties that collectively satisfy some specific normative moral theory T and (2) moral terms supposedly refer to the natural properties to which they bear this relation R, it should be possible to construct a Moral Twin Earth scenario suitably analogous to the one constructed above — in other words, a scenario in which twin-moral terms bear the same relation R to certain natural properties that collectively satisfy some specific normative theory T*, incompatible with T. (I leave this as an exercise for the interested reader.) The above reasoning against CSN should apply, mutatis mutandis, against the envisioned alternative moral semantics.[33]

I am not claiming, by the way, that Moral Twin Earth represents an absolutely conclusive refutation of causal moral semantics; indeed, various defensive stratagems are possible in response to my argument. The principal options, listed in order of increasing retreat against the force of Moral Twin Earth, appear to be the following:

1. *Bold denial*: Claiming that the Moral Twin Earth thought experiment does not describe a genuinely possible scenario.
2. *Avoidance*: Claiming that although people's semantic intuitions about Moral Twin Earth are not suitably analogous to their intuitions about Putnam's original Twin Earth scenarios, these semantic intuitions are just mistaken and hence do not undermine causal moral semantics at all. (Presumably, this response would amount to treating the causal

---

33. Although SSN is not susceptible to the sorts of 'open question' objections that Moore and others raised against analytic semantic naturalism (ASN), ironically, one can construct a revised version of the open question argument that, in effect, packages the Moral Twin Earth thought experiment in such a manner that certain sorts of questions ought to be closed if SSN is true, but instead are open. A discussion of this revised open question argument is presented in Horgan and Timmons, 1992a.

account of moral terms as a revisionist proposal for how such terms
ought to be used.)

3. *Betting on the future*: Granting that Moral Twin Earth refutes Boyd-
   style causal semantic naturalism, but claiming that there may be some
   other synthetic moral semantics that does not succumb to a similar
   Moral Twin Earth scenario.

4. *Relativism*: Granting that Moral Twin Earth makes any version of synthetic moral semantics implausible, and retreating to a relativist version
   of ethical naturalism. That is, claiming that although there are no
   moral properties and facts *simpliciter*, nevertheless, (1) there are moral
   properties and facts *relative to a person or social group*; and (2) that
   these relativized properties (and facts) are natural properties. (One
   might claim, for instance, that on Earth, the terms 'good' and 'right,'
   and so on, refer *nonrigidly* to functional properties whose essence is
   captured by the consequentialist moral theory T^c, whereas on Moral
   Twin Earth these terms refer nonrigidly to different functional properties whose essence is captured by the deontological theory T^d.)[34]

5. *Analytic semantic naturalism revisited*: Again, granting that Moral
   Twin Earth makes synthetic moral semantics implausible, articulate
   and defend a version of analytic semantic naturalism. After all,
   Moore's 'open question' argument seems to presuppose something
   false about the nature of conceptual analysis, namely, that there really
   could not be any genuinely informative conceptual analyses of the
   sort that is often sought in philosophy. (Think of the epistemological
   project of trying to give an adequate definition of knowledge. The var-

---

34. I have found it natural to construe the causal-functionalist account of moral semantics as involving
the claim that moral terms designate functional properties *rigidly*. Let us call this *second-order* causal
functionalism. What I am stressing here in the 'relativism' option is that the rigidity claim is important,
since if one takes moral terms to refer *nonrigidly* to functional properties, picking out different functional properties in different possible worlds, the door to relativism is wide open—something the realist
can not allow. But there is another way one might formulate the causal-functional view. One might
pattern a metaethical view after the version of functionalism—'commonsense' functionalism mentioned above—defended by David Lewis (1972, 1980). Whereas according to psychofunctionalism mental properties are multiply realizable functional properties whose relational essence is fully capturable
by the generalizations of the (ideally complete) empirical psychological theory that happens to be true
of human beings, commonsense functionalism holds that mental properties are first-order realizers of
functional properties and that mental terms nonrigidly refer to such properties. So the analogous
position in metaethics would hold that moral terms nonrigidly refer to first-order natural properties,
and that moral terms are definable via definite descriptions that pick out the relevant properties on
the basis of their distinctive functional role. Let us call this *first-order* causal-functionalism.

The semantic story about moral terms and the concepts they express, apparently favored by
Railton (1993), is a version of first-order causal-functionalism. Although this sort of view may not
succumb to the same troubles that beset the Brink-Boyd view, Horgan and I argue (Horgan and
Timmons, 1996a) that it faces a dilemma: either it is guilty of a chauvinistic form of conceptual
relativism, or it is guilty of radical moral indeterminacy (depending on how the view is worked out).
For a similar critique of this sort of view that stresses the problem of indeterminacy, see Michael
Smith's discussion of so-called network analyses of moral concepts in Smith, 1994: ch. 2.

ious analyses generated in response to Gettier's counterexamples to the 'justified true belief' conception of propositional knowledge were not rejected because they were not obviously true.) Perhaps the naturalistic moral realist should explore further the possibility of providing an adequate conceptual analysis of our moral concepts. What I am calling new wave moral realism embraces synthetic ethical naturalism, so this option represents a return to the good old brand of ethical naturalism.

Option 1 incurs an overwhelmingly heavy burden of proof because of two interrelated facts. First, in order for a Twin Earth thought experiment to serve its intended purpose, the relevant scenario need not be a genuine *metaphysical* possibility, but only a broadly *conceptual* possibility. (Suppose, for instance, that Putnam's original Twin Earth scenarios turn out to be metaphysically impossible: i.e., no physically possible substance other than H_2O can have all the features that Putnam attributes to the mythical natural kind XYZ. This outcome would not alter the *conceptual* coherence of Putnam's thought experiments and hence would not alter their relevance to the semantics of 'water.') Second, the prima facie intelligibility of the Moral Twin Earth story recounted earlier constitutes very strong evidence that the scenario is indeed conceptually possible—whether it is metaphysically possible or not.

Option 2 also carries an enormous burden of proof. Admittedly, people's semantic intuitions about Moral Twin Earth *might* be mistaken. But the ethical naturalist who claims that they *are* mistaken has some hard explaining to do. He owes us explanations of why the intuitions are so strong and so widespread even though they are allegedly mistaken, and why people's intuitions don't work the same way here as they do in Putnam's original cases. Furthermore, even if some kind of moderately plausible-looking explanation could be given, modulo CSN as a background theoretical assumption, nevertheless CSN itself is seriously in doubt because it lacks independent empirical support. So the odds look very good that a *better* explanation of people's intuitions about Moral Twin Earth is that these intuitions stem from people's semantic competence and therefore are correct. That's why they constitute such strong and challenging empirical evidence against CSN. Finally, proposing the causal semantic account as a revision of our understanding of ordinary moral terms amounts to admitting that the realist treatment of moral notions does not fully comport with the presumptions of ordinary moral thought and practice—something realists like Brink want to avoid. (There will be more on this point in the next section.)

Option 3 looks unreasonably optimistic for two reasons. First, no interesting version of synthetic semantic naturalism significantly different from Boyd's is even remotely in sight. Second, as mentioned earlier, there are already good reasons for thinking that any such newly devised account of moral semantics would succumb to its own Moral Twin Earth scenario.[35]

---

35. A defender of moral realism might attempt to avoid Boydian causal semantics and appeal, say, to our linguistic intentions regarding our uses of terms like 'good' and 'right' in trying to give a realist account of moral reference. Again, the Moral Twin Earth argument is a recipe that can be adapted

Option 4 is very unattractive to new wave metaethical naturalists like Boyd and Brink. These philosophers espouse *moral realism*, an adamantly non-relativist position. So this option looks hopeless.

Finally, although option 5 cannot be entirely ruled out, the history of failure to provide any sort of adequate analytic naturalistic definition of basic moral terms like 'good' and 'right' casts serious doubt on this option.[36]

I conclude, then, that the new wave moral realist in particular and, as far as I can see, naturalistic versions of moral realism in general, are not able, after all, to naturalistically accommodate the metaphysical and associated epistemological commitments of the moral realist's view.

X. The Moral of Moral Twin Earth

In light of the Moral Twin Earth thought experiment, one might well ask *why* our linguistic intuitions proceed the way they do. What would explain why, in contemplating the Moral Twin Earth scenario, we are strongly inclined to say that Twin Earthlings and we disagree in moral belief and theory, rather than in the meanings of our moral terms? One hypothesis[37] is that moral truths are necessary and a priori, so moral properties of rightness and goodness must be identical with or be realized by the same sort of natural properties in all possible worlds whose essence is capturable by some one normative moral theory T. However, if a realist adopts this view and wants to square his metaethical view with the constraints of philosophical naturalism, he needs some sort of plausible semantic story about moral terms and concepts to undergird the view in question. We have been examining causal stories, and they won't do. But if not some causal story, then what? Presumably, the realist would have to opt for some version of moral realism based on a conceptual analysis of moral concepts, in short, some version of analytic ethical naturalism. We have already noted the bleak prospects for any such view.

Another hypothesis for explaining why our moral intuitions about Moral Twin Earth go the way they do is that our moral terms (and the concepts they express) are in some sense *evaluative* terms and concepts; they are used in judgments that serve the primary purpose of evaluation rather than description.[38] This idea, of course, is the cornerstone of non-descriptivist treatments of moral discourse, a version of which I will develop in chapter 4. For now, it may help to understand

---

and applied to various realist attempts to nonarbitrarily pin down the referents of moral terms, including proposals that do not make use of causal regulation stories. Copp (forthcoming) gestures in the direction of some non-causal semantic realist story about moral terms, but see Horgan and Timmons (forthcoming a) for a reply.

36. It is perhaps possible to understand Railton's view (mentioned in n. 34) as a version of analytic semantic naturalism. But then I would argue (for reasons already mentioned) that this particular brand of analytic semantic naturalism comes to grief.

37. Suggested to me by Michael DePaul.

38. See Holmgren (1990), who raises the 'why' question and takes this to be the lesson of Moral Twin Earth. The semantic story I tell about moral discourse (in ch. 4) emphasizes its evaluative aspect, though the manner in which I develop my version of non-descriptivism differs significantly in some ways from more traditional versions of non-descriptivism.

how this hypothesis might be pressed into service to explain our linguistic intuitions about Moral Twin Earth, if we go back to some of R. M. Hare's early work in metaethics. A forerunner of the Moral Twin Earth thought experiment is the story Hare used some years ago to criticize ethical naturalism (though, of course, his target was analytic ethical naturalism). He had his readers imagine a group of missionaries landing on a cannibal island and discovering that 'good' in Cannibalese is apparently a correct translation of 'good' in English. However, whereas the missionaries apply the English term to people of genteel spirit, the cannibals use their term 'good' to commend people who, among other things, collect more scalps than average.

Hare finds it natural to interpret disagreements between the missionaries and cannibals over what is good as disagreements in the standards used by these different groups in evaluation, rather than as mere disagreements in the meanings of the English and cannibal uses of 'good.' Hare writes:

> Even if the qualities in people which the missionary commended had nothing in common with the qualities which the cannibals commended, yet they would both know what the word 'good' meant. If 'good' were like 'red,' this would be impossible; for then the cannibals' word and the English word would not be synonymous. If this were so, then when the missionary said that people who collected no scalps were good (English), and the cannibals said that people who collected a lot of scalps were good (cannibal), they would not be disagreeing, because in English (at any rate missionary English), 'good' would mean among other things 'doing no murder,' whereas in the cannibals' language 'good' would mean something quite different, among other things 'productive of maximum scalps.' (Hare, 1952: 148–49)

The moral that Hare derives from this thought experiment is that in addition to any descriptive meaning moral judgments may possess, they also possess what he calls 'evaluative meaning,' and it is the fact that the evaluative meaning of moral terms (and the concepts they express) is primary that explains why we are strongly inclined to say, upon contemplating Hare's scenario, that the cannibals and missionaries mean the same thing in the moral judgments they make.

The view I want to develop in chapter 4 differs in some ways quite significantly from Hare's own moral semantic views, but I do think that Hare's hypothesis here is on the right track. This pretheoretic, vague idea about the evaluative nature of moral language is often represented philosophically as some version or other of internalism, which, as we noted in §VI, is thoroughly criticized by Brink. In fact, Brink argues that internalism misrepresents certain features of ordinary moral thought and practice. So, on the one hand, in light of Moral Twin Earth, we are led to the view that moral discourse is evaluative (at least, that is the lesson I think we should learn), but in light of Brink's critique of internalism, we seem to be led away from that view.

Actually, there is a false dilemma in all of this. First, I do think that the point of Moral Twin Earth is that moral discourse is essentially evaluative discourse. Second, I agree with Brink's assessment of the various internalist theses he considers — they implausibly represent the connection between morality and action. But, from the fact that standard versions of internalism are implausible, we should only conclude that the more standard forms of internalism should be rejected. In chapter 4, I plan to defend a recognizably internalist view that avoids Brink's objections.

I have been arguing that some sort of semantic story—presumably a causal story—is needed by the new wave moral realist in order to fully accommodate the metaphysical and epistemological commitments of naturalistic moral realism. I mentioned earlier that Terry Horgan and I have argued that some such story is needed in order to explain moral supervenience relations and thus to respond adequately to Mackie's second queerness argument, which we understand as the demand that objective moral supervenience relations be naturalistically accommodated. But in light of what the Twin Earth thought experiment reveals about the evaluative nature of moral language, we can also revive the first of Mackie's queerness arguments.

The first queerness argument, you may recall, appeals to the evaluative nature of moral terms (and discourse) and claims that were there objective moral properties corresponding to such terms, they would be, from a naturalistic perspective, ontologically queer. Mackie used the expression 'intrinsic prescriptivity' to express what he detected as the evaluative dimension of ordinary moral language and judgment, which Brink interprets as commitment to some version of internalism. But, (1) if the Moral Twin Earth scenario (and our reactions to it) makes clear that ordinary moral terms and the concepts they express are essentially evaluative and (2) if we represent this fact as commitment to internalism (the way Brink defines this view), then Mackie's first queerness argument is revived: if there were objective moral properties and facts, their normative dimension would make them queer.

So Moral Twin Earth does, indeed, pack a powerful punch. Not only does it deck causal moral semantics, thus leaving the new wave moral realist without the needed semantic underpinning to ground his metaethical view, but it reveals something about the evaluative nature of moral language—a feature of such language that naturally leads one in the direction of moral irrealism.

XI. A Dilemma

New wave moral realists argue that a realist construal of moral discourse fully comports with various commonsense assumptions of moral discourse and practice and that, therefore, their view satisfies the general desideratum that the commitments of a metaethical theory comport with ordinary, commonsense presumptions (D1 from ch. 1). These realists have also argued that their version of moral realism comports with a thoroughly naturalistic metaphysical outlook and that their view is not committed to the existence of non-natural moral properties, facts, and relations, and hence does not raise special epistemological worries about our access to, and (possible) knowledge of, those properties, facts, and relations. That is, they argue that their view is not in any way metaphysically or epistemologically queer and that, in general, it can also satisfy the general desideratum that a metaethical view comport with non-moral principles, theories, and assumptions (D2 from ch. 1).

But in light of the Moral Twin Earth thought experiment and the point to be drawn from it, it would appear that the realist cannot satisfy both D1 and D2. On the one hand, to satisfy D2 and meet the metaphysical and epistemological challenges to realism, a causal moral semantics (or something like it) is needed. But considering the Moral Twin Earth thought experiment, to insist upon a causal construal of moral terms amounts to engaging in revisionist moral semantics (see the *avoidance* strategy from §IX). But this means that, after all, his metaethical view does not neatly comport with the presumptions of ordinary moral discourse, that he can satisfy D2, but only at the expense of failing to satisfy D1. On the other hand, if one develops a metaethical theory that is in keeping with the assumptions of ordinary moral discourse, including how we ordinarily use moral terms, then one will want to recognize the evaluative dimension of such discourse. But to do this, and thereby abandon the causal story, would apparently force the moral realist to become a non-naturalist about moral properties and facts, and hence to construe them as having something like "to-be-pursuedness" built into them.

I conclude that, despite the impressive marshaling of philosophical resources made available by recent work in philosophy of language and philosophy of mind and the ingenuity with which Brink and Boyd apply such work to metaethical concerns, their new version of moral realism has an Achilles' heel. Those interested in the project of naturalistic accommodation in ethics should look to moral irrealism.

XII. Conclusion

After setting the stage for understanding what is perhaps the most plausible contemporary version of naturalistic moral realism, and then going into some of the important metaphysical and semantic details of the view, we have found good reason to reject new wave moral realism. Perhaps I am wrong in thinking that the version of moral realism I have criticized is the most plausible version available to the realist (who accepts naturalism), and some better version can be developed. But until then, I think we are justified in exploring irrealist options in metaethics.

3

The Argument from Moral Error

In this chapter we begin to explore metaethical irrealism. The major philosoph-ical complaint against this sort of view is that it is not able to accommodate adequately various commonsense features and assumptions of morality. Of the various features and assumptions in question (see §II in this chapter), the issue of plausibly accounting for the possibility of *error* in moral judgment and belief rep-resents the most persistent and serious challenge to the form of moral irrealism that I shall defend. This chapter examines what I call the *argument from moral error*, leveled by realists against their irrealist opponents. I attempt to formulate the argument in its strongest version and then survey the prospects for a plausible irrealist reply. Our examination of the argument from moral error will be illumi-nating for what it reveals about a defensible form of moral irrealism, since I main-tain that the argument reveals an important insight about what I call our 'critical practices' that the irrealist should acknowledge. I will argue that the insight to be gleaned from this argument leads the irrealist in the direction of a *non-reductive* form of moral irrealism. In the next chapter, I shall elaborate and provide a (ten-tative) defense of a non-reductive version of irrealism.

I. Moral Irrealism and Accommodation Projects

Since the metaethical commitments of the moral irrealist differ from those of the moral realist, we need to begin with a brief overview of moral irrealism, indicating some of the major varieties of this view, and then consider what sorts of explanatory burdens the irrealist undertakes in attempting to naturalistically accommodate her view.

Some Varieties of Moral Irrealism

You may recall from the last chapter that we characterized the moral realist as holding the following battery of metaphysical and associated semantical theses:

M1   There are moral properties and facts.

M2   These properties and facts are objective.

S1   Moral discourse is fact-stating discourse.

S2   Moral statements are either true or false, depending on whether they correspond to the objective moral facts.

To these theses, we can add a fifth that is obviously implied by them (taken together), namely,

S3   Some (affirmative) moral statements are (correspondence) true.[1]

Since moral realism is, at bottom, a metaphysical outlook, M1 and M2 are at the very heart of this view. Brands of moral irrealism result from rejecting various of the above theses and, in particular, the commitment expressed in M2 to objectively existing moral properties and facts. The three most dominant versions are represented by *non-descriptivism (non-cognitivism)*, *constructivism*, and the *error theory*.

The non-descriptivist, who takes moral discourse (as ordinarily used) as primarily performing some non-fact-stating function, denies S1 and, hence, also denies S2 and S3. As we saw in chapter 1, one main reason for thinking that moral sentences are not fact-stating (despite what the surface grammar of many of them suggest) is commitment to *moral nihilism* — the view that denies that there are any moral properties or facts (denies M1 and, hence, M2). So the typical non-descriptivist denies all of the above tenets associated with moral realism.

Less radical by not denying all of the above theses is the constructivist, who admits the existence of moral properties and facts (accepts M1) but denies that these facts have the sort of ontological status indicated by M2. According to this view, moral properties and facts are to be understood as human constructions — constituted from some constellation of our beliefs and other attitudes. Constructivists can be descriptivists (and usually are) and hence accept S1, but they typically reject the correspondence account of truth (S2) and instead accept some other account of truth (e.g., a coherence account), or devise some substitute semantic notion in place of truth.

The error theory denies both of the metaphysical tenets of moral realism and combines its commitment to moral nihilism with acceptance of both S1 and S2. The idea is that although moral discourse, as typically used, is fact-stating and, moreover, purports to correspond to objective moral facts, nevertheless there are no such moral facts. So none of the (affirmative) statements of the discourse are true — S3 is false.

The version of irrealism I shall defend falls within that rather large territory occupied by non-descriptivists, though, as we shall see in the next chapter, my view differs significantly from standard versions.

---

1. As Walter Sinnott-Armstrong pointed out to me, if we understand a statement as what is said when a declarative sentence is uttered or inscribed, then in light of the fact that systematic error or distortion is possible so that, in fact, no utterances or inscriptions are true, we should qualify S3 to say that some *possible* affirmative moral statements are correspondence true.

Accommodation Projects

Since the moral irrealist denies the existence of objective moral properties and facts, she does not face the dual explanatory burden of first having to naturalistically accommodate such (putative) properties and facts, and then having to explain how we have access to and (possible) knowledge about them. This does not mean, however, that the irrealist incurs no accommodation burdens—quite the opposite. First, there is the task of situating moral discourse within a broadly naturalistic picture of human nature and society. After all, even if moral discourse does not involve (or should not be taken to involve) realist metaphysical and epistemological commitments, there is still the task of making sense of that discourse—of explaining its point and purpose—from within a naturalistic/evolutionary picture of human beings. I have called this the task of external accommodation, and I shall consider the prospects for discharging this burden in the next chapter, once the version of moral irrealism I defend is out in the open.

But the task of accommodation also looks to ordinary moral discourse and practice, and requires that a plausible metaethical view accommodate (as well as possible) the essential features and deeply embedded assumptions of such discourse and practice (D1). So, a second accommodation burden undertaken by the irrealist involves making good sense (if possible) of such features and assumptions, including the so-called objective pretensions (a phrase borrowed from Gibbard [1990]) of moral discourse. Before proceeding to describe those 'objectivist' features and assumptions allegedly embedded in commonsense moral discourse and practice, let us pause for a moment to make a few observations about the strategies pursued by realists and irrealists in attempting to carry out the accommodation projects I have been describing.

The naturalist–moral realist supposedly has an easy time squaring his view with many salient features and assumptions of commonsense moral thought. The main task confronting the realist is to naturalistically accommodate the metaphysical and associated epistemological commitments of his view. The moral irrealist, by contrast, supposedly has an easy time with the metaphysical and epistemological commitments of her view; the real work for the irrealist is in plausibly accommodating various features and assumptions embedded in ordinary moral discourse and practice and, in particular, the ones that seem to indicate that the discourse is, in some sense, objective. And so the typical realist strategy in defending his view is first to argue that moral realism, but not irrealism, can naturally and plausibly accommodate the objective pretensions of ordinary moral discourse and practice, and then go on to discharge the accommodation burdens associated with his view. (See Brink, 1989.) This strategy, if successful, has the effect of placing the burden of proof on the back of the irrealist: if ordinary, commonsense moral discourse and practice involve (or strongly suggest) commitments that are best captured by the moral realist, then the irrealist must explain in what ways commonsense thinking is misleading and why.

Of course, if the argument of the last chapter is correct, then the moral realist is not, in the end, able to accommodate fully the metaphysical and epistemological commitments of his view and remain true to commonsense presumptions. At the end of the last chapter, we left the new wave moral realist with a dilemma: either recognize the evaluative dimension of moral discourse and (in light of Mackie's queerness arguments) give up the project of naturalistically accommodating the metaphysical and epistemological commitments of this view (i.e., combine moral realism with non-naturalism), or hold onto one's commitment to philosophical naturalism and admit that one is, at bottom, proposing a revisionist moral semantics that does not fully comport with ordinary, commonsense moral discourse.

It might now appear as though the realist and irrealist are at a standoff: both metaethical views can naturalistically accommodate their metaphysical and epistemological commitments, and both views can accommodate some, but not all, features and assumptions of commonsense moral thought. Perhaps, then, the metaethical debate ends in a draw; perhaps we should take an agnostic stance over the question of whether there are objective moral facts to which we have access. Perhaps. But we should not come to this conclusion until the irrealist hand has been played out. What remains to be seen is whether the moral realist really does, in fact, have the upper hand in accommodating those features and assumptions of moral discourse and practice that he points to in favor of his metaethical view. I think that if irrealism is properly developed, it, too, can plausibly accommodate such features — or so I shall argue.

II. The Objective Pretensions of Moral Discourse and Practice

Ordinary, commonsense moral discourse displays certain clearly discernible features that presuppose that, in some sense, such discourse is non-arbitrary or 'objective.'[2] Moral discourse is also embedded in a complex network of assumptions and practices that, again, presuppose that moral thought and inquiry are in some sense 'objective.' The various internal considerations that suggest objectivity fall into three broad categories. First, there are those features of moral discourse itself having to do with the form and content of moral sentences. Many moral sentences are expressed in the indicative mood. Examples include: 'Abortion except in cases of rape and incest is morally wrong,' 'James's action of lying to Brenda was, in the circumstances, the right thing to do,' 'Parents have a moral obligation to educate their children,' and so on. Sentences in the indicative mood are naturally interpreted as genuine fact-stating sentences. Moreover, some moral sentences appear to make reference to (putative) moral properties and facts; whereas other moral sentences appear to make reference to moral knowledge. Examples include: 'Moral virtue, wherever it occurs, should be praised,' 'The evil of American slavery was

---

2. I put this term in quotes because I don't think that ordinary moral discourse and practice is best construed as embedding assumptions that only forms of moral objectivism can most plausibly accommodate. So my remarks here should not be taken as conceding that ordinary moral discourse presupposes that such discourse really is objective in the way that the metaethical realist understands moral objectivity. I discuss this matter in more detail in the next chapter.

partly responsible for its demise as an institution,' and 'One cannot be held morally responsible for actions that one could not have known were wrong.' The very content of such sentences — mentioning such things as moral virtue, the evil of an institution, and knowledge of wrongness — presuppose (or strongly suggest) that there are moral properties, facts, and knowledge about various actions, persons, institutions, and the like. Some of these points are nicely summed up by Ewing:

> Ethical sentences are grammatically of the same structure as factual statements. They can go in the indicative except in cases where it would be against the rules of grammar likewise for the latter to do so. It is certainly correct English to speak of them as if they expressed propositions known or believed to be true. It has indeed been asserted that we do not in ordinary speech use 'true' or 'false' of 'ethical judgements,' but all that can be said is that this usage is less frequent than with factual judgements. It certainly does occur, and nobody who employs it could possibly be said to be using language incorrectly. Further, we constantly use phrases such as 'know that' or 'believe that' followed by an ethical sentence, thus implying that the latter expresses a proposition which could be true, and if we *know* it, is true. (Ewing, 1959: 36)

We should add to these points the fact that moral sentences, like ordinary fact-stating sentences, display such 'logical' features as being negated, being antecedents and consequents of conditional statements, and figuring in valid inferences such as *modus ponens* — all of which strongly suggests that they should be construed as making genuine assertions.

A second range of features that suggests that some degree of objectivity attaches to moral discourse and practice has to do with moral phenomenology, including, in particular, moral experiences of all sorts. For instance, our experience of moral obligations typically has an affective component that strongly suggests objectivity: moral obligations are *felt* as something imposed from a source external to and independent of the individual having the experience. We thus often talk of *recognizing* moral requirements, and we also speak about observing value in the world. Here is how David McNaughton puts it:

> Our experience of the world does seem to involve experience of value, both moral and non-moral: we hear the beauty of Mozart's music; we see the children's cruelty to the dog; we witness McEnroe's rudeness on the tennis courts. Can the non-cognitivist give an account of our experience of value which is true to the nature of that experience while denying value any place in the world? (McNaughton, 1988: 19)

Moreover, this vague sense of recognizing moral obligations and observing value in the world is also suggested by our talk of people being more or less *perceptive*. We think that some people, whose moral advice we may well seek, have better and clearer moral vision than the rest of us.

A third range of internal considerations concerns the assumptions associated with such activities as moral deliberation, debate, and argument — that is, with our critical practices. These critical practices are seemingly aimed at arriving non-arbitrarily at true or correct moral views — ones that would (ideally, anyway) resolve intrapersonal and interpersonal conflict and uncertainty about moral issues. Reflection on our critical practices (associated with moral discourse) reveals, then, that they involve at least the following (roughly formulated) assumptions:[3]

> C1   Some moral judgments (beliefs, sentences) are true or correct.
>
> C2   Error in moral judgment (belief) is possible — one can make mistakes. Thus, improvements in one's moral outlook are possible; one can make moral progress.
>
> C3   Genuine conflicts in moral judgment and belief are possible. For example, normally, if one person affirms and another person denies a moral judgment, then they do disagree, and (again, normally) at least one of them is mistaken (has made an error in moral judgment).

These features and assumptions of and about moral discourse, moral phenomenology, and our critical practices seem clearly embedded, and deeply so, in moral discourse and practice. In accordance with D1, we can say that the better any metaethical view accommodates these features and assumptions, the better (ceteris paribus) the metaethical view. So I am interested in exploring the prospects of accommodating as fully and as plausibly as possible these items of commonsense moral discourse and practice. Of course, to what extent, and how plausibly, the irrealist can accommodate these features and assumptions depends on what version of irrealism is in question. In the next chapter, I will consider the features of moral discourse and moral phenomenology that need accommodation. Our immediate concern is with those assumptions associated with our critical practices (C1–C3) and, in particular, with the second assumption, about the possibility of moral error.

III. Irrealism and Error

A clear articulation of the complaint featured in the argument from moral error is to be found in the writings of Marcus Singer:

> [W]henever one criticizes some precept or practice, not with mere irritation or aversion or anger but on the basis of reasons, one is appealing to an idea of a rational morality which provides the basis for the criticism. And at least a glimpse of this rational morality is provided to anyone who has ever changed his or her mind on a moral matter for what one regards as good reason. "I was mistaken," one thinks, "I was in error. It is hard to realize this, and even harder to admit it. But if I am to be honest with myself, if I am to be able to maintain a sense of my own integrity, I must admit that I was mistaken, I was in error." In thinking this one is necessarily thinking that something that was once and perhaps for a long time a part of one's personal morality has to this extent changed, and that the change is in the direction of a more rational or correct morality.
>
>   What is essential to this process is that the change of mind be thought to be rationally based, that it not be conceived of as something resting solely on whim. What I am claiming is that we cannot make sense of a change of moral *belief* or

3. I extend this list of features in the next chapter, in §V.

judgment or *opinion* apart from the conception of a rational or true morality. (Singer, 1986: 18)

If we take Singer's reference to a 'rational' or 'true' morality as being about an objective moral reality in the realist's sense, then the complaint expressed against moral irrealists in this passage is as follows.[4] Our critical practices associated with moral thinking proceed on the assumption that error in moral judgment or belief is possible (C2) and, correlatively, that we can improve (and not just change) our moral outlook. But this assumption presupposes a realm of objective moral properties and facts (in Singer's terms, a "true morality"). The clear implication is that the irrealist, who denies the existence of objective moral properties and facts, cannot make sense of the possibility of error in moral judgment and belief. Furthermore, if the irrealist cannot make good sense of error in moral judgment, then she won't be able to make sense of a judgment's being true or correct (C1), or even make sense of two parties disagreeing in moral judgment and belief (C3).

Moral realists don't face this problem. Even if Singer's claim that the possibility of error in moral judgment and belief *presupposes* a true morality (moral realism) is too strong a claim to make, at least the moral realist can point out that he has a clear and straightforward explanation of this phenomenon. Moral judgments, sentences, or beliefs are true, claims the realist, if, and only if, they correspond to objective moral facts. Moral error occurs, then, when a moral judgment fails to correspond to the facts. However, for the irrealist, things are not as clear and straightforward. It would appear that, in the end, irrealism will not be able to explain adequately the possibility of moral error (or at least certain types of moral error) and hence will not be able to fully accommodate certain assumptions associated with our critical practices. What resources do irrealists have for mounting a defense against this objection?

IV. Moral Error and the Error Theory

Before proceeding, we should begin by clearing away a certain possible confusion about the force of the argument from moral error. Some challenges to irrealism based on an appeal to the objective pretensions of moral discourse have limited targets. For example, challenges based on an appeal to the form and content of moral sentences are directed at non-descriptivist forms of irrealism; they are not directed at versions of constructivism or the error theory, since these latter views allow that moral sentences are typically fact-stating. The argument from error, though, targets all versions of irrealism. But this may not be so obvious since, according to the error theory, all positive moral judgments are false. You may recall that according to this view, ordinary moral statements purport to be about

---

4. Singer does not commit himself, in the essay from which this passage is taken, to moral realism, and it is possible to construe these remarks in a way that does not commit one to moral realism. Brink (1989: ch. 2) is someone who runs the argument from moral error against forms of ethical constructivism. And, of course, the appeal to the assumptions behind our critical practices is typically raised in criticizing versions of moral relativism. See, for example, Stace, 1937.

objective moral properties and to describe objective moral facts, but since on this view there are no such properties and facts, all (affirmative) moral sentences are false. Not only is error in moral judgment ubiquitously possible on this view, such error is ubiquitously guaranteed!

In light of this, the realist could restrict the scope of the argument from moral error and direct it at other versions of irrealism. It would still be a useful weapon in the realist's arsenal, but its targets would be limited. However, this move is unnecessary, and to understand that it is, we need to consider Mackie's error theory in the context of a battery of metaethical questions — questions often enough not clearly distinguished.[5]

The questions are the following:

1. What is the proper analysis of the meanings of moral sentences as ordinarily used?
2. Do moral sentences, as ordinarily used, require that there exist objective moral properties and facts to which such sentences, if they are true at all, must correspond?
3. Assuming that an analysis of ordinary moral sentences presupposes that there are objective moral properties and facts, *are* there any such properties and facts?
4. If not, what are the conditions under which moral sentences are correctly/incorrectly asserted?[6]

Notice that the first question concerns the semantics of ordinary moral discourse. It asks about our commonsense conceptual scheme, and it belongs to what I call *commonsense semantics*. The second question, which again focuses on our commonsense conceptual scheme, asks what sorts of properties and facts that scheme presupposes there are and thus is a question belonging to *commonsense metaphysics*. The third question, on the other hand, concerns the existence and nature of what there really is, and it belongs to what I call *philosophical metaphysics*. The fourth question requires some comment.

Let us suppose that judgments attributing colors to things presuppose that the world contains instances of color properties spread onto objects quite independent of our cognitive-perceptual makeup. That is, let us suppose that the proper analysis of color judgments reveals that they require, for their truth, the independent existence of colors. Let us further suppose that Locke and his followers were right in maintaining that, as a matter of fact, colors are not literally in the world, as common sense supposes, but rather are in some way subjective. Thus, we have

---

5. Here (with some modifications) I follow the lead of John Tienson (1989) in distinguishing the following questions.
6. In using 'correct' and 'incorrect' here, I run some risk of later on confusing my readers, since I proceed in the next chapter to construe truth in terms of *correct assertibility*. In the present context, I am letting truth be understood in terms of correspondence, and so, talk of correct and incorrect assertion is meant to be used in place of talk about the truth and falsity of moral sentences by those who do not think that such sentences are either true or false, or perhaps who think, like Mackie, that all of the affirmative ones are literally false.

an affirmative answer to a type 2 question about commonsense metaphysics and a negative answer to a type 3 question about philosophical metaphysics, which leads us to conclude that ordinary, commonsense color judgments are systematically false.

Still, the color judgments we make aren't arbitrary. Rather, they are keyed to regularities in the objective world, and this fact presumably provides a basis for distinguishing between correct and incorrect color judgments. In this context, the relevant type 4 question asks what the situation must be in the world for it to be correct to assert a particular color judgment. Since this sort of question is not concerned with commonsense presuppositions, it is not a question of either commonsense semantics or of philosophical metaphysics, though one asks this sort of question from within some ontological perspective arrived at as a result of doing philosophical metaphysics. Since proposals in response to question 4 presumably attempt to straighten out our semantic understanding of a certain class of sentences by having that understanding reflect how things are (viewed from an apparently correct metaphysical view of things), we might label such proposals as *revisionary semantics*.

Moral philosophers in this century, until recently at least, have been preoccupied with the first and second questions, and irrealists have typically offered non-descriptivist accounts of the meanings of moral judgments that imply that such judgments do not primarily purport to state or describe any realm of moral facts. However, irrealists like Mackie are descriptivists—they concede that, as ordinarily used, moral judgments purport to describe objective moral facts. Mackie's error theory is the result of combining an affirmative answer to the second question (he thought that descriptivism was true and that truth was a matter of correspondence) with a negative answer to the third question (he was an irrealist about ethical properties and facts).

Thus, the error theory in ethics agrees with (the semantic side of) moral realism in construing moral statements as purporting to state moral facts that, if they existed, would make certain moral statements true. But the error theorist denies the truth of any such statements, since she denies that there are any objective moral properties or facts to which moral statements could correspond or fail to correspond. Granted, the error theory does explain how error in moral judgment—in the sense of failing to correspond to the moral facts—is possible. But Mackie and other error theorists are not *eliminativists* about morals. They do think that moral discourse is useful, and presumably they would wish to preserve the critical stances we take toward the moral judgments of ourselves and others—that is, that people are sometimes correct in their moral judgments and sometimes mistaken: we are capable of both accuracy and error in moral judgment. Thus, the error theorist who would retain moral discourse and our critical practices needs to engage in revisionary moral semantics; she needs to provide a plausible account of the conditions under which moral judgments are (in some sense) correctly assertible and, by implication, an account of incorrect, erroneous moral judgments.

But now it should be pretty clear how the argument from error can be applied to a Mackie-like irrealist view: the realist will argue that the notion of correctness at work here, or whatever substitute notion for truth the irrealist might like to devise, will not yield an account of correctness and error for moral judgments that squares with the possibility of error in moral judgment as expressed in C2. So the argument from error, as I plan to develop it, applies to irrealist views that incorporate the error theory into their overall metaethic, as well as to those metaethical views that would reject, or at least remain agnostic about, the error theory. Views of both type provide some sort of non-correspondence semantic view for moral discourse, and it is against all such views that the argument from moral error takes aim.

V. Passing the Buck: A First Line of Defense

One rather obvious line of response available to the irrealist amounts to "passing the buck" when it comes to error in moral judgment: error in *non-moral* judgment is really to blame for moral error. This is the position that C. L. Stevenson takes in his essay "Ethical Fallibility." Stevenson takes the error challenge, as I have, to proceed from the sort of commonsense assumptions embedded in what I call our critical practices. In particular, he takes seriously the commonsense idea that, as moral judges, our accuracy falls somewhere in between complete infallibility and invariable error. His strategy for dealing with the argument from error involves the attempt to show that his brand of irrealism can mimic the claims of the realist in explaining the possibility of moral error.

Stevenson, of course, defends a non-descriptivist account of moral language and judgment, according to which the primary function of moral judgments is to express the judger's pro or con attitudes toward the objects of evaluation. In this way, they contrast sharply with scientific judgments, whose primary function is to express the judger's beliefs. Nevertheless, moral judgments on Stevenson's view are said to 'contextually imply' a judger's beliefs in the sense that it is on the basis of one's non-moral beliefs about an object of evaluation that one's attitudes are engaged. And so error in moral judgment—that is, error in one's attitudes—results primarily from error in the non-moral factual judgments associated with one's attitude. The blame for moral error is passed on to the associated non-moral beliefs. Thus, in admitting one's ethical fallibility, Stevenson's view is that "the remark, 'Many things that meet with my approval may not be right,' acknowledges in the first instance a fallibility in attitude—though it implicitly acknowledges, as well, a fallibility in belief to whatever extent the speaker's attitudes are guided by beliefs" (1966: 206).

But error in non-moral belief is not the only source of error in moral judgment that a view like Stevenson's can explain. First, and most obviously, in reasoning to moral conclusions, mistakes of non-moral reasoning are possible, that is, mistakes that violate the canons of deductive or inductive logic. For instance, the following argument commits the formal fallacy of denying the antecedent: 'If everyone tells the truth, then you ought to tell the truth also, but since not everyone is telling the truth, you (morally) don't have to either.' Again, one commits the informal fallacy of hasty generalization in the following inductive moral argument: 'Jimmy Swaggart and James Bakker are dishonest people, so all television preachers are dishonest.' The moral judgments in the conclusions of these arguments can be called erroneous, from the non-descriptivist's perspective, since they result from faulty non-moral reasoning.

It is plausible to suppose that there are certain constraints on correct moral reasoning—some formal, some substantive—and that violation of these constraints is another possible source of error in moral judgment. For instance, one plausible formal constraint on moral reasoning is expressed by the principle of universalizability, which involves a consistency constraint requiring that cases exhibiting relevantly similar non-moral properties receive the same moral evaluation. A person who violates this constraint in his moral reasoning is making a mistake; the moral judgments he reaches through violation of the constraint are erroneous. Again (though some would find this controversial), taking the so-called moral point of view involves judging from an impartial stance—giving due consideration to the interests of all relevant parties. If one accepts this as a constraint—presumably a substantive constraint—on moral reasoning, then one errs in moral judgment to the extent that one's moral judgment about a particular case is biased and thereby exhibits partiality.

So irrealists who would, following Stevenson's views, take up a non-descriptivist treatment of moral language can point to a number of possible sources of error in moral judgment: first, some errors in moral judgment are due to errors in associated non-moral beliefs; second, some may be due to errors in non-moral reasoning; and third, some errors can be traced to various errors in moral reasoning.

VI. Is That All There Is? A Realist Rejoinder

No doubt critics of irrealism running the argument from moral error would be unimpressed by irrealist attempts to show how error in moral judgment can result in the ways we have just considered; after all, these errors are not errors in *moral* judgment and belief. In other words, the basic problem with the account of moral error just described is that it doesn't go far enough; it fails to do justice to our commonsense critical practices because it cannot recognize, and hence explain, the possibility of *genuine* moral error.

Let us say that the notion of genuine moral error involves, at a minimum, the idea of an error in moral judgment that is not due to error in non-moral belief or to error in non-moral reasoning or to a violation of any constraints on correct moral reasoning. It certainly appears that there is room left over for criticism of a person's moral judgment, even if we determine that the judgment is not based on any error in non-moral belief or reasoning, and also that it has not resulted from a violation of any other constraints on moral reasoning. We can sensibly judge that the moral principles a person accepts are mistaken, or, if it is a philosopher's fiction to suppose that a person's moral judgments flow in part from *principles* the person accepts, we can judge that the most basic moral convictions that guide a person's moral judgments are mistaken. Stressing the possibility of genuine moral error is simply a way of making clear what is stated in C2: error in moral judgment is possible.

This presumption is also reflected in C3. If two parties disagree about the morality of some particular action, and we judge that neither is guilty of any of the sorts of error described in connection with Stevenson's view, then (in normal cases, anyway) we still believe at least one of the parties made an error; we aren't inclined to suppose that both parties are making correct moral judgments and thus relativize correctness to the principles or basic convictions each party happens to accept. In short, the correctness of a moral judgment is not fully accounted for in terms of an individual reaching that judgment by correctly reasoning from a (consistent) set of moral principles or basic convictions. People's critical practices, when it comes to matters moral, allow them to sensibly judge that even basic principles and convictions can be mistaken; a person can get it all wrong. The irrealist will have to make a better case or admit that the realist is in the lead.

VII. Expanding the Sources of Error: A Second Line of Defense

In light of the shortcomings of Stevenson's view, the irrealist needs to be able to explain genuine moral error—the idea that even a person's most basic moral convictions might be mistaken. And it seems as if there are at least two ways the irrealist might proceed. First, she might follow the lead of Simon Blackburn (1980, 1981, 1984: 194) and make room for genuine moral error by recognizing ways in which a person's *moral sensibility*—the person's disposition to draw inferences from his basic moral convictions—might be improved. A person's basic moral convictions can be mistaken on this view if there is something wrong with the person's moral sensibility—if, that is, the person's sensibility were improved, the person would hold a different set of basic moral convictions. Of course, going this route requires that the irrealist make sense of the idea that a person's moral sensibility may be better or worse.

A second option the irrealist might pursue is to relativize moral correctness to a set of basic agreements or conventions concerning well-being that are operative within a certain social group. Again, since we want to be able to criticize the actual agreements and conventions of groups, the irrealist will be pushed to relativize correctness to those *hypothetical agreements* and conventions that the group would accept under certain *hypothetical conditions*—conditions in which a person is well situated for purposes of deciding which moral principles or norms to accept. That is, just as there can be better and worse moral sensibilities, so the irrealist can insist that there can be better and worse sets of agreements and conventions that constitute a group's moral code. To say that a moral judgment is correct (for a member of a group) is to say that the judgment conforms with the code that the group would accept under specified hypothetical conditions.

And again, going this route imposes on the irrealist the burden of explaining those 'hypothetical conditions' in which one is well situated that give content to the idea that the basic agreements or conventions of a group are correct or incorrect. But this understanding of correctness gives the irrealist some conceptual room for explaining the possibility of moral error at the level of a group's actual moral code.

If we step back for a moment from the evolving dialectic, we can see a certain irrealist pattern emerging that involves the following three steps. (1) To allow for as much error in moral judgment as possible, the irrealist is moved to expand her conception of correctness, going beyond the actual moral convictions of individuals and groups and locating it at the level of hypothetical, improved sets of moral convictions and principles, that is, those convictions or principles that would be accepted by anyone who was well situated. (2) This strategy is typically accompanied by some theoretical account — some specification in terms of necessary and sufficient conditions — of what counts as being well situated in this context. (3) Typically, the notion of correctness becomes naturalized by being understood in terms of what some individual or group would accept under conditions specified in purely descriptive terms. Thus, the typical irrealist proposes a broadly *reductive* account of correctness for moral judgments.[7]

Of course, the realist is not going to be satisfied, but will press the objection further, insisting that it makes perfect sense to suppose that even improved hypothetical convictions and principles might be mistaken. In fact, the realist is prepared to press the basic complaint behind the argument from moral error all day long, no matter what account the irrealist provides about correctness (and error) in moral judgment. But before we pursue this discussion any further, it is time to spell out the argument from moral error. The advantages of doing so will be apparent as we proceed. So given our account to this point, here is the argument.

The Argument from Moral Error

1. If moral irrealism is true, then the correctness of a moral judgment is to be understood reductively by being identified with or determined by some set of actual or hypothetical norms, standards, or convictions of individuals or groups.
2. This means that the irrealist can allow for the following sources of error:
    a. error in relevant non-moral belief;
    b. error rooted in mistakes of non-moral reasoning;
    c. error with regard to various constraints on moral reasoning;
    d. error in moral judgment due to one of the following considerations (depending on what version of irrealism is under discussion): (i)

---

7. In chapter 2, reduction for the philosophical naturalist was characterized quite generically: a reductive semantic account of some term or expression is one that systematically construes (or in some way 'defines') that term or expression in naturalistic terms. Here, we are talking about semantic notions, not moral notions, but the same point applies: a (naturalistically) reductive account of truth or correctness would construe such terms as equivalent to descriptive and, in particular, to naturalistic terms. Hence, in this context, the views in question are reductive views about truth or correctness as applied to moral judgments. Later, in this chapter and the next, I say more about semantic reductionism and contrast it with semantic non-reductionism.

one's moral judgment does not conform with the set of basic moral convictions that one would accept if one's moral sensibility were improved; (ii) one's moral judgment does not conform with the actual, or perhaps improved, hypothetical moral code of one's relevant group.

3. But even moral judgments that do not involve any of the sorts of error described in premise 2 might be mistaken: in particular, error in moral judgment is possible even at the level of hypothetical, improved individual moral sensibilities and hypothetical, improved social moral codes.[8]

Therefore,

4. The possibility of some sorts of moral error cannot be explained if one accepts moral irrealism.

The argument then continues:

5. The adequacy of a metaethical view is judged in part by how well it comports with commonsense moral practice and, in particular, with how well it comports with our critical practices concerning moral judgment, including the presumption that all sorts of error in moral judgment are possible (i.e., D1 is a constraint on an acceptable metaethical view).

6. Moral realism (but not moral irrealism) comports well with people's critical practices, including the presumption that all sorts of error in moral judgment are possible.

Therefore,

7. All other things being equal, moral realism is more plausible than moral irrealism.

I think there are a number of paths the irrealist might follow in responding to this argument, but I will save discussion of those for later. What we need to consider first is precisely how the realist might defend the third premise, since I expect that the irrealist may want to resist at this point. I can think of two considerations the realist might press in defense of this premise. First, and most obviously, he will simply point out that our critical practices (as partially represented by C1–C3) outrun any attempt by the irrealist to explain correctness in terms of even hypothetical sensibilities or social codes. Although I believe the realist is probably wrong in what he attributes to our critical practices in pressing this objection, I do think that there is an important lesson to be learned from the argument from

---

8. There is one species of irrealist view—a version of metaethical rationalism—according to which there are formal constraints on proper moral reasoning that guarantee that if one conforms to the relevant canons, error is not possible. Where metaethical rationalism is wedded to a non-descriptivist moral semantics (like what we find in Hare, [1981]), we get a version of irrealism. Such views would offer a principled response to the argument from moral error. However, I don't consider such views here, partly for brevity's sake, but mainly because I don't think they deliver what they promise. However, if I am wrong about this and some brand of metaethical rationalism is right, that would help my metaethical cause, not damage it. For a discussion on this point, see the appendix.

moral error—fortunately for the irrealist, a lesson that helps her devise a plausible form of irrealism (see later in this chapter at §XI). But second, there is another consideration that we find in Nicholas Sturgeon's criticisms of Blackburn that might be marshaled in defense of the third premise. There are lessons to be learned from Sturgeon as well; let us investigate further.

VIII. The Argument from Hume's Dictum

Against Blackburn's attempt to explain genuine moral error on strictly irrealist grounds, Nicholas Sturgeon (1986) has argued that in the end the Blackburn account comes to grief because it collapses a crucial distinction that realists do accept and that irrealists should accept. Sturgeon's argument can, I think, be generalized and made to apply to irrealist views other than Blackburn's. Since it represents an interesting and separate line of argument that focuses on problems with explaining moral error, it requires separate treatment.

A statement of the distinction in question, and a plea for its importance, can be found in the writings of Hume:

> There is no method of reasoning more common, and yet none more blameable, than, in philosophical disputes, to endeavor the refutation of any hypothesis, by a pretence of its dangerous consequences to religion and morality. When any opinion leads to absurdities, it is certainly false; but it is not certain that an opinion is false, because it is of dangerous consequence. (Hume, 1777: 96)

Put in realist terms, the distinction here is between the *truth value* of a claim, hypothesis, theory, or what have you, and its *acceptance value*.[9] The acceptance value of a claim is the overall value of the consequences (positive or negative) that would result were the claim to be generally accepted. Clearly, in matters scientific at least, we want to heed Hume's advice and not confuse the truth value of a scientific claim with whatever acceptance value it may have. So we might put what I call 'Hume's dictum' as follows:

> For any area of inquiry, the truth values of the claims that make up discourse in that area should be distinguished from the acceptance values of those claims.

The general importance of Hume's dictum for the issue about irrealism and error is the following. According to Sturgeon, if the irrealist is really going to be able to account for the possibility of genuine moral error, she must be able to construct a notion of moral correctness and, correspondingly, a notion of moral error that allows us to make sense of a purely *theoretical* notion of correctness and error—a notion distinct from *practical* correctness and error. This demand is, of

---

9. The distinction, drawn in these terms, is to be found in Railton (1984: 116). See, for example, Paton, 1948, and Blanshard, 1949, for objections to ethical emotivism based on considerations of the acceptance value of this doctrine.

course, being added to what we saw as a minimum requirement of genuine moral correctness and error. So the conception of genuine moral error at work here — an enriched conception — involves two components: first (and minimally) it involves the idea of some moral judgment that is erroneous even though there is nothing wrong with any of the non-moral beliefs or modes of non-moral and moral reasoning associated with that judgment; and, second, it involves the idea that the explanation of error in moral judgment involves considerations distinct from conditions of acceptance value, that truth value and acceptance value be clearly distinguished. (Whether this new, added demand is one the irrealist must concede will be dealt with in the next section.) And, of course, if such error in moral judgment is possible, this provides support for premise 3 of the master argument: even moral judgments that do not involve any of the sorts of error (in non-moral belief, etc.) described in premise 2 might be mistaken.

Of course, irrealists who find some interesting use for moral discourse may not be interested in the *truth value* of moral judgments. But the realist complaint can obviously be restated in terms of the distinction between the correctness and the acceptance value of moral judgments. The complaint is this: in order for the irrealist to devise a genuine notion of moral error, she must be able to distinguish, and plausibly account for, the difference between the correctness value of moral judgments and their acceptance value. To fail to do so would be a serious concession to the realist, and simply to waive the distinction in the case of moral discourse would seem ad hoc, given its strong intuitive support in areas of non-moral inquiry.

If we consider the two sorts of irrealist account described in the previous section, we can see the problem. If the correctness of a set of norms, principles, or basic moral convictions, which constitute either an individual's moral sensibility or the basic moral outlook of a whole society, is not to be understood in terms of its truth, then *in virtue of what* are the norms that constitute any such set correct? One likely irrealist response is to appeal to the functions of a moral code, especially as it bears on well-being. But it is a short step from this sort of consideration to the idea that the correctness of a set of moral norms or basic moral convictions simply is a matter of how effective they would be in promoting the well-being of humans (and perhaps other creatures as well). And this is to construe correctness of those norms or convictions in terms of their acceptance value. The irrealist is thus guilty of not heeding Hume's dictum and, consequently, cannot devise a notion of genuine moral error.

IX. An Irrealist Response: Truth or Consequences

In response to this argument from Hume's dictum, the irrealist has at least two routes to follow. First, she might short-circuit the argument by identifying the correctness of a set of moral norms[10] with the property of *coherence*: norms are

---

10. For convenience, I am going to use the expression 'moral norms' to refer to all sorts of general moral statements and judgments, including moral rules (e.g., 'Lying is (prima facie) wrong') and moral principles (e.g., the principle of utility and Kant's categorical imperative).

true or correct if, and only if, they cohere with an individual's or group's considered moral judgments. Clearly, on a coherence conception of moral correctness (and error), a set of norms might be correct yet be such that, were the norms constituting the set used by individuals to consciously guide their decisions, the value resulting from such acceptance and use would be low. An irrealist need not be guilty of blurring the distinction between correctness value and acceptance value.

But while this short-circuit tactic does avoid the argument from Hume's dictum, it certainly seems to compromise an underlying conception of moral inquiry shared by many irrealists. The underlying conception, already mentioned earlier, is simply that the function of an individual or social moral code has essentially to do with the promotion of well-being or flourishing. An adequate or correct set of moral norms is thus plausibly understood to be largely a matter of its performing its function well. An aim of moral inquiry for the irrealist, then, is to discover such a set of norms. And once the irrealist adopts this conception of moral inquiry, it appears that correctness is being closely tied to, if not identified with, acceptance value.

What I want to argue is that I can see no reason why the irrealist should concede to the realist the claim that, to make sense of genuine moral error, she must be able to distinguish sharply between the correctness value and acceptance value of a set of moral norms. In the end, I suspect that the realist's argument here amounts to question-begging against the irrealist—that Sturgeon's enriched conception of genuine moral error unfairly stacks the deck against the irrealist. But to sort all of this out, we need to clarify some of the theses involved in this issue of truth or consequences.

In this context I will use the term *methodological pragmatism* to represent a general view about theory acceptance in ethics, according to which the correctness of a moral theory (i.e., a set of moral norms together with its implications) is to be judged according to how well it would perform whatever job it is supposed to perform.[11] It is fairly uncontroversial that a practical morality has the social func-

11. Talk about *morality* or *a morality* or, again, *a moral code* is ambiguous. We should distinguish between *positive morality*, the accepted or received morality of some group; *individual morality*, the morality accepted at a time by some individual; and what is variously called *critical*, *ideal*, or *rational morality*, the sort of thing philosophers like to propose and defend as somehow correct or true. (See, for example, Singer, 1986, for a discussion of these notions.) Methodological pragmatism represents a very general standard for comparing and evaluating competing proposals for an adequate or correct substantive moral theory (or set of basic principles or norms). This sort of metaethical outlook takes the primary goal of moral inquiry to be an investigation of what will work. When it comes to comparing and evaluating positive and individual moralities, the methodological pragmatist is primarily interested in the acceptance value of the moralities under consideration: any such morality will count as a rational morality if its acceptance value is good enough. But a moral realist who also accepts some version of moral consequentialism as a correct critical morality will also want to consider the acceptance value of such a moral system. The realist who thinks that, for instance, utilitarianism is a true (critical) moral theory, will want, when it comes to judging the morality of such practices as teaching and promulgating within a particular society some moral code or other, to consider the value of the consequences of such activity and compare the acceptance value of a utilitarian code with the acceptance values of the other, non-utilitarian moral codes that might be taught. And, as realists like to point out, it may turn

tion of promoting, or at least maintaining, the well-being or flourishing of humans (and perhaps other creatures).[12] Thus, the methodological pragmatist is primarily interested in the acceptance value of a moral system, and the fundamental desideratum in evaluating any such system is that it be *functionally adequate*. More precise specifications of this desideratum of functional adequacy result from specifying what counts as a job well done. For example, one might take a maximizing view, according to which a job well done would require maximizing well-being, but non-maximizing versions of this view are also possible. Most obviously, *satisficing* versions are among the options here.[13] But, also, one might hold that the job of the norms represented by some moral theory is to adjudicate interpersonal conflict of interest and do so in a way that respects a constraint of impartiality, whereby respecting this constraint may not consist in simply maximizing or otherwise promoting well-being. Obviously, there are many alternative versions of methodological pragmatism; the acceptance value of a moral theory can be calculated in a wide variety of ways.

Two remarks about this approach to theory acceptance are in order here. First, methodological pragmatism—focusing on the values of consequences of various moral systems—is a version of moral consequentialism. But notice that this consequentialist approach to theory acceptance in ethics is neutral among competing moral systems involving different sorts of norms that might be taught and used by individuals in their practical deliberations. It might turn out that a non-consequentialist moral system, including non-consequentialist moral norms that represent all sorts of deontological constraints, may have a higher acceptance value, for a group, than any of its consequentialist rivals. So, methodological pragmatism does not unfairly favor consequentialist moral theories over their rivals. Second, notice that taking a pragmatist stance toward theory acceptance does justice to the widely shared intuition that consideration of consequences plays a central role in ethics. But just *how* consequences count is a matter of controversy. However, it seems to be relatively uncontroversial, no matter what one's meta-ethical bent, that considerations of consequences play a central role in evaluating a practical moral system. Of course, the realist will insist that the functional adequacy of a moral system is one thing, and its truth is another. The irrealist who rejects the notion of truth as appropriate for moral judgments may well want to construe correctness in terms of acceptance value.

---

out that a consequentialist moral theory would prohibit the teaching and promulgation of that very theory: the possibility of an 'esoteric' critical morality is live. So, when comparing and evaluating positive and individual moralities, both methodological pragmatists and realist-moral consequentialists are joined in considering acceptance value. The difference is that for the realist-moral consequentialist, the interest in acceptance value is motivated by supposing that moral consequentialism is a true critical morality, whereas for the pragmatist, acceptance value is what correctness, as applied to moral systems, is all about.

12. See Boyd, 1988: 208–12, who argues that our preanalytic use of moral terms like 'good' is associated with the notion of human well-being in such a way that considerations of human well-being function as a constraint in the practice of translation of moral discourse.

13. See Slote, 1985: ch. 3, for a discussion of satisficing versions of consequentialism.

I have already noted that the irrealist need not construe correctness of a moral theory in terms of its acceptance value and also need not be a methodological pragmatist. But against a defender of this metaethical view, the argument from Hume's dictum charges that the pragmatist can not recognize the distinction between correctness value and acceptance value of moral theories and so can't recognize a notion of genuine moral error. Granted, a methodological pragmatist ties correctness to acceptance value. But, as far as I can tell, the claim that this counts against this view of theory acceptance in ethics (because the view cannot plausibly recognize and explain a distinction rooted in commonsense) simply begs the question against the pragmatist.

There are three points to be made here. First, the argument from Hume's dictum presumably appeals to commonsense moral thinking as a basis for insisting on maintaining the distinction between truth or correctness value and acceptance value in ethics. But it is very doubtful that Hume's dictum is part of commonsense thinking about morality. The irrealist can grant, for the sake of argument, that commonsense critical practices presuppose that mistakes in moral judgment are possible at the individual and social levels, but such practices do not seem to presuppose anything in particular about the *sources* of error or about how moral error is to be *explained*. Indeed—and this is the second point—one might well suppose that many ordinary folk, upon reflection, would agree that (1) human well-being is the ultimate rationale for having a moral code and (2) a set of moral principles, convictions, or norms is correct if, and only if, they subserve that aim. In other words, methodological pragmatists can, and have, plausibly appealed to commonsense for support. So a methodological pragmatist who wishes to restrict Hume's dictum will plausibly point out that he is not *simply*, and for no reason, waiving the distinction between correctness and acceptance value when it comes to moral discourse.[14]

Third, if the realist *insists* on the distinction between correctness and acceptance value in connection with moral theories, then the argument from Hume's dictum seems to beg the question against the irrealist. Such insistence seems to amount to the insistence that any adequate semantic notion of correctness in ethics *just is* truth in the sense of correspondence, but that is the very issue dividing the realist and irrealist. Put another way, the enriched conception of error in moral judgment that the realist holds over the irrealist's head—a conception that includes the idea that error in moral judgment (not due to error in belief or reasoning) be explained in terms other than acceptance value—is not a conception the irrealist will accept. And her not accepting this enriched conception does not seem to violate any of the assumptions that are involved in our commonsense critical practices concerning moral evaluation.

So it would appear that the irrealist has nothing to fear from the argument from Hume's dictum. An irrealist need not be a methodological pragmatist, and

---

14. See Warnock, 1971: ch. 2, for a defense of the claim that commonsense moral thinking presupposes something like what I call methodological pragmatism.

anyone who is can plausibly maintain that, in ethics, correctness is to be understood (at least partly) in terms of acceptance value.[15]

X. An Option for the Stubborn Irrealist

Let us return to premise 3 of the argument from moral error. Even if the argument from Hume's dictum fails to support that premise, the realist can simply rely on an appeal to our critical practices and maintain that error at the level of hypothetical moral sensibilities and social moral codes is intelligible — we can sensibly inquire about the correctness of the judgments, norms, and convictions that make up such things. And, if so, it would appear that the argument works. What more does the realist need for his argument?

I can well imagine that the stubborn irrealist may want to block this appeal to commonsense critical practices by arguing that there is nothing about such practices that implies that moral error at the level of improved hypothetical moral sensibilities and social moral codes — I call this *deep moral error* — is possible. That is, the irrealist may grant that appeal to commonsense critical practices presupposes that moral discourse is *objective*, in the sense that ordinary moral judgments may be correct (or erroneous) in a way that does not simply depend on what some individual or group happens to think about the matter. But common sense is not fine-tuned to the subtle differences in metaethical positions, and, in particular, common sense does not (so the irrealist might plead) make any distinction between *realist objectivity*, which insists on the possibility of even deep moral error, and an *irrealist brand of objectivity* that might deny this possibility.[16]

In short, the irrealist may want to insist that C2 (which, as stated, does not say that any moral judgment might be false or erroneous and thus subject to

---

15. Sturgeon (1986: 129–32) notes that moral consequentialists, regardless of metaethical bent, have characteristically wanted to sharply distinguish between truth value and acceptance value in order to avoid the embarrassing result of having one's moral theory refuted by considerations of the consequences of a group's accepting that theory. But here we must be careful to distinguish between two levels of moral judgment and the sort of evaluation relevant to each. When it comes to evaluating moral systems that are to function as a practical morality for a group, a thoroughgoing irrealist who espouses methodological pragmatism and also holds that, as far as she can tell, some version of moral consequentialism has as high an acceptance value as any other moral theory, should not be embarrassed by the possibility that her moral theory might prove to be incorrect on the basis of considerations of acceptance value. On the other hand, when it comes to evaluating consequentialism at the metaethical level — that is, as a correct view about theory acceptance at the level of practical moralities — overall coherence of this view with other phenomena decides the issue. I do not see how admitting any of this should prove an embarrassment for the methodological pragmatist.

16. David Copp (1991: 613–14), in his review of Brink (1989), points out that, contrary to Brink's claim that commonsense moral inquiry and critical practices presuppose the truth of moral realism (or at least that realism is the most natural interpretation of such practices), such inquiry and practice, at most, presuppose a descriptivist treatment of moral language, such treatment being, of course, compatible with moral irrealism. I agree with Copp that moral realism is not necessarily implicated in our critical practices, but, as I will argue in the next chapter, I disagree that those practices presuppose some form of descriptivism.

correction) admits of both a strong and a more modest interpretation. According to the strong interpretation—which the moral realist apparently prefers—*any* moral judgment, regardless of the conditions under which it is made, might be mistaken. According to a more modest interpretation of C2, the idea is *almost* any moral judgment might be erroneous and hence subject to correction. The irrealist might point out that certain moral judgments just seem to be immune to error. I am thinking of judgments like: 'It is wrong to torture innocent children for fun.' So, even apart from considerations of being ideally situated, it is far from clear that commonsense moral thinking presupposes that moral error is ubiquitously possible.

Furthermore, the stubborn irrealist who would deny that deep moral error is possible can still plausibly claim that her metaethic does square with a deep-seated intuition presupposed by our critical practices, an intuition that is closely associated with C2. That is, besides C2, there is this idea:

> C2* It is often possible to take a critical stance toward a moral judgment made by some speaker on some occasion, *no matter how well situated the speaker happens to be.*

Notice that C2* seems to represent a more fundamental assumption of our critical practices than does C2, as revealed by the fact that the realist is likely to appeal to C2* as evidence for C2: the only (or best) explanation of why it is possible to take a critical stance toward someone's moral judgment, *even in the case in which that person's moral judgment results from being well situated,* is that for any such judgment, it might be false.

The irrealist proposes an alternative explanation. As we have seen, the reductive irrealist must concede that error in moral judgment is not possible when made under those conditions that according to the particular version of irrealism in question, are good enough for making correct moral judgments. We can express this point by noting that from an irrealist perspective, one cannot grant that some moral judgment was made under the appropriate hypothetical conditions that guarantee, according to the irrealist account, correct moral judgment, and yet sensibly call into question the judgment's correctness. However, in the context of everyday discussion in which we have to judge whether or not to accept the moral judgments of others, we can (often) sensibly raise questions about some moral judgment by raising questions about the judge herself. After all, whatever is involved, according to the irrealist, in being well situated for making correct moral judgments, it is not likely to involve features of the judge and her situation that we can easily detect. For example, part of being well situated would seem to require having all relevant factual information, being free from certain sorts of biases, and properly weighing the interests of parties affected by the action being evaluated. But it is often extremely difficult to determine that someone has all relevant factual information, is free from biases, and has properly weighed the interests of affected parties. Consequently, even if it is not possible for anyone who is appropriately well situated to make a mistake in moral judgment, it is possible for critics (who would acknowledge that such error is not possible) to sensibly raise questions about the correctness of a person's moral judgment.

So the stubborn reductive irrealist can legitimately claim that her theory is compatible with C2*. Furthermore, she will point out that C2* is more deeply embedded in our critical practices than is C2, and will question the realist's inference from C2* to C2 (strongly interpreted). From the fact that we can take a critical stance toward the moral judgments of ourselves and others, it does not follow that we must allow for the possibility that every moral judgment might be mistaken.

In light of the fact that the irrealist (1) can plausibly challenge the claim that commonsense moral thinking presupposes the possibility of deep moral error and (2) can plausibly square her metaethic with C2*—the assumption that it is possible to raise questions about the correctness of a person's moral judgments, regardless of how well situated they might be—the argument from moral error comes up short.

XI. A Lesson for the Irrealist

I am somewhat sympathetic with the stubborn (reductive) irrealist response, but I shall not rest my defense of irrealism on the points just made. Rather, I want to explore another irrealist option, one that represents a departure from standard irrealist accounts of correctness and error. Since the argument from moral error rests on an appeal to our commonsense critical practices, I want to grant, for the sake of argument, that such practices presuppose even the possibility of deep moral error. I am interested, then, in developing an irrealist reply to the argument that concedes as much as possible to the realist about our critical practices. For one thing, this strategy, if successful, will deflate the argument completely. But also, I think that even if our commonsense critical practices do not presuppose anything so recherché as the possibility of deep moral error, we should, on philosophical grounds, admit the possibility of such error.

The sorts of philosophical grounds I have in mind stem from consideration of certain skeptical possibilities. The moral realist correctly points out that moral discourse has many of the trappings of genuine factual discourse: we use it to make what seem like genuine assertions; we take moral disagreements to be genuine disagreements; and so forth. With ordinary empirical discourse, a little philosophical reflection on certain skeptical scenarios (e.g., Cartesian demons, brains in vats, etc.) convinces us that error in factual belief is possible—even if we normally feel absolutely confident in many of the empirical beliefs we now hold. But, as the moral realist might insist, if moral discourse displays the relevant features of genuine factual discourse, then we should admit that moral error is ubiquitously possible—it is even possible that what seem to us unassailable moral judgments really are mistaken. Brink, who argues in roughly this way, points out that just as in the case of empirical/scientific beliefs,

> [t]his possibility of systematic error among our moral beliefs could be realized in different ways. As in the nonmoral case, the cause could be a Cartesian demon who induces in us considered moral beliefs that, when conjoined with nonmoral

beliefs, form a coherent system. Or it could be some more familiar source of distortion such as excessive self-concern or gross imaginative limitations; but, of course, in order to be the source of uncorrectable error, these more familiar sources of distortion would have to be much more widespread and more opaque to us than we believe they are. (Brink, 1989: 34)

Brink's conclusion is that just as certain skeptical possibilities favor a realist construal of empirical discourse, so similar skeptical possibilities regarding moral belief favor a realist construal of moral discourse. I don't agree with Brink's conclusion here, but, as I have said, I do want to grant that moral error—even deep moral error—is possible.

What I claim is that the argument from moral error should teach the irrealist an important philosophical lesson. The lesson concerns what Putnam calls *transcendent reason*, which, he says, "is a regulative idea that we use to criticize the conduct of *all* activities and institutions" (1983c: 234). In the present context, the lesson is this:

> It is a mistake to identify (or in any other way reduce) the correctness of moral judgments with (to) any set of moral standards, principles, norms, or convictions of individuals or groups: the notions of correctness and error, here as elsewhere, "outrun" not only the actual moral standards, and so on, of individuals and groups, but even the standards, and so forth, that would be accepted by individuals and groups under specified hypothetical conditions.

I claim that this is an important truth that underlies premise 3 of the argument from moral error, and one the irrealist should acknowledge. The challenge to the irrealist, then, is to develop a version of irrealism in ethics that is consistent with this lesson. The realist, of course, interprets this lesson as supporting a realist construal of moral discourse. But what the irrealist should learn from this lesson is that it is a mistake to *reduce* by trying to *naturalize* critical notions like correctness and error—the very thing that typical moral irrealists, most notably constructivists (whether of the relativist variety or not), have attempted to do. In other words, the typical irrealist commits a version of the naturalistic fallacy as revealed by the fact that for any set of standards or norms accepted by any individual or group, it is always an open question whether those standards or norms are correct.

Returning to the argument from error, I recommend that the irrealist accept the third premise, heed the underlying lesson, and call the first premise of the argument into question. As we have seen, the first premise of the argument from moral error expresses the typical irrealist approach to correctness (and error) in moral judgment—a *reductivist approach*. Thus, I claim that in responding to the argument from moral error, the irrealist should reject the first premise and attempt to articulate a non-reductivist version of her view. Since the territory of non-reductive irrealism may not be familiar to many readers, and since Putnam himself has attempted to provide a non-reductive irrealist metaphysical/semantic story generally, which he then proposes to use for understanding moral discourse, it will be useful to consider Putnam's views.

XII. Putnam on Methodology and Morals

One of the major critical themes of Putnam's work is that reductive programs in philosophy have not worked, and are not going to work, no matter what sort of reductive program (e.g., semantic or ontological) one has in mind. This is not the place to explore all of Putnam's arguments for his view (though the argument from moral error we have been examining is in the Putnam spirit, and, of course, the philosophical moral I draw from that argument is taken from Putnam). Rather, what interests me here is the post-analytic view of truth or correctness that Putnam labels *internal* or *pragmatic realism*. I should say that I am interested in certain *facets* of Putnam's pragmatic realism, since I am not sure that Putnam's positive philosophical story about truth in general—one that is supposed to avoid both metaphysical (external) realism and relativism—represents a stable philosophical position. (I express my reservations about Putnam's pragmatic realism as it plays itself out in ethics later in this section.) So I shall begin with some remarks on Putnam's metaphilosophical views and then consider some of their implications for understanding moral discourse.

Putnam's Antireductivist Methodology

Before going on, however, I need to straighten out some terminology. Putnam refers to his overall metaphysical and associated semantic view as 'internal realism,'[17] but if we draw the line regarding realism where I have—that is, as making a strong claim about the independence and objectivity of the world that is wedded to a correspondence theory of truth—then Putnam's views count as irrealist. With apologies to Putnam, I will go ahead and construe his view as a version of global metaphysical irrealism. Regardless, what interests me here is the antireductionist theme of Putnam's work.

   One facet of Putnam's view that is important for our concerns is his backing away from traditional ways (at least within analytic philosophy) of tackling philosophical problems by attempting some sort of philosophical *account* of critical notions like truth and justification (rationality)—accounts that, in effect, reduce or define such notions. Another related facet of Putnam's thought concerns what a philosopher may usefully say about such notions as truth and justification if one gives up traditional philosophical projects. After all, even if we abandon these traditional projects, there surely is something philosophically interesting to say

---

17. In his 1994 Dewey Lectures, Putnam expresses some reservations about his internal realism. See especially pp. 461–65. I will not consider any new wrinkles in Putnam's most recent views about matters of truth.

about the notions in question; we don't want to end up saying that these notions are useless or philosophically mysterious. Let us consider these themes in order.

A basic tenet of Putnam's pragmatic realism is his claim that "a statement is true . . . if it would be justified under epistemically ideal conditions" (Putnam, 1983a: 84). The import of this claim is supposed to be that the truth of a sentence is not (contra the metaphysical realist) completely independent of all questions of its justification, yet it is independent of 'here and now' justification (hence, the talk of 'ideal'). Putnam's "truth is idealized justification" slogan has encouraged certain misunderstandings that, in effect, construe pragmatic realism as some sort of reductive account of truth. One such misunderstanding is the suspicion that this view is warmed-over Peirce; that truth is being identified with what would be unanimously accepted in *the ideal limit of inquiry*. But Putnam explicitly rejects this interpretation of what he is saying,[18] and in his most recent writings, prefers to express the view in terms of one's epistemic situation being "sufficiently good" (as opposed to "ideal") for judging whether sentences of a particular sort (e.g., ordinary sentences about the observable properties of physical objects) are true or false. But there are some other misunderstandings of what Putnam is saying that fail, in a fundamental way, to appreciate the non-reductive strain of his thought. Let us briefly consider them.

First, contrary to what some readers of Putnam have thought, Putnam's remarks about truth as ideal warranted assertibility are not intended to provide any sort of definition of truth. That is, it is perhaps tempting to suppose that what Putnam is offering is a philosophical account of truth by filling out the formula, '*p*' is true if, and only if . . . , with a specification of some necessary and sufficient conditions, in epistemic terms, that would turn the resulting statement into some sort of definition of truth. But certainly Putnam is not proposing an analytic definition of the word 'true': he denies that statements of the form: '*p*' is true are equivalent in meaning to (i.e., synonymous with) statements of the form: '*p*' is *ideally warrantedly assertible*. Nor is he offering an 'account' of truth by providing a list of necessary and sufficient conditions that would constitute a specification of the underlying nature of truth, and so would provide some sort of synthetic definition of this notion. Thus, Putnam is not proposing that truth talk be somehow *reductively defined* in epistemic terms. Here is a passage from *Representation and Realism* that makes this point:

> The point is that I am not offering a *reductive* account of truth, in any sense (nor of warrant, for that matter). In *Reason, Truth and History* I explained the idea thus: "truth is idealized rational acceptability." This formulation was taken by many as meaning that "rational acceptability" (and the notion of "better and worse

---

18. The sorts of misunderstanding that talk of 'ideal' epistemic conditions encourages include taking Putnam to be a closet metaphysical realist after all (see Rorty, 1985) and taking such ideal conditions to be humanly unattainable and unknowable. Putnam (1992: 73–74; 1991: 417, 421; 1990: viii; 1988: 115) responds to these misunderstandings. For an interesting discussion of the Peircian-like aspect of Putnam's view, see Wright, 1992: 44–48.

epistemic situation," which I also employed) is supposed (by me) to be *more basic* than "truth"; that I was offering a *reduction* of truth *to* epistemic notions. Nothing was farther from my intention. The suggestion is simply that truth and rational acceptability are *interdependent* notions. (Putnam, 1988: 115)[19]

An important related point is this: Putnam is not proposing that the interdependent notions of truth and justification be naturalistically defined in terms of a list of necessary and sufficient conditions. Putnam often expresses the point by claiming that there is no algorithm that completely specifies, for any arbitrary statement, those conditions under which someone is ideally (or sufficiently) epistemically well situated:

> What is "a sufficiently well placed speaker"? That depends on the statement one is dealing with. There is no algorithm for determining whether a given epistemic position is better or worse for making an arbitrary judgment. But facts of the form "If you have to tell whether S is true, then it is better to be in circumstances C_1 than in circumstances C_2." are not "transcendent" facts; they are facts that it is within the capacity of speakers to determine, if they have the good fortune to be in the right sorts of circumstances. What are "the right sorts of circumstances"? That depends on the statement one is dealing with. (Putnam, 1988: 115)

Given these caveats, we can understand why, in commenting on pragmatic realism and his claim about truth, Putnam remarks:

> Now, the picture I have just sketched *is* only a "picture." If I were to claim it is a *theory*, I should be called upon at least to sketch a theory of idealized warrant; and I don't think we can even sketch a theory of actual warrant (a theory of the "nature" of warrant), let alone a theory of idealized warrant. (Putnam, 1990: 42)[20]

Putnam, then, is quite explicit in his backing away from trying to give a philosophical theory or account (i.e., a set of necessary and sufficient conditions that serve to define the 'essence' or 'nature') of truth and justification. It is worth pausing for a moment to sort out two distinct antireductive claims that Putnam seems to accept, since some antireductionists in ethics accept one and not the other.

Let us first distinguish between strong and weak reductive definitions. A strong reductive definition would have the effect of analyzing some normative concept fully and completely by a battery of non-normative concepts. In chapter 1, you may recall, versions of semantic naturalism were involved in the project of giving strong reductive definitions of moral concepts. By contrast, a weak reductive definition of a normative concept would eschew the attempt to give a strong reductive definition, but would nevertheless propose that (1) with regard to two species of normative concepts, there is genuine conceptual priority between them (in the sense that one species is more basic than the other) and (2) therefore, one species of normative concepts (the less basic) can be usefully defined in terms of the more

19. See also Putnam, 1991: 421.
20. See also Putnam, 1983a: xvi–xviii; 1991: 402.

basic species of normative concepts. So, for instance, Michael Smith (1994) does not think that it is possible to give a strong reductive definition of the concept of moral rightness, but he does propose what I call a weak reductive definition: he analyzes the concept of moral rightness in terms of the concept of full rationality. (See the appendix for some discussion of Smith's view.)

So, it is useful to distinguish between what I call the *thesis of weak anti-reduction* (with regard to some species of normative discourse), according to which it is not possible to give a strong reductive definition of the normative concepts in question, and the *thesis of strong antireduction* (with regard to some species of normative discourse), according to which it is not possible to give a weak reductive definition of the concepts in question. The first quoted passage from Putnam makes it clear that he is a strong antireductivist about the concept of truth. (As is evident in the next chapter, I hold a strong antireductivist view about basic moral concepts.)

But if one takes a strong antireductionist line about some battery of notions, one may wonder what, philosophically, one can do by way of illuminating these notions. In fact, since, as Putnam likes to stress, questions about rationality and justification are at the very heart of philosophical inquiry (1981: 104–5), one wonders what is left for philosophers to do (at least those who do metaphysics, seman-tics, or epistemology) if they abandon offering *theories* about truth and justification.

An answer, along the lines Putnam would, I think, endorse, could be put this way. Although we cannot define (by specifying a list of necessary and sufficient conditions) the notions of truth or ideal justification, nevertheless, we do under-stand talk of being epistemically well situated with regard to statements of a specific sort, and our understanding of these notions, like our understanding of other no-tions, is largely in terms of certain *paradigms* or *prototypes*. That is, through com-ing to learn how to competently engage in a certain type of discourse, we learn (perhaps largely implicitly) a set of norms that guide our judgments of truth about the sentences making up that type of discourse.

These norms, in effect, specify conditions (pertaining both to the judger and his immediate environment) that we take as (partly) articulating 'ideal' or at least 'good enough' conditions for judging the truth or falsity of the type of sentence in question. For example, with regard to mundane statements about ordinary phys-ical objects, Putnam writes:

> By an ideal epistemic situation I mean something like this: If I say "there is a chair in my study," an ideal epistemic situation would be to be in my study with the lights on or with daylight streaming through the window, with nothing wrong with my eyesight, with an unconfused mind, without having taken drugs or been subjected to hypnosis, and so forth, and to look and see if there is a chair there. Or to drop the notion of "ideal" altogether, since that is only a metaphor, I think there are *better and worse* epistemic situations *with respect to particular statements*. (Putnam, 1990: viii)

So we can, as it were, *illustrate* our current conception of what an ideal epistemic situation is with regard to various types of discourse, but this illustration (involving the articulation of a battery of norms) falls short of any reductive definition for two related reasons. First, the various considerations mentioned by Putnam that bear on the truth of ordinary physical object statements are properly expressed as 'ceteris paribus' generalizations—which can be overridden in nonordinary circumstances. And the crucial point here is that there is no decision procedure or algorithm that specifies all of those possible conditions under which all things are equal. In learning physical object talk, for example, we acquire a practice, part of which involves learning (largely implicitly) a battery of norms for warranted assertibility. But, as Putnam points out, in acquiring a practice like this

> [w]hat we acquire is not a knowledge that can be applied as if it were an algorithm. We do learn that in certain circumstances we are supposed to accept 'There is a chair in front of me' (normally). *But we are expected to use our heads.* We can refuse to accept 'There is a chair in front of me' even when it looks to us exactly as if there is a chair in front of us, if our general intelligence screams 'override.' The impossibility (in practice at least) of formalizing the assertibility conditions for arbitrary sentences is just the impossibility of formalizing general intelligence itself. (Putnam, 1983a: xviii)

So, looked at synchronically, those norms that make up our current conception of ideal justification do not amount to a fully specified set of necessary and sufficient conditions defining this notion. But a second related point is this. Our current conception of ideal justification involves norms that may evolve or even be rejected in light of future refinements in our view of the world. That is, looked at diachronically, our conception of ideal justification may undergo revision. This point is perhaps best illustrated in connection with theory acceptance in science.

Scientific inquiry is currently guided by certain ideals such as *simplicity, predictive fertility, comprehensiveness*, and so forth. These ideals can be expressed as very general norms governing theory acceptance in science, whose use in the context of evaluating scientific theories is an important part of our conception of what it is to be ideally situated for evaluating the truth of such theories. In addition to the point that there is no algorithm or definition (in terms of necessary and sufficient conditions) associated with these ideals, there is the point that scientific ideals can change and evolve. For instance, in his book *Science and Values*, in which Larry Laudan describes the dynamics of theory change in science, he points out that some aims or ideals of scientific inquiry have been completely abandoned:

> More or less from the time of Aristotle onward, scientists had sought theories that were demonstrable and apodictically certain. Although empiricists and rationalists disagreed about precisely how to certify knowledge as certain and incorrigible, all agreed that science was aiming exclusively at the production of such knowledge. This same view of science largely prevailed at the beginning of the nineteenth century. But by the end of that century this demonstrative and infallibilist ideal was well and truly dead. Scientists of almost every persuasion were insistent that science could, at most, aspire to the status of highly probable knowledge. Certainty, incorrigibility, and indefeasibility ceased to figure among the central aims of most twentieth-century scientists. (Laudan, 1984: 83)

The point I wish to stress here is that the norms involved in our conception of ideal warrant (in connection with ordinary physical object discourse, scientific discourse, and other kinds of discourse as well) are, in a dual sense, 'open-ended.' First, viewed synchronically, they represent a battery of ceteris paribus norms for which it is not possible to specify, in terms of an algorithm, all of those conditions under which *ceteris* is *paribus*. Second, viewed diachronically, the current set of ceteris paribus norms are liable to change; current norms may be modified or reinterpreted; some may be rejected (as illustrated in the Laudan quote); others may be added. In short, our conception of ideal warrant with regard to empirical sentences is rather loose and fluid—not something for which we have necessary and sufficient conditions—but nevertheless serviceable.

Some recent empirical work by cognitive psychologists on ordinary 'natural object' concepts, and various processes of categorization associated with such concepts, bolsters the claim that we should not expect to find reductive analyses or definitions (in terms of necessary and sufficient conditions) for concepts like truth and rationality. The work of Eleanor Rosch (1973, 1975, 1978) and others has seriously called into question the plausibility of the so-called classical view about how natural object concepts are mentally represented and how these representations are processed.

A good deal of the experimental research has focused on *typicality effects*. These effects on such activities as categorization stem from the fact that people find it natural to classify various members or subsets of a concept according to how typical the member or subset of the concept is. For instance, most people consider robins and sparrows typical birds, hawks and eagles less typical, and penguins and chickens atypical. These typicality ratings provide a basis for predicting how people will perform on certain categorization tasks: typical members or subsets of a concept are more quickly classified than less typical members; the error rate for correctly classifying members and subsets decreases the more typical the members or subsets, and so on. The important point here is that the experimental results conflict with what a classical view would predict.[21] According to the classical view, such concepts have necessary and sufficient defining features, and mental representations of such concepts, as well as processes of categorization, employ these features. Assuming that categorization judgments of the sort studied by cognitive psychologists are a product of and reflect our conceptual scheme, one would expect that people who have and use a concept like bird would find all instances of birds to be good examples of the general concept, and that there would be little or no disparity in reaction times of categorization judgments. After all, on the classical view, the criteria for class membership apply equally well to all instances of the general concept. On the basis of such empirical research, most cognitive scientists studying concepts have given up the classical view of concepts.[22]

---

21. For a good summary of the experimental work and its bearing on the classical view, see Edward E. Smith and Douglas L. Medin, 1981: ch.1, and W. Ramsey, 1992.

22. As Ramsey (1992: 63) points out, the relevant empirical work does not constitute a refutation of the classical view, but provides strong reason for abandoning the view and constructing alternative accounts. The criticism of the classical view of concepts has not gone unchallenged by philosophers,

Various non-classical models of concept representation and processing have been proposed that would explain typicality effects on people's categorization behavior, all of them falling under *prototype theories* of categorization. The implications of the prototype approach for the question about the structure of concepts can be summed up this way: (1) natural object concepts do not have necessary and sufficient defining conditions; rather, (2) in typical cases, some (but not all) instances or subsets of a concept are prototypical instances of that concept; and (3) whether or not a concept correctly applies to some object depends on the degree of similarity between the object and the prototypical members of the concept.

Philosophers, of course, will be familiar with these themes through the writing of Wittgenstein. In fact, in their 1981 book summarizing some of the prominent empirical research on categorization, Smith and Medin distinguish between what they call 'general criticisms' of the classical view and those based on experimental findings of cognitive psychologists. They attribute to Wittgenstein the most forceful of the general criticisms, namely, the fact that decades of analysis of concepts have not been very successful in specifying necessary and sufficient defining features of many concepts:

> One of Wittgenstein's most famous examples was that of the concept of games, and we can use it to illustrate the flavor of his argument. What is a necessary feature of the concept of games? It cannot be competition between teams, or even the stipulation that there must be at least two individuals involved, for solitaire is a game that has neither feature. Similarly, a game cannot be defined as something that must have a winner, for the child's game of ring-around-a-rosy has no such feature. Or let us try a more abstract feature—say that anything is a game if it provides amusement or diversion. Football is clearly a game, but it is doubtful that professional football players consider their Sunday endeavors as amusing or diverting. And even if they do, and if amusement is a necessary feature of a game, that alone cannot be sufficient, for whistling can also be an amusement and no one would consider it a game. This is the kind of analysis that led Wittgenstein to his disillusionment with the classical view. (Smith and Medin, 1981: 30)

If prototype theory presents a more plausible picture of natural object concepts than does the classical view, then one suspects that the same can be said of those concepts like truth and rationality that occupy the attention of philosophers.[23] And if so, Putnam's metaphilosophical views that I have been describing represent a sensible way to proceed in tackling questions about truth and rationality.[24]

---

by the way. Rey (1983, 1985) argues that the critics confuse epistemological issues of cognitive access with metaphysical issues about what a thing really is. How we tend to classify and categorize things for pragmatic purposes is one matter, according to Rey, but the essential features of a thing (which is what we are trying to capture by giving a classical philosophical analysis) is another. For a tidy exposition of and response to Rey, see Ramsey, 1992: 66–68.

23. Putnam (1992: 167) notes (following Rush Rhees) that Wittgenstein's 'game' example was intended by him to apply to terms like 'language' and 'reference'—terms that are of central philosophical concern.

24. As Michael DePaul pointed out to me, since mathematical and logical concepts do not seem to fit the prototype conception of concepts (better suited for understanding 'natural' concepts), one needs

Putnam on Moral Truth

So, if we are interested in following through with the antireductivist theme in ethics, the first place to look is to Putnam himself, particularly since, in recent years, he has proposed to investigate "the standpoint of pragmatic realism in ethics" (1987: 21). Although Putnam has not provided the details of this sort of standpoint in ethics, it is clear that if we focus on his conception of moral truth by simply extending his general epistemic conception of truth to the domain of morals, then to say that a moral statement is true is to say that that statement is ideally warrantedly assertible. The result here is best classified as a non-reductive version of moral constructivism. In fact, Putnam seems to endorse a Rawlsian wide reflective equilibrium approach to moral theory acceptance, according to which basic moral principles that would emerge from this process would specify basic moral truths, and less general moral statements, that in some sense follow from the more basic ones, would (perhaps together with relevant factual information) specify non-basic moral truths. What more can be said to illuminate this conception of moral truth?

According to Putnam, a morality or moral code — comprising in part norms specifying particular goods to be pursued, character traits to be developed, and actions to be done or omitted (call these moral norms) — is best understood as providing guidelines for promoting human happiness or flourishing in the face of interpersonal conflicts of interest. The development of such a code requires that we reason not only about the best way to promote such flourishing, but about the nature of human flourishing itself. Moreover, reasoning about such matters requires the use of standards "that automatically arise once we undertake the enterprise of giving a justification of principles for living" (1978: 84). Thus, "the 'objectivity' of ethical principles, or, more broadly, of 'moralities,' is connected with such things as width of appeal, ability to withstand certain kinds of rational criticism, . . . feasibility, ideality, and, of course, with how it actually *feels* to live by them or attempt to live by them" (Putnam, 1978: 93).

Such desiderata, and associated principles of acceptability for norms, then, are used to evaluate the truth of specific moral norms for promoting human flourishing. They are also used in developing and justifying a conception of human flourishing, or what, in his Carus Lectures, Putnam calls a "moral image":

> A moral image, in the sense in which I am using the term, is not a declaration that this or that is a virtue, or that this or that is what one ought to do; it is rather a picture of how our virtues and ideals hang together with one another and of what they have to do with the position we are in. It may be as vague as the notions of 'sisterhood and brotherhood'; indeed, millions of human beings have found in those metaphors moral images that could organize their moral lives —

---

to argue that the sorts of evaluative concepts in question are more like natural object concepts than mathematical and logical concepts. I won't explore this matter here, but in light of the history of failure to define evaluative concepts on the model of mathematical and logical concepts, we have reason enough to work with the prototype model.

and this notwithstanding the enormous problem of interpreting them and of deciding what it could possibly mean to make them *effective*. (Putnam, 1987: 51)

Though Putnam is not very explicit about what is involved in moral images, it
would seem that they include very general moral principles, for example, 'One
ought to respect others'; 'All persons are of equal moral worth'—principles that
require interpretation in order to yield a system of moral norms.

According to Putnam, moral images themselves are to be justified according
to how well they serve the needs of human beings, which, of course, ties into our
theories of persons and society generally (what Rawls and others call 'non-moral
background theories'). Thus, for example, an excessively utopian moral image that
is simply not livable because it is out of touch with facts about human motivation
would be unacceptable. Moreover, what was said earlier about the manner in
which norms involved in scientific theory acceptance are both synchronically and
diachronically open-ended applies here. Our norms of appraisal for moral theories
(norms involving such notions as feasibility, livability, and the rest) are open to
interpretation at times, and they evolve and change with the process of moral
inquiry itself. Let us call the norms of theory acceptance that would themselves
be accepted under conditions ideal for evaluating those sorts of norms 'ideal
norms'; then we can say that a moral statement (including moral statements at all
levels of generality) is true if, and only if it would be accepted under conditions
in which we employ ideal norms of moral theory acceptance.

As I have said, the result of all this is a version of moral constructivism that
is supposed to be appropriately non-reductive in its construal of moral truth. At
least it is clear that it is a version of moral constructivism and that the description
of a non-reductive approach to philosophical questions about truth and rationality
given in the previous subsection applies as well to Putnam's attempted illumination of moral truth.

If the overall metaethical view can deliver what we are promised, namely, a
view of moral truth that avoids moral realism on the one hand (that is, what
Putnam would call 'external moral realism') and relativism on the other, then it
has a lot going for it; or so I would argue.[25]

However, a worry about the overall stability of Putnam's view remains.[26] The
gist of the worry is that there are (or seem to be) incompatible strains in Putnam's
overall story. Some strains pull in the direction of the sort of external (metaphysical) realism Putnam repudiates; other strains pull in the direction of relativism,
that he also repudiates. If we focus on his views about moral truth, we can bring
out the alleged tension as follows. Truth involves an idealization of norms of
rational acceptance; a true statement is one that would be endorsed by ideal norms
of warrant. However, as Putnam himself notes, there are no epistemic norms (or
norms of any sort) that are, as it were, the world's own norms of rationality; there

25. I tried my hand at explicating in some detail Putnam's metaethical views in Timmons (1991) which
I then employed in an attempt (Timmons, 1993a) to respond to the argument from error. I am now
less sanguine about the view, for reasons I sketch later in this section.
26. For an illuminating discussion of the apparent tensions in Putnam's view, see Throop and Doran,
1991.

is no set of conceptual-scheme/inquiry-independent epistemic norms (see Putnam, 1987: 78). Moreover, as Putnam also insists, norms of rationality are not value free; in fact, they reflect ideals of human flourishing (i.e., they reflect, in part, particular moral images):

> If 'rationality' is an ability (or better, an integrated system of abilities) which enables the possessor to determine what *questions* are relevant questions to ask and what *answers* it is warranted to accept, then its value is on its sleeve. But it needs no argument that *such* a conception of rationality is as value loaded as the notion of relevance itself. (Putnam, 1981: 202)

Putnam's overall view of moral truth allows for a rather robust ethical pluralism — pluralism in the sense that in the ideal limit there may be more than one conception of human flourishing that is acceptable and, so, more than one set of true moral norms: "We agree with Aristotle that different ideas of human flourishing are appropriate for individuals with different constitutions, but we go further and believe that even in the ideal world there would be different constitutions, that diversity is part of the ideal" (1981: 148). But Putnam denies any sort of 'anything goes' relativism, according to which, with different ideals of human flourishing, there are different norms of rational acceptance, and so we have to end up being relativists about moral truth. Thus, he denies that moral truth is a matter of what is acceptable under conditions that are epistemically ideal for assessing moral matters, and that there are many incompatible ideal standpoints and so many sets of incompatible sets of moral truths. "[B]elief in a pluralistic ideal is not the same thing as belief that every ideal of human flourishing is as good as every other" (1981: 148). The problem is how Putnam can cut off the anything goes worry without, at the same time, tacitly embracing some externalist realist view about the nature and status of norms. This worry I am pressing here about Putnam's view of moral truth is an instance of a general worry about his conception of truth that has been pressed by his critics.[27]

Let me try to make the problem clearer by considering Putnam's case of the 'rational' Nazi. The case of the 'rational' Nazi is a litmus test for determining whether Putnam's view can avoid anything goes relativism; surely, if Putnam's pluralism isn't just disguised relativism, then he ought to be able to rule out the 'rational' Nazi outlook as being false. The case in question is one in which we have a group of fanatics who have worked out a coherent moral system. Granted, there may have been many actual Nazis who were such that, had they been made aware of and vividly reflected on the sorts of atrocities they were committing, they would have been led to give up their murderous ends. In their case, we can say that they were mistaken and that they had a reason to give up their Nazi goals.

But there remain the true fanatics who, we are to suppose, have a 'coherently' worked-out system. Putnam explains:

> But doubtless many Nazis would have still been Nazis, because they did not care about the suffering their actions caused and because no matter how vivid they

---

27. See, for instance, the reviews of *Reason, Truth and History* by Nathanson (1983) and Conee (1987).

might make the alternative life seem to their imaginations, it would [not] speak to anything in them. . . . There is no end *in them* to which we can appeal, neither an actual end or even a potential one, one which they would come to realize if they were more intelligent and more imaginative. (Putnam, 1981: 171)

These specific remarks are supposed to indicate that no purely instrumentalist conception of practical reason (according to which, roughly, all reasons for action ultimately flow from ultimate ends one happens to have, or perhaps would have upon some amount of reflection) can help with the case of the 'rational' Nazi, and that we need some non-instrumentalist notion.

But we have also seen that Putnam does not think that any notion of rationality (regarding belief or action) is value free; rather, any notion we can concoct will be partly reflective of views about the good and, in particular, about human flourishing. And now the situation looks difficult because (1) there doesn't seem to be a way of showing that the 'rational' Nazis are really mistaken—we have a conception of rationality that reflects one conception of human flourishing; they have a different conception of rationality reflective of a different conception—and thus (2) there doesn't seem to be a way of blocking the idea that associated with the Nazi outlook is an idealization of their norms, and so, (3) there doesn't seem to be a way of denying that certain moral norms and particular judgments (which we would find morally outrageous) would be ideally warrantedly assertible. Anything goes.

In response, one could insist that, in the ideal limit, Nazi outlooks would not survive, but getting to this result would seem to require going back on the claim that there are no norms of rationality that are the world's own norms (as Putnam submits), and would amount to embracing external realism.[28]

There may be a way of preserving Putnam's conception of truth and blocking the road to anything goes relativism, but I shall not explore this matter here. Rather, I want to call attention to just how Putnam responds to the case of the 'rational' Nazi, because I think it illuminates how one might proceed in developing an appropriately non-reductive version of moral irrealism.

In one place, after noting that his view allows for pluralism, Putnam remarks, "We reject ideals of human flourishing as wrong, as infantile, as sick, as one-sided" (1981: 148). Note the evaluative language: Putnam obviously supposes that we make such judgments from within a moral outlook. Again, here is a longer passage in which Putnam calls attention to the invocation of his (and presumably our) moral outlook in dealing with the 'rational' Nazi challenge:

Suppose . . . that the Nazi *repudiates* ordinary moral notions altogether. . . . I argued that a culture which repudiated ordinary moral notions, or substituted notions derived from a different ideology and moral outlook for them, would lose the ability to *describe* ordinary interpersonal relations, social events and political events adequately and perspicuously *by our present lights*. Of course, if the different ideology and moral outlook are *superior* to our present moral system then this substitution may be good and wise; but if the different ideology and moral

28. This is Rorty's 1985 complaint.

outlook are *bad*, especially if they are warped and monstrous, then the result will be simply an inadequate, unperspicuous, repulsive representation of interpersonal and social facts. Of course, 'inadequate, unperspicuous, repulsive' reflect value judgments; but I have argued that the choice of a conceptual scheme *necessarily* reflects value judgments, and the choice of a conceptual scheme is what *cognitive* rationality is all about. (Putnam, 1981: 212)

What I find interesting about Putnam's remarks here is that, in dealing with fundamental challenges to one's moral outlook (and associated conception of rationality), Putnam freely invokes his own moral outlook and uses it in asserting certain moral views and evaluations over and against those of the hypothetical 'rational' Nazi. Such remarks, then, are 'morally engaged,' we might say—made from within a moral outlook. There is no attempt here to detach from one's moral outlook and ascend to some neutral perspective and attempt to argue, on grounds that would be morally and epistemically neutral, that the Nazis were irrational and had false moral views. Indeed, the idea that our conceptions of rationality are value laden rules out this sort of move. Moreover, in invoking his own moral outlook and making judgments over and against the claims, goals, and norms of the Nazis, Putnam does not intend to construe truth as simply identical to whatever view he (or we) now happens to accept; that would be what Susan Haack (1993: 192) calls 'tribalism'—a view like relativism, but lacking its ecumenical charm. Putnam allows for moral progress.

I believe all of this indicates how, in general, the moral irrealist should attempt to deal with matters of deep moral disagreement and error, and, in the next chapter, I shall attempt to tell a semantic story about moral discourse that incorporates these ideas. However, notice that Putnam's view of truth as an idealization of warranted assertibility really doesn't play an essential role (as far as I can tell) in combating the outlook of the Nazis. As I have said, there is no attempt to ascend to some neutral vantage point, armed with some neutral conception of rationality, in order to show that the Nazi goals are irrational. But notice that when we view things from a morally detached perspective, it certainly looks as if there are going to be multiple and incompatible sets of moral norms and values that are generally acceptable, relative to various incompatible sets of idealized norms. What I want to suggest, then, is that (in addition to his antireductivism) there is something right about the spirit of Putnam's views worth preserving, but as far as I can discern, we should not follow Putnam in construing truth as ideal warranted assertibility. At least, that is part of my plan for the next chapter.

Before leaving Putnam, however, let me call attention to a theme in his thinking about truth and rationality that, despite being fairly vague, touches on something important. In "Why Reason Can't Be Naturalized," Putnam writes the following:

What I am saying is that the 'standards' accepted by a culture or a subculture, either explicitly or implicitly, cannot *define* what reason is, even in context, because they *presuppose* reason (reasonableness) for their interpretation. On the one hand, there is no notion of reasonableness at all *without* cultures, practices, procedures; on the other hand, the cultures, practices, procedures we inherit are not an algorithm to be slavishly followed. As Mill said, commenting on his own inductive logic, there is no rule book which will not lead to terrible results 'if supposed to be conjoined with universal idiocy.' Reason is, in this sense, both immanent (not to be found outside of concrete language games and institutions) and transcendent (a regulative idea that we use to criticize the conduct of *all* activities and institutions). (Putnam, 1983c: 234)

The immanent/transcendent theme, applied to our critical notions like truth and rationality, seems right to me. My own interpretation of it (to slightly anticipate the next chapter) goes as follows. Evaluative statements (and I take truth to be an evaluative/normative notion) generally are immanent, in that they involve judgments made from a normatively engaged stance. This was nicely illustrated by the Putnam quote about what is wrong with the Nazi outlook. On the other hand, truth is not just to be identified with our current outlook, or any with any outlook. Our notions of truth and of rationality have a kind of transcendence that blocks any attempt at some sort of naturalistic reduction of them. (This was the main lesson of the argument from moral error.) This immanence/transcendence dual aspect of such notions as truth and rationality is what needs preserving (so I think) in any plausible philosophical story about these notions. I take Putnam's positive views about truth to be one attempt to capture this duality; the view I sketch in the next chapter is meant to be another.

XIII. Conclusion

The strongest challenge to any version of moral irrealism concerns the project of internal accommodation: there are all sorts of phenomena deeply embedded in ordinary moral discourse, thought, and practice that strongly suggest that such discourse, thought, and practice are in some sense objective. Perhaps the stiffest challenge to any version of moral irrealism is what I have called the argument from moral error, which challenges the irrealist to plausibly accommodate the presumption that genuine moral error in thought and discourse is possible. This chapter has largely been an attempt to state this argument in its strongest form, in order to make clear to ourselves its force and how (if at all) an irrealist can reply to it. I have argued that the argument from moral error contains a lesson for the irrealist—a lesson concerning philosophical methodology. In short, the moral irrealist is best advised to abandon all philosophical attempts to reductively analyze moral sentences and the concept of truth as it applies to such sentences.

To get a somewhat clearer picture of just what following this advice might amount to, we briefly examined Putnam's antireductionist metaphilosophical views and considered how such views play themselves out in the realm of ethics. We found reason to be dissatisfied with Putnam's metaethical views, but this should not, in turn, cast doubt on the antireductionist methodology that Putnam advocates. Rather, what we need to do is to find a different way to implement the antireductionist strain in Putnam's philosophy.

My aim in the chapter to follow, then, is to develop a strain of moral irrealism and, in particular, a story about truth, as predicated of moral sentences, that in some sense captures the sort of immanence/transcendence duality characteristic of normative notions like truth.

4

Contextual Moral Semantics

In this chapter, I begin my articulation and defense of what I term 'ethical contextualism,' so called because the semantic and epistemological components that make up this view represent versions of general semantic and epistemological views that are appropriately classified as contextualist. Specifically, this chapter deals with semantic and related metaphysical issues — the backbone of my view. In the following chapter, I turn to matters of moral epistemology.

My plan for this chapter is as follows. In the first section, I continue my discussion of non-reductivism by explaining what I have in mind in calling a version of moral irrealism non-reductive. Then, in §§II and III, I introduce the reader to a general approach to semantic questions about truth called contextualist semantics, which I then apply to moral discourse in the subsequent two sections. In §IV I set the stage for my own version of contextual moral semantics by considering some familiar metaethical options officially open to the contextualist (since contextual semantics applied to moral discourse does not itself force one into any particular metaethical option). Then in §V, I go on to develop a version of contextual moral semantics that involves, at its core, these ideas: (1) Moral statements, in their primary role, are genuine assertions, but not assertions of a descriptive kind. Rather, they are *evaluative assertions*, but genuine assertions nonetheless. (2) Such statements, by virtue of being genuine assertions with genuine (non-descriptive) content, are also truth-apt; truth ascriptions can be properly made of them, and to some extent they exhibit the semantic features of the statements themselves. (3) However, there are no moral 'truth-makers.' Rather, truth ascriptions in moral discourse are simply governed by the famous Tarski equivalence schema, and so truth talk here operates *minimalistically*. Because the view attempts to show how a non-descriptivist can allow that moral sentences are used to make genuine assertions, I will call the view *assertoric non-descriptivism*.

In addition to these claims about the semantics of moral statements, my brand of contextual moral semantics incorporates the following methodological ideas: (4) I refuse to offer reductive translations or paraphrases of first-order moral statements (or reductive formulations of truth conditions for them) via declarative sentences or even non-declarative sentences such as imperatives. (This is my way of respecting what some have called the 'autonomy' of ethics.) (5) The way to properly understand the semantics of moral language is to focus on the point and purpose of moral language (rather than on its paraphrase or reductive truth conditions).

After presenting my view, I turn in §VI to the dual task of accommodation, and argue for the overall plausibility of my view vis-à-vis competing current metaethical views. In the end, I will not have developed my positive story in full detail and I will not have dealt with all objections (though I tackle what seem to me to be the most serious of them). But I hope I will have made a plausible enough case for my brand of contextual moral semantics to make it a serious contender among leading metaethical theories.

Before going on, however, it might help the reader's philosophical digestive system if I mention that there is some setting up to do in preparation for laying out my story about moral discourse. The stage setting comes in waves. First, because I do not assume that all, or even most, readers are familiar with contextualism in semantics, in §II, I introduce and illustrate what I call the thesis of semantic contextualism. Second, there is the general semantic view itself that I simply call 'contextual semantics,' which follows my discussion of contextualism in semantics. Third, once contextual semantics is out in the open I set up the story about moral discourse by doing two things: (1) making clear how the view I propose to defend involves rejection of a semantic assumption that has gone largely unquestioned in metaethical thinking (viz., the assumption that all genuinely assertive discourse is descriptive discourse) and (2) introducing so-called minimalist themes in recent work in the philosophy of language.

I. Prospects for Non-Reductive Irrealism

Let us recall how the reductive/non-reductive distinction was handled in previous chapters. Cell 1A from the chart of metaethical options that appears in chapter 1 (fig. 1–1) — the cell that represents the intersection of semantic reductionism and realism — was subsequently subdivided in chapter 2 (fig. 2–1) for purposes of making clear some of the interesting metaethical options open to the naturalistic moral realist. We distinguished between narrow and broad reductive semantic views, according to what sort of naturalistic definition was being proposed for moral terms and expressions: narrow reductivist views offering analytic reductive definitions and more broadly reductionist views offering synthetic reductive definitions. We drew a corresponding distinction between narrow and broad reductive ontological views, depending on whether the sorts of natural properties, relations, or facts with which moral ones were being identified were either narrowly natural or broadly natural. A reductionist version of (naturalistic) realism in ethics, then, was explained as any view that takes moral properties, relations, and facts to be identical with natural properties, relations, and facts, and offers a corresponding definition of moral terms and expressions in naturalistic vocabulary — vocabulary that characterizes the natural properties and so on that the moral properties are identified with. A non-reductive version of moral realism, then, is one that does not attempt these ontological and semantic feats.

When we come to moral irrealism, however, there are various complications that block the attempt to simply map the various divisions we have drawn in connection with moral realism into the realm of moral irrealism. Some of the complications arise from the fact that the irrealist asserts a negative ontological claim, namely, that there are no properties, relations, or facts (at least having the sort of strongly objective status the realist supposes), while other complications arise from the fact that within the irrealist's camp there are both descriptivist and non-descriptivist semantic views. Let us consider these matters more closely.

Since the moral irrealist denies that there are any objective moral properties, relations, or facts, the ontological distinction between narrow and broad natural properties to which moral properties are allegedly identical does not figure in sorting types of irrealist views. Granted, some versions of irrealism — for example, constructivist versions — accept the claim (M1, from ch. 2, §I) that there are moral facts and then go on to deny that they have the sort of 'strongly objective' status claimed on their behalf by the realist: such facts are supposed to somehow result from human attitudes and conventions. But 'fact' talk slides easily between semantic talk about the truth or correctness of some realm of discourse, and ontological talk about the items that such discourse is supposed to concern. And when it comes to versions of moral irrealism, talk of moral facts is probably best understood as talk of moral truths, that is, true (or correct) moral statements. So, I suggest that for purposes of distinguishing reductive from non-reductive versions of moral irrealism, we focus on the semantic dimension of this metaethical view. As we shall see later in this chapter, the sort of view I defend allows for talk of moral properties and facts, though such talk is, in a sense, derivative from talk about moral statements being true or correct.

So let me simply provide a working characterization of the reductive/non-reductive distinction as it applies to versions of moral irrealism:

> A (naturalistically) reductive version of moral irrealism is one that attempts to naturalistically define (by specifying a list of necessary and sufficient conditions) the notion of truth or correctness as predicated of moral statements.

A non-reductive version rejects any definition of this sort. In order to get a clearer sense of this division, let us consider some standard versions of moral irrealism (including some addressed in the previous chapter) that fall into the reductivist camp.

Consider, first, descriptivist versions of moral irrealism that construe moral statements as fact-stating. Here, we can distinguish, as we did in connection with the semantic dimension of moral realism, between narrowly reductive semantic treatments of moral terms and more broadly reductive treatments. For example, what is called semantic subjective naturalism — the view that moral sentences of the form 'X is wrong' (when uttered by me) are analytically definable as 'I disapprove of X' — are narrowly reductive. R. Firth's 1952 version of the *ideal observer theory* of ethics is likewise a version of narrow semantic reductionism. Firth analyzed the meanings of moral sentences in terms of what an ideal observer (naturalistically characterized) would approve or disapprove. Although these narrowly reductive semantic views are offered as analyses of the meanings of moral terms and expressions, they in effect define the truth or correctness of moral statements in naturalistic terms and hence count as reductive.

By contrast, broadly reductive versions of descriptivist irrealism would hold that, although moral sentences are not analytically equivalent in meaning to sentences expressed in naturalistic vocabulary, nevertheless, the truth or correctness conditions of such sentences are to be understood in purely naturalistic terms. So, for example, an ideal observer theorist might claim that, although not equivalent in meaning and hence not analytically definable in terms of the reactions of an ideal observer, nevertheless, a moral sentence is true or correct if, and only if, the object of evaluation mentioned in the sentence is an object of an appropriate attitude of an ideal observer.[1] And, of course, the specification of what counts as an ideal observer is defined in naturalistic vocabulary.

Standard versions of non-descriptivist irrealism are also reductive in my sense. Regardless of how moral sentences are analyzed—whether as simple commands, universal prescriptions, or expressions of emotion—so long as some distinction between true or correct, and false or incorrect, moral judgment is preserved, what we typically find is something along the lines suggested by Stevenson: a correct moral judgment is one that would be made by someone who is suitably well situated for making moral judgments wherein, of course, the notion of being well situated is defined naturalistically. (Stevenson's view, and related views, were discussed in the last chapter.)

So, both descriptivist and non-descriptivist versions of moral irrealism—at least those we typically find defended in the literature—are reductive in my sense: they have the effect (whether as a result of analyzing the meanings of moral terms and expressions, or by defining the notions of truth or correctness as they apply to moral sentences) of defining, in naturalistic terms, the truth or correctness conditions of moral sentences. A non-reductive version of moral irrealism, then, attempts no such thing. But one wonders just what sorts of options are open to the so-called non-reductive irrealist in ethics, especially if one takes up the project of naturalistic accommodation.

Referring again to the chart from chapter 1 (fig. 1-1), cell 2B represents the intersection of irrealism and non-reductive moral semantics. Mackie's error theory was mentioned as falling within this cell.[2] But there is room within the general area represented by 2B for developing other, non-reductive irrealist views, ones that avoid error stories. It is one of the main themes of this book that this relatively

---

1. See, for example, the version of the ideal observer view defended by Carson, 1984.
2. Of course, there are apparently two sides to Mackie's metaethical view: first, his analysis of moral statements as ordinarily used (commonsense semantics and metaphysics) and his denial that any affirmative moral statements are true (philosophical metaphysics), but second, there is whatever replacement view about the conditions of correctness and error Mackie would accept (i.e., revisionary semantics). It is the first side of Mackie's view—his error theory—that belongs in cell 2B.

unexplored territory in metaethics is worthy of cultivation. But before exploring this fertile real estate, I want to introduce an approach to semantic questions that my colleague, Terry Horgan, and I call 'contextualist semantics'[3] — a view that represents a particular philosophical orientation toward language/world relations that I intend to press into service in telling a story about the semantics of moral discourse. My immediate plan is to introduce contextual semantics in two stages. In the next section, I introduce, in a rudimentary way, the idea of contextual analysis in semantics, and then in the following section, I sketch the approach to matters semantic that I simply call contextual semantics.

II. Contextual Themes in Recent Semantics

I am going to call any semantic view about an area of discourse that incorporates the idea that the proper workings of the key terms in that discourse operate according to contextually variable parameters a contextual semantic story about that area. In the next section, I will sketch a general approach to language/world relations that features this general contextualist idea applied to matters of truth and falsity. As a prelude to that story, let me introduce you to (or remind you of, as the case may be) contextual themes in recent semantics that one increasingly encounters in the literature. Here is a formulation (at least in rough and ready form) of what I will call the thesis of contextualism about truth (or semantic contextualism) pertaining to sentences that make up some area of discourse:

> CT   The truth value of (some, most, all) sentences that constitute some discourse D can vary from one context to another, owing to the semantic norms governing those sentences. The idea is that, owing to the semantic working of the terms (and the concepts they express) that figure in the sentences of some discourse D, the truth values of those sentences are sensitive to what are appropriately called contextually variable parameters.

This is desperately vague, and instead of trying my hand at precification, it will prove more illuminating to illustrate the thesis. And here there is no better place to find examples than in David Lewis's influential article "Scorekeeping in a Language Game," in which he makes some observations about the phenomenon of the context sensitivity of the truth of certain claims made in the course of ordinary conversation.

Lewis's own characterization of some of the context-sensitive parameters governing ordinary conversation involves the following three themes: (1) It is useful to think of the various linguistic 'moves' that are permissible in a conversation as dependent on what Lewis calls the *conversational score*. Which sentences are literally true (or otherwise acceptable) depends (at least partly) on such factors as any presuppositions being made (what is being taken for granted by the parties), the denotations of any definite descriptions and demonstratives, the point of ref-

---

3. See Horgan and Timmons, 1993. In previous publications, Horgan called this view 'psychologistic semantics.' See Horgan, 1986a, 1986b, 1987, 1990, 1991.

erence that determines such things as what counts as going and coming, and so forth. Such factors determine the score at any particular time in a conversation. (2) Changes in the score of a conversation are, by and large, rule governed. (3) The conversational score tends to evolve in such a way as to make moves in the conversation correct ones. This tendency is represented by what Lewis calls *rules of accommodation*. A few of Lewis's case studies should make these points clear.

Lewis considers the context sensitivity of standards of precision that are operative in conversations in which the truth values of sentences depend on where one draws the line with regard to vague terms and expressions. So, for example, the term 'bald' admits of various precifications, and whether a sentence like 'Fred is bald' is true will depend on where one has drawn the line for what counts as being bald. Lewis notes that we treat a sentence as *true enough* if it is true over enough delineations of some vague term like 'bald.' But when is a sentence true enough?

> This is itself a vague matter. More important for our present purposes, it is something that depends on context. What is true enough on one occasion is not true enough on another. The standards of precision in force are different from one conversation to another, and may change in the course of a single conversation. Austin's "France is hexagonal" is a good example of a sentence that is true enough for many contexts, but not true enough for many others. Under low standards of precision it is acceptable. Raise the standards and it loses its acceptability.
>
> Taking standards of precision as a component of conversational score, we once more find a rule of accommodation at work. One way to change the standards is to say something that would be unacceptable if the standards remained unchanged. If you say "Italy is boot-shaped" and get away with it, low standards are required and the standards fall if need be; thereafter "France is hexagonal" is true enough. But if you deny that Italy is boot-shaped, pointing out the differences, what you have said requires high standards under which "France is hexagonal" is far from true enough. (Lewis, 1985: 244–45)

Other examples of Lewis's that are particularly illuminating concern some of Peter Unger's arguments. Unger argues that very few things are really flat, since (1) 'flat,' he claims, is an absolute term (in the sense that it is inconsistent to say that something is flatter than something else that is flat) and (2) for anything you are inclined to characterize as flat, he can find something else that is flatter. Here is what Lewis says about Unger's argument:

> The right response to Unger, I suggest, is that he is changing the score on you. When he says that the desk is flatter than the pavement, what he says is acceptable only under raised standards of precision. Under the original standards the bumps on the pavement were too small to be relevant either to the question whether the pavement is flat or to the question whether the pavement is flatter than the desk. Since what he says requires raised standards, the standards accommodatingly rise. Then it is no longer true enough that the pavement is flat. That does not alter the fact that it *was* true enough *in its original context*. (Lewis, 1985: 245–46)

There is another feature of conversational score that Lewis notes and is worth adding to our other three features, namely, (4) in cases in which a component of the score involves standards that can be lowered or raised (as in the 'flat' example), accommodating upward goes more smoothly than accommodating in the direction of lowered standards. In commenting on the standards for being boot-shaped and hexagonal, Lewis remarks:

> I take it that the rule of accommodation can go both ways. But for some reason raising of standards goes more smoothly than lowering. If the standards have been high, and something is said that is true enough only under lowered standards, and nobody objects, then indeed the standards are shifted down. But what is said, although true enough under the lowered standards, may still seem imperfectly acceptable. Raising of standards, on the other hand, manages to seem commendable even when we know that it interferes with our conversational purposes. (Lewis, 1985: 245)

One philosophically interesting illustration of this upward accommodation tendency is the case of the skeptic's challenge to ordinary empirical knowledge claims. For almost any empirical claim, for example, 'I know that Sherry is standing over there,' the skeptic is going to respond by introducing knowledge-defeating possibilities that the ordinary person has not ruled out, like demon hypotheses. What is happening here, according to Lewis, is that standards specifying the boundary of possibilities relevant to one's knowledge claim are being raised, and when they are raised by the skeptic, then, at that point in the conversation, the commonsense epistemologist can no longer get away with ordinary commonsense knowledge claims:

> We get the impression that the sceptic . . . has the last word. Again this is because the rule of accommodation is not fully reversible. For some reason, I know not what, the boundary readily shifts outward if what is said requires it, but does not so readily shift inward if what is said requires that. Because of this asymmetry, we may think that what is true with respect to the outward-shifted boundary must be somehow more true than what is true with respect to the original boundary. I see no reason to respect this impression. Let us hope, by all means, that the advance toward truth is irreversible. That is no reason to think that just any change that resists reversal is an advance toward truth. (Lewis, 1985: 247)

As I mentioned, the idea, amply illustrated by Lewis's examples, that the truth of a sentence depends on various context-sensitive parameters (for many sentences involving all sorts of concepts) is an important insight that is meant to be captured by the contextualist approach to truth.

Since I continue in this chapter and the next to work with the contextualist idea beng illustrated in Lewis's work, let me just mention that other writers, including Unger (1986), DeRose (1991, 1992), S. Cohen (1986, 1987), and Foley (1993), have worked with contextual semantic themes in epistemology (see the next chapter for more on this). Unger (1995), by the way, has proposed that we understand judgments about the moral permissibility of actions as governed by contextual parameters. Put in most general terms, his idea is that the truth values of moral judgments about an action's being right or wrong often depend on the specific context in which the judgment is made. (As shall be seen, I agree with this claim.) However, the case he makes for the general claim involves rather specific assertions about the variability of the demandingness of moral standards for conduct, where in some contexts (ethically demanding ones), demands on, for example, one's behavior with regard to helping others in need, are extremely high, whereas in other contexts (ethically lenient ones), the demands regarding such behavior are pretty minimal. Thus, what would appear to be contradictory moral judgments are really not contradictory, once one recognizes the contextually operative parameters involved in making such judgments. Just as in Lewis's mundane examples involving contextual variability in degrees of precision (for being hexagonal, for being flat), Unger claims that there is a similar sort of variability, in at least some moral judgments, having to do with levels of demandingness on one's behavior.

I mention Unger's brand of contextual analysis in ethics partly to indicate to the reader that contextual themes are gaining increasing recognition these days, but also because I want to make clear at the outset that my handling of contextual themes regarding the proper semantic treatment of moral discourse differs importantly from Unger's. I am going to propose (at the metalinguistic level) that correct ascriptions of truth and falsity to moral judgments involve an implicit reference to a 'perspective,' and this idea is quite independent of Unger's specific thesis about the manner in which the demandingness of certain ethical standards varies with context. I can (and shall) remain officially neutral about Unger's specific thesis, and so doubts one may have about the way in which Unger develops contextualism in ethics does not negatively impact how I plan to proceed with this idea. I hope what I've said here is not too cryptic; things should become clearer as I proceed.

What I now want to do is to sketch a general semantic story about truth that incorporates the idea that the norms governing the truth of assertions in various areas of discourse operate according to contextually variable parameters. Then we will be ready to go on and extend the general story to the case of moral discourse.

III. A Contextual Semantics Primer

My plan in this section is to introduce the reader to contextualist semantics by first laying out some of the central tenets of this view, and then explaining, with examples, how this semantic view works. Since I think the broad orientation to semantic issues represented by contextualist semantics is quite attractive (especially compared to alternative views), I will explain why I think this view holds promise; though, of course, I cannot launch into a full-scale defense of it here.

Since contextual semantics deviates from more traditional, referential, and epistemic/pragmatic semantic views, I should say something at the outset about how I understand the relation between the broad semantic orientation that I call contextual semantics and the brand of moral irrealism I wish to defend. After all, it is risky philosophical strategy to defend some controversial philosophical view by appealing to yet some other controversial philosophical view. If I don't really need contextual semantics for purposes of articulating and defending my meta-ethical view about moral language, then why introduce it in the first place? If my metaethical view need not rest on contextual semantics, then am I not asking the reader to digest quite a lot?

My response to these queries is as follows. First, an important part of what I am trying to do here is to break some new ground in metaethics and get away (at least in some measure) from the well-worn traditional options. To accomplish this, my thought is that we should break away from certain ways of thinking about truth that seem to force certain options once one leans toward irrealism in ethics. A lot of traditional metaethical thinking (though not all) seems guided by a correspondence view of truth, which then leads either to relativism, to traditional forms of non-descriptivism that deny that moral sentences have a truth value, or to an error theory. There is reason to be dissatisfied with these options. I am not forgetting coherentist views of moral truth that are featured in versions of moral constructivism, but as I explained in connection with Putnam's metaethical views, I just don't think that such views are satisfactory. Putnam's specific version seems to lead to relativism. I want to avoid relativism but allow that moral sentences are often used to make genuine assertions and, hence, are genuinely truth-apt. One way to break new ground here is to reconsider matters concerning truth.

Second, quite apart from needing new options in metaethics, I think there are other compelling reasons (having to do with making sense of various discourses) to explore new semantic options. So, as I hope to make clear in this section, what I call contextual semantics is well motivated, independent of looking for new metaethical options.

Third, I don't need the machinery of contextual semantics to present my metaethical view about moral language. So even if one were to think that the more general semantic view were mistaken, that would not necessarily damage my metaethical view, though I would have to repackage the sort of non-descriptivist story about moral language I wish to defend. This is not to say that I could adopt any semantic view and tell the same semantic story about moral discourse that I sketch below. If one were to adopt a narrow, referentialist version of the correspondence view of truth, then I would be forced into some kind of error story about moral discourse.[4] So, in addition to being very plausible as a general semantic view, contextual semantics provides a convenient and intuitive way to articulate and defend the sort of non-descriptivist view I favor. In the end, the reader will have to decide whether the brief excursion through contextual semantics was worth it.

Contextual Semantics

Contextual semantics is intended as an alternative to other more familiar semantic stories about natural language, including, most obviously, the correspondence view

---

4. For more on the advantages of contextual semantics compared to other more standard semantic views, see Horgan and Timmons, 1993.

of truth. According to the correspondence theory, truth is a matter of a direct correspondence between language (or thought) and a mind-independent world of entities, properties, relations, or, more simply, facts (construed as constellations of the former).[5] For expository purposes, it will be convenient to adopt Putnam's method of capitalizing such words as 'world,' 'object,' 'property,' and 'fact' in order to make clear that when I am talking about the inhabitants of the mind and discourse-independent world it is part of the correspondence view. As we shall see later on, the moral irrealist can help herself to talk about moral properties, relations, and facts, but, of course, it is part of the irrealist's story that there are no moral PROPERTIES, RELATIONS, or FACTS. So, according to the correspondence view, the truth of any sentence is a matter of its corresponding to the WORLD of OBJECTS, PROPERTIES, RELATIONS, and (if one wants to speak this way) FACTS.

The leading ideas of contextualist semantics are these: (1) The truth of a sentence is a matter of its *correct assertibility*. (2) Correct assertibility, at least for ordinary descriptive sentences,[6] is normally a matter of the often complex interaction of two factors: (a) the various norms and practices that govern a certain mode of discourse and (b) the WORLD. (3) Unlike the correspondence view, a mode of discourse often employs assertibility norms that do not require, for the truth of sentences constituting that discourse, OBJECTS or PROPERTIES in the WORLD to directly answer to the sentences' singular terms, unnegated quantifier expressions, or predicates; nor need there be any 'dedicated' FACTS in the world that correspond to the sentence. (4) Furthermore, the norms and practices for correct assertibility are not monolithic within a language; rather, these norms and practices vary from context to context depending on such factors as the sort of discourse in question (scientific, aesthetic, moral, and so forth) and the specific purposes the discourse is serving at the time. (5) Although truth, in this view, is a normative notion, the view is not a form of verificationism (sometimes called, pragmatism): truth is not radically epistemic; correct assertibility is not the same as warranted assertibility (even 'ideal' warranted assertibility). Let me elaborate and illustrate these themes.

The sorts of norms involved in correct assertibility include syntactic norms — norms of a particular natural language that govern correct formation of meaningful sentences. But, more important for our purposes, norms of correct assertibility include semantic norms — norms that govern the correct usage of the terms and expressions in a natural language. The truth of a sentence, then, results from a combination of the operative assertibility norms together with (in normal cases) the WORLD, wherein, for our purposes, the WORLD is to be construed naturalistically as containing OBJECTS, PROPERTIES, and RELATIONS that can be accom-

5. The correspondence theorist need not countenance property types or relation types as part of her ontological inventory of the world, though presumably she needs some story about the semantics of terms and expressions that purport to refer to properties and relations.
6. In this section, my focus is on non-evaluative, purely descriptive sentences. The more complicated case of the correct assertibility of sentences that constitute evaluative moral discourse is taken up in the next section.

modated by the philosophical naturalist. This much, of course, the correspondence theorist could admit. However, there are two important differences between contextualist semantics and the correspondence view worth stressing here.

First, the correspondence view holds that there is some sort of objective, in-the-WORLD correspondence RELATION between bits of language (thought) and ITEMS in the WORLD. Of course, if the correspondence theorist accepts philosophical naturalism, then the idea is that there is a non-normative, natural RELATION—the correspondence RELATION that links language (thought) to the WORLD. Truth, in this view, has an essential nature locatable in the WORLD. Causal theories of direct reference are typically introduced by advocates of the correspondence view (who are also committed to philosophical naturalism) as providing a causal account of the referential apparatus of natural language and, hence, a naturalistic account of the nature of the correspondence relation.[7] By contrast, contextual semantics does not construe truth as involving an objective, in-the-WORLD RELATION for all modes of discourse; moreover, it does not construe truth as having any sort of interesting essential nature. Rather, the slogan *truth is correct assertibility* is meant to call attention to the normative and context-sensitive dimensions of the manner in which truth talk works in natural language.

A second, important difference concerns the fact that, with contextual semantics, there is a broad spectrum of ways in which a sentence's correct assertibility can depend on the WORLD. At one end of the spectrum, contextual semantics recognizes that the correct assertibility of the statements of some discourse can depend on quite direct language/WORLD relations, while on the other end of the spectrum, there may be discourses in which the semantic norms governing the correct assertibility of statements within the discourse do not require cooperation of the WORLD to yield truth—rather, the statements in question are true by virtue of the semantic norms themselves. Analytic statements (if there are any) would be of this sort, and perhaps the statements of pure mathematics would also work this way. In order to convey an idea of some of the interesting semantic territory in between the extremes, I want to focus on the general case in which the WORLD is implicated in the correct assertibility (and deniability) of statements and to consider the interesting semantic variation within this broad category of statements.

So let us begin with those discourses that involve quite direct language/WORLD relations. As already mentioned, in many, but not necessarily all discourses, according to contextual semantics, statements have correct assertibility or correct deniability status in virtue of two factors: (1) purely semantic assertibility norms, plus (2) the WORLD. Semantic norms satisfying this description will be called *tight*, since intuitively they conspire with certain features of the WORLD to yield the correct assertibility of certain statements; there is no 'semantic slack,' as it were, between the norms and the WORLD for yielding correct assertibility (truth). Discourse governed by tight semantic norms will be called *objective*, and statements that are correctly assertible under such norms will be called *objectively true*. This

---

7. For more on this, see Field, 1972.

usage reflects a fundamental idea embodied in the ordinary pretheoretic notion of objectivity: the idea, as Crispin Wright puts it, "that where we deal in a purely cognitive way with objective matters, the opinions which we form are in no sense optional or variable as a function of permissible idiosyncracy, but are *commanded* of us—that there will be a robust sense in which a particular point of view *ought* to be held" (Wright, 1992: 146).

Within the class of objective discourses, there may be interesting variation in the manner in which tight semantic norms conspire with the WORLD to yield a statement's correct assertibility. At one extreme are discourses whose statements are governed by semantic norms that are not only tight but *referentially strict*; that is, they require quite direct language/WORLD connections. Under referentially strict norms, a statement is correctly assertible only if some unique constituent of the WORLD answers to each of its singular terms and at least one such ENTITY answers to each of its unnegated existential-quantifier expressions. Prima facie, concreta-positing discourse in science, by virtue of the causal explanations it proffers, is governed by referentially strict semantic norms, and a robustly realist treatment of this discourse is called for. However, other discourses that count as objective do not involve referentially strict semantic norms, and consequently, the metaphysical commitments of such discourses are not as robust as in the case of scientific discourse.

Consider an example of Terry Horgan's that nicely highlights this sort of case. The sentence

B   Beethoven's fifth symphony has four movements

is correctly assertible, but its truth does not seem to require that there be any one THING in the WORLD that answers to 'Beethoven's fifth symphony' and to 'has four movements.' Rather, what seems plausible to say here is that there are features of the WORLD—including Beethoven's symphony-composing behavior over a period of time in virtue of which such and such composition counts as a symphony, and counts as his fifth symphony, plus conventions in music having to do with what counts as a movement, and so forth—that make the displayed sentence correctly assertible. If this is right, then it would seem that the assertibility norms governing this sentence, and symphony talk generally, allow for quite indirect language/WORLD relations in determining the truth of sentences like B. Notice that what seems to be the root idea behind the correspondence theory—that truth with regard to a wide range of sentences depends on the WORLD—is preserved, though without the sort of strict correspondence requirements that are part of the correspondence theory.

The Beethoven example helps illustrate the fourth theme characteristic of this view, namely, that the norms of correct assertibility are not monolithic, but can vary from context to context; assertibility norms can vary in what they require of the WORLD for the correct assertibility of a sentence. In an ordinary, non-philosophical context, a sentence like B is correctly assertible, as are sentences that would assert the existence of symphonies. However, in a philosophical context in which the operative assertibility norms are those appropriate for discussing matters of ontology, a sentence that would deny the existence of symphonies may be correctly assertible. In such contexts, the standards of correct assertion for existential claims may invoke direct language/WORLD connections, such that the sentence

B'   SYMPHONIES (SYMPHONY TYPES) do not exist

is correctly assertible, and in fact will be assertible for those who accept a naturalistic ontology that (1) recognizes that symphony talk cannot be reduced to talk about concrete natural ENTITIES and (2) has no place for non-natural, Platonic ENTITIES. But this sort of case lies at one end of a spectrum of ways in which a sentence's correct assertibility can depend on the WORLD. What I have been stressing is that contextualist semantics can recognize rather indirect language/WORLD connections.

We can sum up this little discussion by noting that, ordinarily, the norms operative in connection with discourse about musical works, or at least operative in connection with statements like B, are less demanding of the WORLD than are statements governed by what I call strict semantic norms. So the *sort* of discourse in question has something to do with how language/WORLD relations should be understood. But, what seems to be more fundamental in determining the demandingness of the norms of correct assertibility on a particular occasion has to do with the specific purposes of individuals on occasions of thought and discussion. Differing purposes can be understood as yielding different *perspectives*.[8] From an ordinary perspective (which is itself to be understood in terms of what we take to be the ordinary purposes for engaging in talk about the symphonies), claims like B' are correctly deniable; however, from a philosophical perspective, the operative norms are such that (at least given certain general philosophical views) B' is correctly assertible.

I have been working with the Beethoven example to give the reader a sense of the non-monolithic character of contextual semantics. Many other examples are at hand. For example, talk of institutions, games, corporations, species, and so forth, would be treated by the contextualist as involving (in ordinary contexts) the sorts of *indirect* language/WORLD relations illustrated with the Beethoven example. So, as has been shown, if this orientation toward matters semantic is right,[9] then the truth of any arbitrary sentence can vary from context to context, and will be a matter of the often complex and subtle question of the assertibility norms that are operative in some specific context.

Two questions immediately come to mind. First, although I have been talking about assertibility norms, and have indicated that they are linguistic norms governing syntax and semantics, I have not articulated any of these norms, or even indicated something of the proper form a linguistic representation of them would take. How can we express these norms? Second, although I have spoken about a

---

8. Thinking of different contexts in terms of perspectives will be useful for my purposes both here and in the next chapter, though not all switches in context (e.g., some of Lewis's examples of context sensitivity of definite descriptions) count intuitively as a switch in perspective.

9. And, of course, this will depend on whether the contextualist's claims are, themselves, correctly assertible.

sentence being correctly assertible in a context, I have said very little about the relevant notion of context and, in particular, I have said nothing about the dynamics of context switching—a common phenomenon that involves changes in the operative assertibility norms.

I don't have a full-blown theory about these matters, nor do I think (for current purposes) that I need one. I certainly do not think that one will be able to provide necessary and sufficient conditions specifying just what a context is, and so forth. Instead, for reasons explained in the last chapter (§XII), it is reasonable to expect that I convey the sense of this picture of truth by working with examples. Moreover, though I shall say something about context switching in the next chapter in connection with my epistemological contextualism, this particular issue is, no doubt, complex, and I don't plan to delve into such matters here. So, without pretending to have a fully worked-out story to tell about contextual semantics, I can go on to say a bit more about this kind of semantic orientation, which should help.

To understand contextual semantics, it is important to make clear some of the guiding ideas that motivate the view. Begin with the intuitive idea (already mentioned as behind the correspondence theory) that truth (for ordinary descriptive sentences) is somehow a matter of the WORLD 'making true' a sentence. Then, given a naturalistic WORLD-view, ask yourself just how our semantic norms must be in order for various sorts of garden-variety sentences to be true, given the context in which they are uttered or thought. We can say, rather trivially, that the semantic norms must be whatever way they need to be in order for language and the WORLD to conspire to make for truth. This is what guides the story about the Beethoven example. Of course, just how such semantic norms are to be articulated is wide open here, and one suspects that the norms governing various bits of language may be quite varied in content. No doubt some terms of English (but probably not very many) are governed by necessary and sufficient defining conditions, but in light of the empirical work by cognitive psychologists cited in the previous chapter, it is likely that a good many terms and expressions are governed by prototype norms.

Of course, apart from the question of how semantic norms might be expressed, there is the question of what distinguishes semantic norms from other norms that may be operative in a context and affect, in some sense, the assertibility of a specific sentence. In an ordinary context of conversation, it may be inappropriate to comment upon your interlocutor's irregular haircut, though, of course, it is norms of politeness that would prohibit such an action, even if the comment were true. Many other types of norms, including epistemic and moral norms, will normally be operative in almost any context. What distinguishes semantic norms from these other sorts of norms has to do with their function: semantic norms are those that bear on the literal truth of what one says.

How does this view differ from verificationist views of truth? According to the verificationist, the truth of a sentence is a matter of the sentence's being warrantedly assertible (or, ideally warrantedly assertible); truth, for the verificationist, is radically epistemic. Although what is correctly assertible may (for some discourses, in some contexts) coincide with what is ideally warrantedly assertible, and although, in general, norms for correct assertibility and norms for warranted assertibility are intertwined, semantic norms should not be confused with epistemic norms.

In principle, semantic norms governing the correct assertibility of some mode of discourse is one thing and epistemic norms governing justified or warranted assertion is another thing. Unlike some versions of verificationism, contextual semantics does not attempt to reduce truth to epistemic notions.[10] Of course, in becoming competent language users we learn norms of both sorts — norms that are no doubt intertwined in various ways. But we should not assume that semantic norms governing such discourse are just epistemic norms. At least for certain classes of statements, it is plausible to suppose that the relevant norms of correct assertibility are quite strict and require that singular terms denote PROPERTIES and that predicate expressions apply to some OBJECT in the manner featured in robustly realist versions of referential semantics. In such cases, there is a conceptual gap between correct assertibility and warrant, even ideal warrant.[11] So, at least until someone has convinced us that all norms governing the correct assertibility of statements are epistemic norms, we should resist any sort of conflation of matters semantic with matters epistemic.[12]

Although this sketch of contextual semantics is fairly rough (I haven't, for instance, described norms of correct assertibility in any sort of detail), I hope I have said enough to give the reader a feel for the view. In the next section, in which I turn to matters of moral semantics, I will be more explicit about the semantic norms governing moral discourse. Let me conclude this section with a few remarks advertising this view.

First, I have already noted (in the previous section) that the phenomenon of context variability owing to matters semantic seems to be a quite widespread phenomenon to be incorporated into a general semantic theory. The view now being sketched, of course, does this. But, second, another clear advantage of this view concerns its role in naturalistically accommodating various modes of discourse. If one adopts a naturalistic ontological perspective, and hence thinks of the WORLD as populated with natural OBJECTS and PROPERTIES, then one confronts the question of what to do with all sorts of seemingly unproblematically true sentences, whose singular terms, quantifier expressions, and predicates do not distinguish any identifiable OBJECT or PROPERTY in the WORLD. Were one to construe sentences like B in a strictly correspondence manner — whereby the expression 'Beethoven's fifth symphony' purports to denote some one OBJECT, namely, BEETHOVEN'S FIFTH SYMPHONY — the apparent ontological commitments of such sentences

---

10. Putnam's brand of verificationism (as we saw in the last chapter) repudiates any sort of reduction of truth to epistemic notions.

11. Of course, if one wants to invoke the so-called God's-eye view as an ideal epistemic vantage point, and then identify truth with this sort of epistemic perspective, there will be a convergence of semantic correct assertibility and ideal-warranted assertibility. But verificationists do not idealize in this way beyond any ideal human perspective.

12. For more on the relation between the notions of correct assertibility and epistemic notions, and, in particular, between semantic norms and epistemic norms, see Horgan, 1991.

would violate the ontological scruples of the naturalist: SYMPHONY TYPES are not included in the naturalist's ontological inventory. The naturalist who wanted to hold onto a strict correspondence view might try to paraphrase symphony discourse, and other problematic discourse, into some more austere idiom that avoids reference to any unnatural entities. Or, instead of (or perhaps in addition to) a paraphrase, the naturalist might try to affect an ontological reduction of symphony types to, for example, classes of performance instances, or whatever. But there is good reason for being very skeptical about the likely success of these (semantic and ontologically) reductive programs.[13] In light of this, the naturalist who accepts the correspondence theory of truth would seem to be forced into adopting, for the problematic mode of discourse in question, an error theory: sentences like B, which are to be interpreted as purporting to be about SYMPHONY TYPES, are simply false, since there just aren't any such things in the natural world. But error theories seem particularly desperate here.

In a contextualist story, as we have seen, symphony discourse, as well as discourse about all sorts of subject matter that does not neatly 'match' a WORLD of natural OBJECTS and PROPERTIES, turns out to be unproblematically true (at least as uttered in ordinary contexts), since what would appear to be the relevant assertibility norms governing such discourse, plus the WORLD, conspire to render some sentences of symphony discourse correctly assertible, and other sentences of this discourse correctly deniable. Thus, all sorts of seemingly unproblematic discourse can be ontologically accommodated by the philosophical naturalist.

A similar point applies concerning the epistemological accommodation of various modes of discourse. Since, for the contextualist, the truth of a sentence like B depends on various concrete, natural happenings with which we come into causal contact, there is no serious problem in understanding how we have the right sort of epistemic contact with what in the WORLD is relevant for knowing about Beethoven's fifth symphony. Contextualist semantics, then, has fairly obvious advantages over its correspondence rival when it comes to the ontological and epistemological accommodation of various modes of ordinary discourse, from the naturalistic perspective.

I think it is worth lingering a bit longer over these matters in order to make clear how the problem of accommodation typically gets generated. In a nutshell, then, it occurs as follows. We sensibly predicate truth and falsity of various modes of discourse (empirical, moral, aesthetic, legal, mathematical, etc.). If one assumes that truth in any area of discourse must work in the same manner that it does in any other area in which the truth predicate is appropriately used—that is, if one construes truth monolithically—then one ends up in the position of either having to force a single semantic story on all modes of seemingly truth-apt discourse, or else claim that those discourses that fail to fit the preferred semantic story about truth are not, despite appearances to the contrary, really truth-apt. The way in which this usually works is that a philosopher provides some story about ordinary

---

13. For reasons why, see Horgan, 1986a, 1986b.

empirical discourse about macrosized physical objects (correspondence stories are very attractive here) and then, using this particular view as a model for truth, approaches other areas of discourse, assuming that if truth is to be had in these other areas, the same sort of semantic story must hold in such areas.

A perfect example of this phenomenon is nicely described in Paul Benacerraf's 1973 "Mathematical Truth." In this paper, Benacerraf argues that the demand that we stick to what he calls a 'homogeneous' story about truth (i.e., that truth works the same way in all genuinely truth-apt discourses) is in tension with a reasonable epistemology (by which he has in mind an epistemology that makes sense of how we have access to mathematical truths in a way that comports with our naturalistic view of ourselves). He writes:

> [A]ccounts of truth that treat mathematical and nonmathematical discourse in relevantly similar ways do so at the cost of leaving it unintelligible how we can have any mathematical knowledge whatsoever; whereas those which attribute to mathematical propositions the kinds of truth conditions we can clearly know to obtain, do so at the expense of failing to connect these conditions with any analysis of the sentences which shows how the assigned conditions are conditions of their *truth*. (Benacerraf, 1973: 662)

The dilemma here stems in part from assuming that the detailed story about truth in mathematics must be essentially the same as the detailed story about truth in any other genuinely truth-apt discourse (empirical discourse being the important touchstone of truth here). Of course, theoretical simplicity has its strong attractions, but why not consider the possibility that the manner in which truth works in one area may differ (in significant details) from how it works in another? Why not suppose, for example, that for empirical discourse, truth involves rather robust language/WORLD relations, but that in other areas of inquiry, truth does not involve such relations?

One likely answer is that allowing for this possibility would result in having to countenance different *concepts* of truth, so that talk of truth in the realm of empirical discourse would involve a concept of truth that differs from the concept involved in truth talk about some non-empirical realm of discourse. And the problem with this is that we don't seem to have different concepts of truth; truth is truth, no matter what sort of sentence is true.

I agree that we shouldn't multiply concepts of truth, but the sort of semantic pluralism that contextual semantics allows does not proliferate concepts in this way. Rather, the idea is that there is a single, univocal concept of truth — truth is correct assertibility — and the story to be told about correct assertibility in one discourse may differ in important ways from the story to be told in another area of discourse. Indeed, as we have already seen in connection with ordinary descriptive modes of discourse (the Beethoven example), there can be important variations in how language interacts with the WORLD to yield determinate correct assertibility. One result of being more flexible in how we think about truth across domains is a kind of semantic pluralism about truth similar to what is advocated in Crispin Wright's work. He endorses the idea that any area of discourse that satisfies certain semantic platitudes is a truth-apt discourse, and he notes that this allows for a kind of semantic pluralism:

The proposal is simply that any predicate that exhibits certain very general features qualifies, just on that account, as a truth predicate. That is quite consistent with acknowledging that there may, perhaps *must* be more to say about the content of any predicate that does have these features. But it is also consistent with acknowledging that there is a prospect of *pluralism*—that the more that there is to say may well vary from discourse to discourse. (Wright, 1992: 37–38)

So, everything considered, although there is much more to be said about contextual semantics, I hope that I have been able to convey a clear enough sense of the view (at least with respect for how it works in the realm of descriptive discourse) and that I have been able to convey its attractiveness as a general semantic story. I turn now to moral discourse.

IV. Contextualist Moral Semantics: An Overview of Some Options

Contextual semantics, as a general approach to matters of truth and ontology, is fairly neutral about the metaphysics and semantics of moral discourse, and thus various treatments of moral discourse are compatible within the generic framework. Any semantic interpretation of moral discourse in terms of this broad semantic picture would be a version of contextualist moral semantics (CMS, for short). I want to work my way toward the sort of non-reductive metaethical view I am proposing by considering how certain standard metaethical options would be understood from the perspective of contextualist semantics. In particular, I want to focus on *objectivist* versions of CMS (including versions of moral realism), as well as *relativist* versions of CMS. The view I favor is a non-objectivist, non-relativist version of CMS.

Objectivist Versions of CMS

The basic assumption behind objectivist versions of CMS is the following:

A   Semantic norms governing moral discourse conspire with the world[14] to yield determinate correct assertibility and correct deniability status (i.e., truth or falsity) for moral statements.

This semantic construal of moral discourse assimilates it to descriptive discourse whose semantic norms are, as explained in the previous section, tight. Intuitively, then, semantic norms governing moral discourse work together with features of the world to yield determinate moral truth. As I explained in connection with such discourses governed by tight semantic norms, the sort of language/world connections may be more or less direct, and thus versions of objectivist CMS may vary

---

14. I find that the capitalization technique gets tiring after a while, so I shall not bother to capitalize 'world,' 'entity,' 'property,' and other such words when they are used to refer to denizens of the mind- and discourse-independent WORLD. Context should make clear when these terms have this sort of significance, and when it does not, I shall revert to using capitals.

in how ontologically robust they are. Some versions of CMS would hold that the semantic norms are not only tight but also referentially strict, hence requiring that there be moral property types in the world. However, and perhaps more plausibly for the metaphysical naturalist, less demanding versions of CMS would hold that although the semantic norms governing moral discourse are tight—they do not allow any semantic slack—the manner in which the world and the norms conspire to yield correct assertibility of moral statements may be much like how things work with musical discourse.[15]

Although versions of moral realism are the most obvious examples of objectivist versions of CMS, some versions of moral constructivism also deserve to be included here. You may recall that, according to the moral constructivist, there are moral facts, and a moral statement is true if, and only if, it expresses a moral fact. However, the facts in question are facts somehow rooted in the attitudes of some actual or perhaps ideal individual, or group of such individuals. Assuming that there is a single set of attitudes that, together with the semantic norms governing moral discourse, more or less fix the correct assertibility of moral statements, we have a clear sense in which certain worldly facts—namely, dispositional facts about the attitudes of certain individuals—conspire with the relevant semantic norms to yield correct assertibility and correct deniability. My discussions in chapters 2 and 3 explain why, in general, and why, within the confines of contextual semantics, I reject what I am here calling objectivist construals of moral discourse. I think that a correct semantic take on moral discourse will fall within the broad range of non-objectivist construals.

Relativist Versions of CMS

One rather obvious way to develop a non-objectivist version of CMS is to work with the idea that moral truth is relative to a moral outlook. Here I use the term 'outlook' to encompass the various sorts of things to which moral statements can be relative, under various brands of relativism. I shall be talking about semantic norms and the *person's* moral outlook, but this should be taken to mean whatever moral outlook (the outlook of the individual, or perhaps the outlook of his group, or whatever) the person's own moral discourse is supposed to be relativized to, under a given version of relativism. (I elaborate on the notion of a moral outlook in this section and in the next chapter.)

In terms of the general contextual semantics framework, relativism involves three key claims. First, the semantic norms governing moral discourse are not tight: it is not the case that these norms conspire with the world to render moral statements determinately correctly assertible or correctly deniable. But, second, the semantic norms plus the world do interact with a third factor—namely, a person's moral outlook—to render moral statements semantically appropriate to assert (or

---

15. Horgan (1987) proposed a modest version of objectivism within CMS, though he no longer thinks that view is plausible since the sorts of considerations marshaled in ch. 2 against new wave moral realism (a robustly realist view) apply mutatis mutandis to more modest versions.

to deny) *for the person*; that is, semantic norms plus the world do conspire to yield outlook-relative semantic appropriateness for moral statements.[16] So, for instance, given that a person's moral outlook includes a moral norm prohibiting all intentional killing of innocent human beings, certain specific moral judgments about cases that involve intentional killing would be semantically appropriate for the person to make. Third, truth for moral statements (i.e., correct assertibility for them) is identical to the relation of semantic appropriateness between moral statements and moral outlooks; thus, moral statements are not true or false *simpliciter*, but are only true or false relative to the speaker's moral outlook. Thus, in the example just mentioned, given the fact that some innocent person, for example, Jones, was intentionally killed, the statement 'The killing of Jones was wrong' is true for those whose moral outlook includes the moral norm (or a norm with the same implications, in this case) that proscribes intentional killing.

Although relativist CMS denies that the semantic norms governing moral discourse are tight in the sense characterized earlier, it does attribute to them a property I will call *relativized* semantic tightness: namely, the semantic norms conspire with the world to render moral statements true or false, relative to the speaker's moral outlook. And according to relativism, this relativized truth is the only kind of truth to be had in matters moral. So principle A, the core idea within objectivist versions of CMS, gets replaced in relativist versions of CMS by a similar core idea:

> A*   The semantic norms governing moral discourse conspire with the world to yield outlook-relative correct assertibility and correct deniability status (i.e., outlook-relative truth or falsity) for moral statements.

An insuperable problem for any version of relativism is that it simply does violence to a deeply embedded feature of ordinary moral discourse, namely, the fact that from within an engaged moral stance, we assert moral statements and make truth ascriptions to moral statements *categorically*. That is, in ordinary contexts of moral thought and discussion, we judge that actions, persons, institutions, and other objects of moral evaluation are either right or wrong, good or bad — period. In thinking that apartheid is morally wrong, for instance, we do not just think that this practice is wrong for anyone who happens to share our particular moral outlook (or one relevantly like ours); it is wrong (we think), full stop.

Again, if we ascend to the metalinguistic level and say that the statement 'apartheid is morally wrong' is true, we do not mean that it is true relative to some moral stance — we mean that the statement is simply true. I hope that this categorical feature of moral discourse in focus here is fairly obvious and uncontroversial; I maintain that it would be a virtue of any metaethical view to be able to accommodate this feature (as opposed to having to explain it away). However, for anyone whose relativist leanings have had a distorting effect on their grasp of

---

16. Since a person's moral outlook is part of the world, my way of expressing the relativist's view is not quite right. I would need to distinguish a narrower and broader notion of 'world' to make things precise. But I trust the reader understands what I am proposing in contrasting moral realism and moral relativism.

ordinary moral discourse, I suggest that he or she consider cases of deep moral disagreement—cases in which the parties to the disagreement do not differ over any non-moral facts that may be relevant to the issue under dispute, but are having an irreducibly moral disagreement.[17] Parties to the dispute, even if they realize the nature and depth of the disagreement, do not ordinarily think that their own view is true for them and that their opponent's view is true for their opponent. (I consider an example of this sort of disagreement later in this chapter, in §V.) Rather, in such cases of conflict, one asserts one's moral convictions over and against one's opponent and thinks that the conflicting moral views of the opposing party are just mistaken.

I take this categorical use of moral discourse (and associated truth talk) to be at least partly definitive of what it is to use moral discourse in a morally engaged manner—that is, in a manner in which one makes sincere and genuine moral claims. Relativist stories about moral truth cannot accommodate this feature and, consequently, must chalk it up to a deeply embedded error involved in moral discourse.[18] Moreover, because they can't accommodate this feature of moral discourse, relativist stories cannot satisfactorily accommodate the possibility of genuine moral disagreement. Those who know their history of twentieth-century metaethics will note that problems in accounting for the possibility of moral disagreement were stressed by Moore (1912) and other non-naturalists (particularly in connection with semantic ethical subjectivism), but they were also stressed by Stevenson, Hare, and other non-descriptivists.[19]

If we pause for a moment and reflect on the present discussion, the first thing to notice is that both objectivism and relativism embrace, in their own way, a picture of moral discourse according to which the semantic norms that govern moral terms and expressions conspire with the world to yield some form of correct assertibility and deniability of statements—either absolute correct assertibility (objectivism) or relativized correct assertibility (relativism). Within the framework of contextual semantics, it is natural to say that a statement is *descriptive* in content only if the semantic norms work in one of these ways—that is, only if the semantic norms are tight *simpliciter* or relativistically tight; for only then does the world's being a certain way make the statement true or false (albeit perhaps only relativistically true or false). Given the various distinctions I have drawn (between objectivist and non-objectivist discourses, and descriptivist and non-descriptivist discourses) I present figure 4-1 as a visual aid, summarizing the interrelations among these distinctions and the various metaethical views mentioned so far.

Although I have not completely solidified my case (since I have not considered all versions of objectivism), I do think that my critique of new wave moral realism in chapter 2 provides strong reasons for supposing that the semantic norms gov-

17. Ayer (1946: 110–12) denies that there are ever such disagreements, but his doing so seems mainly driven by his brand of metaethical emotivism.
18. See Wong, 1984, for the articulation and defense of a version of moral relativism that attempts to explain away the categorical feature of moral discourse.
19. Stevenson (1937, 1944: ch. 1, 1948), for instance, made it a constraint on any adequate analysis of moral sentences that it allow for genuine moral disagreement—including deep disagreement.

Robust Objectivism (Realism)	Modest Objectivism	Relativism	Non-Descriptivism

Objective Discourse	Non-Objective Discourse

Descriptive Discourse	Non-Descriptive Discourse

FIGURE 4–1 Interrelations among distinctions between discourses and metaethical views

erning moral discourse are not tight—at least not tight in the way demanded by moral realism. Moreover, not only are there no dedicated moral properties, relations, or facts corresponding to moral terms and statements, but even a more modest non-minimalist treatment of moral discourse (as relevantly analogous, for example, to 'Beethoven's fifth symphony has four movements') will not do, either. In the last chapter, I considered reasons that make other objectivist views, like certain brands of constructivism, implausible. And problems mentioned already in this section (in addition to those from the previous chapter) also make relativism untenable.

Given all this, I think an adequate treatment of moral discourse should recognize the following: the semantic norms governing moral discourse are not semantically tight *simpliciter*, as is required for moral objectivism; nor are they relativistically semantically tight, as is required for relativism. So I reject descriptivism in all its various forms, and thus think that the area to search for a plausible metaethical view is within the region of non-descriptivist views. However, my view does differ importantly from more traditional non-descriptivist views, in ways that I shall now proceed to explain.

V. Assertoric Non-Descriptivism: A Version of Contextual Moral Semantics

Declarative sentences are the standard linguistic vehicle for making assertions. Moral discourse typically employs the declarative form of speech, a form especially well suited to the *categorical* nature of moral talk. Furthermore, moral sentences can figure as constituents of logically complex sentences in all the standard ways: they can be negated; they can be embedded in conditionals; they can combine with verbs of propositional attitude; and so on. Taken together, these considerations provide a strong prima facie presumption in favor of the contention that declarative moral sentences are typically used to make genuine, full-fledged *assertions*. So, we want to accommodate this presumption (if we can) in our metaethical account of moral discourse.

One way of doing this is to opt for some objectivist treatment of moral discourse, but I have been urging that we should reject all forms of moral objectivism.

So the presumption about genuine moral assertion combines with the reasons for rejecting descriptivism to suggest a view about moral statements that embraces both non-descriptivism and the contention that moral discourse is fully assertoric — a view claiming that the evaluative meaning of moral sentences subserves genuine assertion, but also claiming that evaluative meaning is not a species of descriptive meaning. Such an approach to moral semantics, although it would appear to be a dramatic departure from the standard menu of semantic options in metaethics, cries out for articulation and defense. My plan is to develop just such a metaethical view, within the framework of contextual semantics.

On the view I advocate, there are two distinct kinds of assertion, neither one a species of the other: descriptive and evaluative. Evaluative assertions, including moral assertions (in their primary usage), do not describe the world or purport to describe it, but play a fundamentally different sort of role in human discourse — broadly speaking, an action-guiding role. Since moral statements make genuine assertions, they are truth-apt; that is, truth and falsity are properly predicated of them. Likewise, when one person sincerely utters a moral statement and another sincerely utters the negation of that statement, they thereby make two assertions that directly contradict one another. However, unlike discourse whose sentences are typically used for the primary purpose of representing or describing in-the-world states of affairs — and which therefore, in order to be true, makes demands of the world — moral discourse, by contrast, makes minimal demands of the world. So what I am searching for is a metaethical view about moral discourse that belongs in the non-descriptivist camp (broadly construed), but that recognizes that moral sentences are typically used to make genuine assertions and are thus truth-apt. Before laying out the view, it will be useful to do two things. First, since my view represents a metaethical option that, owing to certain deeply held assumptions, has been obscured from view, I plan to indicate exactly how my view departs from previous views. Second, since part of the story I tell about moral discourse involves so-called minimalist themes from recent philosophy of language, I want to say something about such ideas, particularly as they have been articulated and used recently by Crispin Wright. We will then be ready for the view I defend.

Rejecting an Underlying Assumption of Traditional Metaethics

Before launching into my positive story, I want to bring to the surface (i.e., 'thematize,' as my continentally trained colleagues would say) and question a certain deeply embedded assumption of traditional metaethical thinking (indeed, a deeply embedded assumption in philosophical thinking about meaning and truth generally) that, when brought into question and rejected, puts one in position to develop a version of non-descriptivism that differs significantly from more standard versions.

The assumption is simply that all sentences that have or carry genuine assertoric content (make genuine assertions) thereby have or carry robustly descriptive content: they purport to describe worldly states of affairs and so are true if, and only if, they successfully do so. Given the framework of contextual semantics, we can express the same idea by saying that the assumption amounts to claiming that all discourse with genuine assertoric content is governed by tight semantic norms (either tight *simpliciter* or relativistically tight). If one accepts this idea and then construes, as the non-descriptivists did, moral sentences as not possessing descriptive content (or at least not featuring such content as semantically primary), then one is led to deny that sentences that make up moral discourse are genuinely (or primarily) assertoric. But, then, since the grammatical surface features of moral sentences are just like the grammatical surface features of sentences that constitute ordinary empirical discourse, one is forced to make a distinction between surface features of a discourse and its presumably deeper semantic features. And this is just what traditional non-descriptivists did, and so were obliged to dismiss the grammatical and related logical features of moral discourse as misleading in regard to its true semantic workings.

Let us call the assumption we are focusing on simply the *semantical assumption*, or 'SA' for short:

SA   All genuinely assertive discourse is descriptive discourse.

To see this assumption as a deeply embedded assumption of traditional meta-ethical thinking—shared by both descriptivists and their non-descriptivist opponents—let us formulate what I will call the *thesis of semantic unity* ('SU' for short):

SU   The grammatical and logical trappings of the sentences that constitute a discourse are indicative of the real semantics of those sentences. Or, to put it differently: if one wants to distinguish between the surface features of some discourse and its 'deep' features—features that reveal its true semantic workings—then the thesis of semantic unity says that there is no difference between surface and deep features of the discourse in question.

We can represent the basic (no doubt simplified) line of thought behind the thinking of the metaethical descriptivist in the following way (letting 'D' stand for the descriptivist idea in metaethics that moral sentences, in their primary usage, have descriptive content):

1. Moral discourse manifests the sorts of grammatical and logical features that indicate that it is genuinely assertive—that its sentences have genuine assertive content.
2. SU
3. SA
Therefore,
4. D

At least the descriptivist can present this argument as a strong presumption in favor of construing moral discourse as having primarily descriptive content—an argument that, barring very compelling reasons for denying one of its claims, should carry the day.

We can represent the non-descriptivist's participation in this dialectic as follows. She has reasons for rejecting D—whatever those might be—and, so, is led to argue as follows:

1. Moral discourse manifests the sorts of grammatical and logical features that indicate that it is genuinely assertive—that its sentences have genuine assertoric content.
2. SA
3. Not D
Therefore,
4. Not SU

And so the non-descriptivist is led, by this line of reasoning, to reject the idea that moral discourse conforms to the thesis of semantic unity, and thereby must distinguish, for moral discourse, between surface features of the sentences that make up the discourse and deep features that reveal its true semantic workings. Hence, the project of the non-descriptivist is to characterize (often through reductive-meaning analyses) the deep semantic features of moral discourse.

My proposal is to reject the underlying, deeply embedded common assumption operating in the little dialectic just sketched—the basic semantic assumption that weds genuine assertoric content for sentences in a discourse to the idea that those sentences have (or have primarily) descriptive content. The line of thought I employ, then, could be expressed this way:

1. Moral discourse manifests the sorts of grammatical and logical features that indicate that is is genuinely assertive—that its sentences have genuine assertoric content.
2. Not D
3. SU
Therefore,
4. Not SA

If one accepts this line of reasoning, then one can agree with the descriptivists that the surface features of moral discourse really do indicate that the discourse is genuinely assertive (and hence can save oneself the burden shouldered by traditional non-descriptivists of having to tell a story about the genuine semantic features of the discourse that differ from the surface features) and yet not have to prove that moral discourse has descriptive content.

So I plan to make a set of proposals: (1) that we reject the fundamental semantic assumption that ties genuine assertoric content to descriptive content; (2) that we accept the thesis of semantic unity and allow that, unless there is good reason for thinking otherwise, any discourse that has the grammatical and logical trappings of genuine assertoric discourse be treated as genuinely assertoric; (3) that since moral discourse has the relevant trappings, and since it is not to be construed as descriptive discourse, we should recognize that there is a species of assertion that is not descriptive, but rather evaluative; and (4) that evaluative assertions are, in a sense, semantically sui generis; their content cannot be reduced to or decomposed into any other, more primitive kind of content.

Just how this will proceed, I will cover in a moment. But before turning to my positive story, let me make a remark or two about the proposal to reject SA.

I would like to suggest that quite apart from the line of thought represented by my third displayed argument that leads from certain assumptions (including the metaethical thesis of non-descriptivism) to the rejection of SA, one can find non-philosophically motivated reasons for being suspicious of SA. What I have in mind is simply that it seems pretty clear to commonsense thinking that there are at least two basic modes of assertion—two basic sorts of speech acts: description and evaluation. Again, operating on an intuitive, commonsense level of thought, there seems to be a difference between describing something—saying what sorts of observable properties and relations it has—and evaluating something as being good or bad, right or wrong. Granted, we have terms that are, in a sense, hybrid: they are partly descriptive and partly evaluative. I have in mind so-called thick ethical concepts like honest, courageous, and so forth. But I have been focusing on what I take to be the primary terms of moral evaluation, and when we use words like 'good,' 'bad,' 'right,' and 'wrong,' we are not, so it seems, primarily describing, but evaluating. And granted, we evaluate in light of the sorts of observable features an object of evaluation has, but the activity of evaluating differs from mere description. (For those who need to get in touch with the sort of basic difference between describing and evaluating I am calling attention to here, there is no better place to go than Hare's *The Language of Morals*, part 2.)

In addition to the two different sorts of speech acts, there is the fact that we typically express moral evaluations by uttering sentences that have, or at least seem to have, genuine assertoric content. So why not suppose, on the front end, that typical moral sentences, and the statements we make by their use, have a kind of assertoric content, namely, *evaluative assertoric content*? I do not see a reason against it, though admittedly there is philosophical work to be done in telling a convincing story about evaluative assertions. These reflections alone are not enough to overturn a deeply embedded assumption like SA, but they are a start. Moreover, I think one can find in recent work in the philosophy of language more philosophically motivated reasons for rejecting SA. Here, my plea to the reader is simply not to dismiss the suggestion out of hand.

Operating within the Spirit of Minimalism

My own positive story about moral discourse is, as I have said, semantically minimalist, and as one more bit of preliminary business, I should explain what I have in mind in calling my view minimalist. Any minimalist view about discourse holds that the sentences that constitute the relevant area of discourse have (in their primary usage) genuine assertoric content (they are used to make genuine assertions) and, consequently (given the analytic connection between assertion and truth), are genuinely truth-apt. So minimalism is not equivalent to semantic eliminativism. There are really two distinct ideas that come together in the semantic view about moral discourse that I defend that make the term 'minimalism' an appropriate label for the view.

First, moral discourse is non-descriptive discourse and, in contrast to descriptive discourse, it makes minimal demands of the world in its proper semantic operation. That is, moral terms like 'good,' 'right,' and 'ought,' do not purport to pick out or denote (either directly or indirectly) some in-the-world (i.e., WORLD) properties or relations. They simply do not have that kind of linguistic function, and so we can say of sentences containing these terms (in their primary usage) that they involve a kind of assertion that makes minimal demands of the world. Correlatively, although moral sentences (in their primary usage) are genuinely truth-apt, proper ascriptions of the truth predicate to moral sentences do not require that there be in-the-world moral facts to which true moral sentences correspond. Again, moral sentences involve a kind of truth ascription that makes minimal demands of the world. Hence, viewing moral discourse from the sort of irrealist semantic-metaphysical perspective being defended in this book, calling the semantic story minimalist is appropriate.

The second idea involved in my brand of minimalism concerns the sorts of answers that are appropriate in response to certain sorts of questions about the content and truth of moral discourse. I have in mind philosophical questions about the content and truth of sentences wherein the expectation is that any adequate response will provide a certain sort of semantic illumination. For instance, questions of the form 'What is the content (or meaning) of p?' (where p is some sentence of the discourse) are typically posed with the expectation that, in response, one will provide an illuminating analysis of p, perhaps by giving a synonymous sentence (or set of sentences) in which the terms for philosophically troubling concepts that appear in the analysandum sentence are replaced in the analysans sentences by other, less troublesome terms. But given my overall metaethical view, one is not going to be able to provide any such analysis, and so the appropriate response to questions of the form 'What is the content of p?' is simply the minimalist response: p.

The reasons for the appropriateness of this response are, I hope, fairly obvious. First, if the expectation behind the question is that one needs to provide some illuminating analysis in descriptive terms, then clearly this is one demand that the non-descriptivist repudiates. Second, if the expectation is that, as a non-descriptivist, one at least needs to analyze moral sentences as equivalent (or roughly equivalent) in content to some other kind of non-descriptivist sentences, then, again, one ought to repudiate the (essentially reductive) demand. Given, then, the sort of philosophical expectations that questions about content normally carry, and given the general antireductivist line being pursued here,[20] the appropriate response to the sorts of questions I have in mind is the minimalist response.

The same goes for typical questions about truth of moral sentences. In response to such questions (which usually are asked with the expectation that one

---

20. The view is intended to be a version of *strong* antireductivism, in the sense explained in ch. 3, §XII.

needs to provide some interesting account of truth in the relevant domain), the proper response is simply to invoke Tarski's T schema: 'p' is true if and only if p.

In giving these sorts of minimalist responses to certain sorts of questions about the content and truth of moral discourse, it does not mean that there is nothing one can do to illuminate the semantic workings of moral discourse. Quite to the contrary, there is a lot one can do, and, indeed, being the sort of minimalist about moral discourse that I am here advocating means that one has some work to do, since the standard ways of telling a semantic story about this sort of discourse are closed off. As will be shown in the next section, such illumination comes from examination of the point and purpose of the discourse. Here we should note that the sort of minimalism that I propose for moral discourse is friendly toward certain projects in the philosophy of language, in allowing that there is semantic illumination to be had for various types of non-descriptive discourses if one knows where to look. Unfriendly minimalism (sometimes called 'quietism'), by contrast, is an extreme view that would dismiss such philosophical projects altogether. My brand of minimalism is friendly.

So my proposal for non-descriptive discourses (that display the right sorts of grammatical and logical features as does moral discourse) is that they are best construed minimalistically. If we put this idea together with my rejection of meta-ethical descriptivism and consequent denial that typical moral sentences have descriptive content, then we are pushing toward the joint recognition that moral discourse has some sort of non-descriptive assertoric content and, by implication, that what I have called the semantic assumption (SA) that ties genuine assertion to description is to be rejected. But now one might want to question my proposal with regard to moral discourse, specifically, my proposal to (1) treat moral discourse as having genuine assertoric content (and all that goes with genuine assertion) and (2) then turn around and treat the discourse minimalistically. After all, I first deny that moral discourse has descriptive content; then I insist that it has genuine assertoric content anyway; but then when one might expect me to provide an interesting story about the sort of non-descriptive assertoric content enjoyed by moral statements, I go minimalist and turn my back on any such project. Is this just a cheat?

No, it is not, and I hope by the end of the chapter I can convince the reader that the general semantic view I have to offer about moral discourse is entirely reasonable, if not entirely correct. In the meantime, let me stall the worry I have just raised by making a few brief remarks about minimalism.

First, if I am right in positing that moral discourse is not descriptive discourse, then it is not surprising that it would demand a semantic treatment that differs in some ways from a proper semantic treatment of descriptive discourse. Second, since it is descriptive discourse that seems to lend itself to certain kinds of interesting and illuminating analyses, and since moral discourse is not descriptive, it perhaps should come as no surprise that such discourse is not susceptible to such analyses. Third, in treating moral discourse minimalistically, one repudiates any need to provide illuminating analyses of the contents of moral sentences or to provide some deep account of the truth predicate as it applies to such sentences, but (to repeat) this does not mean that there is nothing of interest to say about the workings of these sentences. Quite a bit of illumination is provided by inquiring into the typical point and purpose of the discourse—an inquiry into the sorts of speech acts we perform with this type of discourse. And it will be part of my overall story to say something about point and purpose. Fourth, and finally, minimalist semantic stories have gained in respectability quite recently, particularly in light of the work by Paul Horwich (1990) and Crispin Wright (1992). Some of Wright's views are worth mentioning here since they tie in nicely with some of the ideas I plan to present later.

In *Truth and Objectivity*, Wright defends the idea that a necessary and sufficient condition for a predicate defined over a discourse to count as a truth predicate for that discourse is simply that the predicate satisfy a handful of a priori platitudes that express conceptual connections between such notions as assertion, truth, negation, and the like. The platitudes include: *to assert is to present as true; any truth-apt content has a significant negation that is likewise truth-apt*; and *to be true is to correspond to the facts*. Here I want to call attention to three ideas from Wright's work on minimalism.

1. One immediate implication of this sort of minimalism,[21] according to Wright, is that there is no further metaphysical question concerning whether a truth predicate that satisfies the relevant set of platitudes really captures the concept of truth. And so, in response to a plea that in addition to the platitudes there must be something more to say that would identify truth, Wright responds:

> This line of objection betrays an important misunderstanding. It presupposes that minimalism is offering an *account* of the meaning of "true," in the traditional sense in which giving an account of the meaning of a word involves provision of an illuminating *analysis* of the concept it expresses—an account, in this case, of what truth most fundamentally consists in. Traditional—"correspondence" and "coherence"—theories did hope for such an account. But minimalism has no such ambition. (Wright, 1992: 37)

So on Wright's view, truth is not, as he puts it, "intrinsically a heavyweight metaphysical notion" (1992: 72), and thus a discourse may be genuinely truth-apt without any commitment to realism about that discourse.

2. Furthermore, according to Wright, understanding a truth predicate in the way he proposes is not inconsistent with *pluralism*—the idea that what more there may be to say about the truth predicate (in addition to its satisfaction of the relevant set of platitudes) may vary from discourse to discourse. Some discourses may demand a robustly realist treatment, though others may not. (You may recall the brief discussion of this theme at the end of §II earlier.)

3. Another interesting feature of Wright's view is that there is no significant appearance/reality distinction to be drawn with regard to the semantic workings of a discourse. The idea is that if a mode of discourse displays all of the grammatical and logical trappings of genuine assertoric discourse, then it *is* genuinely assertoric.

---

21. A terminological point: Wright's use of 'minimalism' is not quite the same as my use of the term, though the differences between us will not matter here. See Wright, 1992: 24–29, 33–61.

This means that someone who accepts minimalism will not see the point in the projects of traditional metaethical non-descriptivists. So whereas traditional non-descriptivists hold that although the surface grammar of a mode of discourse may display all of the trappings of genuine assertoric discourse, it yet may still fail to be genuinely assertoric, a minimalist will reject this possibility. As Wright puts it, for the minimalist, there is no "well-conceived deeper notion of assertoric content" (1992: 36) other than what goes along with the capacity of the sentences of the discourse to be featured in embedded contexts, to be capable of negation, and so forth—features with which genuine assertoric discourse is associated.

These three ideas from Wright about assertion and truth are ones I embrace. The contextualist semantic picture that I have proposed as a general framework for thinking about truth does not take the truth predicate (correct assertibility) to be an intrinsically heavyweight notion, and the openness to pluralism is part of the general contextualist picture. So there is dialectical space for developing semantic stories about some area of discourse that construes them as operating quite minimalistically. Moreover, as I have been stressing, the view I want to propose parts company with traditional metaethical non-descriptivists in refusing to draw a philosophically significant distinction between the mere surface features of the sentences of a discourse and their deeper, semantically revealing features. In line with Wright's brand of minimalism, I propose to accept the thesis of semantic unity and to take the surface features of moral discourse as indicating what they seem to indicate, namely, genuine assertoric content.

I hope these brief remarks about minimalism are enough to get started. Let us now proceed to the positive story about moral discourse.

Assertoric Non-Descriptivism: A Sketch

As I have mentioned, on the view I advocate, there are evaluative assertions, which are not a species of descriptive assertion. They do not purport to describe a world of facts (in the way in which typical descriptive statements do); rather, their primary role is choice and action guidance. Since moral sentences are used to make genuine assertions, they are truth-apt. I am calling the view *assertoric non-descriptivism*, which contrasts with more traditional versions of non-descriptivism that tended to deny that moral sentences (as typically used) have genuine assertive content. Let me begin, then, by simply laying out some of the main ideas that constitute the view and then proceed to elaborate them.

There are two sides to the view. First, there is the negative claim:

1. The semantic norms governing moral discourse do not, together with in-the world facts, yield objective correct assertibility (or correct deniability) for moral statements. Nor do these semantic norms conspire with the facts to yield *relativized* correct assertibility (or correct deniability) for moral statements. That is, the semantic norms governing moral discourse are not, in the sense explained above, semantically tight; nor are they relativistically tight. Thus, I am neither an objectivist nor a relativist.

The other side of the view — the preservative side — involves these claims:

2. Moral statements make genuine assertions. These are *evaluative* assertions, which are not a species of descriptive assertion.

3. Truth ascriptions to first-order moral statements are a legitimate aspect of moral discourse. Thus, I reject any version of *eliminativism* about moral truth talk in favor of a version of *preservativism* about such talk.

4. The positive story to be told about moral discourse is two-pronged: (a) In order to get a handle on the workings of moral discourse, we need to focus on the point and purpose of the discourse (as well as the point and purpose of the typical psychological states that moral assertions reflect). (b) When it comes to certain questions about moral assertion and moral truth, I repudiate certain reductive demands that would require that we 'analyze' moral concepts and the sentences that contain them, or that we give some substantive 'account' of moral truth. Rather, given that moral discourse is not fundamentally descriptive but evaluative, the appropriate responses to such questions are minimalistic. So, for example, what one should say about truth ascriptions in moral discourse is simply that they are governed by the Tarski equivalence schema: '*p*' *is true if and only if p*.

I proceed now to elaborate these core tenets.

The first thesis claims that the semantic norms governing moral discourse do not, together with facts in the world, yield correct assertibility for moral statements. Or, to put it in the terms introduced in connection with contextual semantics: semantic norms governing moral discourse are not tight — they are not tight *simpliciter*, as the realist would have it, nor are they relativistically tight, as the relativist would have it. I have already argued for this thesis, but a quick review may be useful.

The key idea behind talk of semantic norms being in some sense tight, you may recall, is the idea of the discourse being fundamentally descriptive. (The distinction here between tight and non-tight semantic norms is the basis, within CMS, for distinguishing descriptive from non-descriptive discourse.) Moral discourse, I am claiming, is not fundamentally descriptive, and so this assertion raises the question of just how we are to understand the semantic workings of non-descriptive discourse. Traditional non-descriptivists in ethics were inclined to engage in the project of paraphrase: those more reductively inclined attempted to paraphrase moral sentences into sentences that were overtly non-assertoric (e.g., exclamations, commands).[22] As I have been explaining, a key semantic assumption

22. Hare is an interesting exception, since he repudiates semantic reductionism in ethics and seeks to shed light on the semantics of moral discourse by drawing analogies between the workings of moral language and the workings of overtly non-assertoric discourse. For instance, in the last chapter of *The Language of Morals*, Hare writes: "[I am not] committing the sin of 'reductionism' which, because of its excessive prevalence, has become a fashionable target for philosophical heresy-hunters. I am not, that is to say, trying to analyse one kind of language in terms of another" (1952: 180). Taken in this non-reductive spirit, there is quite a lot of similarity between key aspects of his early view and the view I want to defend.

at work in traditional metaethical thinking is that all genuinely assertoric discourse is descriptive discourse. If we question this assumption, conceptual space is opened up for combining the claim that moral discourse is genuinely assertive discourse with the claim that it is fundamentally non-descriptive. Rather than being in the business of purporting to describe in-the-world properties and facts, moral discourse is fundamentally in the business of evaluation. Hence, we should characterize typical moral sentences as being used to express evaluative assertions, and this is the second thesis on my list. So let me proceed to elaborate this claim.

My basic semantic hypothesis for understanding the workings of moral discourse is this: (1) Moral sentences (in their primary usage) are used to make evaluations—they have evaluative content. (2) Moreover, they are used to make genuine assertions and, so, have genuine assertoric content: they are used to make evaluative assertions. (3) This sort of content is not a species of descriptive content (nor is descriptive content a species of evaluative content). (4) But since moral assertions do have genuine assertoric content, we should recognize the fact that moral assertions are of a primitive, sui generis kind.[23]

So to understand moral language, we need to zero in on the phenomenon of evaluation, specifically moral evaluation. Evaluation has as its typical point and purpose both personal choice and guidance vis-à-vis the behavior others. It is also *reasoned* choice and guidance. Thus, one wants a story about the phenomenon of evaluation both in terms of the sorts of mental states characteristic of moral evaluation and also in terms of the typical linguistic manifestations of these states. The two stories (psychological and linguistic) should fit together in a way that would shed some light on the proper semantic workings of moral language. Let us begin with the psychological side of things and then move to matters linguistic.

Moral Judgment

A fully developed moral psychology is not something I can deliver here. Rather, what I shall do is focus on moral judgment—a psychological state that consists in taking a moral stance about some issue. Here it will be useful to do two things: first, say something about the general psychological background, as it were, in light of which one comes to take a moral stance on some issue and, second, say what I can about the psychological state of moral stance taking, that is, moral judgment, in terms of the kind of prototypical causal role it plays in a normal person's cognitive economy.

But first, a note on terminology. I plan to use 'judgment' here to refer to a contentful psychological state whose linguistic expression is typically a declarative

---

23. I believe the main lesson to be learned from the traditional metaethical non-naturalists is that although moral discourse has genuine assertoric content, it cannot be reduced to some other type of discourse. But I want to take things further: not only can moral discourse not be reduced to or analyzed in terms of discourse about the natural world or even supernatural world, it cannot be understood as a species of descriptive discourse, either. From my perspective, then, the non-naturalists were in the grip of the idea that all genuine assertion is descriptive assertion; hence their countenancing of non-natural truth makers.

sentence. So I am interested primarily in the product sense of the term and not the process sense.[24] I might have simply spoken in terms of belief states and their contents, but because of the unwanted philosophical baggage that belief talk carries with it, namely, that beliefs are representational in nature (not that I think that this feature really is built into the generic conception of belief), I shall, for the time being, avoid such talk and stick with talk of judgment. I will comment on talk of moral belief later.

In the interesting cases in which one takes a moral stance, and hence forms a moral judgment on the basis of her or his own moral thinking (or at least as a result of employing one's own moral sensibility), one does so by bringing to bear one's overall *moral outlook* on the case at hand. Typically, one's moral outlook is a complex matter that includes: (1) having a developed sensitivity to various features of one's environment that, according to the outlook in question, are morally relevant features and, so, the basis of moral evaluation; (2) having various emotional responses in connection with objects of evaluation, for example, experiencing feelings of guilt and resentment toward certain of one's own actions and the actions of others; (3) being acquainted with certain exemplars, that is, paradigmatic cases of moral and immoral actions, persons, institutions, and so forth; (4) having learned various moral generalizations that encapsulate the most morally relevant features to which one has a developed sensitivity; and (5) having learned basic patterns of moral reasoning, for instance, golden rule/reversibility reasoning, as well as learning to reason from moral generalizations to particular cases.[25]

Coming to take a moral stance, that is, coming to form a moral judgment, then, is a matter of thinking about (or at least reacting to) some moral issue in a morally engaged way (employing one's moral outlook) and 'coming down' on the issue at hand. There are four basic characteristics typical of moral judgment that, if not collectively sufficient to distinguish moral from other kinds of judgment, at least come close to staking out this kind of judgment.

First, moral judgments (like all judgments) are contentful psychological states whose content can be expressed by the use of 'that' clauses. One judges, for example, *that* abortion is not always wrong, or *that* actions motivated by benevolence are morally good, and so on. Moral judgments have what I will call *cognitive content*.

Second, these sorts of stance-taking psychological states are not representational — moral judgments are not aimed at representing or describing a world of facts. Their content is not representational but evaluative — aimed at choice and guidance of action. Moral judgments are, in other words, essentially tied to motivation.[26] A moral judgment, then, is the type of psychological state whose role

---

24. In ch. 5 I discuss a notion of judgment, which I call the 'virtue' sense of the term, that is associated with the process of judging.

25. I do not mean to suggest that these are the only forms of moral reasoning that are acquired in typical moral learning.

26. Of course, from the fact that some judgment is not representational, it does not follow that some judgment is evaluative — nor does it follow from the fact that it is evaluative that it is motivational. I

in the overall cognitive economy of a person can be elucidated in terms of certain action-oriented psychological generalizations. Specifically, a moral judgment typically has certain (defeasible) causal tendencies, including, especially, certain first-person choice-guiding tendencies and tendencies toward the actions (or possible actions) of others. Its typically having these tendencies is part of the very concept of moral judgment, as I suggest, but here it is crucial to understand what this claim does not force me to accept.

The idea that moral judgment is essentially action-guiding is an old one that usually gets articulated as some version or other of what is called 'ethical internalism.' In perhaps its most common form, ethical internalism is the thesis that sincere moral judgment entails that the one making the judgment is appropriately motivated. The idea is that there is a conceptual connection between the notion of moral judgment and the notion of being motivated: motivation 'is internal to' moral judgment. Internalism, in its various guises, is often criticized as tying motivation too tightly to moral judgment and thus being implausible. Evidence of this is the so-called amoralist objection, according to which (1) the amoralist—that is, someone who, either chronically or on occasion, sincerely judges that such and such act would be wrong (or right), but is not at all motivated to avoid (or to do) the act in question—is at least a conceptual possibility, but (2) this conceptual possibility is ruled out by ethical internalism, and so (3) internalism overdraws the connection between moral judgment and motivation. Critics who raise this objection[27] then go on to conclude that ethical externalism (the denial of internalism) must be right.

It seems to me that there is something about the spirit of ethical internalism that is correct, but I do find the amoralist objection pretty persuasive. The way to be an internalist yet avoid this objection is not to overdraw the connection between moral judgment and motivation—to make the connection looser by insisting that although moral judgments are themselves motivational, they are *softly motivational*. Let me explain.

Speaking most generically, internalism is the idea that there is a conceptual connection of some sort between sincere moral judgment and motivation. This generic internalist thesis allows some room for interesting variation regarding both the strength of the conceptual connection and how one understands associated folk psychological notions. Consider, first, strength. Traditional ethical internalists typically accept what I will call 'hard internalism'—the claim that there is a conceptual connection between moral judgment and motivation that is exceptionless.[28] On this view, lack of appropriate motivation on some particular occasion

---

hope I will not be accused of arguing in these ways. Rather, as I hope to explain presently, it is plausible to understand moral judgments as typically functioning in an evaluative role (not that they always do) and that this sort of role has to do with motivation (though the tie here does not amount to there being exceptionless connections). (I thank Walter Sinnott-Armstrong for raising the concerns mentioned here.)

27. Brink (1989: ch. 3) marshals this objection forcefully against various forms of internalism.

28. Hare counts as a hard internalist. See especially Hare, 1952: ch. 11. Interestingly, Nowell-Smith is not a hard internalist. He claims that there is what he calls a 'quasi-logical' connection between moral judgments and action-oriented attitudes, and that therefore there can be exceptional cases in which

entails the absence of sincere moral judgment: the connection is a hard-and-fast one. By contrast, a soft internalist will claim that there is a conceptual connection between the notions of moral judgment and motivation but insist that the connection here should be understood as involving ceteris paribus generalizations. Moral judgment, then, is characterized by the overall typical role it plays in the cognitive economy of a person, which, as I have been stressing, has to do essentially with certain choice-guiding tendencies. These tendencies are (1) typical of the psychological state of moral judgment but (2) defeasible owing to other psychological causal tendencies (e.g., fear, greed, lust, etc.) that can co-occur with moral judgments and can generate competing causal tendencies.

I have expressed internalism in terms of there being a conceptual connection between the moral and the motivational, but the view gets its name from a certain metaphor that is also used to gloss the view, namely, that motivation is internal to moral judgment. As long as one has in mind the idea that if one concept is conceptually related to another, then either they are identical or one is contained in the other, then the generic way of expressing internalism and the metaphorical are the same. But, strictly speaking, one could accept the generic internalist thesis and yet reject the idea (or the apparent implications of the idea) that motivation is internal to moral judgment. The difference here concerns different possible views that an ethical internalist might hold about the nature of moral judgments: on one view, they are motivational states themselves; on the other view, they need not be. My point is that accepting the main, generic idea of internalism does not commit one to some particular story about the nature of moral judgment, and this is important because it cuts off certain objections that might be raised against internalism. But I must explain all this further.

If one is guided by the internalist metaphor, then one is going to construe moral judgments themselves as intrinsically motivational. The expression 'hot cognition' in circulation these days, particularly in the field of philosophy of psychology, is apt here. Moral judgments on this view are hot, motivationally charged, cognitions. There is a variety of possible views about the sort of motivational state in question, but I need not take sides on this issue of philosophical psychology.[29] But, and this is my main point here, internalists are not forced to reject the joint idea that (a) judgments, beliefs, and other such cognitive states possess no dynamic

one sincerely makes a moral judgment but fails to have the appropriate attitudes. See Nowell-Smith, 1954: 88–89, 95, 103, 146.

29. Some of the possibilities about the nature of moral judgment qua motivational are that they are: (1) a species of belief that is motivational, but not a species of desire; (2) a species of desire, but not a species of belief; (3) a species of belief *and* a species of desire; (4) a complex state involving both a belief and a desire; and (5) a psychological state that is neither, strictly speaking, a belief nor a desire, that we might call a 'besire.' (For some discussion of at least some of these options, see McNaughton, 1988: ch. 7, and Michael Smith, 1994.) Although I can be neutral over whether the psychological state of moral judgment is intrinsically motivating, my view would insist that if such states are to be construed as themselves motivational, they must also be construed in a way that is compatible with their having cognitive (assertive) content. Hence, options 3, 4, and 5 are among the possible construals of moral judgment compatible with my overall view about moral judgment. (See the discussion of moral belief later in this section.)

motivational role in the cognitive economy of agents, and (b) this role can only be played by desires, or sentiments, or other such non-cognitive, 'conative,' psychological states. Instead, it is perfectly in order for an internalist to downplay the internalist metaphor and maintain that (1) moral judgments are not intrinsically motivational, however, (2) it is part of their typical role in a person's cognitive economy to causally generate corresponding desires (or sentiments, etc.) and (3) their having this particular typical role is a conceptual truth about moral judgments qua moral.

To conclude this little digression about internalism, here are the key points. (1) Construing moral judgments as evaluative judgments means that their typical role has to do with choice and action guidance. (2) Furthermore, this means that I am committed to some form of ethical internalism (if the internalist thesis is understood broadly). (3) However, I reject any version of hard internalism that would overdraw the connection between moral judgment and motivation, and I accept, instead, a version of soft internalism, according to which ceteris paribus generalizations that tie moral judgment to motivation serve to characterize the sort of psychological state in question. (4) Moreover, I can be a (soft) internalist, accept the idea that moral judgments have assertible content, and not have to take a stand on the debate between Humeans and non-Humeans over questions about folk psychology.

Returning, then, to the discussion of the characteristics of moral judgment, if we put the first two characteristics together, we get the idea that such judgments are essentially evaluative cognitions — cognitions whose role in an agent's cognitive economy is not representation but, rather, the choice and guidance of action. Thus, their evaluative content is not a species of representational or descriptive content. To make a moral judgment is (normally) to take a certain sort of committed stance, psychologically; the specific evaluative content of a given judgment is reflected in the specific defeasible causal tendencies toward choice and toward action guidance that are typically generated by judgments with that particular content.

The two features I have discussed so far — namely, that the judgments in question are intentional psychological states whose content is expressible with 'that' clauses, and that they are non-representational in content — really apply to evaluative judgments in general, with moral judgments being a special case. So let us turn now to a third and fourth feature that are characteristic of moral judgments specifically, as distinct from certain other kinds of evaluative judgment. The third feature is this: moral judgment, that is, moral stance taking, is *categorical* in nature. In other words, in the typical case, one has a certain kind of commitment — a categorical commitment — that serves to distinguish moral stance taking from having a preference, or a taste, or a personal ideal. It is the sort of commitment that typically manifests itself in being disposed, for example, to assert and uphold one's stance over and against the conflicting stances of others, and so to categorically deny conflicting moral views rather than regard them as true or correct for those individuals who sincerely hold them (and who are not guilty of some factual or logical blunder).

Fourth, in the typical case, one's moral evaluation is *reasoned* evaluation, by which I mean that, in normal situations, one bases one's moral judgment about a particular case on her or his beliefs about the morally relevant non-moral features of the item being evaluated. One has reasons for her or his judgment and is thus disposed to engage in the practice of reason giving and criticism generally. Hence, the psychological state characteristic of moral judgment is a state that is (normally) motivating, reason guided, and held with a certain degree of categorical commitment.

A moral judgment, then, is a certain contentful psychological state that is implicated in a web of defeasible psychological tendencies aimed primarily at choice and guidance of action, not representation. Moreover, such judgment is a psychological stance-taking that is categorical: the agent is disposed to uphold and implement his stance vis-à-vis others and their behavior, whether or not those others share the agent's own stance. And it is typically a reason-guided state, for whose evaluative content the agent is prepared to argue.

I mentioned at the outset of this section my intention to avoid talk of belief and to talk instead of moral judgment in discussing the psychological dimension of my story. According to a very pervasive philosophical view about belief, beliefs are (in the phrase used by Armstrong) 'maps by which we steer.'[30] This conception of belief goes hand in glove with the standard view that all assertion is descriptive. I reject the latter presumption, and so there is really no reason not to say that moral judgments are a kind of belief—whether a motivationally charged kind of belief or a kind of belief whose typical causal role is to generate appropriate desires. Moreover, the notions of assertion and belief are conceptually connected. As Wright puts it, "[A]ssertion has the following analytical tie to belief: if someone makes an assertion, and is supposed sincere, it follows that she has a belief whose content can be captured by means of the sentence used" (1992: 14).[31] So, if indeed there can be genuine modes of assertion that are not descriptive but instead evaluative, and there really is an analytic (or at least conceptual) connection between assertion and belief, then moral utterances express genuine moral beliefs. We just have to get over the idea that all beliefs are representational (that they are all *maps* by which we steer). *Descriptive* beliefs are maps by which we steer; evaluative beliefs do not map the world, but instead typically serve to regulate our choices of routes.[32]

Note that if we allow that there are genuine moral beliefs that sincere moral assertions normally express, then it is appropriate to use the term 'cognitivism' for the view in question. As I explained in chapter 1 (see §IV, especially n. 15), this term, although often used to characterize semantic options in metaethics, has (given its etymology) primarily to do with belief and knowledge. A cognitivist view in metaethics, then, is one according to which the sorts of mental states charac-

---

30. Armstrong (1973: ch. 1) elaborates a view about belief that he attributes to Ramsey (1931).

31. Wright's claim that there is a tight analytic connection between assertion and belief may overstate things. It is enough to claim that the link in question is broadly conceptual thus allowing for a 'soft' connection of the sort explained in connection with internalism.

32. If one insists on tying belief to representation, then we should distinguish the sort of representation associated with descriptive belief and contrast it with the sort associated with evaluative belief. We might then say that moral beliefs represent how to act. But I have been using 'description,' 'representation,' and their cognates in an intentionally robust, non-minimalist way.

teristic of having moral convictions are beliefs. This idea is preserved in my view, so I am advocating what may be called a version of non-descriptivism that embraces (in the manner just explained) cognitivism.

Moral Assertion

When we turn from our psychological story to matters linguistic, we see that the linguistic neatly mirrors the psychological. First, moral sentences are typically used to express or reflect one's moral judgments. I am not saying by this that moral sentences are used to *describe* one's moral stance on some issue. If they were, then such sentences would have descriptive content and my view would be a version of semantic subjectivism that I described in chapter 1 — a rather crude form of relativism that makes nonsense of typical moral disagreement. Though moral sentences are not used to describe, they do share with sentences that have descriptive content this feature: both are used to express certain sorts of judgments (evaluative judgments in one case, descriptive judgments in the other). When I assert that apartheid is practiced today in certain countries, this assertion, if sincere, is a linguistic expression or reflection of my belief that apartheid is practiced today in certain countries; it does not *describe* me as thinking or believing this claim. So, likewise, when I sincerely say that apartheid is wrong, my assertion reflects my moral judgment (belief) that apartheid is wrong; it does not *describe* me as having such a moral stance.

Second, those sentences used to make genuine assertions are not descriptive; rather, they are evaluative — aimed primarily at choice and guidance. We judge that so and so is good or bad, right or wrong, and the typical linguistic manifestation of the activity of judging is a declarative sentence. As I explained in the previous section, I see no reason to deny that moral discourse has genuine assertive content. Remember, it is part of my strategy to accept the thesis of semantic unity (unless there is very good reason for denying it with regard to some discourse). Along with Wright, I hold that when it comes to interpreting some area of discourse, the default should be that if its surface features indicate genuine assertive content, then ceteris paribus it should be taken to really have those features. Furthermore, given that moral judgment displays the sort of reason-guided, action-oriented tendencies characteristic of evaluation, we should simply admit that moral sentences (in their primary usage) are used to make evaluative assertions.

Third, moral assertions are categorical assertions reflecting the categorical nature of moral judgment itself. I have been stressing this aspect of moral language all along, a crucial feature of moral discourse that versions of relativism cannot handle. But, as I have been saying in connection with moral judgment, moral thought and discourse involve a kind of commitment that manifests itself in such linguistic activities as willingness to assert one's moral stance on some issue over and against conflicting stances of others. This does not mean that one's commitment is dogmatic since, after all, moral judgment is (typically) reasoned stance taking (see the fourth point in the next paragraph), and this involves tendencies to give and respond to reasons and to adjust one's moral outlook accordingly, changing one's mind on the specific issue at hand if necessary. And, of course, one's level of commitment can vary from issue to issue, depending on one's level of confidence in one's moral judgment about particular cases. Nevertheless, even in cases in which one is not completely confident in one's moral judgment, one is disposed to assert one's moral stance over and against conflicting stances, though one is also disposed in such cases—if one is not dogmatic—to be persuaded to change one's mind on the issue.

And so, these assertions are typically reason guided (the fourth aspect of such assertions). In fact, one notable feature of moral discourse is that the basic moral concepts it employs—the concepts of moral goodness, rightness, and so forth—are supervenient concepts. If moral terms like 'good' and 'right' (and the concepts they express) are not descriptive terms, how should we understand their proper semantic working? In response, it is clear, as Hare (1952) pointed out long ago, that statements employing these terms conform to a principle of supervenience that requires that one have reasons for particular moral assertions—that one base one's evaluations on reasons and do so consistently. This much seems to be at the very heart of the semantic norms governing moral discourse. These concepts are exactly what is needed to express reasoned evaluations.[33]

In sum, moral statements make genuine assertions whose content is not descriptive, but instead is categorically evaluative. What is asserted by a moral statement is not a proposition purporting to represent how the world is, but rather a moral judgment, that is, a specific moral stance held by the agent; the asserted judgment is reflected or expressed by the moral statement, but not described by it. Such moral-evaluative assertions typically are reason guided.

Comparisons with Other Metaethical Views

The non-descriptive, categorically evaluative nature of moral assertions can perhaps be further elucidated by comparing the present treatment of moral language with traditional non-descriptivist approaches. Uttering a moral sentence is not a linguistic act of merely 'emoting'—that is, linguistically revealing one's stance without really asserting anything. On the contrary, in uttering a moral sentence, one not only reveals one's stance but *asserts* it—categorically. Among the features that are semantically central to such categorical stance assertion (but not to mere emotings) are the following. First, moral statements typically effect a *demand*, of those to whom the statement is addressed, to behave in ways that conform to the moral stance being asserted. Second, they typically signal the speaker's readiness to back the moral stance being asserted with *non-subjective reasons*, in other words, reasons that do not appeal to matters of individual taste, personal preference, or

---

33. Here, I can be non-committal on the issue of whether moral supervenience is to be understood 'thinly,' in the sense of denying that particular moral judgments entail interesting moral generalizations, or 'thickly' (as amounting to the so-called thesis of universalizability) in affirming that they do. Ethical particularists like Dancy (1993) construe supervenience thinly; ethical univeralists like Hare (1963) construe it thickly. For a brief overview of the difference between Hare and Dancy on this topic, see Timmons, forthcoming.

the like. Third, they typically *challenge* the listener, insofar as he adopts some conflicting moral stance, to provide non-subjective reasons in support of that stance and against the speaker's own stance. To construe moral utterances as mere emotings is to misconstrue them; categorically asserting a moral stance is a semantically much richer kind of speech act.

Categorically asserting a specific moral stance by uttering a moral sentence also is not a linguistic act of *prescribing*—that is, issuing a command or quasi command (or a universalized command or quasi command), without really asserting anything. For again, in issuing a moral utterance, one does assert something, and one asserts it categorically vis-à-vis one's audience: namely, one's moral stance itself. And again, the features mentioned earlier are semantically central to moral discourse, but not to commands or prescriptions. In particular, the authority the speaker appeals to, when uttering a moral sentence, is not the authority of the speaker himself as commander or prescriber, but rather the authority of non-subjective reasons.

It is well worth pausing here to stress that my view is not a version of relativism. I have already noted that, on my view, moral assertions express or reflect one's moral stance on some issue—they do not serve to describe it. But one might worry about relativist implications of my view, even granting that moral assertions are not descriptive assertions. The worry could be understood in the following way. On the view I am offering, moral judgments and moral assertions 'flow,' as it were (barring errors in non-moral belief and errors in moral reasoning), from one's general moral outlook. As I have explained, coming to form a moral judgment is, in the typical case, a matter of bringing one's moral outlook or sensibility to bear on some topic or issue. In making moral judgments and assertions, it is semantically appropriate, given how moral thought and discourse work, to judge and assert in accordance with one's moral outlook. One might be tempted to reason as follows: on the view being proposed, although we get genuine moral assertion and, hence, genuine moral truth, it looks as if moral truth is a matter of judging in accordance with one's own moral outlook. So we get a version of what is usually called *individual moral relativism*: a moral sentence uttered by an individual at a particular time is true if, and only if, that sentence follows from (in some sense) that person's moral outlook together with relevant non-moral facts.

But my view does not boil down to this (or any) form of relativism. This objection conflates the idea of a moral judgment and corresponding assertion being what I call *semantically appropriate* (a notion introduced in §III) with moral truth. On some occasion, the semantically appropriate thing for one to do (if one is being sincere) is to make assertions that reflect one's moral judgments, which in turn depend on one's moral outlook at the time. But I do not equate semantic appropriateness with truth, and since the argument under consideration equates the two, it fails to convict me of being a relativist. (I come back to the issue of relativism in the next section.)

In the story I have been telling so far, I have made a point of avoiding certain sorts of questions about the assertoric content of moral statements and their truth-aptness that are standardly asked when one proposes some view about the semantic workings of some discourse. Dealing with such questions is where my minimalism about moral discourse, to which I now turn, comes into play.

On Analyzing Moral Assertions

Moral discourse, I am claiming, is genuinely assertoric discourse, and since to assert something is to present it as true, such discourse is thus genuinely truth-apt. My plea has been that we follow what seems natural to say about such discourse, namely, that it is genuinely assertoric and truth-apt, yet also essentially evaluative discourse. We should recognize a kind of assertion — evaluative assertion — that is distinctive of moral thought and discourse. The philosophical pressure against doing so comes from the semantic assumption that all assertion is descriptive, and it is this deeply embedded assumption that should be given up to clear the way for the sort of view I am proposing.

But there are certain questions about assertive content and truth-aptness that will be raised about any area of discourse that purports to have these features that I must now address. For instance, with regard to alleged moral assertions, there are questions about this brand of content, such as 'What is the content of an utterance like "Apartheid is wrong"?' And associated questions will arise about the truth of moral sentences, for instance, 'What is the account of truth as predicated of moral sentences that is being offered here?' When one is dealing with descriptive modes of discourse, one can legitimately expect substantive and illuminating analyses of content (in descriptive terms) and substantive stories about truth.[34] But if the discourse is not descriptive, and thus is not in the business of representing the world, the sorts of philosophical expectations that questions about content and truth usually raise should be questioned. That is, since moral discourse is not descriptive discourse, one cannot be expected to provide an account of their semantics that takes the form of truth conditions expressed in descriptive language. Although there is indeed a way to articulate the content of a moral sentence via truth conditions, this way is disquotational. In response to questions of the form 'What is the content of p?' (where p is a moral sentence), the reply is simply p. The content of 'Apartheid is wrong' is apartheid is wrong.

To reinforce this point, think for a moment about philosophical analyses of content and how they unfold. One familiar project is to take some problematic concept like the concept of knowledge or free will and attempt to decompose the concept (analyze it) into simpler, less problematic constituent concepts that would illuminate the content of sentences that contain terms that express the troubling concepts. The aim, presumably, is to come up with illuminating and content-preserving paraphrases of sentences that constitute some troublesome area of discourse. (Of course, this kind of analysis can be practiced on any sentence in which

---

34. However, I already expressed my reservations about such traditional projects in the previous chapter.

a term for a complex concept is used; being philosophically troublesome is not a prerequisite for practicing this form of semantic analysis.) And although there is an interesting history of attempts to paraphrase moral sentences into sentences in which moral terms are replaced with non-moral terms (while attempting to preserve content), these projects are generally recognized as failures. For that matter, virtually all attempts at philosophical analysis have met this same fate.

Some such paraphrases construe moral discourse as descriptive discourse, whereas other paraphrases attempt to reduce moral language to some familiar form of non-descriptive discourse. And, of course, there have been attempts at hybrid reduction—attempts to analyze moral discourse as partly descriptive and partly non-descriptive. Stevenson's metaethical view is as follows. According to one of his two 'patterns' of analysis, moral sentences of the form 'X is good' (when uttered by me) are roughly synonymous with 'I approve of this, do so as well,' wherein there is a combination of a descriptive statement ('I approve of this') with an emotive component ('do so as well'). Presumably, the urge to attempt some hybrid analysis is the presumption that if an utterance has genuine assertoric content, then that content must be descriptive content. And so one might be inclined to react to my claim that moral sentences are used to make genuine assertions by attempting some kind of division between the purely descriptive content of the sentence and the purely non-descriptive content of the sentence. But why not suppose that moral language simply cannot be reduced or analyzed in these ways? For one thing, it seems more natural and less forced simply to admit that moral sentences have a primitive kind of content: evaluative content. Furthermore, as I have pointed out, the history of attempts at philosophical analysis of moral (and other interesting) concepts is largely a history of failure.

But in addition to the type of analysis that features conceptual decomposition, another familiar way to illuminate the content of assertions and assertoric discourse (at least discourse that exhibits simple subject-predicate structure) is to specify the referents of their singular terms and predicative expressions. But this mode of analysis does presuppose that the discourse in question is in the business of representing or describing the world, and so with non-descriptive discourse this sort of project is out of the question.

Thus, the urge to provide some sort of illuminating analysis of moral discourse is guided either by the reductive urge or the assumption that if it has genuine assertoric content, it must be a species of descriptive content. Since the reductive urge should be resisted, and since moral discourse is not descriptive discourse, it is quite appropriate to respond to questions about the content of moral discourse in the minimalist manner I have advocated. In answering a question about the content of a moral sentence, the proper response is to simply repeat the sentence.

This is not obscurantism, or philosophical quietism. There are indeed philosophically illuminating things to say about evaluative content in thought and discourse. Philosophical understanding is to be had not by means of reductive paraphrases or decompositional analyses of moral statements, but rather in ways like those recently exhibited in this chapter: characterizing moral judgments as psychological stance takings of a certain kind; delineating the typical role of these states in a moral agent's cognitive economy, by reference to certain soft psychological generalizations true of such judgments; characterizing moral statements as assertions of specific moral stances; focusing on semantically central features of moral statements, involving their role in guiding choice and action within a context of reason giving and reason having; and so on. To do all of this is to do quite a lot, and it provides (I claim) sufficient philosophical illumination of the discourse for understanding its workings. No more is needed, except by way of elaboration.

'True' as Predicated of Moral Assertions

A similar minimalist tack is appropriate for questions about the truth of moral sentences. When genuine assertion is present in a discourse, the statements of that discourse are truth-apt—they are subject to proper application of the truth predicate. This much is guaranteed by the fact that to assert something is simply to present it as true. What is interesting is just how the truth predicate works in cases in which the semantic norms governing the discourse are not semantically tight, and in which the discourse itself is categorical.

Moral statements do not, of course, have truth conditions that can be set forth in purely descriptive language. As I have explained, moral discourse is not in the business of describing how the world is, and so one should not expect to find such truth conditions associated with truth ascriptions to moral statements. Rather, truth talk in moral discourse operates minimalistically, in accordance with Tarski's schema T. Let me elaborate.

Just as first-order moral statements are not governed by tight (or relativistically tight) semantic norms, truth ascriptions to such statements are also not governed by tight (or relativistically tight) semantic norms. Just as first-order moral statements make moral-evaluative assertions, the corresponding truth ascriptions make them, too. This does not mean that the truth ascriptions ascribe moral correctness *instead* of semantic correctness, or even that they ascribe a *hybrid* kind of correctness that consists of a semantic component and a moral component. Rather, it means that semantic and moral assessment become *fused* when one attributes truth to moral statements: one's semantic evaluations are made from within one's moral outlook and thus express metalinguistically the specific moral stances that accompany the outlook. Although the truth predicate is still being used to ascribe correct assertibility (and hence has the same *meaning* that it has in other contexts), the correctness in question is not a matter of purely semantic norms; it cannot be, since the semantic norms are not tight. Rather, 'true' is being used in a morally committed way.

It is crucial for understanding this view that I not be taken for a relativist about moral truth. I mentioned this in the previous section, but it is worth saying again. In one important respect, there is a similarity between my view and relativism: on my construal of moral discourse, as in relativism, moral statements possess a relativized kind of *semantic appropriateness*. A moral statement used by a speaker is semantically appropriate, relative to that speaker's own moral outlook, provided it is used to assert a moral stance that accords with that moral outlook. Unlike relativism, however, my view does not identify *truth* (i.e., correct assertibility) with this relation of semantic appropriateness between a statement and a speaker's moral outlook. On the contrary, truth ascriptions to moral statements, like first-order moral statements themselves, are categorical rather than implicitly relativistic.

Since my view includes a notion of outlook-relative semantic appropriateness, it can and does allow for another kind of semantic evaluation of statements, distinct from truth ascription. One can ask an explicitly relativistic question: Is someone who is using moral discourse speaking in a semantically appropriate way, relative to his own moral outlook? (One can also ask whether someone else is making truth ascriptions to moral statements in a semantically appropriate way, relative to his own moral outlook.) But to ask such questions is not to ask whether the person's moral statements are *true* relative to his moral outlook; for, the semantically appropriate way for the questioner to use the truth predicate is (1) categorically rather than relativistically and (2) in such a way that one's truth ascriptions reflect one's *own* moral outlook. Thus, the semantically appropriate thing to say about someone whose moral statement accords with his moral outlook but not with one's own is this: 'Although his statement is semantically appropriate relative to his own moral outlook, it is false.'

So from the fact that people can and do judge that opposing moral statements can be semantically appropriate relative to different moral outlooks, one should not infer that truth as predicated of moral statements is relative. This inference is tempting if one rejects moral objectivism and wants to allow the legitimacy of moral truth talk. Let us call it the *relativist's fallacy*. My view is an irrealist approach to moral semantics that avoids this fallacy, while also accommodating the categorical nature of both moral statements themselves and truth ascriptions to these statements.

Contextual Variability in Ascriptions of Truth and Falsity to Moral Assertions

Let us return now to the wider theoretical framework in which assertoric non-descriptivism is situated: contextual semantics. You may recall that part of this general approach to semantics is that semantic norms frequently involve contextually variable parameters. Contextual variability can manifest itself not only among different kinds of discourse involving different subject matters, but also within a single kind of discourse. Specifically, it can manifest itself with respect to the norms governing the contextually appropriate uses of 'true' and 'false' as applied to moral statements. I also noted that, for many purposes, it is useful to think of the sort of context variability in operation as a matter of there being different perspectives, which reflect various purposes we have in thought and discussion and from which such ascriptions can legitimately be made.

Perhaps the two most obvious perspectives from which to judge the correct assertibility of moral statements are what we can call the *detached perspective* and the *engaged perspective*. (These terms aren't entirely satisfactory, but they will do for now.) From a morally detached perspective, one uses 'true' and 'false' in such a way that a statement counts as true (false) if, and only if, it is correctly assertible (correctly deniable) solely by virtue of the operative first-order semantic norms, plus the world. One asks, in effect, whether the semantic norms governing the discourse conspire with features of the world in order to yield correct assertibility (or deniability) of statements in the discourse; thus, 'true' and 'false' are used in such a way that they are only applicable to statements governed by tight semantic norms. Given my irrealist story about moral discourse, when one judges from a morally detached perspective, and thus simply in light of semantic norms, moral statements are neither correctly assertible nor correctly deniable, and so they are neither true nor false. In other words, under the contextual parameters operative in judging from a detached perspective, the truth predicate does not properly apply to moral statements.

However, people can and do judge the truth of moral statements from within a morally engaged perspective, and in these more ordinary contexts, the use of 'true' runs in tandem with the object-level discourse. When speaking and judging metalinguistically in a morally engaged way, one's use of 'true' and 'false' in connection with moral statements becomes morally assertoric itself, so that truth ascriptions are a fusion of semantic and moral evaluation. That is, the contextually operative parameters on 'true' are such that (1) the semantically appropriate use of moral statements is reflective of one's own moral outlook, and (2) the semantically appropriate use of truth talk for moral statements is in accordance with schema T.

I have been at pains to explain just how and why my view is not a version of moral relativism, and in doing so, I have distinguished between considerations of semantic appropriateness of moral claims and considerations of their truth. And although what I am about to say does not in the least take back my antirelativist stance, there is a legitimate use of truth talk that is relativistic. There is nothing incoherent about making semantic assessments of moral statements that explicitly (or implicitly) relativize them. My ethics students quite often talk about such and such moral claim being true for this or that person or group. When they do so, what I find is that they detach, as it were, from their own moral outlooks (at least in cases in which the moral statement is one they do not accept) and view things from the perspective of the person or group in question. Semantic claims (ascribing truth or falsity) about a moral statement that are relativized to some person other than one's current self (it can even be one's former self) are made from what we might call the *egocentric perspective*; those relativized to some group are made from a *sociocentric perspective*. And, again, judging from my students, it is pretty clear what point there might be in making egocentric or sociocentric semantic evaluations: we often do so when we are inclined to evaluate them charitably. Note that, typically, when one makes one or other of these relativistic semantic evaluations, one does so from a detached, non–morally engaged perspective, which means that there are many quite different perspectives that are appropriately called detached. Earlier, I introduced the notion of semantic appropriateness and contrasted it with the notion of truth in order to call attention to what I take as the standard use of the truth predicate—in effect, to make genuine, categorical moral assertions at the metalinguistic level. Here I am calling attention to the fact that, as far as the semantics of truth talk goes, there is nothing incoherent in using such talk in an overtly (or covertly) relativistic manner.

Indeed, it is possible, under contextual semantics, to use truth talk in a way that comports with how the moral realist (of the sort under scrutiny in chapter 2) thinks about things. Suppose that some community really does use moral predicates in a thoroughly consistent manner, so that ascriptions of good and right are generally made in response to the presence of certain natural properties of actions, persons, institutions, and anything else that is subject to moral evaluation. Through consistent use of their moral language, a term like 'good' might come to be so strongly associated with whatever natural features those folks use to make judgments of moral goodness, that this term figures mainly in descriptive claims about objects of moral evaluation. Here again, we can talk about this or that moral statement being true for the group in question, perhaps in order to indicate something about the implications of the moral outlook of the group. So there is nothing that stands in the way of using the truth predicate for such purposes. But to use the truth predicate in this way is (normally) to use it in a morally detached way. All I would insist is that this is not the way in which we normally use the truth predicate; we use it in a morally engaged way.[35]

So, in answer to questions about moral truth, the view being proposed here is, in short, the following. We can usefully distinguish between morally detached and morally engaged ways of using the truth predicate in connection with moral statements. From a certain detached perspective—in which we are engaged in metaphysical speculation—there is no moral truth (or falsity) since semantic norms alone do not conspire with the world to yield correct assertibility or deniability status to moral statements. But there are other detached perspectives—for example, the egocentric and sociocentric—and from these perspectives one uses the truth predicate in a relativized way. This relativized use of truth talk in ethics is not primary, however. From an engaged perspective, 'true' as predicated of moral statements results in a metalinguistic assertion that is a fused semantic/moral evaluation rather than a detached semantic evaluation. All of these ways of employing the truth predicate are legitimate in context, by virtue of the contextual variability of the parameters in the semantic norms governing truth talk. One can properly use truth talk any of these ways, but not in the same breath.

Fact Talk without FACTS

The remarks in the last two paragraphs about the contextually variable uses of terms like 'true' and 'false' are very closely related to what should be said, in my view, about fact talk in ethics. (Here, for clarity, I revert to the capitalization technique to indicate commitment to metaphysically robust entities, properties, relations, and facts—that is, ENTITIES, PROPERTIES, RELATIONS, and FACTS.) As I have been saying, in contexts in which we detach from our moral outlooks and view things from a morally disengaged point of view (as, for example, when considering matters of what exists), truth and falsity as predicated of moral statements

---

35. Hare makes similar remarks about the use of 'good.' On his view, moral judgments involving terms like 'good,' 'ought,' and 'right' have both descriptive and evaluative meaning, and he notes that in communities in which a certain standard for judging things good becomes widely accepted, the evaluative-meaning component may be lost, with the result that 'moral' judgments for this group become purely descriptive. See Hare, 1952: 120, 124–25, 147–50.

is empty. That is, under the contextually operative parameters governing the correct assertibility (deniability) of moral statements for which one does not invoke one's moral outlook, moral statements are properly said to be neither true nor false. This reflects the metaphysical aspect of my view—its irrealism—that there are no moral FACTS, PROPERTIES, or RELATIONS. The claim just made about there being no moral facts and so forth is itself correctly assertible under the intended assertibility norms, since I mean to be making a comment about ontology from the point of view of my philosophical naturalism. But even if it is correctly assertible (in the sort of context just mentioned) that there are no moral FACTS and PROPERTIES, one can still correctly assert that there are moral facts and properties (the different sizes of script here are meant to signal that different assertibility norms are operative when one makes such remarks). When I say that there are moral facts and properties, I mean to be speaking from within a morally engaged perspective, a perspective within which there are genuine moral assertions; truth and falsity are properly predicated of moral statements; and, of course, it is proper to say that there are moral facts and properties. If, for example, I say that apartheid is wrong, I make a genuine moral assertion, and so it is proper for me also to mention that sentence and go on to predicate truth of it, and it is also proper for me to refer to the *fact* that apartheid is wrong and to say of its practice that it has the *property* of wrongness.

A related point can be made concerning the idea that essentially truth has to do with correspondence to reality. Earlier in this section, I noted that one of Wright's truth platitudes is the idea that true statements correspond to the facts. A minimalist can accommodate this platitude by understanding it in a metaphysically non-committal way. The realist will prefer to understand the idea this way:

CP   'P' is true if and only if 'P' corresponds to the FACTS.

The minimalist, however, will want to deflate the metaphysical punch intended by reference to the facts (indicated by the capitalization) and simply talk about facts in the manner I have been suggesting. Or, better, the minimalist can follow the suggestion of Wright and express the correspondence platitude like this:

CP'   'P' is true if and only if things are as 'P' says they are.

As Wright points out, the minimalist has "no difficulty in accommodating intuitions about the relationship between truth and correspondence so long as doing so is held to require no more than demonstrating a right to the *phrases* by which those intuitions are characteristically expressed" (Wright, 1992: 27).

In short, it is legitimate, and fully within the spirit of minimalism, to help oneself to moral fact talk and to the idea that a true statement corresponds to the facts, so long, of course, as one treats such talk in a metaphysically minimalist manner and does not suppose that in talking about moral facts (and properties) there must be some in-the-world FACTS and PROPERTIES to which such talk must be responsive.

Two clarificatory comments are in order here. First, I am not denying that there are in-the-world FEATURES possessed by actions, persons, institutions, practices, and so forth that are the basis for our moral evaluations—such a denial would be crazy. Of course our moral evaluations are based on beliefs we have about the natural features of items in the world around us. What I reject is any attempt to identify a realm of moral facts or properties with such FEATURES. To do so and then claim that moral statements function primarily to report or describe such FEATURES (and thereby perhaps guide choice and action) would be to accept a version of descriptivism, which, I have argued, is not the way to go.

Second, I am not advocating a Mackie-style error theory, according to which moral statements purport to make assertions about moral FACTS and PROPERTIES, but since no such things exist, affirmative moral statements are all false. Moral statements, in their primary use, do not purport to make such ontological claims; rather, their primary function is to evaluate, not describe. So, as explained a few paragraphs back, the proper thing to say about the truth values of moral statements, when viewed from the perspective of realist ontology, is that they do not have truth values—they are neither true nor false.

Summary

With the rudiments of assertoric non-descriptivism on the table, let me make a few summary remarks. I have rejected all forms of metaethical descriptivism, and so I fall squarely within the non-descriptivist camp. My general proposal, then, is in the spirit of traditional non-descriptivism in two respects: (1) my view is staunchly irrealist in denying that there are any objective moral properties, relations, or facts that moral discourse purports to report or describe, and (2) the proper way to get a handle on the workings of moral discourse is to focus on its typical point and purpose. However, I part company with the traditionalists in claiming that, despite the fact that moral sentences lack descriptive content, they are nevertheless typically used to make genuine assertions and hence are genuinely truth-apt. I claim they have (in their typical uses) evaluative assertoric content—that they are typically used to make evaluative assertions. One upshot of this view about content (and this is a second major way in which I differ from the traditionalists) is that I can accept the thesis of semantic unity and need not follow traditionalists in the project of reductively analyzing moral sentences in terms of some non-assertoric form of language.

Against the background of contextual semantics, I proposed a two-pronged approach to moral semantics. First, we find illumination about the workings of moral discourse by focusing on its point and purpose, which, I claimed, should be understood in relation to the phenomenon of taking a moral stance; a moral statement not only expresses one's stance, but also categorically asserts it. Second, I have also stressed that moral discourse be construed minimalistically, in the sense that questions about the assertive contents of moral statements as well as questions about their truth are properly referred to Tarski's schema T. This is not surprising, I argued, given that the discourse is not descriptive. Putting all of this together, it is perhaps not too misleading to say that my view is non-descriptivist at heart but fully recognizes the grammatical and logical features of moral discourse that make it genuinely assertoric and truth-apt.

Robust Objectivism	Modest Objectivism	Relativism	Assertoric Non-Descriptivism	Traditional Non-Descriptivism

| Objective Discourse | | Non-Objective Discourse | | |

| Descriptive Discourse | | Non-Descriptive Discourse | | |

| Genuine Assertoric Discourse | | | Non-Assertoric Discourse | |

FIGURE 4–2 Interrelations diagram modified to include assertoric non-descriptivism

Another way to bring out the contrast with traditional forms of non-descriptivism is by going back to my chapter 1 characterization of descriptivism as involving two main claims: (1) Moral terms purport to denote or designate moral properties and relations that actions, practices, persons, institutions, and so forth may or may not possess, and moral sentences purport to describe or report moral facts — facts about which actions, persons, practices, institutions, and so forth do (and which do not) possess certain moral properties. (2) Consequently, moral sentences containing such terms and expressions have genuine assertoric content — they are used to make assertions about what is true (or false) and so have truth values. I went on to point out that non-descriptivists deny the first tenet, claiming instead that typical moral sentences are used to perform some non-describing function and, so, are led to conclude that the second tenet of descriptivism is false. And, of course, if one is working with the assumption that all genuine assertions are descriptive, then the conclusion is inevitable. I have challenged that assumption to open the door for a version of non-descriptivism that denies claim 1 but embraces claim 2.

Since assertoric non-descriptivism is not on the traditional menu of metaethical options, let us modify figure 4–1 from earlier in this chapter to incorporate this sort of view (fig. 4–2).

Before moving on, I would like to situate my view in relation to more traditional metaethical views. There is something I like about all three traditional views — ethical naturalism, ethical non-naturalism, and traditional non-descriptivism — that I am trying to preserve in my own view. I share the ethical naturalists' broad metaphysical orientation, but I do not think this broad metaphysical view can be combined with moral realism or any other (narrowly or broadly) naturalistically reductive metaethical view. My partial alliance with ethical naturalism is reflected in my overall project of naturalistic accommodation of moral discourse. I share the ethical non-naturalists' staunchly non-reductivist stance about moral discourse, as well as the idea that typical moral utterances represent genuine assertions. I reject, of course, the non-naturalist moral metaphysics that the non-naturalists thought they were committed to as a result of construing moral utterances as genuinely assertoric and rejecting any reductive analysis of such assertions. I share the non-descriptivists' rejection of the idea that moral discourse is primarily descriptive discourse and their emphasis on the action-guiding role of such discourse.

So, consider it this way: with philosophical naturalism providing the general metaphysical background, my metaethical view attempts to combine some aspects of non-naturalism (moral sentences are typically used to make genuine moral assertions, but assertions of a sui generis speech act that has to do with action guidance). The particular metaethical blend of views I am advocating requires that we reject a deeply embedded assumption of traditional metaethics, namely, the idea that all genuine assertoric discourse is a species of descriptive discourse. Splitting apart this connection between genuine assertion and descriptive discourse allows us to combine the idea that moral discourse is genuinely assertive (and that it possesses all the associated linguistic phenomena that go with genuine assertion) with the idea that it is primarily evaluative and not descriptive discourse. I have employed a particular semantic orientation — contextual semantics — that I think is, in general, plausible and suggestive of the sort of metaethical view that I favor.

Much of what I have done so far in this chapter is to stake out a metaethical view. Let me try to convince you that it is a correct view, or at least a view that deserves serious consideration, by turning to the dual accommodation project in which the basic view will receive further elaboration. Hopefully, in what follows, I will adequately address certain objections that have likely occurred to many of my readers.

VI. Accommodation

Commitment to philosophical naturalism requires that the metaphysical and associated epistemological commitments of 'higher order' discourse, including moral discourse, fit into a broadly naturalistic picture of the world that includes human beings and their activities. This is the project of external accommodation (guided by D2). There is also the project of internal accommodation (guided by D1), that is, the project of making sense of various assumptions that are deeply embedded in commonsense moral discourse and practice. Of course, there is no guarantee that each of these projects of external and internal accommodation will go smoothly; it may well turn out that each of these projects tends to make trouble for the other. Thus, one's commitment to naturalism might lead one to claim that some of the deeply embedded assumptions of commonsense moral discourse are mistaken. Mackie's error theory seems to fit this pattern. Again, upon reflection, one might find that if a metaethical view is going to accommodate the assumptions of commonsense moral discourse and practice, then one must give up naturalism. However, as I mentioned in chapter 1, any metaethical theory that can accomplish both accommodation aims is more plausible than one that cannot. I think the sort of irrealist view I have been developing can fairly meet both accommodation demands, or so I shall proceed to argue.

External Accommodation

As I mentioned in §I, the external accommodation burdens of moral irrealism differ importantly from those of other metaethical views. The moral realist who is committed to naturalism needs to be able to accommodate putative objective moral properties, relations, and facts, as well as to explain how human beings have access to those items so that moral knowledge is possible. Descriptivist positions other than robust moral realism—views of the sort that fall within the middle range in figures 4–1 and 4–2 earlier in this chapter—need to be able to explain how naturalistic properties and facts conspire with the semantic norms governing moral talk to confer determinate correct assertibility (for relativists, outlook-relative correct assertibility) upon moral statements, and again must also explain how knowledge of moral truth is possible.

The irrealist, who rejects the metaphysical commitments incurred by the various forms of descriptivism, does not shoulder the rather weighty metaphysical and epistemological burdens that come with such positions. But there is some accommodating to be done. Human beings, with their capacities and proclivities for certain kinds of cooperative social structures, are evolved creatures, products of natural selection. From a naturalistic perspective, then, one important philosophical project of naturalistically accommodating moral discourse and practice involves situating such discourse and practice within a broadly naturalistic/evolutionary picture of human nature and society: explaining the dynamics of the discourse and practice, and its point and purpose, in broadly naturalistic/evolutionary terms. This aspect of accommodation is obviously continuous with science itself—indeed, with various branches of science, from neurology through sociology. Accordingly, what philosophers, qua philosophers, have to contribute to it will usually involve a certain amount of speculation.

Humans are creatures who can, and do, coordinate their behavior so as to achieve mutually beneficial ends and lessen the likelihood of individually or collectively harmful occurrences. Coordinative behavior, and hence the capacity and proclivity to engage in such behavior, has obvious benefits from a pragmatic/evolutionary naturalistic perspective. Many kinds of coordinative behavior involve these features: (1) each member of a social group adopts certain kinds of normative stances toward himself or herself and others that reflect aspects of a person's moral general normative outlook, and (2) each member of the group behaves and judges, and is disposed to behave and judge, in ways consistent with his or her own normative outlook. Humans, that is, very often act and judge qua normative stance takers—that is, from *within* a normative outlook.

Various kinds of normative stance taking can provide obvious pragmatic/evolutionary advantages to creatures who are sophisticated enough to be capable of them. The immediate concern here is with *moral* stance taking, though there are other kinds of normative stances, including legal stances, linguistic stances, and stances of etiquette and social grace that admit of the same general treatment I am describing in connection with moral stance taking.[36] One salient feature of having a moral outlook is the degree of seriousness and felt commitment we normally attach to our moral views when we take a moral stance on some issue. It is commonly believed that moral outlooks and particular moral stances have a

---

36. See Horgan and Timmons, 1993, for a discussion of how semantic discourse and linguistic stance taking can be naturalistically accommodated.

kind of importance often manifested in our dispositions to think that moral obligations override non-moral obligations in cases of conflict.[37] So one way to begin to understand the point and purpose of moral discourse and practice, and indeed, the point and purpose of having a moral outlook, is to inquire about the basis of the special status that our moral views have for us as human beings.

And the answer is fairly clear. There is a rather obvious pragmatic/evolutionary advantage of humans having a moral outlook, and having one that is shared across one's community, namely, to promote, in a fundamental way, human well-being (or at least the well-being of a certain group) by providing norms that serve to guide behavior in ways that are crucial to the stability and cohesion of groups of human beings. Because of the importance of certain patterns of behavior (and emotional responses), one would expect that humans, capable of complex coordinative behavior, would evolve more or less shared normative systems that have the sorts of features characteristic of a typical moral outlook. In short, given what human beings are like, the setting in which they find themselves, and that they are capable of quite sophisticated coordinative behavior, one would expect them to develop strategies that would most effectively solve problems of coordination crucial for group survival. Viewed in this pragmatic/evolutionary way, moral stance taking, moral discourse and practice, and the characteristics of having a moral outlook make sense from the point of view of naturalism.[38]

Internal Accommodation

Though the burdens of external accommodation for the irrealist (at least the version I favor that does not countenance any moral PROPERTIES or FACTS) are less burdensome than they are for the moral realist, it is with the project of internal accommodation that the irrealist finds her stiffest challenge. Supposedly, the realist has the upper hand, here especially with regard to the task of making sense of those so-called objective pretensions of moral discourse and practice. So my plan to explain how my brand of non-reductive irrealism can fairly accommodate such pretensions.

The project involves three steps. First, I need to remind the reader of the sorts of phenomena deeply embedded in moral discourse and practice that presumably have a strongly objectivist flavor. Second, I need to show how my brand of irrealism can accommodate these presumptions. And third, I need to explain, from the perspective of my irrealist view, *why* moral discourse has these features. (Ideally, explaining these features would include explaining any differences between moral discourse and other types of normative, stance-taking discourse, including, for example, epistemic discourse, aesthetic discourse, prudential discourse, and so forth. However, I will be able to make only a few brief remarks about this matter.)

37. See, for example, Brandt, 1979: ch. 10, and Ladd, 1957: 101–8, for discussions of this aspect of having a moral outlook.
38. Of course, I have only scratched the surface of what is a long and complicated story about these matters. See Gibbard, 1990, for much more detail.

Objective Pretensions

Since the objective pretensions have already been mentioned in the previous chapter, let me just review what I take to be the main features that an irrealist would like to be able to accommodate. There are three general types of these features.

First, there are those features having to do with the form and content of ordinary moral discourse, most importantly:

1. Typical moral sentences, for example, 'Apartheid is wrong,' are in the indicative mood and so appear to make genuine assertions. Consequently, such sentences are truth-apt.
2. Some moral statements, for instance, 'The evil of apartheid is the principal reason for its demise,' make putative reference to moral properties and facts.
3. Furthermore, simple moral sentences are embedded in all sorts of grammatical constructions. Most notably, they can be embedded in truth functional constructions: negations, disjunctions, conditionals, and so forth. They thus appear embedded in arguments that seem to be either straightforwardly valid or invalid as, for example, in the argument:[39]
   a. It is wrong to kill.
   b. If it is wrong to kill, then it is wrong to pay someone to kill.
   Therefore,
   c. It is wrong to pay someone to kill.

Second, there are those features of moral discourse and practice that have to do with what I have called 'moral phenomenology,' features that are a bit harder to characterize clearly but that involve certain affective and perceptual dimensions:

4. Most individuals have affective moral experiences. For example, they experience obligations as somehow externally imposed, and seem to observe value out in the world; for example, one can see a child's cruelty toward a playmate.

Third, there are those features of moral discourse and practice that have to do primarily with our so-called critical practices. In the previous chapter, I mentioned three interconnected features:

5. Moral sentences (judgments, beliefs) are sometimes genuinely true, or 'correctly assertible' (C1 from ch. 3).
6. Whatever moral outlook one may have at a time, it might be improved; in some respects, one's current moral views might well be mistaken, including various moral assumptions that are fundamental to one's

---

39. This particular example is from Sinnott-Armstrong (1993).

outlook. In other words, moral error (including 'deep' moral error) and, correspondingly, moral progress are possible (C2).

7. Genuine conflicts in moral belief are possible. For example, normally, if one person affirms a moral statement and another person denies it, then they genuinely disagree (C3).

To these three, we should add a fourth:

8. Moral thought and discussion can be, and often are, guided by the practice of giving reasons for and against moral statements.

Moral realists, of course, have made much of these features in defending their metaethical view and have argued that irrealists cannot plausibly accommodate these features. It has been the main burden of this chapter to develop a version of irrealism that can accommodate these features as well as possible. So I will now take up these features one by one and explain how, if it is not already obvious, my view comports with each of the items on this list.

Accommodating Matters of Form and Content

In the metaethical view I have been advocating, moral sentences are a species of genuine assertion, and so, it is no surprise that they are expressed in the indicative mood. This fact about moral discourse, then, is not something relegated to the realm of mere appearance that somehow must then be explained away. Moreover, since moral statements are genuine assertions, and since the very notion of assertion is tied to truth, moral sentences are properly understood to be truth-apt. Thus, my brand of irrealism apparently has no trouble accommodating item 1 from the above list of features.

The second item on the list has to do with matters of content rather than the form of moral sentences, and specifically with the fact that some moral sentences make putative reference to moral properties and facts. Again, I hope that it is fairly clear how my view accommodates this phenomenon. Although there are no moral PROPERTIES or FACTS, property and fact talk have their proper place in moral thought and discussion. As explained in §IV, fact talk (and the same can be said of property talk) is proper and legitimate, when made from within a morally engaged perspective; such talk is simply part of a complex web of notions that includes talk of truth and falsity and genuine assertion. The brand of irrealism I favor does not have trouble accommodating reference to moral properties and facts.

So far my view has dealt entirely with those linguistic contexts in which one categorically asserts some simple moral statement, for example, 'Apartheid is wrong.' But such simple statements allow embedding—they can be negated, as in 'It is not the case that apartheid is wrong'; they can be parts of conjunctions, disjunctions, and conditionals, as in, for instance, 'If apartheid is wrong, then any country that allows or condones this practice ought to be the subject of international censure'; and they can be the objects of propositional attitudes, as in 'John believes that apartheid is wrong.'

Of course, descriptivist views have no problem accommodating such phenomena. But what about non-descriptivist views? Geach (1960, 1965) objected to forms
of non-descriptivism, claiming that they had failed to make good sense of embeddings of simple moral sentences. He made his point by focusing on certain simple
argument forms like the one featured in item 3. In connection with, say, metaethical emotivism, the problem is as follows. According to emotivism, the meaning
of the simple sentence 'It is wrong to kill' is to be understood in terms of what
one does when one asserts it, namely, express emotion (such sentences have 'emotive meaning'). But in the conditional sentence 'If it is wrong to kill, then it is
wrong to pay someone to kill,' the same simple sentence, now embedded, does
not normally function to express a speaker's feelings and emotions about killing,
and so it must differ in meaning from its unembedded occurrence. Thus, if one
accepts the emotivist's analysis of the meaning of simple moral sentences, then in
arguing from these two sentences to the conclusion that it is wrong to pay someone
to kill, one commits the fallacy of equivocation: the meaning of 'It is wrong to
kill' is not the same in its two occurrences. But surely the argument is valid, an
instance of the *modus ponens*. Emotivism, then, at least owes us an explanation
of the meanings of sentences that embed simple moral sentences. This is the gist
of Geach's objection.[40]

The challenge to the non-descriptivist is to make sense of embeddings of
simple moral sentences, and do so in a way that jibes with our intuitions about
the validity and invalidity of various moral arguments.

Hare (1970), Blackburn (1988), and Gibbard (1990) have all made interesting
and, I think, plausible enough proposals for answering the Geach challenge head-
on by explaining how, in a non-descriptivist view, we can understand the sorts of
embeddings in question. They each take the challenge seriously and try to answer
it. However, some philosophers (e.g., Stoljar [1993] and Horwich [1994]), sympathetic to non-descriptivist views in ethics, employ an evasive tactic in relation to
the Geach problem and attempt to defuse the challenge. They maintain that the
emotivist can help himself to minimalism about truth and, in so doing, does not
face the Geach challenge. Stoljar, for instance, argues that (1) we should recognize
that the basic semantic thesis of emotivism (simple moral sentences lack realist
truth conditions) allows the emotivist to embrace minimalist truth conditions for
such sentences and that (2) the semantic thesis should be sharply distinguished
from its pragmatic thesis, namely, that such sentences are asserted with the primary
purpose of expressing emotion. Presumably, keeping these aspects of emotivism
straight is enough to deflate Geach's challenge. Stoljar writes:

> Geach . . . claims that this pragmatic difference between the premises [in an ar-
> gument like the one about killing mentioned earlier]—this difference in emotive
> meaning—affects the validity of the argument. From the emotivist's point of view,
> however, this is to quite illegitimately blend the pragmatic and the semantic. The

---

40. Geach attributes the basic idea of this objection to Frege. Searle (1969: 136–41) also pressed this
objection.

emotivist can reply that whatever the pragmatic difference between its premises, and however this pragmatic difference is expressed, [the argument] is still valid. For validity is a matter of the truth conditionality of the premises, that is, it is a matter of the *semantic* features of the premises. Moreover, the emotivist can argue, the truth conditionality of the premises is logically distinct from our purpose in asserting them; truth conditionality, that is to say, is logically distinct from the pragmatics of the premises. (Stoljar, 1993: 93)

So, apparently, once it is realized that emotivists, and non-descriptivists generally, can help themselves to minimalism about truth, the embedding problem does not arise.

If Stoljar and Horwich are right that the embedding problem is really a pseudo-problem for the non-descriptivist, then well and good. But this sort of dismissal of the problem is controversial (see later in this section), and it is better to play it safe and provide a sketch of how a non-descriptivist might go about tackling Geach's challenge head-on. What I have to offer here is not a full-blown account of the phenomena of embedded contexts; rather, I will indicate in a rough-and-ready manner how my sort of non-descriptivist might answer the Geach challenge head-on.

If we focus on conditional sentences for the time being, it seems that there are two main things to be done in telling a non-descriptivist story about them. First, one wants to understand something about what one is doing when one asserts such sentences since, as I have been saying, the way to gain some understanding of moral language is by focusing on the point and purposes of moral thought and speech. Second, one would like some assurance that it even makes sense to talk about logical inference and, hence, the validity of moral arguments like the one featured above, if one embraces a non-descriptivist view like mine. Let me deal with these in order.

Consider, then, the conditional, 'If it is wrong to kill, it is wrong to pay someone to kill.' In asserting this sentence, one does not assert its antecedent, just as, in general, one does not assert the antecedent of a conditional statement. However, one does assert the whole conditional sentence, and normally does so from within a morally engaged stance. What we have, then, is the expression of a second-order stance — a stance that expresses commitment to a combination of possible first-order stances. One way to think about the assertoric content of such second-order stances is to focus on their role in deductive arguments, including *modus ponens* arguments. One might, that is, appeal to so-called inference rule explanations of the connectives, according to which connectives, and the statements built out of them, are to be understood in terms of the inference rules for them. Thus, to understand conditional statements, we appeal to their role in argument forms like *modus ponens*. So the idea is that it is partly *constitutive* of the assertoric content of conditional moral statements that they interact with simple moral statements in such a way that anyone who sincerely asserts both premises of a *modus ponens* argument is committed to an overall moral outlook that includes the specific moral stance expressed by the argument's conclusion.

How does this help with the embedding problem? In the case of conditionals, we have a quite general story about how to understand their content, and now we can add that, when embedded, simple moral statements like 'It is wrong to kill' are to be understood in terms of their typical action- and choice-guiding roles. However, when embedded, they are not asserted, and so their typical expressive function is suspended. Thus, in arguments like the one we have been considering, there is no equivocation.

But more needs to be said, since we need to have some assurance that with this mode of non-descriptive assertion we have the basis for a logic in which some moral statements can be legitimately inferred from others. James Dreier (1996) nicely illustrates the need to say more by having us consider an expression, 'hiyo,' which is used to perform the speech act of accosting someone. He points out that we can help ourselves to the inference-rule model of connectives to say something about conditionals that embed simpler sentences using 'hiyo' as a predicate, and so mimic what the non-descriptivist says about the embedding of sentences with moral predicates. Yet we have not really gained illumination of these conditionals since inferences involving the speech act of accosting do not make sense. Thus, according to Dreier:

> We [i.e., non-descriptivists] may announce that material conditionals always me-
> diate inference, and claim victory. We can then say that we have explained what
> the conditionals mean, that the embedded normative sentences still have the same
> function they have when unembedded, for they still express an attitude, only their
> expressive function is (as Hare puts it) encaged. And *of course* the formal logic
> will work out right. But will the idea of an inference actually make sense? Can
> we understand the idea that someone uttering the conditional is committed to
> the consequent on condition that she accepts the antecedent? We need some
> assurance. (Dreier, 1996: 42)

This brings us to the second main task to be performed in responding to the embedding challenge. Can we make sense of the validity and invalidity of arguments involving both embedded and unembedded moral statements? Indeed, as Dreier puts it, can we make sense of inference if we are non-descriptivists?

One way to deal with this problem that takes its inspiration from Hare (1952), is to make use of the logic of imperatives to argue that inference in connection with moral sentences is legitimate for the non-descriptivist. Here is how we might proceed. First, we note that it makes perfect sense to talk about inferences that involve imperatives: from the premises 'Take out all the boxes' (expressing an imperative) and the belief 'This is one of the boxes,' I may legitimately infer the imperative, 'Take this out.' The basis of imperative logic is the notion of satisfaction. Imperatives may be satisfied or not, and what is preserved in valid arguments involving imperatives is satisfaction: if the first premise is satisfied, and the claim expressed in the second premise is true, then the imperative expressed in the conclusion must be satisfied.

Next, we note that even if moral sentences are not equivalent in meaning to imperatives, nevertheless, there is enough similarity between them to be able to use the logic of imperatives to help illuminate certain facets of moral discourse.

After all, in the story I have been telling, moral judgments express a kind of practical commitment and, so, something like satisfaction is appropriate here. If I think that I ought to take out all the boxes, and I believe that this particular object is a box, then it seems pretty clear that I am committed to taking out the object in question. To make sense of this, we could introduce a notion of satisfaction or realization of a moral commitment in a way analogous to what we have in connection with the logic of imperatives, though, on my view, one can legitimately talk about truth being preserved in valid moral arguments. (There are other approaches one might take. Gibbard employs possible worlds semantics to represent the contents of normative statements; Blackburn works with a logic of goal satisfaction.)

So, it would appear that the non-descriptivist can make sense of inference involving moral statements. Moreover, the non-descriptivist can plausibly explain what is wrong with having inconsistent moral beliefs. Beliefs with descriptive content have as their goal correct representation of the world. Two descriptive beliefs that are inconsistent with one another cannot both represent the world. The problem with such inconsistent beliefs is that having them frustrates one of our main cognitive goals. Moral beliefs do not purport to describe; they are involved in reasoned action guidance. The sort of inconsistency involved with moral beliefs can be understood in terms of possibility of action: inconsistent moral beliefs cannot coherently guide our behavior. And, in failing to guide our behavior, they frustrate one of our main practical goals: effective action in the world.

So, all things considered, it would appear that the non-descriptivist can plausibly respond to Geach's challenge. She has a way of making sense of embedded contexts, and she can make sense of inferences involving moral statements.

Of course, this is but a sketch of how to deal with Geach's challenge; much more needs to be said to provide a fully satisfying response. But perhaps enough has been said to accommodate (at least presumptively) the phenomenon of embedded contexts.

Accommodating Matters of Moral Phenomenology

I have noted at least two related phenomena regarding moral experiences: (1) the felt sense of independence and objectivity associated with moral obligations and (2) the sense that we sometimes genuinely observe moral value in the world and that there is such a thing as better and worse moral perception. Let me focus first on the phenomenon of moral observation.

Our moral reactions to what we see in the world are often quite spontaneous. As Gilbert Harman's asserts in his well-known example, "If you round a corner and see a group of young hoodlums pour gasoline on a cat and ignite it, you do not need to *conclude* that what they are doing is wrong; you do not need to figure anything out; you can *see* that it is wrong" (1977: 4). But, as Harman goes on to ask, do you literally see the wrongness of what the hoodlums do, or is your reaction a result of your moral upbringing? It seems to me that an irrealist can perfectly well accommodate such moral experiences by fleshing out a sufficiently robust notion of what it is to have a moral outlook, including the fact that having one involves being responsive to those natural features of our world that are, according to the outlook in question, associated with certain modes of moral evaluation. Having internalized a moral outlook, we are able to respond spontaneously in morally significant ways to what we see going on around us. And our being able to do so does not seem to create a presumption in favor of moral realism.

You may recall that Hume challenged anyone to find some in-the-world property denoted by moral terms. He wrote:

> Take any action allow'd to be vicious: Willful murder, for instance. Examine it in all lights, and see if you can find that matter of fact . . . which you call *vice*. In which-ever way you take it, you only find certain passions, motives, volitions and thoughts. . . . The vice entirely escapes you, as long as you consider the object. You never can find it, till you turn your reflexion into your own breast, and find a sentiment of disapprobation, which arises in you, towards this action. (Hume, 1739: 468–69)

You certainly do not see some property like wrongness in the manner in which you see the sorts of qualities of objects like colors and shapes. But, of course, moral realists would want to insist that moral properties and facts are more like many sorts of scientific properties and facts in that they are complex causal properties and facts, not the sorts of things that are detectable by simple sense perception. In order to detect these more complex moral properties, and thus in order to discern moral facts, one must have a developed moral sensibility, not unlike the way in which certain scientific observations are only available to those who have the proper scientific training. I grant that Hume's remarks may not be sufficient to impugn the legitimacy of there being in-the-world moral properties that we can unmysteriously detect, but here we are concerned with the sort of presumption that moral 'observation' provides in favor of moral realism and against moral irrealism. As I have said, I do not think any of the phenomena to which one might point here truly helps out the realist. It seems to me that both realists and irrealists can fairly accommodate whatever there is to our moral observations.[41]

With regard to having certain affective experiences, like the felt sense that obligations are externally imposed, the irrealist can again appeal to a number of related phenomena that make sense of this feature of moral experience. First, our typical moral judgments have categorical force, and so we do not take them to be mere expressions of taste or mere expressions of what some group thinks about moral matters. And second, we make such judgments in light of certain natural features of the objects of evaluation (or at least in light of our beliefs about those features) — features that are, in the relevant sense, 'external.' These facts about typical moral judgment gives those judgments (at least judgments of obligation) the sort of externally imposed, non-arbitrary 'feel' that we normally experience when we judge that some action is obligatory or forbidden.

---

41. One writer who attempts to argue for moral realism by appealing to moral observation is Werner (1983). But for what I think is a telling response, see Wong, 1986.

No doubt there is much more that could be said about matters of moral phenomenology, especially when it comes to fleshing out my brief remarks. But, all things considered, the sort of moral irrealism I am defending can handle, at least as well as any version of moral realism, various 'objectivist' features of moral phenomenology. If any of my readers feel that my discussion fails to appreciate the real force of the appeal to moral phenomenology in favor of moral realism over moral irrealism, my challenge to them is to make their case. (My following discussion of moral commitment is also relevant to matters of moral phenomenology and helps explain how my view can make sense of the difference between mere matters of taste on the one hand and moral matters on the other.)

Accommodating Our Critical Practices

Item 5 on the list of features to be accommodated states that moral sentences are sometimes true (correctly assertible), and it is unproblematic, on my metaethical view — especially given the contextual semantics that undergirds that view — that indeed some moral sentences are correctly assertible (true). Moreover, it should be clear how my view accommodates the presumption that genuine conflicts in moral belief are possible (item 7). I have already stressed problems with relativistic moral views on this count and how my view avoids relativism. Moral disagreements, according to my brand of irrealism, are disagreements in moral stance. In categorically asserting moral statements, one asserts one's stance over and against the conflicting moral stances of others (including one's hypothetical selves); one's disputants do the same vis-à-vis oneself. This categorical feature of our moral discourse and practice makes possible genuine disagreement in the assertoric content of moral statements uttered by different speakers, and that disagreement, in turn, reflects the underlying disagreement in the moral stances themselves.[42]

Item 8, to the effect that moral thought and discussion is often enough guided by the practice of reason giving, does not seem to be particularly problematic for my view. Part of having a moral outlook, as I have indicated, is learning various patterns of moral reasoning. We sometimes reason deductively from principle to particular case, sometimes inductively from case to case, and so forth. In reasoning in these ways we cite features of, for example, particular actions that, from the point of view of one's own moral stance, is a right-making or wrong-making feature of actions generally, or at least in the case at hand. Again, the irrealist can accommodate the practice of moral reason giving.

We come finally to the presumption that error, even deep moral error, is possible (item 6), which, in the previous chapter, I claimed to be perhaps the

---

42. Disagreements in moral stance bear an obvious family resemblance to what Stevenson calls disagreement in attitude. Stevenson (1944: ch. 1) distinguishes disagreement in attitude from disagreement in belief, and he also maintains that purely moral disagreement involves only the former and not the latter. The view I am defending differs from Stevenson's with regard to moral belief, however. I maintain that moral disputants have genuine moral beliefs that genuinely conflict, but the content of these beliefs, like the content of the corresponding moral statements, is evaluative rather than descriptive.

most difficult for the irrealist to accommodate. So let me begin with the sort of worry that a critic might wish to raise against my view concerning the possibility of moral error.

A critic might claim that there is a tension in my overall metaethical view. On the one hand, I have been stressing the categorical aspect of moral discourse and the fact, that on a minimalist view of the sort I advocate, moral truth talk runs in tandem with first-order moral discourse. As already noted, normally one asserts one's moral views over and against the contrary views of others, including even one's hypothetical selves. This seems to imply that one takes one's current moral views as true *and regards any change in those views as a movement away from what is true.* But, if so, then we really are not able to make good sense of certain modal claims that express the kind of non-dogmatic openness one normally has toward one's current moral views — claims like: 'Some of my current moral beliefs might be mistaken or false' and 'My current view about abortion might be mistaken.' The problem of making sense of such modal claims seems particularly trouble-some for my brand of irrealism since I deny that there are any objective moral properties, relations, or facts to which one might appeal in trying to make sense of such claims. The upshot of this line of objection is that whatever merits my brand of irrealism may possess, it is committed to a distasteful brand of moral dogmatism that does not allow for the possibility of error in moral belief and, correspondingly, does not allow for the possibility of improvement in one's moral outlook. Indeed, on this count, my view may look decidedly worse than the sorts of standard irrealist views mentioned in the previous chapter, since some of those views could at least account for the possibility of a great deal of error in moral judgment and belief.

To respond to this line of objection, I want to focus on a dimension of my overall view that I briefly mentioned earlier, namely, the fact that one can take a moral stance on a particular issue in a non-dogmatic way and likewise have a non-dogmatic attitude toward one's entire moral outlook. Since this non-dogmatic at-titude toward particular moral stances and associated outlook is expressed in the sorts of modal statements just mentioned, what I really need to be able to do is to make sense of such modals without, of course, sacrificing the basic tenets of my irrealism. What I claim is that modal statements expressing the idea that one's moral beliefs might be mistaken involve a sort of speech act that is interestingly complex. One expresses, in typical categorical manner, one's moral stance on some issue (e.g., 'Abortion is not always wrong'), but one also makes explicit in one's overall statement the sort of non-dogmatic respectful manner in which one asserts one's own moral stance ('but I might be mistaken'). So, such modal statements do not serve simply to express one's current moral stance on some issue, but in addition they serve to express a kind of attitude toward one's current outlook, an attitude of openness to the possibility that it might evolve into a different moral outlook as a result of new and persuasive arguments, as well as new experiences. This non-dogmatic, change-receptive attitude is possible, despite the fact that one's present moral outlook operates as one's present moral touchstone. The relevant sort of potential improvement would not be a matter of bringing one's moral outlook into closer approximation to some putative objective moral reality, since my position, after all, is a staunchly irrealist metaphysics of morals. Nor would it be a matter of judging, from within some transcendent moral outlook, that one's present moral outlook is inferior to some other one; there is no such transcendent moral vantage point, according to my position. Rather, it would be a matter of a certain potential kind of evolutionary transition from one's present moral outlook to another one.

One variant of such potential evolutionary change fits the image of Neurath's boat: we make piecemeal revisions over time to some, or perhaps eventually to a great many, of our current moral beliefs. Such local revisions, insofar as they are rational, can be viewed as more or less following the method of reflective equilibrium, in which the changes we make are guided by various coherence-relevant constraints. The fact that the changes are guided by certain constraints and are not haphazard or arbitrary, and that one currently approves morally of employing such methods, is the basis for prospectively viewing such a potential successor-outlook as a possible improvement over one's current moral outlook.

A second, more radical form of revision would involve rather massive global changes in the fundamental assumptions of one's moral outlook about which it is proper to say that one has undergone a moral conversion. Here I am thinking of a moral conversion as involving a discontinuous change in moral belief, one that is not reached by arguments but that involves coming to 'see' things differently.[43] To think of being mistaken about one's current fundamental moral assumptions is to consider what I have been calling the possibility of 'deep' moral error. When one regards such possible discontinuous change not as mere change but as a potential *improvement*, one is envisioning the possibility that one's present moral outlook would be regarded in a particular way from that potential new outlook. The core idea is that the new outlook would include the sense that one has achieved a clearer moral view of situations, not merely a different view. The following remarks by Crispin Wright, in discussing the prospects for a 'minimalist' account of moral discourse (of broadly the sort I am proposing here), are very similar in spirit to the conception of moral error and moral improvement I am recommending:

> It is, so far as I can see, open to minimalism to maintain that the sensibilities on which moral discourse is founded are capable of *progress*—that morals can undergo significant development, and that, in response to our efforts, the story of our moral development can unfold better than it might otherwise have done.
>
> *But*: the minimalist will have to admit that such ideas of progress, or deterioration, are ones for which we can have use only from *within* a committed moral point of view; and that the refinement of which our moral sensibilities are capable can only be a matter of the approaching of a certain equilibrium as appraised by the exercise of those very sensibilities. There will be no defensible analogue of the scientific realist's thought that the real progress of science is measured by the extent to which our theories represent a reality whose nature

---

43. See DePaul, 1993: ch. 1, for a useful discussion of moral conversions and their epistemic import.

owes nothing to our natures or the standards that inform our conception of responsible discourse about it. (Wright, 1992: 200; see also Wright, 1995, and Blackburn, 1980, 1985a, 1996)

In order, then, to make sense of the possibility of moral improvement and avoid the charge of dogmatism, my view recognizes the sort of non-dogmatic speech act associated with modal statements that assert that one might be wrong about matters moral. Such statements express an openness to certain potential kinds of evolutionary alteration in one's moral outlook. This non-dogmatic attitude is associated with various dispositions to make potential changes (even discontinuous changes) in outlook in response to potential persuasive new arguments or sensibility-altering new experiences.

Since the objection to forms of moral irrealism based on the alleged problem of accommodating the possibility of various forms of error in moral judgment is quite important, let us pause for a moment to consider the general form of response to the argument from moral error that I am advocating. The reader with realist proclivities when it comes to moral discourse will not be entirely satisfied here, since I have not told the sort of story that would address a notion of error like the notion operative for the scientific realist or the commonsense realist about ordinary macro-sized objects. The realist critic wants me to tell a story about error that would directly address the question, '*In virtue of what* is a moral sentence mistaken, erroneous, or false?' And, of course, as Wright points out, the sort of irrealist who supports a minimalist treatment of moral discourse is not going to try to tell a story that is a direct response to this sort of question. After all, the question really loads the dice in favor of the realist, since it demands that one tell a story about 'truth makers' for moral discourse — that one indicate some interesting truth conditions (presumably descriptive ones) that make true moral statements true.

I understand moral constructivists as tackling head-on the question posed by the realist, but we saw in chapter 3 where this leads. So instead of tackling the 'in virtue of what?' question on its own terms, I have posed the error challenge in terms of making good sense of certain modal claims. Posing the challenge in this way does not beg any questions: the moral realist will tell a realist story all about truth makers in making sense of such modals; the moral irrealist will follow the route I have suggested. So an important part of my response to the argument from moral error is to cast the challenge in a way that does not beg questions at the outset against moral irrealism. (We already saw in chapter 3 how questions are apt to be begged here in connection with Sturgeon's objections to Blackburn.)

Finally, I want to return to a theme mentioned at the end of chapter 3 — the immanence/transcendence theme found in Putnam's views about critical notions like rationality and truth. My proposed way of handling issues about moral error and moral progress perhaps captures a sense in which the notion of truth here is both immanent and also transcendent. Truth is immanent because truth ascriptions to moral statements are morally engaged. As explained earlier in this chapter, to assert that some moral statement is true is (normally) to do so from one's own moral outlook, whereby one uses one's outlook as a touchstone of moral truth.

But, as I also noted, the fact that truth ascriptions are in this way immanent does not commit us to some form of relativism. Far from it. Our notion of truth is also transcendent in that it cannot be identified with one's current moral outlook (or the moral statements that somehow follow from that outlook together with relevant facts). It cannot be identified with any other outlook, either (this was the main lesson of the argument from moral error). When it comes to moral assertions, we make them from some particular view (there is no moral view from nowhere), but we can also judge that we might be wrong, thus envisioning the possibility of moral progress and an improved moral outlook.

Moral Commitment

I suppose that, at this point, a critic might voice concerns about earnest moral commitment and the fact that people take morality very seriously. In fact, a critic might want to point out that my list of objective pretensions is seriously incomplete and that we should add the following:

> 9. The manner in which we assert moral claims and engage in moral discussion reflects a kind of importance and associated commitment we have with regard to our moral outlook in general and to the specific moral stances we take. We take our moral views seriously.

The worry about moral error and moral progress just considered was a worry that I cast in terms of my view's being dogmatic. The current worry that arises from my response to the dogmatism charge is focused on the suspicion that if my view is not dogmatic in its implications, then it yields an overly casual attitude toward our moral views and hence is really not compatible with 9.

One way in which the worry might be pressed is by calling attention to the possibility of there being two incompatible moral outlooks, each of which being internally consistent. If we envision the proponents of these opposing outlooks engaging in discussion and debate, we recognize that there arises a kind of symmetry here: each party can explain and justify his own particular moral stances on various issues from within his own outlook. Putnam gives an example of the sort of symmetry in question:

> One of my colleagues is a well-known advocate of the view that all government spending on 'welfare' is morally impermissible. On his view, even the public school system is morally wrong. If the public school system were abolished, along with the compulsory education law (which, I believe, he also regards as an impermissible government interference with individual liberty), then the poorer families could not afford to send their children to school and would opt for letting the children grow up illiterate; but this, on his view, is a problem to be solved by private charity. If people would not be charitable enough to prevent mass illiteracy (or mass starvation of old people, etc.) that is very bad, but it does not legitimize government action.
>
> In *my* view, *his* fundamental premises—the absoluteness of the right to property, for example—are counterintuitive and not supported by sufficient argument. On *his* view I am in the grip of a 'paternalistic' philosophy which he

regards as insensitive to individual rights. This is an extreme disagreement, and it is a disagreement in 'political philosophy' rather than merely a 'political disagreement.' (Putnam, 1981: 164)

Reflection on this scenario might prompt the following objection. Since in my view there is no metaphysical backing that 'validates' one or the other of the competing moral outlooks, people should not take their moral views as seriously as they do. After all, if there are not any objective in-the-world moral facts that determine who is right—Putnam or Nozick—should not one conclude that matters moral are like matters of mere taste? People do not normally express their tastes in a committed, serious manner in which they assert their opinions about taste over and against the conflicting tastes of others. In stressing the categorical nature of moral discourse, I have stressed the strong, committed manner in which one normally asserts one's moral views, but does not my irrealism undermine this moral commitment that I have expressed in presumption 9?

It is indeed part of my metaethical position that there is no metaphysical backing to moral discourse that would adjudicate the sorts of deep moral disagreements represented by cases of moral symmetry. But I deny that this fact about my view should undermine serious moral commitment. Why *should* it? The argument under discussion rests on a normative premise to the effect that if one is my kind of irrealist, then one ought not (or, at least, need not) take one's moral views seriously. What the critic needs to do is offer a persuasive *moral* argument for this premise, and I doubt there is one. Meanwhile, I am certainly prepared to argue morally against the premise, and in support of fully serious moral commitment, despite the lack of metaphysical backing for it. Here is one such argument: It is morally important to have modes of discourse that promote the broad purpose of guiding behavior so that humans might coordinate their efforts in ways that will tend to promote survival and well-being; moral discourse fulfills this function, but only insofar as people employ it categorically and with full seriousness; therefore, people ought to take their moral views seriously, even in the absence of metaphysical backing.

To this, the critic might reply as follows: 'Granted, it is morally important to have a moral mode of discourse in civilized society and to employ it seriously, insofar as one's moral views conform with everyone else's. But how, in the absence of metaphysical backing, can one morally justify privileging one's own moral views over the *competing* moral views of others?' Here again I would answer with a moral argument: namely, that deferential tolerance of competing moral views can often have morally unacceptable consequences. To underscore this point, consider what Putnam has to say in contemplating his dispute with Nozick:

> What happens in such disagreements? When they are intelligently conducted on both sides, sometimes all that can happen is that one sensitively diagnoses and delineates the source of the disagreement. . . . But what of the fundamentals on which one cannot *agree*? It would be quite dishonest to pretend that one thinks there are no better and worse reasons and views *here*. I don't think it is just a matter of *taste* whether one thinks that the obligation of the community to treat its members with compassion takes precedence over property rights; nor does my co-disputant. Each of us regards the other as lacking, at this level, a certain kind

of sensitivity and perception. To be perfectly honest, there is in each of us something akin to *contempt*, not for the other's *mind*—for we each have the highest
regard for each other's minds—nor for the other as a *person*—, for I have more
respect for my colleague's honesty, integrity, kindness, etc., than I do for that of
many people who agree with my 'liberal' political views—but for a certain complex of emotions and judgments in the other. . . . 'Respectful contempt' may
sound almost *nasty* (especially if one confuses it with contemptuous respect,
which is something quite different). And it *would* be nasty if the 'contempt' were
for the other as a person, and not just for one complex of feelings and judgments
in him. But it is a far more honest attitude than *false relativism*; that is, the
pretense that there is no giving reasons, or such a thing as better or worse reasons
on a subject, when one really does feel that one view is reasonable and the other
is irrational. (Punam, 1981: 164–66)

Putnam's attitude of moral seriousness in light of the symmetry phenomenon
seems right on target. Although being non-dogmatic does require remaining open
to the possibility of having one's moral standpoint altered by persuasive arguments
or formative experiences, it does not require passive deference toward competing
moral standpoints. Even in the absence of metaphysical backing, moral stance
taking is, and should be, respectfully assertive, and one's attitude toward moral
standpoints seriously at odds with one's own is, and should be, as Putnam puts it,
respectful contempt. Those who deny this are making a *moral* claim, and they
bear the burden of providing a good moral argument for it.

Explaining the Objective Pretensions

The third step in internal accommodation is to explain, from within my metaethical perspective why the discourse should embody those pretensions listed.
Many of the features (1–4) reflect the categorical aspect of moral stance taking and
discourse that we have already mentioned, and feature 8 reflects the fact that such
judgments (and the statements that express them) are *reasoned* evaluations. The
core idea, you may recall, is that the manner in which we judge morally (take a
moral stance), as well as moral statements expressing one's judgment, are such
that we take those moral statements to be binding on anyone (including our hypothetical selves), and thus we assert our moral stance over and against the conflicting moral stances of others. And this manner of categorical assertion is manifested in the first three sorts of ordinary presumptions embedded in moral
discourse. So the question here is how we can explain the categorical aspect of
moral stance taking—a question whose answer adverts to the general point and
purpose of moral discourse and practice.

In short, my answer to the question is this: if the whole point and purpose of
moral practice is action guidance in ways that promote survival-enhancing coordinative behavior, it makes sense that we engage in assertion that is categorical in
pressing our moral views. Moreover, the typical manner in which one takes a
moral stance and categorically asserts one's moral views is *respectful* in the sense
that (typically) one is prepared to give reasons for her moral convictions and ex-
pects others to do likewise. Failure to be respectful of the views of others, by

dogmatically clinging to whatever moral views one currently holds, often cuts off the possibility of fruitful exchange and mutual agreement on matters of deep importance. Failure to express one's views categorically over and against competing views of others manifests a kind of timidity that tends not to contribute to the fruitful pursuit of mutual rational agreement on matters of deep importance, and also tends not to advance the fundamental point and purpose of moral discourse as a social practice: namely, guiding behavior so that humans might coordinate their efforts toward survival and well-being. (Thus, one would fully expect that moral discourse exhibit features summarized in items 6 and 9.) So, in general, it is no surprise, then, that moral discourse should have the characteristics it does, manifested in various ways—including the sorts of objective pretensions we find embedded in moral discourse.

I think the same general sorts of remarks apply in connection with the pretensions associated with moral phenomenology. The feeling that moral requirements are non-arbitrarily imposed on oneself, for instance, goes hand in glove with the other pretensions having to do with the categorical aspects of moral discourse.

What is of particular interest is how we might explain any differences between the objective pretensions involved in moral discourse with any that are involved with other forms of evaluative discourse, including stances reflecting self-interest, epistemic stances, and aesthetic stances, to name a few. In the section on external accommodation, I already hinted at how an explanation might proceed. As noted, one interesting feature of moral discourse and practice is that moral requirements apparently 'trump' all competing non-moral requirements.[44] We need not take a side on how exactly to understand this claim or whether it is true or false, but we can explain why the categorical feature of moral practice and its associated objective pretensions are thought to have this trumping feature. If the point and purpose of moral discourse is to guide behavior so that humans might coordinate their efforts in ways that would tend to promote survival and well-being, one would expect that the categorical force of moral requirements would be felt to have the sort of strength that many people actually feel.

A Final Comment about Accommodation

I have been trying to show how my version of irrealism can accommodate the so-called objective pretensions of moral discourse. Some readers with realist leanings are probably going to think that, despite what I have done, my attempts at accommodation really miss something that is there in moral discourse and that requires (or at least strongly suggests) a realist interpretation of that discourse. (In particular, the realist might point to how I handled the issue of moral error.) So the realist

---

44. The thesis that morality is somehow overriding is the subject of some controversy. Perhaps a sufficiently qualified statement of the thesis is true. In this connection, it may be important to distinguish between the claim that moral *considerations* override all non-moral considerations in cases of conflict from the claim that all moral *requirements* override conflicting non-moral considerations and requirements. For a discussion of the importance of this distinction, see McNaughton, 1988: 114–15.

might react to my view as being a kind of error theory, perhaps not as radical as Mackie's, but an error theory nonetheless. Before I conclude this chapter, let me address this concern.

The issue concerns how we should understand the various commitments (in particular, the metaphysical commitments) of moral discourse. Graham and Horgan (1994) set forth a broadly empirical conception of philosophical inquiry into concepts (and the semantics of terms that express concepts) that they call 'ideological inquiry.' They distinguish between *austere* and *opulent* interpretations of concepts, particularly those of perennial philosophical interest (concepts of knowledge, free will, and the like). An opulent interpretation of a concept (or mode of discourse involving some concept) would be one that construes the concept and associated mode of discourse as involving strong metaphysical (and perhaps other) commitments. An austere interpretation would be one that does not impute such commitments to the concepts and discourse in question. Of course, the opulent/austere distinction is one of degree, but we can ignore this for now and just focus on the issue of the metaphysical presumptions (if any) that are implicated in ordinary moral concepts and associated moral discourse. More significantly for our purposes, Graham and Horgan defend the following (empirical) claim:

> [I]n general, the correct ideological account of any given philosophically interesting concept will fall toward the austere end of the associated range of competing ideological construals. I.e., . . . key concepts in philosophical problems will normally be relatively austere ideologically; the commitments of statements employing these concepts will normally be no more opulent than is required by the purposes for which the concepts are employed in thought, in discourse, and in social practices and institutions. (Graham and Horgan, 1994: 232)

If this hypothesis about philosophically interesting concepts is correct, then the default view should be that fundamental moral concepts and associated moral discourse should be construed in a metaphysically austere way and not in the way that the moral realist proposes to construe it.

Moreover, there is an argument (a version of what Graham and Horgan call 'the argument from ideological conservatism') that can be used to defend an austere reading of moral discourse. It is as follows. Moral discourse and moral notions employed in such discourse play an indispensable role in human life that would survive rejection of the idea that there are objective moral facts that moral statements purport to describe or report. (Recall that after arguing in chapter 1 of his 1977 book that affirmative moral statements are systematically false because they involve rather opulent metaphysical assumptions about moral facts and properties, Mackie goes on to set out a normative moral theory; he does not opt for an eliminativist position.) If we assume that human concepts in general evolve in a broadly pragmatic way, and are thus not likely to have application conditions that are more opulent than is required by the purposes they serve, then the fact that moral discourse would survive the rejection of objective moral facts and properties is some reason to suppose that such discourse does not have built into it opulent metaphysical assumptions. I grant that this argument is not, by any means, decisive, but it provides some reason to construe moral discourse austerely.

Moreover, the idea that ordinary moral discourse requires (or at least strongly suggests) an opulent construal has seemed to many philosophers quite suspicious. I have mentioned a number of times that Mackie claimed that ordinary folks competent with the proper use of moral terms and concepts tacitly, if not explicitly, purport to ascribe objectively prescriptive moral properties to objects of evaluation when they say such things as 'Apartheid is wrong.' This is to read some pretty heavy-duty metaphysical baggage into ordinary moral discourse — it is to construe moral concepts opulently. But, as Hare points out, although it may be true that many moral philosophers, asking themselves what moral language means, have developed semantic views according to which moral sentences purport to describe objective moral facts, still "from the fact that philosophers have thought this it does not in the least follow that ordinary people have thought it" (Hare, 1981: 80). Again, David Copp (1991), in his review of Brink's book, makes a similar point. Copp claims that Brink is reading too much into ordinary moral discourse when he assumes that moral realism is the natural rendering of that discourse (at least in terms of its metaphysical commitments). Copp claims that moral discourse presupposes some form of objectivity, not necessarily the kind the realist seeks. As I have said, my general opinion on such matters is that typically the default interpretation of many concepts of philosophical interest should be the austere interpretation, so I would not even go as far as Copp in interpreting moral discourse.

I have been talking about the pretensions in question as being 'objective' pretensions, but I do not think (and hope I have persuasively argued) that we need to construe moral discourse as a mode of objective discourse (according to how I understand talk of objective discourse from within the perspective of contextual semantics). So, for instance, I do not believe I was cheating in the section on moral error when I construed the challenge in terms of making sense of certain modal claims; I just do not think that ordinary moral discourse presupposes that ethics is objective *in the sense that realism and some versions of constructivism attempt to capture*. Or, if you like, I could distinguish between 'thin' and 'thick' senses in which a mode of discourse might display objective pretensions. Any discourse that displays the grammatical and logical trappings of genuine assertion can be said to manifest objective pretensions in a thin sense of the term, because its doing so is compatible with an irrealist interpretation of the discourse. Any discourse that displays not only objective pretensions in this thin sense, but also involves more metaphysically robust presumptions, could be said to manifest objective pretensions in a thick sense. Wright (1992) gives the example of humor discourse that manifests thin objective pretensions but not thick ones.

Using the thin/thick terminology, I can phrase what I have been saying this way. The moral realist notes the various objective pretensions of ordinary moral discourse, reads those pretensions thickly, and then claims that moral realism best accommodates the pretensions in question. But once it is noted that a mode of discourse can manifest objective pretensions in the thin sense (and not also in the thick sense), then the door is open for telling a semantic (and associated metaphysical) story about the discourse that fully respects the pretensions but does not involve robust metaphysical commitments. This is what I have been doing for moral discourse.

So, I read moral discourse as involving only thin objective pretensions and thus I propose that we read moral discourse as involving moral concepts that should be interpreted austerely, not opulently. However, I confess, apart from the considerations I have been rehearsing, I do not know how to decisively argue for this claim.

VII. Conclusion

In this chapter, I have put forth a version of moral irrealism that (I claim) can satisfy reasonably well the demands of internal and external accommodation. After surveying the prospects for developing a non-reductive version of moral irrealism, I proceeded to sketch a particular view about language/world relations that Horgan and I call 'contextual semantics.' Within this general semantic orientation, I was able to distinguish between descriptivist semantic views about moral discourse and non-descriptivist views. If one thinks (as I do) that both major variants of descriptivist views—that is, both realism and relativism—are mistaken, then one needs to explore the options open to non-descriptivism. Thus, my aim has been to articulate and defend a non-descriptivist story about moral language that fully recognizes the fact that typical moral discourse has as its main point or purpose the guidance of choice and action, but at the same time is genuinely assertoric. In my view—assertoric non-descriptivism—moral sentences are typically used to make genuine assertions: evaluative assertions. They are hence truth-apt.

As I have explained, my story about moral discourse takes a page from traditional non-descriptivists (the influence of some of Hare's views, particularly his early views, is obviously present). However, to make room for my view, I have rejected the assumption that all genuinely assertive discourse is descriptive discourse, and I have argued that certain projects, like the project of philosophical analysis (as it has been traditionally conceived) should be rejected (or, at least we need not feel constrained to tell a philosophical story about moral discourse that engages in this sort of project). With the rudiments of my view on the table, I finally moved to questions about accommodation and argued that my assertoric non-descriptivism satisfies reasonably well both external and internal accommodation demands.

Again, since defending a metaethical theory is partly a matter of showing that it beats out the competition, and since in this book I have not discussed all of the competitors to my view, I cannot claim to have fully shown that the view I have defended really is superior to all other prevailing views. But beginning in chapter 2 and continuing in chapters 3 and 4, I have tried to expose the shortcomings of some of the most plausible competitors to my view and develop an alternative. My hope is that I have at least carved out a stable and interesting metaethical position worthy of discussion and debate. However, what I have been able to accomplish is but a sketch of a position—not something fully worked out. There are many difficult issues that my view (and any metaethical view) engages: issues about truth, assertion, belief, commitment, motivation, and evaluation, just to mention some. Much more work would be required on such topics in order to have a fully satisfactory philosophical view about moral discourse, work that is yet to be done in filling out the project I have started.[45]

To complete my metaethical story, then, I turn to matters of moral epistemology in the next chapter.

45. See Horgan and Timmons, forthcoming b, for more discussion on the parts of the general view being defended here.

Moral Justification in Context

At the foundation of well-founded belief lies belief that is not founded.[1]

Wittgenstein

In this final chapter, I turn from questions about the metaphysics and associated semantics of moral discourse to issues relating to moral epistemology. 'Moral epistemology' is sometimes used to refer to the whole field of metaethics,[2] but here I use it more narrowly to refer to that area of metaethics that is concerned with philosophical questions about the epistemic appraisal of moral statements and moral beliefs. I am primarily interested in the justification of moral belief, though I shall have some things to say about moral knowledge as well. In particular, I want to focus on questions about the structure of justified moral belief. Traditionally, foundationalism and coherentism have represented the two main alternative views about the structure of justified belief generally, and of moral belief in particular. But I think there is reason to be doubtful of the plausibility of both of these alternative views (in all of their varieties), and I want to propose instead a contextualist moral epistemology—a view that claims (in the spirit of the Wittgenstein quote) that justified belief is ultimately based on beliefs that are not, themselves, justified.

Before I consider questions about the epistemology of moral belief, I spend the first five sections of this chapter dealing with important preliminary matters. I begin in §I by distinguishing questions about the epistemology of moral belief from questions about the epistemology of moral theory acceptance. Then, because epistemological contextualism is perhaps less familiar in ethics than are other epistemological views, but also because there is a variety of so-called contextualist themes and theses that have been featured in recent epistemological debate, I devote §II to sorting and clarifying the most important of them, focusing, in par-

---

1. Wittgenstein (1969: 33).
2. One can understand why 'moral epistemology' has been used in this broad way in light of the tendency, particularly during the days of analytic metaethics, to take questions about justifying or proving ethical principles to be the most pressing in metaethics. See ch. 1.

ticular, on the thesis of structural contextualism, which will be of primary interest in our examination of moral belief. In §III, I explain that ascriptions of rationality and justification that will be featured in my work involve certain contextually variable parameters, and I explain what those parameters are. Then, in §IV, I set forth the rudiments of a specific notion of doxastic appraisal—a notion of *epistemic responsibility*—that will be the focus of my thinking about the justification of moral belief. After having clarified epistemological contextualism and the specific notion of epistemic appraisal I wish to discuss in connection with moral belief, I return in §V to the thesis of structural contextualism, in order to clarify what that thesis involves. After doing all of this preliminary work, I turn in §VI to the issue of the doxastic justification of moral belief and sketch a contextualist story about the structure of such belief. After the basic story is presented, I briefly remind the reader in §VII of the project of accommodation by which we are to measure the success of an epistemology of moral belief, and then I turn to the project of arguing that my contextualist story satisfies both internal and external accommodation constraints and that it does a better job of it than foundationalist and coherentist rivals. In §VIII, I make some remarks about the nature and possibility of moral knowledge, and §IX contains my concluding thoughts.

I. The Epistemology of Moral Belief and of Moral Theory Acceptance

It is important for present purposes to distinguish questions about the epistemology of moral belief from questions about the epistemology of moral theory acceptance. Let me begin with the epistemology of moral belief.

Questions about the epistemology of belief, in general, concern the conditions under which an individual's beliefs are justified. In contemporary jargon, the term *doxastic justification* is used to refer to the sort of justification predicated of an individual's beliefs, and so questions about the epistemology of belief are questions about the doxastic justification of individuals' beliefs. Epistemologists typically distinguish between doxastic justification and what is called *propositional justification*. Propositional justification is concerned with questions about what sorts of propositions would serve to justify in the sense of *proving, demonstrating, showing true*, or in some sense *validating* some other proposition or set of propositions.[3] In short, questions about propositional justification concern abstract evidential relations among propositions.

One reason for noting this distinction between justification that is predicated of beliefs and justification that is predicated of propositions is that talk of *beliefs' being justified* is ambiguous. In claiming that a certain belief is justified for some

---

3. Actually, we should distinguish between *objective* conceptions of propositional justification that have to do with what propositions objectively serve to prove, demonstrate, and so on some other proposition(s) and *non-objective* conceptions of this notion that do not presuppose an external, objective point of view, but rather view connections among propositions from some non-objective perspective. I discuss this matter of perspectives in §III.

person S, we may or may not mean to imply that S, in fact, holds the belief at some time t. Consider, first, cases in which an individual does not hold a certain belief. For instance, suppose that Jane has a number of beliefs that, in fact, provide excellent evidence for believing that Holmes committed the murder. But suppose also that it would take some reflection, which Jane has not done, in order for her to put two and two together and come to the conclusion that Holmes committed the murder. If, at t, Jane fails to believe that Holmes is the murderer, we can still say of Jane that the belief that Holmes is the murderer is justified for her. Here, what we are doing is predicating justification of a *belief type* — not of a *belief token*. Since belief types are individuated by their propositional contents — same propositional content, same belief type — we can understand this sort of justification as having primarily to do with the propositional contents of beliefs and, thus, having essentially to do with propositional justification. In cases like the one just described, in which the individual has beliefs whose propositional content justifies some proposition that she does not at the time believe, we can say that the belief (type) is propositionally justified for her. So, returning to the case of Jane, we can say of the belief (type) that Holmes is the murderer that this belief or, more precisely, its propositional content, is propositionally justified for her. Although issues concerning propositional justification are obviously important to epistemology — think of the project of devising an inductive logic — epistemologists also want to inquire into those conditions under which an individual's beliefs are justified wherein the implication is that the individual does possess the beliefs under scrutiny. Here the concern has to do with the justification of *token beliefs*, and the sort of justification at issue here is called *doxastic justification*.

There is disagreement among epistemologists about the correct relation between propositional and doxastic justification, but one plausible view of their relation is that the notion of propositional justification is more fundamental than the notion of doxastic justification, and thus the former notion can be used to define the latter. The basic idea is that being doxastically justified in believing some proposition p at some time t entails: (1) believing that p at t, (2) being propositionally justified in believing p at t, and (3) basing one's belief on the evidence that serves to propositionally justify p.[4] For the time being, we need not enter into debates about which of the notions of justification is more basic (assuming one is) or how exactly either of these notions can be defined. For present purposes, I am going to assume that being doxastically justified in believing some proposition entails that one is also propositionally justified in the belief in question. Given this assumption, I want to consider the bearing of the epistemology of moral theory acceptance on questions about the epistemology of moral belief.

A great deal of metaethical work has been devoted to questions about the propositional justification of moral statements — of answering the question of how (if at all) we can justify in the sense of proving, demonstrating, showing true, or validating moral statements. Since moral principles are at the heart of normative

---

4. For an excellent discussion of the distinction in question and of this issue of priority, see Kvanvig, 1992: ch. 4.

moral theories—a normative moral theory is understood to be composed of a set of moral principles—the attempts of philosophers to prove or demonstrate moral statements are concerned with questions of *theory acceptance* in ethics.

Here is a short list of recent philosophers and their projects that mainly concern questions of theory acceptance in ethics: Marcus Singer's 1961 attempt to prove the generalization argument principle, based on an appeal to the logic of moral discourse; Gewirth's 1978 attempt to prove the so-called principle of generic consistency, based on claims about the nature of rational action; Donagan's 1977 attempt to prove a Kantian respect for persons principle, based on claims about the nature of practical reason and the nature of moral agents; Brandt's 1979 attempt to justify a kind of rule utilitarian principle, based largely on empirical considerations from cognitive psychology; Rawls's 1971 attempt to defend his two principles of justice, based on considerations of overall coherence broadly conceived; and Hare's 1981 attempt to justify a utilitarian moral principle (or at least a broadly utilitarian method of moral thinking), based on the logic of ethical concepts.

What I wish to argue is that we should not assume that engaging in moral theory acceptance is required for an individual's being doxastically justified in holding particular moral beliefs. Let me first show why someone might think otherwise, and then explain my position.

The claim that an individual must have evidence of the sort that would propositionally justify moral principles if he is to be doxastically justified in holding particular moral beliefs would seem to depend on three assumptions. (1) For an individual to be doxastically justified in holding some particular moral belief about the moral quality of some concrete action, person, or institution, the moral proposition believed must be propositionally justified for the individual. (2) The propositional justification of a particular moral proposition depends (at least in part) on general moral propositions (moral principles).[5] (3) The propositional justification of general moral propositions depends on still other propositions. The implication of these assumptions taken jointly is the claim under scrutiny.

I am willing to grant that one way in which an individual might come to be doxastically justified in holding some particular moral belief is by learning, for example, Gewirth's proof for the principle of generic consistency and then using that principle to derive other, more specific moral propositions that one then comes to believe as a result of one's derivation. But my point is that we should not assume without good argument that being able to prove, show true, or validate some moral principle is necessary for coming to have justified moral beliefs about particular matters. As mentioned above, I am willing to grant assumption 1, but the other two assumptions are not obvious and would require some argument. So-called particularists in ethics hold that the justification of particular moral beliefs does not derive, even in part, from moral principles. Rather, according to the particularist, it is the other way around: justified moral principles receive their justification inductively from justified particular moral propositions. So assumption

---

5. See Griffiths, 1967, for a concise and representative argument for this claim.

2 is not obvious; nor is 3. Some defenders of epistemological intuitionism in ethics like W. D. Ross[6] would apparently accept 1 and 2 but reject 3, arguing that general moral principles can be intuitively known and, hence, known or justifiably believed without being evidentially based on other propositions. According to Ross and other intuitionists, such principles are self-evidently true and can be immediately grasped by a kind of intellectual intuition.

Notice that if one were to insist that being doxastically justified in holding particular moral beliefs requires that one have the sort of evidence for general moral beliefs featured in a particular epistemology of moral theory acceptance, then the result would be that most ordinary people fail to be justified in any of the moral beliefs they in fact hold. It is safe to say that very few people have ever studied the epistemology of moral theory acceptance, and it is also safe to say that very few people accept moral principles on the basis of the sorts of considerations featured in the arguments that philosophers offer for their favored moral principles. Of course, it may be that in order to be justified in believing that certain forms of moral skepticism are false, one must be able to do the sort of thing that moral epistemologists do when they set forth justifications of fundamental moral principles. But again, we should not assume without good argument that in order for an individual to be doxastically justified in holding a particular moral belief, she must also be justified in holding certain epistemological views about moral skepticism. (Or so I will argue in §§IV and V.) I am making an issue of this because, in developing a story about the epistemology of moral belief, I am not going to engage in the epistemology of moral theory acceptance.

II. Epistemological Contextualism

Epistemological contextualism, which has its roots in the writings of pragmatists like Peirce and Dewey and in the later writings of Wittgenstein, is often characterized as an alternative to the more traditional approaches in analytic epistemology. In opposition to both foundationalist and coherentist views about the structure of justification and knowledge, the contextualist claims (in the spirit of the Wittgenstein epigraph) that justified belief is ultimately based on beliefs that are not themselves justified. But other so-called contextualist claims, not having to do with structural issues, have gained increasing recognition and discussion by analytic epistemologists in recent years. One such claim (vaguely expressed) is that possession of such epistemic goods as knowledge and justification depends importantly on one's circumstances or 'context,' including, in particular, certain facts about one's social group. Unfortunately, 'contextualism' and talk of justification and knowledge being sensitive to context is used to cover a variety of themes and theses—some of them fairly uncontroversial, others quite controversial. The first order of business, then, is to sort out and clarify the most important contextualist themes.

6. I have in mind Ross's 1930 generalist view and not his 1939 view, in which he apparently gave up generalism in favor of particularism. See Ross, 1930 and 1939.

I am going to distinguish among what I will call *circumstantial contextualism*, *normative contextualism*, and *structural contextualism*. The first two theses are roughly analogous to familiar relativist views in ethics. The third represents a response to the infamous regress of justification problem and, so, rivals foundationalist and coherentist responses to that problem. However, there is a fourth contextualist thesis now in circulation that represents a version of semantic contextualism about correct epistemic ascriptions. In the previous chapter (§II), I presented what I called the thesis of semantic contextualism (CT), according to which, roughly, the truth values of sentences that constitute some discourse can vary from one context to another, owing to semantic norms governing those sentences. The idea (roughly) was that the key terms operative in some discourse may involve contextually variable parameters as part of their meaning. In epistemology, philosophers like Unger (1986), DeRose (1991, 1992), and S. Cohen (1986, 1987) have proposed analyses of epistemic concepts that make correct ascriptions of epistemic claims sensitive to matters that may vary from context to context. (Later in this chapter, I construe Foley's recent proposal for understanding ascriptions of rationality in a contextualist manner.) Since I have already discussed the thesis of semantic contextualism and I am going to propose (following Foley) a way of understanding ascriptions of epistemic justification that represents a version of semantic contextualism, I will not spend time in this section presenting and illustrating this thesis with regard to epistemic discourse.

Circumstantial Contextualism

One contextualist theme in recent epistemology (applied to the issue of justification) I will call 'circumstantial contextualism,' and it can be expressed this way:

> CC   Whether one has knowledge of or, indeed, justifiedly believes some proposition is partly dependent on certain facts about oneself and certain facts about one's environment.

It is uncontroversial that whether one knows or justifiedly believes some proposition depends on 'internal' (psychological) features of one's circumstances such as evidence one has (whether in the form of other beliefs or certain experiential states), and whether one possesses any undermining evidence, and so forth. But many epistemologists have called attention to certain 'external' features of one's circumstances that may affect the epistemic status of one's beliefs. Goldman's 1976 case of the papier-mâché barns is a well-known example. In that example, one has excellent perceptual evidence that there is a barn in the field, though one is unaware of the fact that the surrounding countryside is populated with papier-mâché barn facsimiles. In this case, one apparently fails to know that there is a barn in the field because of facts about one's immediate environment that represent relevant evidence one does not possess. This is a case in which knowledge is sensitive to one's *physical* environment.

The idea that knowledge and justification depend on facts about one's *social* environment—that epistemic appraisal has a 'social dimension'—has been of particular interest in recent epistemology. According to Stewart Cohen and Ernest

Sosa, there is an interesting connection between certain social facts—facts about one's community—and requirements related to the use of an individual's cognitive faculties that nicely illustrates how knowledge and justification can depend on one's social circumstances.

Cohen's contextualism emerges from his study of the conditions under which evidence one *does* possess undermines one's knowledge. He argues, first, that whether defeaters one possesses undermine one's knowledge of a particular proposition depends on the reasoning abilities of a normal member of a relevant social group and whether, in particular, the fact that some evidence one possesses is a defeater would be obvious to normal members of that group. Thus, in Cohen's view, one component of knowledge is determined by certain psychological facts about society. But which social group or society serves as the basis for judging the obviousness of defeaters? Cohen's own proposal is that "the standards in effect in a particular context are determined by the normal reasoning powers of the attributor's social group" (1986: 579). In light of this social dimension of knowledge, Cohen proposes that ascriptions (and denials) of knowledge are best construed as indexical or context sensitive: the set of intersubjective standards of obviousness that apply in ascriptions of knowledge can vary from context to context, depending on which group counts as the attributor group. The idea that knowledge involves a socially determined level of reasoning ability perhaps also applies to the cognitive faculties of memory and perception.[7]

Not only might epistemic requirements for dealing with counterevidence be gauged by certain social facts having to do with cognitive abilities, but other social factors may play a role in knowledge. Sosa, for example, argues that the extent to which members of one's social group possess some bit of information affects one's knowledge. If, for example, most everyone in one's community has information that defeats some true proposition that one otherwise has excellent evidence for believing, then arguably one fails to know. According to Sosa, reflection on such cases makes it "plausible to conclude that knowledge has a further 'social aspect,' that it cannot depend on one's missing or blinking what is generally known" (1974; reprinted in Sosa, 1991: 27; see also Sosa, 1988).

Normative Contextualism

Another contextualist claim is that justification (rationality, knowledge) depends on, or is relative to, the social practices and norms of communities of inquirers. Some contextualists like to point out how our knowledge-gathering practices are social in nature and importantly tethered to the epistemic practices and norms of

---

7. For instance, it is at least initially plausible to suppose that whether a long-forgotten defeater d of evidence e—evidence that otherwise is adequate for justifiably believing some true proposition p and on the basis of which one currently believes p—undermines one's knowledge of p depends on facts about the normal memory abilities of one's social group. If no normal member of one's group would remember d, then the fact that one used to possess a defeater of e does not undermine one's knowledge of p. See S. Cohen, 1987, for a discussion of the cases of memory and perception.

the members of our group (however 'our group' is to be understood). Construed as a descriptive claim about our epistemic evaluations, this claim is perhaps (with some qualifications) correct since it amounts to the claim that, *as a matter of fact,* our epistemic evaluations are typically made on the basis of ('relative to') the practices and norms generally accepted and used by the community of inquirers to which we belong. However, the contextualists I have in mind intend the claim normatively, that is, as a claim about the conditions under which one knows, or is justified in holding, some belief. If we let 'context' refer to some community of inquirers and the relevant evaluative practices and norms they share, then we can formulate a working characterization of normative contextualism this way:

> NC   A person S is justified at time t in believing some proposition p in context C if, and only if, S's holding p at t conforms to the relevant set of epistemic practices and norms operative in C.

Depending on how we specify the context, we get various versions of the generic view. Here is a formulation of what we might call 'egocentric normative contextualism':

> ENC   A person S is justified at time t in believing some proposition p if, and only if, holding p at t conforms to those epistemic norms accepted by S at t that govern the class of beliefs of which p is a member.

If we replace talk of epistemic norms accepted by S at a particular time with talk of norms accepted by S's society, we get a version of sociocentric normative contextualism. Both egocentric and sociocentric versions of NC represent epistemological analogues of ethical relativism about moral truth.

I am calling particular attention to the idea that there is a social dimension to epistemic evaluation because the idea that knowledge and justification depend on one's social group can be taken in two ways. First, as we saw with Cohen and Sosa, it can be taken as a feature (or set of features) of one's circumstances that is relevant for epistemic appraisal. But, as just explained, it can also be taken as the idea that knowledge and justification *are relative to the epistemic standards of one's social group or community,* so that whether one has knowledge or is justified in believing some proposition depends on whether or not one's belief conforms to the epistemic norms of one's group. The thesis of circumstantial contextualism, then, should not be confused with this sort of relativist claim.

In ethics, it is standard to distinguish between circumstantial (situational, environmental) relativism and ethical relativism. The former is analogous to what I am calling circumstantial contextualism and is often expressed as the general thesis that the rightness and wrongness of particular actions, practices, and so forth depend in part on facts about the agent's circumstances. So, for instance, whether it would be wrong for an onlooker to refrain from jumping into the deep end in an effort to save a drowning child depends (in part) on facts about that person and, in particular, on whether he can swim. Ethical relativism, by contrast, represents a normative theory that, in perhaps its most common variety, relativizes moral truth to the moral standards of groups: the moral standards of a group (together with relevant factual information) determine which particular moral statements are true for members of that group. The epistemological analog of ethical relativism is what I am calling normative contextualism. My point here is that just as we should not confuse circumstantial relativism in ethics with normative ethical relativism, so we should not interpret the circumstantial contextualism of Cohen and Sosa as equivalent to, or entailing, normative contextualism.[8]

I should mention at this point that it is not my intention to defend some version of normative contextualism over and against non-relativist epistemological views.[9] As we shall see later in this chapter, it may be legitimate in some contexts and for some purposes to evaluate the epistemic status of an individual's beliefs relative to the epistemic norms of that person's community. But there are contexts in which we intend to make non-relativized, categorical epistemic evaluations, even if, in doing so, we obviously employ epistemic norms that we accept.

Structural Contextualism

In the last two decades, work in analytic epistemology has been dominated by structural issues relating to justification and knowledge. What is called contextualism is often taken to be a thesis about the *structure of justification* intended as one response to the infamous *regress of justification* problem. That problem gets generated when we notice that some of the propositions that we (presumably) justifiedly believe owe their justification to other beliefs that we accept—such beliefs forming an epistemic chain. But unless these further, justifying beliefs in the chain are themselves justified, we only seem to have what we might call *conditional justification*: the original link in the chain is justified *if* the further links are justified. But then how are we to understand the nature of unconditional justification? The standard options mentioned in the literature[10] in response to this question are these:

> *Epistemic foundationalism*: the regress stops with a certain class of beliefs that are somehow non-inferentially justified in the sense of not owing their justification to other beliefs. These regress-stopping foundational beliefs provide the epistemic basis for inferentially justified beliefs.[11]
>
> *Epistemic coherentism*: there are no regress stoppers; rather, justification is a matter of the interconnectedness of a finite set of beliefs.

---

8. Sosa (1991: 10, n. 14) is explicit about this. So we can think of Cohen and Sosa as proposing what they take to be universally correct epistemic principles that imply that the truth of certain specific epistemic appraisals is dependent on facts (including social facts) about one's circumstances.

9. Some critics either simply equate epistemological contextualism with what I am calling normative contextualism and criticize it for being a version of relativism, or they think that what I call structural contextualism entails, or at least ends up being, a form of normative contextualism. For examples, see Moser, 1985: ch. 2, and Haack, 1993: ch. 9.

10. See Alston, 1976a and 1976b, reprinted in Alston, 1989.

11. Inferential justification must be distinguished from the process of psychologically inferring one proposition from another. Moreover, such justification does not require any such process of inferring. See BonJour, 1985: 19–20, for a discussion of this point.

Epistemic ex nihilism: the regress ends with beliefs that are unjustified. This option is typically associated with Wittgenstein's remark about well-founded beliefs resting ultimately on beliefs that are not well founded. If one construes this option as attempting to provide a non-skeptical structural story about justified beliefs, then the idea seems to be that somehow justification is generated ex nihilo from beliefs that are not themselves justified.

Epistemic infinitism: the chain of justifying beliefs continues infinitely. Again, if one construes this option as attempting to provide a non-skeptical story about the structure of justified belief, then the idea is that infinite epistemic chains ground the justification of members of the chain.

The so-called regress argument is an argument-by-elimination for foundationalism. Epistemic infinitism is usually just written off, and so is the ex nihilist option. Coherentism is taken more seriously, and so the debate over structural issues tends to be presented as a face-off between foundationalism and coherentism. Actually, the ex nihilist option, when taken seriously, is developed in such a way as to make the label 'contextualism'[12] appropriate, though, strictly speaking, epistemological contextualists do not seem to embrace the ex nihilist position as I have stated it. What this suggests is that the set of four recognized responses to the regress problem is too restrictive; we need more options, especially in light of problems (so I would argue) with all of the standards.[13] The view I am going to call contextualism bears some kinship to foundationalism, but it also attempts to run with the spirit, if not the letter, of Wittgenstein's remark. So the view is not any sort of something-from-nothing ex nihilist view. Here, then, is an addition to the menu:

Epistemic contextualism: the regress of justification ends with beliefs that, in a given context, are not in need of justification.[14]

So what I am calling structural contextualism may be informally characterized as follows:

SC   Regresses of justification may legitimately terminate with beliefs, which, in the context in question, *are not in need of justification*. Let us call these latter beliefs *contextually basic beliefs*.

This admittedly rough formulation at best only conveys the basic structural picture of justification that the contextualist favors. For one thing, talk about 'con-

---

12. See Moser, 1985: ch. 2, for a general discussion of epistemic contextualism.

13. Susan Haack (1993) is someone else who is not satisfied with the standard options and develops a hybrid view that she calls 'foundherentism.'

14. Foundationalists sometimes talk about foundational beliefs not being in need of justification, by which they mean that such beliefs, because they are, for example, 'self-justifying,' do not need to receive justification from other beliefs. The structural contextualist, however, means something more radical here, namely, there are certain beliefs that, in certain contexts at least, do not need to have the sort of epistemic status of enjoying positive evidential support (either inherently or from other beliefs and experiences) in order to play a regress-stopping role in the structure of justified belief. For recent defenses of structural contextualism with regard to empirical belief, see Annis, 1978; Williams, 1980; and Henderson, 1994.

text' is left unexplained, as is talk about beliefs not needing justification. I will save the task of clarifying these crucial notions until I have first clarified (in the next section) the specific notion of epistemic appraisal operative in my thinking.

However, before going on, note that SC, as formulated, does not *require* that all inferentially justified beliefs be based on contextually basic beliefs; rather, it allows that regresses *may* legitimately terminate with such beliefs. This means that the contextualist can allow (strictly speaking) that an individual's justified beliefs may exhibit either a foundationalist structure or a coherentist structure, though, of course, the contextualist will deny any claim by the foundationalist that having foundational beliefs (as the foundationalist conceives of them) is *necessary* for having any justified beliefs at all, and she will likewise deny any claim by the coherentist that having a coherent set of beliefs is *necessary* for having any justified beliefs at all. What the contextualist claims is that the contextualist picture represents a realistic and largely correct picture of the actual structure of an ordinary individual's justified beliefs. And this, indeed, is what I plan to argue in connection with moral belief.

But before proceeding further, I want to deal with an objection that would dismiss the view as an obvious non-starter. The objection, I suspect, is guided by a certain assumption that plays a powerful role in some philosophers' thinking about justification. The assumption is that justification is a property that a belief can have and that it can pass on to other beliefs under the right conditions. One metaphor that captures this assumption is the idea that a belief can have an 'epistemic charge' that it can pass along to other beliefs under the right conditions. If this assumption is correct, then contextualism is clearly not a serious alternative to either foundationalism or coherentism since the idea that inferentially justified beliefs can receive an epistemic charge from beliefs that do not have such a charge to pass on seems utterly mysterious. Guided by this sort of metaphor about justification, contextualism appears to be immediately ruled out as a serious contender.

However, instead of allowing our theorizing about structural questions to be guided by certain assumptions and metaphors, I propose that we first observe our actual epistemic practices and see how they operate. In particular, I propose that we examine the sorts of requirements they impose concerning such matters as gathering evidence, checking for counterpossibilities to what we believe, and so forth. My suspicion is that this sort of investigation will reveal that there is something right and important about the thesis of structural contextualism. Of course, many recent contextualists have, in fact, wanted to insist that we should pursue epistemology by reflecting on our actual epistemic practices and have often proposed accounts of the very notion of justification itself that makes being justified a social matter. I am thinking here of the so-called challenge-response model of justification, according to which being justified in holding some belief is a matter of having successfully responded to all challenges to that belief coming from some specified objector group.[15] Contextualism is supposed to look quite plausible in

15. Both Annis (1978) and Wellman (1971) are advocates of this model. Talk of 'objector group' is found in Annis (1978), who characterizes this group as verifically motivated inquirers who, given some specific 'issue context' in which a question arises about whether a particular person is justified in

light of this conception about the nature of justification since, presumably, one's relevant objector group will not challenge everything one believes at once. And so some beliefs are allowed to play a regress-halting role in the process of justifying one's beliefs to the group in question.

But from the assumption that we should take our actual epistemic practices seriously in developing a normative epistemology, we need not—and, I would argue, should not—accept the challenge-response model of justification. For one thing, the model really only seems to fit those cases in which we are interested in testing some controversial or novel hypothesis or idea and in which the appropriate thing to do is to submit it to some relevant community of inquirers.[16] But also the distinction between showing justification—something one does by rehearsing reasons and so forth—and simply being justified, which does not require explicit reasons or proof, seems worth making, and the challenge-response model does not seem to give us a very plausible story about merely being justified.

Annis argues that the challenge-response model does not conflate being justified with showing justification: "[T]he theory offered does not ignore the distinction between being justified and showing that one is justified. It is not required of S that he be able to state the standards of justification and demonstrate that he satisfies them. What is required is that he be able to meet real objections" (1978; reprinted in Moser, 1986: 210). But talk of showing justification is ambiguous. It can refer to the process of justifying a claim by producing considerations in support of it. Let us call this 'simple showing.' But often talk of showing justification is taken to refer to the process of *showing that one is justified in believing some proposition.* Let us call this 'iterative showing.' Simple showing requires only that I state my reasons; iterative showing requires that I do this and much more: I have to be able to justify a claim about the epistemic status of my situation, which requires that I do some epistemology. Clearly, to be justified in holding some (non-epistemic) claim does not require that one be able to justify a correlated epistemic claim. And this is the point that Annis is making. But being justified also does not seem to require that one engage in the process of simple showing either. I might be justified in holding many of the beliefs I hold even if I have never rehearsed those reasons to myself or really paid any attention to them.

So my brand of epistemological contextualism does not depend on the challenge-response model of justification. Instead, for our purposes, it will be useful to think about being justified as a matter of conforming to a relevant set of epistemic norms, and so our main focus should be on the content of those norms and what they require of believers. We begin by examining our actual epistemic

---

believing some proposition, are qualified to raise objections to the person's putative justified belief in the proposition. The function of the objector group is thus to determine which sorts of counterpossibilities to the belief under scrutiny one must be able to eliminate if one really is justified in holding that belief.

16. Brown (1988) apparently endorses this model of justification (rationality); at least, he claims that regresses of justification stop with assumptions and beliefs that go unchallenged. It is significant that Brown's views about rationality are guided by questions about justifying or rationally accepting scientific beliefs—just the sort of context in which it is crucial to publicly submit one's hypotheses, theories, and experiments to the scientific community.

practices and how they work. Of particular interest is whether one is permitted to hold beliefs—beliefs that can play an epistemic role in providing a justificatory basis for other beliefs—even if one does not have reasons or grounds for those justifying beliefs. If the answer is 'yes,' and if one can mount some sort of defense of the norms that permit such beliefs, then structural contextualism, as I understand that doctrine, will have been vindicated.

To conclude, we should recognize three general contextualist theses. I take the general thesis of circumstantial contextualism to be fairly uncontroversial, though epistemologists may disagree over the sorts of circumstantial factors that affect the epistemic status of an individual's beliefs. As we shall see, the moral epistemology that I proceed to defend stresses the importance of one's goals, as well as one's social circumstances in coming to have justified moral beliefs, and these claims cause dispute. Normative contextualism (i.e., epistemological relativism) is quite controversial and should not be confused with circumstantial or structural contextualism. The contextualist moral epistemology I plan to defend is not intended as a version of normative contextualism. Finally, I do plan to defend a version of structural contextualism about justified moral belief that will occupy most of my attention in what follows.

In order to set the stage for the version of epistemological contextualism that I propose to defend, I first need to discuss the notion of epistemic appraisal with which I am concerned.

III. Some Parameters of Epistemic Appraisal:
Goals, Perspectives, and Resources

As explained earlier in §I, my primary interest in this chapter is with questions about the justification of moral belief and not with questions of moral theory acceptance. But before launching into a discussion about the epistemology of moral belief, I need to say something about the notion of justification (rationality) at work in my thinking. As I will explain, ascriptions of justification (and rationality) are best interpreted as involving certain contextually variable parameters. Making these matters clear will allow me to clarify the specific notion of doxastic appraisal that interests me, namely, the notion (or *a* notion) of *being epistemically responsible* in what one believes.

In contemporary epistemology, there is a variety of accounts of doxastic justification. Here, I am interested in a notion that captures the idea of a believer's being *epistemically responsible* in what he believes. To clarify the notion I have in mind, I intend to adopt a certain way of understanding epistemic ascriptions involving notions like rationality and justification that has been proposed by Richard Foley.

In *Working without a Net*, Foley (1993) points out that ascriptions of rationality should be understood to involve (at least tacitly) reference to (1) a goal or set of goals, (2) a perspective, and (3) a set of resources. According to Foley, claims about the rationality of an individual's belief that make all of these parameters explicit have this form:

It is rational for you to believe _____ because you have resources R and because from perspective P it seems that, given R, believing _____ is an effective way to satisfy goal G.[17]

I am primarily interested in a notion of doxastic justification that can be usefully understood in terms of Foley's schema for rational belief. Whether the notion I am interested in is identical to Foley's notion of rational belief, I leave open. What I propose, then, following Foley, is to think of ascriptions of doxastic justification as involving certain contextually variable parameters.[18] Let me briefly comment on the parameters in question, and then I will be able to characterize more precisely the notion of doxastic justification featured in my thinking.

Goals

In the generic conception of justification with which we are working, evaluations that employ talk of justification normally invoke, either explicitly or tacitly, some goal or goals to be promoted in having justified beliefs. But there are various goals one might have, relative to which a belief might be properly characterized as justified. And here it is standard to distinguish properly epistemic goals, such as having true beliefs and avoiding false ones, from various non-epistemic goals such as survival. Correspondingly, we distinguish between epistemic justification and non-epistemic justification. So, for instance, if we fix on the goal of having true beliefs and avoiding false ones — and from now on, let me refer simply to the goal of having true beliefs — then whether a particular belief is justified depends on whether or not it (in some sense) leads to or points to what is true. By contrast, if we fix on some pragmatic goal, like survival, then whether having a belief is justified depends on how that belief contributes to the goal in question. If, for example, believing that I can tread water for at least an hour will be instrumental in my being able to muster the strength and determination to do so, thereby allowing the rescue boat to reach my position in the middle of Lake Michigan, then having such a belief will be pragmatically justified for me. It will be pragmatically justified, relative to the goal of survival, even if I have no good evidence supporting the claim that I am able to tread water for at least an hour (or indeed, even if I possess evidence that the claim is false).[19]

17. Quoted from Foley, 1993: 34.
18. There are two ways one might understand the manner in which epistemic evaluations are context sensitive. One might hold that reference to these parameters is part of the very *content* of such evaluations, or one might hold that although not part of their content, epistemic ascriptions are governed by the contextual parameters in question. Construing such evaluations in the second way amounts, of course, to a version of semantic contextualism, which is how I prefer to interpret Foley's remarks about ascriptions of rationality (even if he does not). For some discussion of the difference between these two readings of the semantics of epistemic terms, see Sosa, 1988.
19. There are other non-epistemic goals besides survival, relative to which beliefs may be, in some non-epistemic sense, justified. Sinnott-Armstrong (1996) illustrates how a belief can be prudentially justified with the example of someone offering me a million dollars if I believe that there are aardvarks on Mars. BonJour (1985: 6) illustrates how a belief can be morally justified with the example of

So, epistemic justification is conceptually linked somehow to the goal of truth. This, anyway, is how the notion is typically glossed in recent epistemological literature. But the issue of proper epistemic goals turns out to be fairly complex and somewhat controversial. One source of controversy concerns the claim, often made by epistemologists, that the goal of truth is the sole epistemic summum bonum, as opposed to there being a plurality of goals. The complexity has to do with exactly how to understand the conceptual connection between justified belief and truth. This is not the place to launch into a full discussion of these matters, but it will be worthwhile for our purposes to say a little about both issues.

Although some epistemologists describe the notion of epistemic justification (and related notions) in terms of a single goal of having a system of beliefs in which there is a high percentage of true beliefs and a low percentage of false ones, many epistemologists do recognize that, strictly speaking, this is not our only cognitive goal as inquirers. We also want a system of beliefs that is, in some sense, interesting and presents as comprehensive a view of our world as possible.[20] But recently, Michael DePaul has argued that we ought to recognize a more complex goal associated with epistemic evaluation: "This goal involves at least four key components: true belief, warranted belief, rational belief, and beliefs with a coherent, systematic structure" (1993: 66).[21] Here is not the place to detail DePaul's reasons for wanting to conceive epistemic evaluation as involving a complex summum bonum, though it is worth noting that viewing epistemic evaluation the way DePaul does has an important bearing on evaluating methods of inquiry. If the goal of such inquiry is complex, and if it is possible that a method of inquiry might bring us some, but not all, of the goods that make up that complex goal, then evaluating such methods will also be a complex matter. For the most part, I wish to remain as neutral as possible about disputes concerning how exactly to understand the goal associated with epistemic evaluation. On all accounts, the goal of truth is at least part of the epistemic summum bonum, and I plan simply to conduct my discussion in terms this goal.

However, there are various ways to understand the connection between justification and truth. I have expressed the connection vaguely in terms of justified beliefs leading to or pointing to the truth.[22] It is now standard to distinguish between 'objectivist' and 'subjectivist' interpretations of the connection in question.[23]

---

someone who is justified out of loyalty in believing that a friend is innocent of some crime of which he has been accused.

20. See, for example, Alston, 1989: 83–84, and Foley, 1993: ch.1.

21. DePaul does not employ the term 'justified' or its cognates, but rather prefers 'rational' and its cognates. He distinguishes warrant from rationality, construing the former as that necessary component in knowledge that, barring Gettier worries, elevates true belief to knowledge. Rational belief is not necessary for knowledge, but rather has to do with an individual's beliefs' conforming to that individual's 'true' epistemic standards (i.e., the standards she would avow upon suitable reflection).

22. Audi (1993b: 301) puts it in terms of epistemic justification *counting (in some way) toward truth*.

23. See DePaul, 1993: ch.2. Audi (1993b: ch. 10) distinguishes between 'ontological' and 'teleological' interpretations of the connection between epistemic justification and truth, which seems to be roughly quivalent to the objective/subjective distinction that I am describing here.

According to an objectivist interpretation, a person (at a particular time) is episte-mically justified in believing some proposition only if that person believes the proposition in such a way that his belief is objectively likely to be true. In the subjectivist interpretation, a person (at a particular time) is epistemically justified in believing some proposition only if having that belief apparently promotes the goal of having true beliefs (wherein we are letting talk of what 'apparently' pro-motes the goal in question to be something judged from that person's perspective). These characterizations are rough, but we need not refine them here. Moreover, if we insist on classifying interpretations of the connection in terms of the objec-tive/subjective distinction, then I suspect we will have to recognize a variety of possible, more specific interpretations of the connection that fall under these head-ings. There may also be hybrid interpretations of the connection, according to which there are both objective and subjective elements in a species of epistemic appraisal. Later, in §IV, I will say more about how I propose to explain the link between concepts of epistemic appraisal and the notion of truth; here, I am just calling attention to various ways of conceiving the link between truth and justifi-cation.

Perspectives

Ascriptions of justification presuppose some perspective. Foley characterizes a per-spective as a set of beliefs or body of opinion possessed by some actual or imaginary individual or group. Presumably, this body of opinion includes epistemic beliefs that reflect a set of epistemic standards that figure in the perspective in question.[24] There are various epistemic perspectives from which epistemic evaluations pro-ceed. Some of the more familiar include: the subjective or egocentric perspective of an individual agent, the intersubjective or sociocentric perspective of some community, the perspective of some group of experts, and the perspective of an ideally knowledgeable observer. The fact that justification talk is perspectival often goes unnoticed since we often do not make explicit the perspective from which justification evaluations are made. But the various perspectives operative in our ascriptions of justification and rationality simply reflect various evaluative interests and purposes we have. For instance, when we are interested in understanding some belief held by a particular person (perhaps oneself) on some past occasion, and when in retrospect that belief seems pretty clearly mistaken, we often are interested in how things looked to the agent on the occasion in question (at least if we are disposed to view the person charitably). Here, it is natural to invoke an egocentric perspective and ask whether, given the agent's epistemic perspective at the time, she was justified in holding the belief in question.

---

24. This matter is not so clear in Foley. Judging from some perspective involves judging relative to the epistemic standards that partially characterize the perspective in question. Although not explicit about the matter, Foley seems to think that the epistemic standards of a perspective are represented as beliefs (perspectives, after all, are defined as sets of beliefs). I suspect that a better way to construe a perspective would not be simply in terms of beliefs, but we need not get into this issue here.

However, for certain purposes, we might be interested in evaluating an individual relative to the epistemic standards prevalent in her community, in which case our evaluation would involve a sociocentric perspective. Still, in other contexts, we might have an interest in questions about justification apart from some subjective or intersubjective perspective, and the perspective of an ideally knowledgeable spectator—a way of capturing an objective perspective—is appropriate. The most important lesson to learn from all this talk about perspectives is nicely expressed by Foley: "There is no single perspective that is adequate for understanding the entire range of our judgments of rationality. We make such judgments for a variety of purposes and in a variety of contexts, and the kind of judgment we are inclined to make varies with these purposes and contexts" (1993: 14).

Resources

Finally, justifiedly believing some proposition depends in part on one's resources—that is, on those cognitive faculties and methods available for use, as well as such psychological states as one's beliefs, experiences, and memories. Just which resources are relevant for certain sorts of epistemic evaluation is one important issue separating reliabilists, foundationalists, and coherentists. Reliabilist stories take one's cognitive processes and methods as crucially involved in having justified beliefs; foundationalist stories typically feature a range of psychological states including, especially, one's experiences as well as one's beliefs; while coherentist stories typically restrict one's resources to beliefs.

Obviously, there is much more to be said about these contextually variable parameters of doxastic justification, and an indication of how they operate will receive some refinement as we proceed. But having sketched a proposal for understanding ascriptions of doxastic justification, I am now in a position to indicate a bit more precisely the focus of my thinking about moral justification.

First, I am interested in the *epistemic* appraisal of individuals' *beliefs*—doxastic epistemic appraisal—wherein a primary goal (if not *the* primary goal) involved in such appraisal is the possession of true beliefs and the avoiding of false ones. Second, I am particularly interested in the sort of epistemic appraisal that is operative in our everyday, common epistemic appraisals of individuals. The sort of appraisal I have in mind concerns questions about how one might be *epistemically responsible* in the beliefs one holds. One illuminating way of evaluating the epistemic responsibility of an agent is to invoke the perspective of what we might call an 'epistemically responsible agent' similar to the idea of the 'reasonable person' standard from Anglo-American law. The idea is to use this model as a foundation for investigating the basic epistemic norms (and general epistemic sensibility) that we normally do and should use in evaluating the epistemic status of moral belief. Finally, the resources implicated in epistemic appraisals from this perspective are simply those possessed by epistemically responsible agents, which, as we shall see shortly, are simply those cognitive capacities characteristic of 'normal' individuals.

There are two crucial features that this model must have if it is going to serve in this role. First, if it is to have any sort of normative bite, and thus be useful as a measure of a person's being epistemically responsible in the beliefs he holds, then it must take on the character of an idealization. The epistemically responsible agent is one whose epistemic activities serve as a norm for our epistemic activities: we *ought* to conform to those norms characteristic of the responsible agent. Second, given our interest in characterizing a notion of epistemic justification that is applicable to human beings, we want a notion of epistemic responsibility that is not overly idealized. In short, we want a model of epistemic responsibility that represents a 'realistic ideal.' With these constraints in mind, let me now proceed to sketch (part of) a model of epistemic responsibility.

IV. Epistemic Responsibility

Broadly speaking, being epistemically responsible has to do with such activities as: (1) gathering evidence, (2) considering and dealing with counterpossibilities, and (3) dealing with internal conflicts of belief. We normally criticize agents whose beliefs are not based on adequate evidence, who have not checked out relevant counterpossibilities to what they believe, and who fail to eliminate certain conflicts of belief. To be epistemically responsible in what one believes, one must not fall below certain standards or norms governing these activities. What do the norms require? More specifically: How much evidence is enough to have a justified belief? Which counterpossibilities is one epistemically required to check? Which conflicts of belief must one eliminate? Since we are interested in the perspective of the responsible epistemic agent, these are questions about the most general epistemic norms characteristic of this representative agent.

Limitations of space do not permit a full treatment of these matters here, but we can provide a sufficiently rich characterization of a model epistemically responsible agent by focusing primarily on those epistemic responsibilities and associated norms that have to do with checking counterpossibilities. (Responsibilities and associated norms for gathering evidence and eliminating internal inconsistencies will be touched upon along the way.)[25] In addition to sketching a partial account of epistemic responsibility, which I argue comports nicely with our commonsense epistemic appraisals, I will briefly consider the project of justifying the sorts of epistemic norms featured in the account. Here, questions about the connection between conforming to the relevant norms and truth come to the fore.

In considering the issue of responsibility for checking counterpossibilities, there are three questions we must consider. (1) What is the basic epistemic norm for checking counterpossibilities that the responsible agent would employ? (2) What is the rationale for having a norm that demands a certain level of responsibility for counterpossibility checking? (3) Since, as we shall see, what I am calling the 'basic norm' is quite general, how can it be made more precise and hence serve as a useful requirement for responsible belief? Let us address these in order.

Responsibility for checking counterpossibilities to propositions we currently believe (or propositions we are considering) can range from very strict require-

---

25. Actually, responsibilities that have to do with gathering evidence and with eliminating inconsistencies seem, for the most part, to derive from responsibilities to deal with relevant counterpossibilities.

ments corresponding to a norm that would require persons to check all logically possible counterpossibilities (including the sorts of fanciful skeptical scenarios devised by philosophers), to very lax requirements for which, in the limit, there would be a complete freedom from doing any checking at all. In between the extremes is a range of possible norms requiring more or less of an agent. There is a fairly convincing argument for thinking that an in-between norm that would require that agents check some but not all counterpossibilities is correct. The argument, to be found in Cherniak (1986) is based on the claim that in a society in which information is not homogeneously distributed (some individuals, because of their circumstances, are in a better position to know particular things than are others), conveying useful information is one of the main purposes of language. The argument then proceeds by way of exhaustion of the three options under consideration:

> (1) On the one hand, utterers cannot be free of all demands to check and eliminate counterpossibilities to their claims, because the claims would then be without value for conveying information. . . . (2) On the other hand, if utterers are held to a perfect standard and are required to eliminate all counterpossibilities, including "Cartesian" ones that are presently regarded as extraordinarily unlikely, no one can ever actually make a satisfactory unchallenged assertion. . . . The whole assertion-making enterprise thus becomes unusable and again worthless. (3) Hence, the only possibly useful option is a standard of some, but not perfect, care. (Cherniak, 1986: 105)

Of course, a basic norm requiring that we check and eliminate some but not all counterpossibilities is worthless unless we have some way of specifying which counterpossibilities must be checked if one is to be epistemically responsible. In other words, we need to make what I am calling our basic norm governing responsibility for checking counterpossibilities more precise. A first step in doing so is to consider some representative proposals.

According to a radically internalist or psychologistic standard, one is responsible for checking all (and only) those counterpossibilities to some belief or claim that in fact occur to one at the time of entertaining the belief or making the claim. However, this internalist standard is both too strong and too weak. To see why, let us consider a simple example. John's wife asks him to make sure that the house keys are in their usual place on the refrigerator door, hanging from a magnetic hook. From across the kitchen, John sees some keys bound by a simple wire band from which they hang on the refrigerator door. Is he justified on the basis of his present visual evidence in believing that the house keys are in their usual place? Suppose that just yesterday John gave his young daughter, Tina, a bunch of old keys, bound by a simple wire ring that cannot be distinguished from the set of house keys unless one takes a good look. In addition, suppose that Tina often plays in the kitchen, likes to get a stool and play with all of the magnets on the refrigerator door that is used to display her drawings, and so forth. In other words, John, were he to think of it, has some beliefs that should prompt him in this situation to rule out the possibility that somehow the old set of look-alike keys is now hanging on the refrigerator. His failure to do so is basis for fair criticism. According to the internalist standard, were John simply to fail to think of this possibility, owing to sloppiness or whatever, then it is not a relevant possibility that he is responsible for checking. So the proposal is too weak. It is also too strong, because if John just happens to think of some wild and crazy alternative—say, that he is really looking at a hologram of a kitchen refrigerator, or countless other logically possible scenarios that would defeat his current visual evidence—he is not being irresponsible if he ignores these possibilities since (we are supposing) he has no real reason for thinking that they apply in this case.[26] So the sort of radical internalist proposal under consideration will not do.

According to an externalist proposal, one is responsible for checking all and only those counterpossibilities that are objectively likely to now obtain. Since it is not objectively likely (let us suppose) that John is looking at a hologram, he is not required to consider and then check this counterpossibility. Moreover, since Tina's activities make it fairly objectively likely that the wrong set of keys is now hanging from the refrigerator, John is required to take a closer look. So this proposal appears to be an improvement over the internalist proposal. However, again, this proposal is both too strong and too weak. Suppose that instead of giving the old keys to Tina, she had found a set of look-alike keys in an empty lot behind their house (something neither John nor his wife knew anything about) and she had been playing in the kitchen with both sets of keys, as before. It is objectively likely that the keys now on the refrigerator are not the house keys, but we would not want to criticize John for his failure to consider this counterpossibility, since all of this information was outside his knowledge and thus we would not expect him to propose to himself this very specific alternative. The externalist proposal is too strong, but it is also too weak. Suppose that in fact Tina had not been playing with a look-alike set of keys, that no such set was anywhere nearby, but that John had reasons to believe that Tina had a set of look-alike keys that she was recently playing with in the kitchen. Surely he would be irresponsible, given what he has to go on, to fail to consider and then check this possibility. But in the current proposal, he is not required to do so since it is not objectively likely. The externalist proposal will not do either.

A proposal that squares with our epistemic judgments about these cases is an 'in-between' proposal—a modest internalist proposal—that requires (roughly) that we check all and only those counterpossibilities whose seriousness is implied by our current belief set. In the case in which John has recently given the look-alike keys to Tina, and also in the case in which he falsely believes that Tina has been playing with the keys, his current beliefs do imply that the look-alike-keys alternative is a serious possibility. He ought to look more closely. In the case in which he is totally oblivious to the look-alike-keys alternative, he is not required to consider this possibility, even if in fact it is objectively likely. Something like the following modest internalist standard, if not this exact standard, seems right.

---

26. This is not to say that there are not contexts in which such unusual scenarios might become relevant given various goals and purposes. For more on this, see §V.

ER   A person S is epistemically responsible in believing some proposition p at
time t only if S checks all of those counterpossibilities whose seriousness is indicated by S's background beliefs at t.[27]

This is a start, but it will not do as it stands. For one thing, insofar as the
epistemically responsible agent is a projection of normal human beings with normal cognitive powers, ER is too strong—it fails to take into consideration normal
human powers of, for example, inference and memory. Moreover, it ignores those
counterpossibilities whose seriousness is implied by information we *ought* to be
aware of, even if we lack the information in question. Let us proceed to refine
ER in light of these remarks.

In some respects, our model epistemic agent represents an idealization of actual
human epistemic practice. So, for instance, our model does idealize away from certain factors that would interfere with or distort the judgment of our epistemically responsible agent. First, the epistemically responsible agent is presumed to always conform her beliefs to the relevant set of epistemic norms, just as in the law, the
reasonable person "is not to be identified with any ordinary individual who might
occasionally do unreasonable things; he is a prudent and careful person, who is always up to standard" (Keeton et al., 1984: 175). Second, in characterizing the activities of our model agent, we ignore drunkenness, being drugged, being tired, being
distracted, and other such inhibiting factors that would impair the normal judgment
of a normal person. Third, our model agent is free from the sorts of pressing emergency situations that would interfere with her focusing and reflecting adequately on
some proposition or belief whose epistemic status is in question.

However, in other respects, we want our imaginary agent to reflect normal
human abilities. Just as in the law, in which the representative reasonable person
is expected to have cognitive capacities that are 'normal' for human beings, our
model of a representative epistemic agent should be similarly constituted. We can
begin by noting that there are all sorts of deductive inferences that are completely
unfeasible (because of their complexity) for normal human beings to perform, and
similarly for non-deductive inferences. If some such inferences are impossible for
normal humans to make or are, in some looser sense, unfeasible, then we should
not hold people responsible for counterpossibilities that would require that they
make unfeasible inferences from their current belief set. We do expect people to
make inferences from their current belief set that are humanly feasible—feasible
for normal human beings. And here is where empirical considerations yielding
theories of deductive and non-deductive *feasibility*, as Cherniak (1986: ch. 2) calls
them, or theories of *obviousness*, as S. Cohen (1986, 1987) calls them, come into
play in helping to set acceptable standards of epistemic care for checking counterpossibilities. Moreover, in setting the level of epistemic responsibility for dealing
with counterevidence, we expect individuals to be able to recall relevant information from memory, though again, we do not hold people to standards of mem-

27. Talk of 'counterpossibilities whose seriousness is indicated by S's background beliefs' needs clarification. But here I will have to rely on the reader's intuitive understanding of this talk.

ory recall that exceed what is feasible for normal human beings. Theories of feasible inference and feasible memory, then, also help to set levels of epistemic responsibility appropriate for normal human beings.

For convenience, let us use the expression 'obvious counterpossibilities' to refer to those counterpossibilities a normal human being with normal cognitive powers could be expected to recognize. Thus, our original proposal should be revised so that we are required to check some but not all of those counterpossibilities implied by what we believe, where limits on counterpossibility checking are partly determined by our empirical views about 'normal' cognitive capacities.

However, there is more to our understanding of epistemic responsibility for dealing with counterpossibilities. That is, merely checking all of those obvious counterpossibilities whose seriousness is implied by one's current belief set does not mean that one is being epistemically responsible, since (1) one might simply lack certain general information that anyone can be expected to know or (2) be negligent in acquiring evidence that bears on some specific issue or claim. (Here is one place in which responsibilities concerning the gathering of evidence characteristic of the epistemically responsible agent come into play.) With regard to general information one ought to have, there are certain things anyone is expected to know, for which we rely, in particular, on such social phenomena as common experience (e.g., fire burns; water will drown; and countless other bits of information); widely shared educational experiences (e.g., elementary facts about history, physical science, and so forth); and information gathered more informally, such as through the media. Again, this general knowledge requirement is reflected in the doctrine of the reasonable person: "there is a minimum standard of knowledge, based upon what is common to the community" (Keeton et al., 1984: 184) that the reasonable person possesses and thus ordinary agents ought to possess.

With regard to quite special information bearing specifically on some claim or belief, again, what is common to a community normally helps determine the extent of one's responsibility for being aware of that information. A slightly modified example from Austin (1961: 84) makes the point clear. If I look out my window and see what I take to be a goldfinch in my front yard, ordinarily I would be justified in believing that there is a goldfinch there. But suppose that stuffed toy goldfinches have become all the rage with children in my neighborhood and everyone is talking about it, though I have been oblivious to this fact. Nothing that I currently believe implies that there is a decent chance that the goldfinch I am looking at is a toy; however, I am subject to fair epistemic criticism since I should have known about the fad. Of course, sometimes information that I ought to acquire is something that is indicated by the beliefs I currently hold, but in this case, the information one ought to have is information possessed by folks in one's immediate community. Thus, as Sosa (1974, 1988) and others have argued, we are normally held responsible for information representing counterpossibilities that is generally known in our community—ignorance of such information is typically no excuse. This fact about our epistemic practices reflects the importance of the idea that there is a social dimension to epistemic responsibility. Indeed, this social dimension plays an important part in the contextualist's picture of epistemic responsibility, as shall be seen in the next section.

If we let the expression 'adequate set of background beliefs' refer to the background beliefs the agent possesses, plus any that he ought to possess, we can reformulate ER to reflect the point about socially available information, as well as the point about obviousness of counterpossibilities:

> ER*   Normally, a person S is epistemically responsible in believing some proposition p at time t only if S checks all of those obvious counterpossibilities whose seriousness is indicated by an adequate set of background beliefs at t.

In order to avoid misunderstanding, there are three comments I wish to make about this norm. First, I have inserted the qualifier 'normally' to indicate that ER* is not intended to be a hard-and-fast, necessary condition on being epistemically responsible. In epistemology, as in the law, there may be extenuating circumstances. The law recognizes a category of emergency situations in which the actor is not held to the normal reasonable-person standard of conduct because "the actor is left no time for adequate thought, or is reasonably so disturbed or excited that the actor cannot weigh alternative courses of action and must make a speedy decision" (Keeton et al., 1984: 196). The normal reasonable-person standard ignores the pressures of emergency situations because such situations are presumed not to be representative of the circumstances in which we typically find ourselves. The reasonable-person standard thus serves as a default measure of responsible and non-negligent action, though the law is flexible enough to allow emergency considerations to factor in. In such cases, "[t]he conduct required is still that of a reasonable person under the [emergency] circumstances" (Keeton et al., 1984: 196).

Like the reasonable-person model from law, I intend our model of the responsible epistemic agent to represent a default standard of epistemic appraisal that can, in special circumstances, be tailored to fit such circumstances. You may recall that I have characterized the model epistemic agent as one who is not abnormally distracted, and so has time to consider the epistemic status of her beliefs. In cases in which the agent lacks adequate time or is in a situation that would distract or agitate a normal person, we can make charitable judgments about the epistemic status of the agent's beliefs. Our everyday notion of epistemic responsibility and justification is as flexible as we need it to be.

The second point I want to make about ER* and my characterization of a model epistemic agent generally is that I am not trying to provide a full analysis of the notion of epistemic responsibility. And my characterization of an epistemically responsible agent and norms like ER* are not intended to provide some sort of reductive partial analysis of the notion of epistemic responsibility. For example, in characterizing the notion of an 'adequate' set of background beliefs, I did so in terms of the sorts of socially possessed information an agent *ought, epistemically speaking*, to possess.[28] Rather, our task has been to partially describe the

---

28. As Foley (1993: ch. 3) points out, this sort of notion is 'reason saturated.' Of course, it is not suitable for projects that would seek to define or otherwise reduce epistemic notions to descriptive notions, though it is suitable for present purposes of simply characterizing in an intuitive way the sorts of responsibilities and norms characteristic of the perspective of a certain type of epistemically ideal agent.

epistemic sensibility of a representative epistemic agent that will be genuinely useful in evaluating the epistemic status of individuals' beliefs.[29]

Third, I wish to clear up a possible misapprehension that my characterization of a model epistemic agent admittedly encourages. I have been focusing on the sorts of epistemic norms characteristic of the epistemic behavior of our model agent. Focusing exclusively on norms suggests that good epistemic judgment can be completely understood in terms of conformity to some set of epistemic norms, and so the task is to formulate the norms. I strongly suspect that this way of thinking about epistemological matters is mistaken. Rather, important room in epistemological theorizing must be made for *epistemic judgment* — a capacity to form justified beliefs and come to justified conclusions in ways that are not strictly governed by rules or norms. (The notion of epistemic judgment is analogous to the notion of moral judgment that we find in such moral philosophers as W. D. Ross and recent defenders of particularist moral epistemologies. There is more discussion of moral judgment in §VI.) For instance, there may be no algorithm or rule for reasonably weighing evidence for and against a claim — it may be a matter of judgment. Again, I will not argue the case for epistemic judgment. Here, the point I wish to make is that in characterizing our model agent, we should be thinking in terms of a model epistemic sensibility that can be partially described in terms of norms to follow, but that also includes a capacity for epistemic judgment. So, although I have managed to formulate but a single general norm, and no doubt there are other norms we might formulate, we should not expect to come up with a finite list of norms that completely characterize the activities of a responsible epistemic agent.

There is much more to be said about this principle, and about the notion of epistemic responsibility generally, but I hope what I have said is clear enough for our immediate purposes.

An Epistemic-cum-Pragmatic Rationale

Up to this point in this section, I have been engaging in what I take to be a largely descriptive enterprise of accurately characterizing an important feature of our actual, everyday epistemic evaluations. But I also think that there is good reason to endorse this norm and other, related norms. I have in mind an epistemic-cum-pragmatic rationale that views epistemic norms in terms of their point and purpose for limited creatures like us. I did mention Cherniak's rationale for ac-

---

29. What about norms governing the activities of checking for internal inconsistencies in belief and norms for gathering evidence? Here, I can be brief since the story to be told about these activities of an epistemically responsible believer will follow the same general lines as the earlier story about responsibility for dealing with counterpossibilities. Thus, it is plausible to suppose that the epistemically responsible believer is one who would be required to consider and eliminate some but not all inconsistencies within his current belief set. So, for example, we would not expect a responsible agent to recognize and then eliminate inconsistencies within his belief set that would require superhuman powers of reasoning to even detect. Here again, empirical theories about normal human reasoning are brought to bear in curbing one's responsibility.

cepting a very general epistemic norm that would require that we check some, but not all, counterpossibilities to what we believe (or to some proposition we are entertaining). I then went on to specify more precisely what such a norm requires of normal human beings in normal, ordinary contexts. But there is more to be done by way of arguing that the norms in question are worthy of our allegiance. In brief, I propose a two-part rationale that involves an epistemic and a pragmatic dimension.

I shall address the epistemic aspect or dimension first. A norm like ER* is fashioned with the goal of truth in mind. In fact, this norm seems to capture part of what we take good epistemic practice to be all about. Here, the thought might be: if checking for possible counterevidence to one's beliefs does not promote the goal of having true beliefs, then what does? But this plea glosses over an important distinction between two ways in which a proposed norm might be related to the goal of truth.[30] In an objective construal, an adequate norm must be such that conforming to it is objectively likely to yield a high percentage of true beliefs and a low percentage of false ones. In an alternative construal, an adequate norm must be such that conforming to it is, from the perspective of some individual (or perhaps group), apparently likely to yield truth. The contrast here between the objective and subjective tasks of providing an epistemic rationale for one's norms of justification, rationality, or responsibility is not altogether clear and, regardless, needs to be reworked in light of what was said earlier about perspectives in epistemic appraisal.

Let us first consider the project of providing an objective rationale for some set of epistemic norms. If the project is understood to be one of trying to provide some sort of non-question-begging argument for the claim that the norms in question are such that conforming one's beliefs to them objectively guarantees true belief or, more modestly, that conformity to them is objectively likely to lead one to have by and large true beliefs, then I suspect the prospects for success are bleak. For present purposes, let us focus on this project as it arises in connection with medium-sized physical-object beliefs, and let us assume that truth is evidence-independent in the way a realist about truth supposes, so that truth about a subject matter is not being identified with, for example, an ideally justified theory about that subject matter. Certainly, however one understands the project of objective justification, one is not able to take the set of beliefs that would emerge from conformity to the relevant epistemic norms and then compare those with the truth; we simply do not have the sort of unmediated access to reality that this task requires. The point is nicely illustrated by Susan Haack (1993: 214), who points out that unlike checking one's proposed solution to today's crossword puzzle against the solution published in tomorrow's edition, we cannot check beliefs endorsed by a set of epistemic norms against the world.[31]

---

30. I have already mentioned these two ways of relating to truth in connection with beliefs.
31. See Haack, 1993: ch. 10, for her attempt to grapple with this problem, which she calls the 'ratification project.'

Laurence BonJour (1985: ch. 8) deals with the objective rationale project in a discussion in which he attempts to argue that conforming empirical beliefs to coherentist epistemic standards will, in the long run, lead one to a proportionally high percentage of true beliefs. His strategy is to argue (1) that conforming one's beliefs to the standards he proposes will, in the long run, yield a coherent and stable web of belief and (2) that the best explanation for the sort of coherence and stability that would emerge is the hypothesis that those beliefs reflect an independent world of objects, properties, and facts. His best-explanation argument is supposed to employ premises, all of which are knowable a priori (so as not to beg any questions), and proceeds by way of eliminating various skeptical hypotheses that might explain the coherence and stability of a set of beliefs. I have serious doubts about BonJour's main argument, intriguing as it is, though I will not stop here to sort it all out. Suffice it to say that the argument is quite controversial.[32] In general, I am inclined to think that the prospects are dim for providing a non-question-begging argument for the claim that some set of epistemic norms is objectively likely to yield truth.

One might then take up the project of providing what I have called a subjective rationale for some set of epistemic norms. The project would apparently involve showing that a particular set of epistemic norms would lead some individual or group of individuals to have beliefs that, judged from *their* perspective, are true. The idea is to stand in the shoes of the individual or group in question, view things from their perspective, try to decipher what they take to be uncontroversially true, and then propose epistemic norms, the following of which would reliably lead them to have a high percentage of (what they take to be) true beliefs. This might be an interesting exercise for coming to understand and interpret an individual's or group's epistemic practices, but engaging in this sort of project really will not help us in our attempt to provide a rationale for the sorts of epistemic norms that I am proposing. I want to be able to provide an endorsement of norms like ER*, and not just point out that they tend to be presupposed in our epistemic evaluations. But now it looks like there remain for me only two unpalatable options: the apparently hopeless option of pursuing an objective rationale and the unhelpful option of pursuing what I am calling a subjective rationale.

Fortunately, I think there is a way out of this pickle. I want to be able to say that norms like ER* are good ones, judged from the point of view of counting toward truth, though I realize that in arguing for such a claim, I am limited in what I can do. I have to proceed according to my own lights (which I take to be largely shared in my culture, and perhaps largely shared, period), but even so, I am not left just having to say that we happen to use such and such norms. I can point out that norms like ER* are partly definitive of what we take to be good epistemic practice: if checking for counterpossibilities does not move us in the direction of the truth, then what could possibly do so for humans? I cannot show that conformity to such norms yields truth, but I can point out that, given our

32. See Plantinga, 1993: ch. 5, for a critical discussion of BonJour's so-called metajustification.

best take on what sorts of beliefs are true, norms like ER* seem to get us to those beliefs. And here I go beyond just stating that norms like ER* are ones we use and ones that we believe will move us in the direction of truth. Granted, I am saying this much, but I mean to say more, namely, that regardless of what other individuals or groups may do in their search for what is true, their epistemic practices ought to conform to norms like ER*. In saying this, I speak from my own egocentric perspective, but I mean to be endorsing ER*, stating that it is likely, so far as I can tell, to move us in the direction of truth (though for reasons already mentioned in connection with the project of providing an objective rationale I cannot show this).[33]

Having said about all I can regarding the epistemic dimension of my rational for ER*, let me turn to the pragmatic dimension.

A norm like ER* is not a purely epistemic norm; it reflects the fact that we are more than just purely cognitive beings with cognitive goals. That is, we are finite creatures with limited cognitive resources and with all sorts of non-epistemic goals in life, and we would expect any genuinely useful set of epistemic norms to reflect such facts. We have explicitly fashioned ER* so that it reflects our limited cognitive abilities. Moreover, the fact that our epistemic norms do not normally require of us that we devote inordinate amounts of time to checking our claims and beliefs for possible error (but instead require only that we expend a 'reasonable' amount of time doing so) reflects the fact that we are not purely intellectual beings whose only concern is with having an interesting stock of true beliefs. Life is short, and there are other things to do. Given the need for some epistemic norms, but also given what we are like (including limitations), a norm such as ER* seems to be the very sort of norm we would want and expect to be operative in everyday life. So, once we think about norms in these broadly pragmatic terms, we can see that the sorts of norms we do tend to use are ones for which there is a good rationale. Note that because part of the rationale for ER* is pragmatic does not mean that the sort of justification possessed by beliefs conforming to this norm is not primarily epistemic. The primary goal here is truth. Pragmatic considerations enter the picture to help constrain the extent of one's responsibility for eliminating counterpossibilities.[34]

I hope it is clear from my discussion that the view about epistemic responsibility that I am defending is not being run as a version of normative contextualism (epistemic relativism). That is, my rationale should make it clear that I am not simply saying that we happen to accept ER* or something like it, and hence one is epistemically responsible in holding a belief if, and only if, it conforms to our

---

33. For some discussion of how first-person ascriptions of reasons, made from one's egocentric perspective, can be construed as purporting to make objective claims about those reasons, see Foley, 1993: 12–13.

34. With regard to a notion of responsible belief, Foley remarks that non-epistemic goals "shape what it is reasonable for you to believe in an indirect way rather than in a direct Pascalian way. They do so by imposing constraints on inquiry, but subject to these constraints your aim will normally be to determine what beliefs would be true, not what beliefs would be useful" (1993: 108).

norms. To say this would be to advocate what Haack (1993: 192) calls 'tribalism' (which, by the way, is what she thinks contextualism comes to).

Finally, before leaving this section, I want to raise a question that is directly related to what follows. First, I need to say something about the connection between the notions of responsible belief and epistemic justification at work here. There are various notions of epistemic justification. Here, I intend to employ a notion of epistemic justification that is directly tied to the notion of epistemic responsibility. This responsibilist notion of justification is nicely described by Hilary Kornblith:

> When we ask whether an agent's beliefs are justified we are asking whether he has done all he should to bring it about that he have true beliefs. The notion of justification is thus essentially tied to that of action, and equally to the notion of responsibility. Questions of justification are thus questions about the ethics of belief. (Kornblith, 1983: 34)[35]

As I am using the term, 'epistemic responsibility' is a broader notion than the notion of justified belief. For an individual to be positively epistemically justified in believing some proposition, requires that he have reasons or grounds for that proposition and that he base his belief on the reasons or grounds. Being epistemically responsible in holding a belief does not necessarily require that one be justified in holding the belief. So, in light of our characterization of epistemic responsibility, we might ask whether one is always required to have evidence in the sense of having justifying reasons for all of the beliefs one holds, and holds without being epistemically irresponsible. Perhaps in some contexts, at least, certain beliefs that one is not irresponsible in holding and that play an epistemic role in the justification of other beliefs, do not themselves *need* justification. Whether there are cases like this will depend on the epistemic norms and practices characteristic of our epistemically responsible agent. It might be the case, after all, that, in some contexts, we are epistemically responsible in holding certain beliefs that can serve as a basis for holding other beliefs, even if we do not have justifying reasons for the justifying beliefs in question.

In fact, I do think this is the case and that the sort of pragmatic rationale just sketched in defense of ER* can be extended to explain why our epistemic practices are this way. In brief, given such facts as that we have non-epistemic goals, that we are not able to remember everything we have learned, and that any intellectual endeavor takes time, we simply should not spend time investigating and gathering evidence for all of our beliefs; in fact, we could not possibly do so. We have no choice but to rely on all sorts of beliefs, skills, and abilities we do have when we engage in any intellectual pursuit. Reflection on our finite predicament, then, makes it plausible to suppose that one is epistemically responsible in holding a belief unless there are concrete reasons for suspicion. And this allows that one

---

35. Kornblith goes on to note that since beliefs are not freely chosen, the ethics of belief will not issue rules and prescriptions for belief acceptance; rather, it will issue rules of conduct.

may be responsible in believing some proposition, even if one no longer has—or indeed, has never had—positive evidence of a sort that would serve as justifying reasons for the proposition in question.

The idea that one may be epistemically responsible in holding certain beliefs without needing justification is central to what I have been calling structural contextualism. Let us consider that thesis in more detail.

V. Three Basic Tenets of Structural Contextualism

Having partially sketched a notion of epistemic responsibility that is the basis for the sort of epistemic evaluation I am interested in describing, I want to return to structural contextualism for purposes of clarifying that thesis. You may recall that according to structural contextualism, certain beliefs, at least in certain contexts, do not need justification, although they may provide one with justifying reasons for holding other beliefs. Let us take a closer look at the claim that certain beliefs, at least in certain contexts, may not need justification.

As I understand the basic structural contextualist thesis, it comprises three fundamental tenets. (1) One may be epistemically responsible in holding certain beliefs at some time t, even though one has no justifying evidence or justifying reasons for holding those beliefs at t. (2) Such beliefs may serve as an epistemic basis for being justified in holding other beliefs. (3) Which beliefs need justification depends crucially on certain facts about one's context, including certain social dimensions of one's context. Let's take these one by one.

1. The thesis that it is possible for someone to be epistemically responsible in holding a belief without justification is one way to express what has come to be called *epistemic conservatism*. The epistemic conservative claims that mere doxastic commitment may be enough to create some degree of epistemic respectability for certain beliefs. There are two basic versions of this conservative doctrine. According to *first-order conservatism*, epistemic respectability may accrue to a belief as a result of simply holding that belief or, more plausibly, as a result of holding that belief as long as it does not conflict with other beliefs one has. According to *second-order conservatism*, second-order beliefs—beliefs about beliefs—are necessary for creating some degree of epistemic respectability for a first-order belief. So, for example, according to one possible version of second-order conservatism, in order for one to be epistemically responsible in holding some belief (for which one has no justifying reasons or grounds), one must not only have the belief, but one must also believe of it that there is something that, in some sense, makes obvious (e.g., something that justifies or shows true) the belief in question.[36] In short, one must take the belief to be epistemically sound.

36. Here I am being intentionally noncommittal about what other requirements (if any) might be involved in a notion of responsible belief for which one has no justification. For example, one might require that someone in one's community have justifying reasons for the proposition in question and that the possibility of non-justified responsible belief reflects one of the ways in which our epistemic practices indicate a kind of division of epistemic labor.

This is not the place to launch into a full-scale investigation of epistemic conservatism, but some indication of its merits is in order. Jonathan Kvanvig (1989) has convincingly argued that versions of first-order conservatism are not defensible, but that any fallibilist epistemology needs to recognize a version of second-order conservatism. The main problem with first-order conservatism is simply that it is susceptible to counterexamples—no matter how one attempts to articulate the view, it implies that certain irresponsibly held beliefs are nevertheless responsibly held. Certainly, we do not allow that any old belief someone holds without justifying reasons or grounds is responsibly held. So, at the very least, a proponent of first-order conservatism would have to specify certain restrictions on non-justified belief if it is to qualify as being responsibly held. But the problem is that there do not seem to be any proposals in sight that will save the first-order version of the view from counterexamples.

For instance, in Chisholm's 1981 version, a non-justified belief is responsibly held (at some time) so long as it does not explicitly contradict any other beliefs held by the individual at that time. But if an individual believes some proposition that does not explicitly contradict anything else she believes (let the proposition in question be something like 'there are little green men on Mars') and has no positive evidence in its favor, but does have evidence against the proposition, her belief is simply not being responsibly held—she has evidence against it and none in favor of it! If we additionally require that she also *not* believe that the belief in question is epistemically dubious (that she lack a certain second-order belief), we still do not have an account that is adequate, since one might come to be absolutely convinced that there are little green men on Mars as a result of being hit in the head by a falling brick, and yet realize that there really is no reason at all (no reason she or anyone else has) to suppose that the proposition believed is true. Again, the belief in question does not seem to be responsibly held. Other proposals might be suggested for constraining the sorts of beliefs that can count as responsibly held without having justification, but the prospects for success look rather poor. It seems that what one needs to do is bring in second-order beliefs—beliefs about first-order beliefs.

According to Kvanvig (whose discussion of this issue I am following), second-order conservatism is not susceptible to counterexamples of the sort that beset first-order versions of the view; moreover, in its favor, conservatism is implied by a robust fallibilism about justification. A fallibilist (about justification) holds that the link between justification and truth is indirect: justifiedly holding some belief does not entail the truth of that belief. Kvanvig's argument focuses on cases in which one infers one belief from another set of beliefs, but in doing so, one either follows a bad rule of inference or is careless with one's evidence base and commits some fallacy like hasty generalization, or perhaps just misinterprets the strength of the evidence. His argument for claiming that such beliefs, even though they are not properly based on good evidence, may nevertheless be responsibly held is that once we recognize, as fallibilists, that a justifiedly held belief might be false, there is no reason to require that beliefs that an individual mistakenly takes to be properly based on good evidence are not responsibly held:

The instructive implication of fallibilism is that the links between truth and justification are at best indirect; nothing follows about the justificatory status of a
belief merely given that it is false. But, if we can have justified false beliefs,
why not about the rules of inference we employ? If our beliefs about inference
patterns are not infallible (and they surely are not), what possible reason could
be given for insisting that unless inferences are correct, they and the results of
following them cannot be justified? Such a position is caught between a rock
and a hard place: it is known that infallibilism is false, and yet it is insisted that
an unwarranted implication of infallibilism be maintained. (Kvanvig, 1989: 156)

Kvanvig's case focuses exclusively on beliefs for which one (mistakenly) takes
oneself to have justifying reasons or grounds. I am concerned with beliefs that one
does not take oneself to have justifying reasons or grounds for believing. One might
take such beliefs to be just obvious and not in need of justification. Or one might
take such beliefs to be supportable by justifying reasons or grounds, and also believe that some other individuals in fact have such reasons or grounds. Perhaps
one thinks both that such beliefs are not in need of justification, but that they are
capable of being justified and that other individuals do have the relevant justifying
reasons or grounds. In any case, such beliefs of the sort I am concerned with seem
to be in the same class as those for which one mistakenly thinks one has evidence:
in both cases, one takes the beliefs to be epistemically sound.[37]

There is a further reason for thinking that some form of conservatism is correct. In the previous section, I offered a tentative and admittedly sketchy defense
of conservatism that appeals to our finite predicament: given limits on our cognitive abilities and our time, it makes sense that our epistemic practices do not
always require of believers that they have evidence or justifying reasons for everything they responsibly believe. As we shall see in §VI, our epistemic practices
regarding moral belief exhibit this same sort of conservatism. Though there is
obviously much more to be said about this topic, I shall proceed on the assumption
that second-order conservatism is correct.[38]

   2. The second fundamental tenet of the structural contextualist—what we
might call the thesis of *epistemic adequacy*—claims that beliefs that one is epistemically responsible in holding, but for which one has no justification, are sometimes

37. Robert Audi suggested to me that the defender of conservatism need not demand that believers
possess second-order beliefs and instead can get by with the requirement that believers be disposed to
have the relevant sort of second-order belief. I excuse myself from fussing with the details of an
adequate formulation of second-order conservatism.
38. Commitment to a particular version of epistemic conservatism is not distinctive of contextualist
epistemology; at least, one finds both self-described foundationalists and coherentists taking a conservative line. As already noted, Chisholm's brand of foundationalism embraces a version of first-order
conservatism. He writes that *"anything* we find ourselves believing may be said to have *some* presumption in its favor—*provided* it is not explicitly contradicted by the set of other things that we
believe" (1981: 14). Harman's brand of coherentism also embraces what seems to be a version of first-
order conservatism. He writes that "beliefs do not usually require any justification. Justification is taken
to be required only if one has a special reason to doubt a particular belief" (1986: 29). So my commitment to epistemic conservatism is shared widely enough among epistemologists of various epistemological persuasions; it is not peculiar to contextualism.

enough, epistemically speaking, to serve as a basis, or partial basis, for justifiably believing other propositions.[39] Regresses of justification can legitimately terminate with beliefs that one does not have justifying reasons for holding. If I am right, and our actual epistemic practices conform to the thesis of epistemic adequacy, this fact about the thesis provides, I would argue, some presumptive reason in its favor. I suppose a critic might try to rule out this thesis by restricting what can count as justifying evidence to that set of beliefs that is positively justified. If this restriction were to hold, it would defeat the thesis of epistemic adequacy.

Why impose such a restriction? One possible reason is the following.[40] From any belief, we can logically infer that same belief. If we allow (as per the thesis under attack) that non-justified but responsibly held beliefs can serve as justifiers, and if we allow that the relation of logical entailment can be a basis of support between beliefs, then it appears as if any responsibly held, non-justified belief can be raised to the level of being a justified belief simply from being inferred from itself. I certainly do not want to allow that non-justified, responsibly held beliefs can end up justified simply by being inferred from themselves, but I really do not have to. The thesis of epistemic adequacy (as stated) does not allow the possibility under discussion; it claims that non-justified, responsibly held beliefs can sometimes serve as a basis for justifiably believing *other* propositions. The idea behind this thesis can perhaps be put the following way. One thing we learn from coherentists about justification is that certain logical and non-logical relations among different beliefs can serve to increase the epistemic status of those individual, cohering beliefs. But the fact that any proposition entails itself does not mean that if one believes a proposition and realizes that it entails itself, then whatever epistemic merit the proposition originally possessed is somehow increased as a result of inferring it from itself. So I do not think the line of argument now under consideration does anything to bring the thesis of epistemic adequacy into question.

3. Finally, whether a belief needs to be justified in order to serve as a properly basic belief depends crucially on context. More generally, whether one justifiedly believes some proposition depends crucially on context. I will call this the *context sensitivity thesis*. Let me begin with this more general claim.

The general idea that correct epistemic appraisals are context sensitive in the sense of being dependent upon one's circumstances is not exciting and, as we saw in §II, not particularly controversial. In general, whether an individual is justified (or, if not justified, then at least epistemically responsible) in holding some belief will depend on certain features of his circumstances. This much is compatible with almost any epistemological view. What makes contextualism (of the sort I am attempting to defend) distinctive is the claim that correct epistemic appraisal and,

---

39. A foundationalist or a coherentist who is an epistemic conservative may or may not accept the thesis of epistemic adequacy. A coherentist, for example, might allow that certain beliefs one holds without justification have some epistemic merit but might claim that they do not have enough such merit to qualify as being justified and that, consequently, they cannot serve as part of one's justification for holding other beliefs.

40. This was suggested to me by Walter Sinnott-Armstrong in conversation.

in particular, whether one's belief needs justification, can vary in ways that depend upon such things as one's goals and purposes that are operative on some occasion — goals and purposes that may not be operative, or operative in quite the same way, on a different occasion. This is all pretty vague, so let me try to clarify matters.

Let us begin with some questions about this matter of context sensitivity that are particularly pressing. (1) How should we individuate contexts? (2) Within any context, what are one's epistemic responsibilities? (3) Under what conditions is one ever epistemically obligated to enter into some particular context? I will not be able to address any one of these questions thoroughly, but I hope to say enough to make the context sensitivity thesis tolerably clear for our purposes here. I shall address these questions in order.

I have been working with a notion of responsible belief, and so let us continue to focus on it. I have explained this notion mainly in terms of norms that concern one's responsibilities for recognizing and then checking certain counterpossibilities to one's beliefs. In order to convey a sense of what I have in mind by the context sensitivity thesis, let us compare an ordinary context having to do with medium-sized physical-object beliefs and a non-ordinary, philosophical context in which skeptical questions about such objects are likely to arise. The most important and obvious difference between these contexts, for our purposes, is simply the range of counterpossibilities that is relevant for epistemic assessment. Most obviously, certain skeptical counterpossibilities that are relevant in a philosophical context are not relevant in a more mundane context. Moreover, what helps determine the relevance of counterpossibilities has to do with one's goals on some occasion. In ordinary contexts, as we have seen, epistemic and non-epistemic goals conspire, as it were, to set limits on the range of relevant counterpossibilities. According to my account of the epistemically responsible believer, in normal, ordinary contexts, one is required to consider and check all of those counterpossibilities whose seriousness is indicated by one's background beliefs. In skeptical contexts, however, certain counterpossibilities whose seriousness is not normally indicated by one's background beliefs come into view and are relevant. Why? One obvious suggestion is simply that in such situations (in which we are waxing philosophical in our thinking and are not engaged in day-to-day practical affairs), our goals are different, or at least their relative importance changes. Suppose, then, that one is taking seriously questions about the reality of what one normally understands to be physical objects populating a mind-independent external world. One prominent goal in an inquiry into the justification for believing our commonsense picture of the external world is the goal of unbiased belief about such things — unbiased in a strong sense that would require that we not take for granted ordinary physical-object beliefs and that we take seriously the hypothesis that we might be subject to some grand delusion by an evil demon, or that one might be a brain in a vat, or whatever. In such contexts, dominated by this sort of goal, certain counterpossibilities whose seriousness is not indicated by anything we now believe do become relevant.[41]

---

41. This discussion of the contrast between ordinary and philosophical contexts is developed by William Throop (unpublished). Throop convincingly argues, by the way, that skeptical hypotheses can-

Shifts in goals, or shifts in their relative importance, then, sometimes bring with them a change in the range of relevant counterpossibilities that bear on the epistemic appraisal of what one believes. Here is another example to help illustrate the context sensitivity of epistemic appraisals. Those who are fond of the context sensitivity theme in epistemology often point out that things like expertise in some area of inquiry, one's occupation, and the importance of being right in one's beliefs about a certain matter affect the range of counterpossibilities for which, in a context, one is responsible for checking.[42] Suppose, for example, that there is a plant—let us call it X—that is plentiful in some region of the country, but that there is another plant—let us call it Y—that has outward features almost indistinguishable from X-type plants but is almost never found in the same region of the country. A botanist taking a weekend hike along a trail through the region where the plant is plentiful would be justified in believing, on the basis of casual inspection, that the plants along the trail are X-type plants. However, in another, more professional context, it might be important to eliminate the possibility that some plant picked from the region is really a Y-type plant. In this context, in which the goal of eliminating the possibility of error is far more important than in a more casual context, the possibility that the plant under scrutiny is a Y plant becomes relevant and must be checked. In the more mundane context, in which not much is at stake in coming to believe that the plant one is looking at is X and not Y, the possibility that it is Y is not relevant; in less mundane contexts it is. And so, whether one is justified in believing of some plant that it is an X plant depends on context. Incidently, this same context sensitivity that I am claiming is part of our normal epistemic practices is also part of the reasonable-person doctrine in the law. Professionals, when working within a professional context, are expected to have special knowledge and skills that normally increase the level of care they must exhibit in certain of their professional dealings. "Professional persons in general, and those who undertake any work calling for special skill, are required not only to exercise reasonable care in what they do, but also to possess a standard minimum of special knowledge and ability" (Keeton et al., 1984: 185).

Having said this much, I hope the answer to question 2 is obvious. Within any context, one's responsibilities essentially involve recognizing and checking any relevant counterpossibilities. Of course, talk about 'checking' counterpossibilities is vague, and there are interesting questions about what it would take, in a context, to have checked out a relevant alternative to something one believes or some hypothesis one is considering. Again, I will not pursue details here.

The third question, about when one is epistemically required to enter some particular context, is a hard one, and I am afraid I won't be able to say much about this matter that will be particularly illuminating. All sorts of factors may come into play here. Obviously, the goals that one has on some occasion will play

---

not be refuted in philosophical contexts, and so in such contexts we fail to have empirical knowledge.

42. See, for example Annis, 1978, and Cherniak, 1986.

a role. But there will be cases in which there are goals one ought to have, or goals that one ought to give special weight, even if one does not have those goals on that occasion or one fails to give them their due weight. I am thinking here of cases in which one's occupation may impose certain epistemic demands, owing to the fact that, normally, individuals with that occupation are expected to have and attach certain weight to certain goals. Doctors, lawyers, scientists, professional car mechanics, and so on, are members of professions that have widely shared standards of expertise that members of those professions are expected to meet. Regardless of the goals one happens to have or the relative weight one happens to attach to, say, the goal of avoiding error in one's professional judgment, one is expected to conform to epistemic standards that are appropriate given certain goals. Obviously, there is much more to be said about this matter, but again, I will have to leave things at an intuitive level, hoping that my few illustrations will suffice for present purposes.

I have been focusing on the general thesis that epistemic appraisal is context sensitive. My general claim is that whether one is justified in holding some belief on some occasion depends on context, which in turn determines the range of counterpossibilities one is responsible for recognizing and eliminating. In some cases, I am suggesting, there are beliefs one holds for which one may have no positive justifying reasons (and so which are, strictly speaking, not justified) but which one is responsible for holding anyway since, in the context, one is not required to have justifying reasons. I will say more about context sensitivity in general, and about responsible non-justified belief in particular, when we get to questions of moral epistemology in the next section.

Before moving on to questions about moral justification, let me relate the main contextualist themes of this section to the notion of epistemic responsibility sketched in the previous section. An individual is epistemically responsible vis-à-vis some belief she holds only when she has adequately dealt with those (obvious) counterpossibilities whose seriousness is indicated by her own background beliefs and with those indicated by relevant information widely shared by a relevant community. Those cases in which one holds some belief without having a justifying reason for that belief, and there are no relevant counterpossibilities of the sort just mentioned, are candidate cases in which it seems appropriate to say that one is epistemically permitted and, hence, responsible in holding that belief. But, in light of the distinction between first-order and second-order conservatism, I think we should add the following proviso to our description of contextually basic beliefs: not only should it be the case that there are no relevant counterpossibilities to the belief in question, but the belief in question, to be properly basic, must also be one that the believer (and perhaps her social group) takes to be epistemically sound. The implication about contextually basic beliefs is that their status as basic depends crucially on social context and what sorts of epistemic demands one is expected to meet, as well as on the group's level of epistemic commitment to the belief in question.

VI. Moral Justification in Context

In this section, I want to articulate and partially defend contextualism about the structure of moral belief.[43] My case involves both a descriptive and a normative dimension. First, I am interested in characterizing our actual epistemic practices when it comes to moral belief—in particular, those epistemic practices that bear on being free from or deserving epistemic blame. My descriptive hypothesis is that our epistemic norms, as they apply to moral belief, do not normally require that epistemically responsible agents have justifying reasons for all of their responsibly held moral beliefs. Some moral beliefs, especially those that are partly constitutive of one's moral outlook, serve as a body of very basic moral assumptions that, in ordinary contexts of moral thought and discussion, are not in need of justification. If this descriptive thesis is correct, then it is correct to characterize the structure of moral justification implied by our epistemic norms as contextual. My normative thesis is that there is good reason to reflectively endorse such norms.

In order to make a case for my descriptive claim, my plan is to describe a picture about our practices of justifying moral beliefs that, while it may not represent a complete picture, is quite familiar. The picture I have in mind is to be found in the writings of W. D. Ross. Once we have the picture before us, I want to indicate briefly some reasons for thinking that we often do reason and think about moral matters as the Rossian picture suggests, and then I will elaborate some of the epistemically relevant features that represent what I will call 'the ordinary context of moral thought and discussion.' What emerges from the picture is a contextualist account of the structure of justification. However, I do not want to be misunderstood in my use of Ross. My contextualism is not wedded to those aspects of Ross's views that are featured later in this section; I use some of Ross's views to help illustrate the sort of picture of the structure of justified moral belief I am defending. Recently, ethical particularists have argued against the Rossian view that justification of moral belief rests with appeals to moral rules—*general* moral beliefs (about what actions are prima facie duties)—and insist instead that the justification of moral belief can legitimately rest with particular moral beliefs about particular cases. My contextualism is intended to be neutral with regard to this dispute between Rossians and particularists—indeed, the thoroughgoing contextualist should be willing to say that what sorts of moral beliefs play a regress-stopping role depends on context. I shall return to this issue later, after I work through the basic outline of my moral contextualism.

---

43. Wellman (1971), Larmore (1987), and Stout (1993) all profess some version or other of structural contextualism about moral belief. In Timmons (1993b), I defend this view, but do so from an egocentric epistemic perspective, whereas here (and in Timmons, 1996) my focus is on a non-egocentric perspective.

A Cue from Ross

Even if Ross's views about the nature of justification in ethics are not wholly correct, they do seem to be at least partially correct, and I use those views to develop a contextualist picture of justification in ethics—a picture or model that seems to gain some support from recent empirical work. The picture I have in mind features moral rules as providing a basis for the justification of particular moral beliefs. And although I do think that rules have *a* role to play in a full story about the justification of moral belief, my version of contextualism is not committed to the claim that moral rules are, in all contexts, necessary in accounting for an individual's moral belief's being justified.[44] Thus, again let me emphasize that the picture to follow is meant only to illustrate my version of ethical contextualism.

Ross, of course, was an ethical foundationalist who advocated a version of ethical pluralism. His specific version of ethical foundationalism involved these two claims: (1) that in ethics, as in mathematics, there are certain "propositions that cannot be proved, but that just as certainly need no proof" (1930: 30) and (2) that such propositions are self-evident, necessary truths describing non-natural moral facts and properties that can be known a priori. His ethical pluralism also involved two central claims: (3) There is a plurality of irreducible mid-level generalizations that express prima facie moral obligations. (These are the propositions that need no proof.) (4) In specific cases, these prima facie moral obligations may conflict, and when they do, there is no procedure, rule, or algorithm by which one may adjudicate these conflicts.

I accept (again, tentatively and with some modification) Ross's claims 1, 3, and 4; what I do not accept is the foundationalist epistemology and associated metaphysics of 2. My idea is that we can rework some of Ross's views by stripping away the foundationalist epistemology and non-naturalist metaphysics and reinterpret the other claims in light of contextualist epistemology. In fact, claims 1, 3, and 4 represent what I take to be a roughly accurate picture of a good part of the structure of justified moral belief—at least for many people in our culture. Embedded in a contextualist moral epistemology, the structural view involves the following four central theses.

> T1   There are a number of irreducible moral generalizations that are defeasible and that we acquire as a result of moral education. In the ordinary context of justification in ethics, these are often epistemically basic.

> T2   However, they are contextually basic: they do not represent self-evident moral truths knowable a priori, nor do they result from the deliverance of some faculty

---

44. So, for example, in specific contexts, the justification of a moral belief may involve an ultimate appeal to moral exemplars or perhaps just an appeal to the particularities of some specific case under scrutiny, and moral rules may play no role at all. I am thinking here of the epistemological views of so-called moral particularists. See, for example Dancy, 1993: chs. 4–7. As I have said, my contextualism can allow that the sort of belief that plays a contextually basic role in the justification of moral belief is itself a contextually variable matter.

of moral intuition. Rather, their status as basic is relative to context in a way to be elaborated below.

T3   The contextually basic beliefs provide (along with relevant non-moral factual beliefs) the justificatory basis for justified belief in other, non-basic moral propositions. Thus, (ceteris paribus) other, non-basic moral beliefs are justified if they are appropriately based on some of the contextually basic ones.

T4   However, going from basic moral beliefs—the mid-level moral generalizations—to more specific moral beliefs about particular cases is not always a matter of simply taking the moral generalization together with relevant empirical information and deducing a moral conclusion. In many cases, two or more morally relevant considerations expressed by the basic moral generalizations will be present in a single case, and for these cases we need have no algorithm or ordering system to which we can appeal to adjudicate the conflict. In these cases, moral *judgment* takes over—something that one can do better or worse but something for which we need not have a covering rule that would dictate what, in particular, it is rational to believe. Nevertheless, in ordinary contexts of moral thought and discussion, individuals can be justified in coming to hold certain moral beliefs in cases calling for moral judgment.

Let me elaborate the view.

Tenets T1 and T3 together comprise a very familiar idea about the structure of ethical justification—a view common to both foundationalism and contextualism. Support for these tenets comes from commonsense observation and from empirical work in moral psychology.

So what does available evidence suggest? If we examine actual bits of human moral reasoning, it is plausible to suppose that doxastic justification in ethics rests with epistemically basic beliefs of some sort. We naturally assume that in honestly stating our reasons for holding some moral belief we are expressing the epistemically relevant structure of our moral beliefs. And when people are asked to articulate their reasons for holding some particular moral belief about a specific case, they by and large reason according to the familiar pattern of bringing forth general considerations bearing on the specific case that they take to be morally significant in that case. Such considerations are usually formulated as mid-level moral generalizations like, for example, 'Lying is wrong' and 'Hurting others is wrong.' Moreover, there are two noteworthy features of these mid-level moral generalizations. First, when asked about these moral generalizations, people by and large report that such claims strike them as intuitively *obvious*. Related to this bit of phenomenology is the fact that people treat these generalizations as being *non-arbitrary*. That is, most people are not inclined to take challenges to these beliefs at all seriously—they represent a person's moral bottom line. These facts suggest that many people do not have justifying reasons for these bottom-line moral beliefs.[45]

45. As Walter Sinnott-Armstrong pointed out to me, the fact that people do not take certain challenges seriously does not show that they lack reasons or justification for the belief's being challenged; in some cases, we do not take challenges to certain beliefs seriously because we have overwhelming justifying reasons for those beliefs. However, as I go on to explain, I think part of the reason for not taking

(As I explain later, this does not mean that one cannot detach from his moral beliefs, hold them at arm's length, in order to raise Nietzschean questions about one's own moral outlook. But this does not affect the point I am making here about moral phenomenology or its bearing on contextualism.) I base these remarks on the observations I have made listening to students (who have not been tainted by an introductory course in normative ethics), but also there are the observations reported by, for example, the authors of *Habits of the Heart*, as well as empirical research on moral development by such psychologists as Carol Gilligan.[46]

One of the interviewees featured in *Habits of the Heart*, when asked about some of his general moral beliefs that he was using to justify more particular moral beliefs, said this: "Why is integrity important and lying bad? I don't know. It just is. It's just so basic. I don't want to be bothered with challenging that" (Bellah et al., 1985: 7). He was simply dumbfounded by the question and took his general moral beliefs in question to be obvious. I suspect one would find this to be a pretty typical answer. Another sort of response to questions about a person's general moral beliefs is to be found in Gilligan's work. The responses she tended to get from subjects, when they were asked to provide a rationale for those general moral beliefs typically used by them to justify more particular moral beliefs, were, as Dreyfus and Dreyfus point out, "tautologies and banalities, e.g., that they try to act in such a way as to make the world a better place in which to live. They might as well say that their highest moral principle is 'do something good'" (1990: 252).

My reading of all this (not that it is the only reading) is that, in many contexts at least, there are moral beliefs—general moral beliefs—that provide the basis for one's coming to justifiably hold other moral beliefs, but beliefs for which most ordinary people have no (justifying) reason. In these (rather typical) cases, I do not think it is plausible to criticize such agents for being epistemically irresponsible. They have particular moral beliefs that rest for their justification on certain other moral beliefs that represent the core of their moral sensibility. Moreover, they take these beliefs to be obvious and non-arbitrary, and so display the relevant sort of second-order doxastic commitment characteristic of what I am calling contextually basic beliefs. There is, of course, much more to say about all this (including the addition of some important qualifications), but my suggestion here is that reflection on these ordinary cases helps reveal something important about our epistemic norms when it comes to moral belief, namely, that in what I am calling 'ordinary contexts of moral thought and discussion,' one need not have justifying reasons or grounds for certain moral beliefs that play a crucial epistemic role in one being justified in holding other moral beliefs.

---

certain challenges seriously in the case of moral beliefs (at least, many such beliefs) is that ordinary people do not have justifying reasons for those beliefs.

46. Gilligan, 1982, 1988; and Gilligan et al., 1988.

Contextually Basic Moral Beliefs

Claim T2 is what distinguishes contextualism about structure from foundational-ism. As we have seen, the contextualist maintains the following two claims.[47] (1) In ordinary contexts of doxastic justification, epistemically basic beliefs *are not in need of justification*. (2) Beliefs that are basic in one context may, in a different context, require justification. What follows is an elaboration of these two claims. In addressing the first claim, we must clarify the notion of *context* as I use it here. We must also say something about the role of contextually basic beliefs in ordinary contexts of moral thought and discussion.

I want to begin by focusing on ordinary, engaged contexts of moral thinking — contexts in which we bring to bear on some moral question or issue a moral outlook — and I want to fill out some of the epistemically important detail of this context. With regard to moral belief, then, an important part of the context when it comes to questions about being justified in holding various moral beliefs involves the role of one's moral outlook.

In the previous chapter, I described a moral outlook as (roughly) a way of viewing and responding to one's environment from a moral point of view; it is a perspective from which one takes a moral stance. You may recall some of the main ingredients. One comes to have a moral outlook through a process of moral education, and some of the more salient features of this process include: (1) developing a sensitivity to various features of one's environment that, according to the particular outlook being taught, are morally relevant and, so, the basis of moral evaluation; (2) learning to associate various emotional responses with objects of moral evaluation, for example, learning to have feelings of guilt and resentment toward certain of one's own actions and the actions of others; (3) becoming acquainted with certain exemplars, that is, paradigmatic cases of moral or immoral actions, persons, institutions, and so forth;[48] (4) learning moral generalizations that encapsulate the most important morally relevant features to which, through training, one develops a sensitivity; and (5) learning basic patterns of moral reasoning, for instance, golden rule/reversibility reasoning, as well as learning to reason from moral generalizations to particular cases.

Having some particular moral outlook provides (part of) the 'context' within which one ordinarily comes to have justified moral beliefs. But notice that in normal cases it is a richly social context — moral education takes place within a certain social environment, normally a large community whose members more or less share certain moral values and beliefs. In what I am calling engaged moral

---

47. Here I am just concerned with what I have called the thesis of epistemic conservatism and the thesis of social context sensitivity. The thesis of epistemic adequacy does not figure in this discussion.
48. Kuhn uses the term 'exemplar' to refer to one of the crucial ingredients involved in what he calls a *disciplinary matrix* — those elements shared by a scientific community that enable them to communicate professionally and arrive at nearly unanimous judgments on scientific questions. As part of a disciplinary matrix, exemplars are "concrete problem solutions, accepted by the group as, in a quite usual sense, paradigmatic" (Kuhn, 1977: 298). Learning a moral outlook involves, I am suggesting, a rough equivalent of learning a disciplinary matrix.

contexts, in which one brings one's moral outlook to bear on some specific case calling for a moral response, certain moral beliefs—what I am calling mid-level moral generalizations—often enough play a special justifying role, and it is by seeing how these moral beliefs function in one's moral outlook that one can understand more clearly the epistemic status of those beliefs. Let us then consider the role of mid-level general moral beliefs in a moral outlook.

The five features of a moral outlook represent (at least part of) what we might call 'formal' features of a moral outlook—features that characterize any (or almost any) moral outlook. But particular moral outlooks differ in content, and one useful way to characterize some *particular* moral outlook, and distinguish it from other moral outlooks, is in terms of those morally relevant features mentioned in 1 and 4. Let us say, then, that those morally relevant features of actions, persons, institutions, and so forth—that represent according to the outlook the most fundamental morally relevant features of things that are the basis of moral evaluation— are distinctive of that particular moral outlook. Mid-level moral generalizations, as I understand them, connect those morally relevant features of things with terms of moral evaluation. Hence, we can say that a set of these mid-level generalizations is (partly) *constitutive* of a particular moral outlook. Thus, in many ordinary, engaged contexts of moral thinking about specific moral questions and issues, these general moral beliefs help structure and organize our moral experience and thought—we think in terms of them. When our focus is on specific issues, they are part of a large body of assumptions that we employ in our thinking. Moreover, such moral beliefs in such contexts are taken for granted: no serious doubts or challenges are considered or taken seriously by the relevant community. Since a large part of being epistemically responsible is a matter of being able to detect and deal with 'relevant' challenges—and in the ordinary context of moral justification, challenges to mid-level moral generalizations are not relevant—one's holding such beliefs and basing other, non-basic beliefs on them is not subject to epistemic criticism, and so one is epistemically responsible in holding them without having justifying reasons.

So, if I am right, our actual epistemic norms and practices do not, as a matter of fact, require that individuals have justifying reasons for some of their moral beliefs—moral beliefs that often play a crucial epistemic role when it comes to being inferentially justified in holding specific moral beliefs.

Context Sensitivity

The second feature of contextually basic beliefs to be considered here is the idea that being basic is context sensitive, and so what is basic in one context may not be basic in another. Let us begin by considering different social contexts involving different communities that have and inculcate different moral outlooks. Although one would expect that almost any two moral outlooks would share many of the same basic moral assumptions (e.g., presumptions against killing humans, theft, and so forth), there may be some differences in the specific moral assumptions that these groups by and large take for granted, as well as the moral weight that is attached to the various morally relevant considerations the rules encapsulate.[49] If so, then one way in which being basic is context sensitive is simply that different groups may take (some) different moral beliefs for granted. For example, in comparing the basic moral outlook of the Amish culture with the outlooks of many non-Amish westerners, we see striking differences.[50] The underlying spirit of the Amish moral outlook—what is called *Gelassenheit*, translated as 'submission'— puts primary emphasis on the values of submission and obedience to God and community as fundamental for leading a morally proper life. The moral requirement to lead a properly submissive life (which the Amish take as basic and applying to *all* persons) is understood to imply that individual achievement, self-fulfillment, personal recognition, and other manifestations of the modern spirit of individuality are morally perverse. Even if submissiveness and obedience are morally valued by people generally, nevertheless, these values need not, and often do not, have the sort of fundamental status and importance that they have in the Amish moral outlook. Amish justifications for specific moral beliefs about actions and practices rest with claims to the effect that such and such actions and practices are required (or forbidden) by Gelassenheit. So, one rather obvious way in which beliefs that do not need justification are context sensitive is where talk of different social contexts refers to different communities with differing moral outlooks.[51]

A more interesting possibility to explore is the extent to which our epistemic evaluations might be context sensitive in a manner that would imply that an individual might be epistemically responsible in holding some moral belief without justification in one context, though not responsible in holding that same belief in a different context—wherein differences in context here involve different social groups. Of course, over time an individual may come to have a moral outlook whose basic moral assumptions differ markedly from the assumptions of his former

49. Here I skip over important complexities that would need to be considered before we could confidently say that all or most communities share many of the same basic moral assumptions. As Snare (1980) argues, the scope and importance that certain moral rules have in different cultures signifies real differences in the moral values and associated moral rules of those cultures. So, for example, merely from the fact that two cultures subscribe to *a* prohibition on lying does not mean that they both accept the same moral rule about lying.

50. See Kraybill, 1989, for a detailed description of Amish culture.

51. Incidently, the fact that we can and do positively evaluate the epistemic status of the moral beliefs of other groups that differ in some significant ways from our own does not imply that we must embrace the implications of any sort of epistemic relativism (normative contextualism). Earlier I explained why the view of epistemic responsibility is not a version of relativism. Here, I should point out that just as in Anglo-American law—in which there are limits to what, given the reasonable-person doctrine, we are willing to recognize as non-culpable behavior—so in the proposed conception of epistemic responsibility, there are limits to what we would allow as a responsibly held moral belief. Thus, a crazy 'moral' outlook with outrageous 'moral' norms would not qualify as an outlook relative to which individuals who conformed their moral beliefs accordingly would count as epistemically responsible. Part of the notion of an epistemically responsible agent involves having certain information and certain skills and abilities, the lack of which does not excuse. The same applies in connection with moral belief. For more on this issue as it pertains to the law, see Keeton et al., 1984: 170 ff.

moral outlook (perhaps as a result of a radical moral conversion not mediated by argumentation).[52] This sort of case is much like the one described in the previous paragraph. But even for an individual whose moral outlook remains relatively unchanged over a period of time, and for whom certain moral beliefs are basic in ordinary, engaged contexts of moral thought and deliberation, there may be special contexts in which those moral beliefs are not basic. One kind of case that fits this description is a context in which one is confronted with skeptical challenges to one's moral outlook—challenges that are aimed at those moral beliefs that, in engaged contexts, are contextually basic. Let me spell out the kind of case I have in mind in a bit more detail.

Let us distinguish between what I have called an engaged context of moral thought and a detached context, in which one is not thinking and deliberating entirely from within her or his moral outlook but is instead looking at it from the outside, as it were. In an engaged context of moral thinking, wherein skeptical challenges to that outlook are not in focus, one is (ceteris paribus) epistemically responsible in holding (without justification) those basic moral beliefs and assumptions more or less fundamental to the outlook. However, once skeptical challenges are taken seriously, then the context has been switched (in the sense that the relevant social group or community crucial for epistemic evaluation is the group of skeptics). In this relatively detached context in which, we are supposing, the core moral assumptions of one's moral outlook are being challenged, those ordinarily basic moral beliefs are no longer basic. For example, suppose we are considering skeptical challenges to the deepest aspects of a person's moral outlook, and imagine that this person is confronted by a group of Nietzscheans who argue, in effect, that democratically structured societies produce a false moral conscience and that, therefore, many of the moral beliefs taken for granted in such societies are mistaken or at least questionable. In such detached contexts, what often seems to happen is that the epistemic norms operative in them differ from those operative in engaged contexts; in particular, in contexts of the former sort, one is not permitted to take for granted the moral beliefs that one may take for granted in contexts of the latter sort. The reason for the difference in epistemic norms governing these contexts is fairly obvious. In engaged contexts, in which the point and purpose of the context is (speaking roughly) to negotiate one's way around in a social world, one is not required to have reasons (so I have argued) for certain moral beliefs that are fundamental to the outlook. In detached contexts, in which the point and purpose of the context is to examine one's moral outlook in an effort, for example, to detect and correct any cultural or idiosyncratic biases, one is not allowed to take one's core moral beliefs and assumptions as basic.

Here is an example of this sort of phenomenon. A few years ago, I served as a member on an ad hoc university committee in charge of coming up with a code of ethics for the university. The group was represented by various faculty members from different colleges in the university. In our very first meeting, in which we were

---

52. See DePaul, 1993: ch. 1, for a description of such radical moral conversions that result from a 'discontinuous' shift in one's moral outlook.

discussing how to proceed, one member voiced skepticism about morality in general. The skeptic did not get around to explaining the source of his skepticism, but in that context the challenge to morality he was voicing was not taken seriously by the members of the committee (the chair of the committee managed to quickly turn the discussion to other matters)—and properly so, since in that context, the point and purpose of the committee was to come up with a code of ethics to be submitted to the president of the university. The committee's discussion proceeded against a background of shared moral beliefs, and we discussed not only matters of how to write up a code of ethics, but we discussed certain substantive moral issues about professional conduct, over which there was some disagreement (at least initially). The conclusions we came to as a result of discussion (and against a background of common moral assumptions) were, I submit, epistemically responsible, though I doubt seriously that very few, if any, on the committee would have been able to rebut the sorts of challenges being voiced by the skeptic (at least, had they been voiced by someone armed with some reasons in their defense). In the ethically engaged context in which the committee members found themselves, certain moral beliefs were taken for granted as a basis for our deliberations about certain moral issues. Regardless of whether members of the committee could defend their basic moral beliefs against skeptical challenges, or even whether they had justifying reasons that they might be able to rehearse, I submit that the moral conclusions reached by the committee were justified ones. In more of a detached context, in which skeptical challenges get their hold, those same beliefs would be in need of justification.

Cases that fit the general description in which one enters a so-called detached context raise interesting questions about the conditions under which it becomes appropriate, or perhaps required, to enter such a context, as well as questions about the sorts of epistemic norms operative in such contexts. Investigating these matters would require that we consider specific cases in some detail, which we cannot pursue here.

Moral Judgment

We come finally to tenet T4. According to the version of structural contextualism I am articulating, basic moral beliefs often provide the justificatory basis for other, inferentially justified beliefs. Often, talk of inference is taken to be a matter of deductive connections between statements or beliefs. But a realistic account of moral reasoning must, I think, recognize Ross's claim that, in many instances, moral reasoning does not follow a simple deductive pattern; in fact, in many instances such reasoning is not governed by rules that dictate what in particular it is rational to believe. Ross's view has been the subject of philosophical dissatisfaction partly because he refuses to provide any algorithm or general procedure for arriving at justified moral beliefs in cases in which two or more morally relevant considerations are present and at least one of them supports one moral evaluation of the action and one of the others supports an opposing moral evaluation. The problem is supposed to be that unless there is some general covering rule or procedure that is to be followed in coming to some overall moral evaluation about the action, then any resulting moral judgment on the agent's part will be arbitrary and hence unjustified.

I think Ross is right about how we often *do* reason about moral matters: we work with a handful of irreducible mid-level moral generalizations that cannot be lexically ordered, so as to provide a super rule for adjudicating conflicts among the generalizations. Nevertheless, moral thought and deliberation that is not rule governed in this way often yields moral beliefs that one is justified in holding. For instance, with issues such as abortion (in which various relevant considerations pull in opposite moral directions), people reason about the morality of that practice (or specific instances of it) using basically the same stock of general, mid-level moral beliefs, even though individuals can differ in their moral assessment of this practice and be justified in their differing individual responses. Moreover, in addition to cases of conflicting moral generalizations, there are many cases in which it is unclear whether some moral generalization correctly applies to a particular case. After all, moral generalizations are expressed in terms of such notions as *harm, lying, innocent person*, and so forth, that are vague. Like cases of conflict, these cases of application require that what I am calling *moral judgment* play an important epistemic role in coming to have justified moral beliefs. What we must do, then, is square our moral epistemology with these facts.

First I will make a brief terminological remark. In chapter 4, I told a story about moral judgment, but in that context, the term 'judgment' was being used to refer to a certain psychological state that, I went on to suggest, might just as well be called a moral belief. ('Judgment' is also sometimes used to indicate the content of the relevant state.) However, in the present context, talk of moral judgment is being used to refer to a kind of capacity (or related set of capacities) to come to decisions, form beliefs, and do it well. (See Brown's characterization in the next paragraph.) We can call this sense of 'judgment' the virtue sense of the term, and it is this sense of the term that is here under discussion.

To resume: there are both philosophical and empirical considerations that support my contention that non-rule-based moral thinking can yield justified moral belief. The main philosophical consideration has to do with the recent work of some philosophers on the notion of rationality. H. I. Brown (1988), for instance, has criticized what he calls the 'traditional' conception of rationality, according to which all rational belief is belief according to some rule. Brown persuasively argues that the traditional view involves an impossible ideal implying that even rigorous scientific inquiry must be counted as irrational. What Brown proposes is a new model of rationality, one that makes a place for what he simply calls *judgment*: "the ability to evaluate a situation, assess evidence, and come to a reasonable decision without following rules" (137).[53] So, this general model of rationality that assigns a significant epistemic role to judgment comports well with the view that scientific inquiry is rational, and also comports well with the claim that weighing

---

53. This same theme is stressed by Putnam in connection with explaining the success of science. He points out that attempts to formalize the scientific method have not worked and are not going to work, and so we should get over what he calls 'method fetishism' in trying to make sense of scientific rationality. Rather, according to Putnam, scientists work with a set of non-algorithmic, informal 'maxims' that require "informal rationality, i.e. intelligence and common sense, to apply" (1981: 195).

up competing moral considerations and, on the basis of this weighing, making a judgment (which is not a matter of conforming to some specifiable rule) can result in rational or justified belief. I suspect that one of the reasons that philosophers have been so unsympathetic to Ross is because they take science as our paradigm of rational inquiry, assume that such inquiry is rule governed, and so conclude that in a view like Ross's, moral thinking has to be epistemically defective. This line of thought is thoroughly undermined by Brown. Indeed, if Brown is right, then the role of moral judgment in coming to have justified moral beliefs is not some isolated and otherwise epistemically queer phenomenon peculiar to moral thinking, but merely an instance of a quite general phenomenon.

The relevant empirical consideration bearing on this issue can be found in the 1990 paper by the Dreyfus brothers mentioned earlier. In that paper, they argue that moral thinking and judging are activities much like many physical and intellectual activities (they discuss driving a car and playing chess), in that doing them well is a skill that develops through stages. When starting out, a novice chess player is taught to consciously follow rules that, with experience, are no longer consciously entertained, until eventually she or he can just 'see' how to react to the various types of chess positions. The Dreyfus brothers' main point, which they apply to the case of moral reasoning, is that an individual's becoming increasingly adept at some complex activity involves acquiring a skill—coming to *know how* to do something, wherein one does not consciously rely on rules (which is not to say that rules play no justificatory role at all in coming to have justified moral beliefs about specific cases). But they make a further Rossian point, namely, that adept moral judgment and reasoning in complex cases, in which a number of morally relevant considerations come into play, is not grounded in any algorithm or super rule that would rationally determine some outcome. They write:

> [I]f the phenomenology of skillful coping we have presented is right, principles and theories serve only for early stages of learning; no principle or theory "grounds" an expert ethical response, any more than in chess there is a theory or rule that explains a master-level move. As we have seen in the case of chess, recognizing that there is no way to ground one's intuitions in an explanation is an important step on the way to acquiring expertise. (Dreyfus and Dreyfus, 1990: 252)

The phenomenology of moral thinking that the Dreyfus brothers present supports that dimension of the Rossian view that emphasizes the role of moral judgment in coming to make reasonable moral decisions, and in coming to have justified moral beliefs.

These remarks about moral judgment comport well with my contextualist moral epistemology. In cases in which an expert moral thinker mulls over some issue and comes to a belief about the morality of some action or whatever, she is engaged in an activity of weighing and balancing various morally relevant considerations—considerations reflected in her general moral beliefs that I have been saying are contextually basic. The moral belief she eventually settles on is not dictated by any algorithm she has; trained moral judgment is operative here. Nevertheless, the expert is reasoning about the case, and she can, if asked, state those reasons that, in the end, were decisive. Of course, at bottom, her reasons are represented by mid-level moral beliefs. So, after the fact, our expert can provide a justification for her belief, terminating in her mid-level moral beliefs, but there is no covering rule she followed that dictates that one sort of general moral consideration should trump competing moral considerations in this case. What this reveals about those epistemic norms governing moral belief is that we operate according to epistemic norms, some of which permit one to hold moral beliefs, in certain circumstances, on the basis of an exercise of one's moral judgment.[54]

VII. Accommodation

Having outlined my contextualist moral epistemology, I now want to provide a defense of my view. Let me begin with a reminder of some general methodological constraints governing metaethical theorizing.

Some Remarks about Methodology

You may recall from chapter 1 that metaethical theorizing is constrained by two very broad desiderata: a plausible metaethical view should comport with ordinary assumptions about moral discourse and practice (D1), and it should comport with plausible general views and assumptions from other areas of philosophy, as well as with plausible views and assumptions from other disciplines (D2). Part of a comprehensive metaethical view includes a view about the epistemology of moral belief, and so our epistemological theorizing should be governed by D1 and D2. D1, suitably modified for purposes of evaluating epistemological views, involves the project of what I have been calling 'internal accommodation'—one's epistemological view ought to comport with various deeply embedded presumptions of commonsense epistemic discourse. And here it is relevant to compare contextualism with its foundationalist and coherentist competitors to see whether there is any advantage in one of these views over the others. I argue below that the contextualist has the edge.

D2—involving the project of 'external accommodation'—has two dimensions: one metaphysical, one methodological. Regarding the requirement that one's epistemology about moral belief comport with various other philosophical views and assumptions, I am interested in the project of naturalistic accommodation, which, as explained in chapter 1, requires that we respect what I called the thesis of epistemological accommodation (N3): all knowledge (and justification) associated with non-scientific discourse must comport with the sort of naturalistic interpre-

---

54. Of course, there is much to say about moral judgment and what makes such judgment *good* judgment, even if it is not rule governed. Space does not permit treatment of this topic here, but the importance of *exemplars* (mentioned earlier in describing a moral outlook) figures importantly here. Good moral judgment is judgment that one would expect the moral experts to make. This is the sort of story we find in Brown (1988) and in Dreyfus and Dreyfus (1990), which, as the Dreyfus brothers point out, is circular—but (they claim) not viciously so.

tation we use to explain our access to, and knowledge of (and justified belief about), the natural, physical world generally. This is the metaphysical dimension of external accommodation. The idea is that in telling a story about the epistemology of moral belief, postulation of, for example, non-sensuous faculties of intuition and the like (that would violate naturalistic metaphysical scruples) are not allowed. Of course, I have denied that there are any objective moral facts, properties, or relations in the world, so I do not shoulder the sort of accommodation burden that a moral realist must shoulder; I do not have to provide a naturalistically acceptable account of our access to such facts, properties, and relations. Nevertheless, there is still accommodation work to be done since one must be able to make sense of the point and purpose (from a naturalistic perspective) of epistemic discourse and practice in connection with moral discourse, whose primary function is not to describe features of an independent world.

The other element of D2, namely, that one's epistemological view comport with views and assumptions from various disciplines other than philosophy, concerns matters of methodology in developing a plausible epistemology. Here, we naturally look to empirical work in psychology, physiology, and perhaps sociology and anthropology as well, to inform our epistemological theorizing. Allowing empirical assumptions, views, and theories to influence one's epistemological theorizing is to embrace the methodology of 'naturalized epistemology.'[55]

Internal Accommodation

Applied to epistemological theorizing, then, D1 requires that we examine the workings of ordinary epistemic evaluations of moral claims and beliefs. Focusing on justification for the time being, people do, on occasion, assert that some of their own moral beliefs and some of the moral beliefs of others are justified, and they sometimes withhold ascriptions of justification or outright deny that some of their own moral beliefs or those of others are justified. In short, we ordinarily assume that some ascriptions of justification to moral beliefs are true and others are not true. All other things being equal, an epistemology of moral belief that can preserve these general assumptions, and do so in a way that preserves the truth or correctness of those epistemic evaluations that we take to be obviously true, is to be preferred to one that does not.

I have been assuming all along that many ordinary people are often doxastically justified (in some sense) in a good number of the moral beliefs they hold, and I have been asking what sort of epistemology provides the most plausible story about the epistemic status of ordinary moral belief. Thus, I began my epistemological investigation with an admittedly antiskeptical stance—at least when it comes to the possibility of the doxastic justification of moral belief. And so, as I

---

55. Naturalized epistemology is a methodological view and not a metaphysical view. What we might call 'epistemological naturalism'—the epistemological analog of ethical naturalism—is a metaphysical view about the nature of epistemic facts and properties. Employing the naturalized epistemological method does not imply commitment to epistemological naturalism.

see it, one (admittedly overridable) constraint on any adequate epistemology of moral belief is that it comport with this antiskeptical presumption. I hope I have made an adequate case for thinking that my contextualism comports with this antiskeptical presumption. What I want to argue is that versions of foundationalism and coherentism do not do as well on this count.

Moral Foundationalism: Some Varieties

First, let us consider versions of moral foundationalism, according to which regresses of justification are halted by basic moral beliefs—basic in the sense that they enjoy positive epistemic justification that does not derive from inferential relations to other beliefs. There is quite a variety of foundationalist views—views that differ on one or more of the following issues.

1. The epistemic status required of epistemically basic beliefs. For instance, one might demand that foundational beliefs be indubitable, incorrigible, or perhaps infallible in order to serve as an adequate foundation, while more modest views might only require that such beliefs be adequately justified by being, for example, self-evident.
2. The sorts of connections required of basic and non-basic beliefs in order for the former to serve as an adequate foundation for the latter. Strict versions would require that the connections between foundational beliefs and justified inferential beliefs be deductive; more liberal views would allow non-deductive connections.
3. The types of beliefs that can serve as an adequate foundation, whereby in ethics the types in question have to do with the level of generality of the belief. Sidgwick (1879) distinguished among *perceptual intuitionism*, according to which particular moral beliefs—beliefs about the moral status of token actions, specific persons, and institutions—are properly basic; *dogmatic intuitionism*, according to which moral rules (e.g., the Ten Commandments) are properly basic; and *philosophical intuitionism*, according to which high-level moral principles (e.g., the principle of utility or Kant's categorical imperative) are properly basic. (These days, philosophers distinguish *particularist* versions of intuitionism [perceptual intuitionism] from *generalist* versions [Sidgwick's other two categories].)
4. The specific story to be told about the justification of basic moral beliefs. As I explain later in this chapter, classical versions of foundationalism (versions of ethical intuitionism) require that basic moral beliefs be non-inferentially justified, but, interestingly, it is possible for a foundationalist to reject this idea.

So, given the variety of possible foundationalist views in ethics, one must be on guard against leveling criticisms that only affect some, but not all, versions of foundationalism. I do not plan to treat each conceivable version of moral foundationalism (or even all of the versions that find defenders) and argue against them one by one. Rather, my plan is to distinguish *intuitionistic* versions of foundationalism from *non-intuitionistic* versions and then argue that specific versions of both general kinds—versions that are fairly representative of moral foundationalism—tend to impose very demanding epistemic burdens on ordinary agents and thus do not comfortably comport with the antiskeptical presumption in question.

Intuitionistic Versions of Moral Foundationalism

According to intuitionistic versions of foundationalism, certain moral beliefs are non-inferentially justified on the basis of some sort of direct grasp, intuition, or intellectual cognition of certain moral statements at which one arrives through a process of reflection.[56] One might be inclined to argue that such views do not comport with D2 since they presuppose that humans are capable of some mysterious, non-natural mode of cognition. Apparently, the source of this worry is that intuitionism, which I am here construing as a strictly epistemological doctrine, has been associated with non-naturalism in ethics, and so the idea seems to be that in order to have any sort of direct grasp of non-natural facts and properties, one would have to have some special mental capacity to accomplish such grasping of a sort that runs afoul of D2. But it should be clear that intuitionism is not saddled with any such commitments that would run afoul of a thoroughgoing naturalism.[57]

Again, some critics of intuitionism argue that there cannot be non-inferentially justified moral beliefs because all justified beliefs must involve inferential relations with other beliefs. For example, Brink (1989: 116–22) understands moral intuitionism to be committed to the idea that some moral beliefs (the foundational ones) are self-justifying. He then argues that since a justified belief is one for which the individual holding the belief has a reason, the very idea of a self-justified belief is the idea of a belief's being a reason for itself, which, as he points out, results in an unacceptable, vicious circle of justification. *If* such a criticism can be made to apply,[58] then foundationalism is hopeless. But I do not need to argue for any such strong claim in order to make my case for contextualism over and against intuitionism. I can allow that there are, or can be, non-inferentially justified moral

---

56. Actually, one should distinguish at least three types of view that might be offered about the non-inferential justification of foundational beliefs. In addition to appealing to intellectual cognition or reflection as a basis for explaining the epistemic status of foundational moral beliefs, a foundationalist might instead appeal to certain sorts of emotions as a basis for explaining the non-inferential justification of foundational moral beliefs, or, again, she might attempt to tell an externalist story about such beliefs. I plan to limit my discussion to reflectionist versions of intuitionism since I think the general sort of worry I have about these versions also applies to the other versions. For a brief but useful discussion of all three versions, see Sinnott-Armstrong, 1996.

57. See Brink, 1989: 109–10, and Audi, 1996, for discussions of this point.

58. There is a serious problem with Brink's characterization of foundationalism as requiring that foundational beliefs be *self-justifying*. If talk of a belief's being self-justifying means that somehow the justification for the belief is the belief itself (which is the basis for Brink's dismissal of foundationalism), then except perhaps for simple analytic truths (assuming there are any), no beliefs are self-justifying. But, as many defenders of foundationalism point out, "Minimal Foundationalism does not require that any belief be self-justified, but only that some beliefs be immediately justified; and the former is only one possible form of the latter" (Alston, 1976a, reprinted in Alston, 1989: 48).

beliefs, for example, moral beliefs that are, in some sense, self-evident, and I can allow that individuals may come to have a battery of self-evident moral beliefs that serve as an adequate basis for their coming to have justified moral beliefs that are not self-evident. I claim (1) that having the sort of structure of moral belief described by intuitionism is not necessary for having any justified moral beliefs and that, moreover, (2) intuitionism either tends to impose unnecessary epistemic burdens on ordinary individuals, or it is really not significantly different from my contextualism in its account of the epistemic status of basic moral beliefs. Let me take these points one by one.

I hope I have made a convincing case that one can come to have justified moral beliefs through their being based on non-justified, though responsibly held, moral beliefs. This much has been the main burden of this chapter. If I have been successful, then, by implication, intuitionism is not necessary for justified moral belief. I grant that a crucial part of making my case for contextualism is working with a certain conception of justification that has to do with being epistemically responsible, and perhaps the foundationalist has some other, stronger notion of justification in mind. Perhaps. But, as I have stressed all along, I am interested here in whatever notion of justification (or rationality) is appropriate for evaluating ordinary moral belief, and I take the relevant notion to be one of responsible belief. (I say more about these matters later in this chapter.)

My second claim — that intuitionism tends to impose unnecessary epistemic burdens on individuals for purposes of being adequately justified (in ordinary contexts) in holding moral beliefs — requires distinguishing older, more traditional versions from newer, more modest versions of the view. The trend among foundationalists — both in moral epistemology and epistemology generally — has been to defend modest versions of the view that tend to minimize the epistemic burdens on individuals. So let me first explain why older versions of the view tend to impose unrealistic epistemic burdens on ordinary believers and then turn to more recent, modest versions.

One way to show that certain moral beliefs are (or can be) non-inferentially justified would be to demonstrate that they enjoy a kind of epistemic privilege that suffices for an individual's justifiedly holding such beliefs apart from their being inferentially justified. In the history of the epistemology of empirical belief, certain types of empirical belief (usually beliefs about one's own mental states) have been thought to enjoy such properties as being *infallible, indubitable,* and *self-evident.* Presumably, beliefs that have some or all of these properties ensure that the believer justifiedly holds such beliefs.[59] Let us briefly consider versions of moral foundationalism that would appeal to one of these properties in telling a story about epistemically basic moral beliefs.

---

59. There are other varieties of epistemic privilege that I do not plan to discuss here. The three I have chosen to discuss will be sufficient for what I have to say about intuitionism. For a discussion of the many varieties of epistemic privilege, see Alston, 1971.

Basic Moral Beliefs as Infallible

To say that a person is infallible with regard to a type of proposition (and, hence, to say that a person's belief of the relevant type is infallible) is to say that it is not possible for the person to believe a proposition of the relevant type and yet be mistaken in one's belief. In short, infallibility in one's belief guarantees its truth.[60] One general question about infallibility concerns whether a belief that has this property really does suffice for the believer's being justified in holding the belief since, unless the believer realizes that he is infallible with regard to some class of propositions, he would not seem to be justified in his belief.[61] But waiving this worry, we need to ask whether there are, or even could be, any infallible moral beliefs.

It is relevant to note that were there any (non-trivial) propositions at all about which one was infallible, it seems that propositions ascribing some occurrent mental state to oneself would be prime candidates. However, some philosophers[62] have plausibly argued against infallibility with regard to even this subject matter, which should make us antecedently dubious about the prospects of infallibility with regard to moral propositions. Moreover, some metaethical views simply rule out moral infallibilism. If one is a moral realist and holds that the truth of a moral statement is independent of the attitudes, beliefs, and conventions of human individuals and groups no matter how epistemically well situated they might be for purposes of moral thought and deliberation, then these individuals cannot be in a state of infallibility with regard to (non-trivial) moral statements; error in moral belief is always possible. Even if one were to accept a constructivist view of moral truth, according to which certain moral statements are true by virtue of being accepted under certain circumstances, moral infallibilism would not be secured in a way relevant to our present discussion. We are interested in the possibility of there being non-inferentially justified moral beliefs, and we are considering infallibilism as one way in which we might make sense of such beliefs.

We are understanding infallibilism as roughly the idea that for a certain class of statements, one can be such that merely believing one of them is sufficient for its truth. So, if we consider the most plausible forms of constructivism—forms according to which (roughly) basic moral truths are those statements that would be accepted by individuals who are ideally situated—then it is clear that although

---

60. Here I plan to skip over complications that concern the kind of modality involved in talk about impossibility—whether what is intended is logical impossibility, nomological impossibility, or impossibility of some other kind. Although important for certain purposes (see the discussion later in this chapter), skipping this complication will not affect my discussion here. Again, see Alston, 1971, for a discussion.

61. As Alston (1971; note C added in the reprinted version in Alston, 1989) points out, whether infallibility entails justification depends on the sort of conception of justification one is working with and, in particular, whether one is working with an internalist, as opposed to an externalist, conception of justification.

62. See, for example, Aune, 1967: ch. 2, and Armstrong, 1968: ch. 6.

such individuals are infallible (they cannot possibly be mistaken) with regard to the moral statements they accept, their believing those statements is inferentially justified since those beliefs are accepted on the basis of other beliefs they hold. I conclude that it is doubtful that there could be any infallible (non-trivial) moral beliefs, and so we can eliminate infallibilist intuitionism from consideration.

Basic Moral Beliefs as Indubitable

To say that an individual's belief about some subject matter (type of proposition) is indubitable is to say that it is not possible for that person to believe a proposition of the relevant type and yet have any grounds for doubting that the proposition is true. The idea would then be that indubitable moral beliefs are foundational and can serve as a basis for the justification of the other moral beliefs. Here, we need to pay attention to the sort of modal claim being made. There are at least three possibilities to consider. First, the claim might be that it is *logically (conceptually) impossible* for one to believe some proposition and at the same time have grounds for thinking that it is false. But surely, for any non-trivial moral statement, this claim is false. For one thing, one might believe some moral proposition p, have grounds for thinking that p is false, and yet simply not realize that one has grounds for doubt. Maybe one just has not made the relevant connection between the belief in question and the undermining grounds one has, or maybe one could not normally be expected to recognize that those grounds undermine one's belief. Thus, perhaps we should revise things so that the indubitability claim is that it is not logically possible for one to hold some belief (of the relevant type) and at the same time *recognize* that one has grounds for doubting the truth of that proposition.

But however we precisely characterize this notion of logical indubitability, it is not plausible for moral propositions. Surely, for any non-trivial moral proposition, it is at least logically possible for someone to believe it and fully recognize that one has grounds for doubting the proposition. The moral claim that it is wrong to torture babies for fun is about as uncontroversial a moral claim as can be. The moral claim that it is prima facie wrong to intentionally take the life of another human being is another. But neither of these claims is logically indubitable; it is possible for people to believe these propositions and at the same time realize that arguments for the claim that morality is a sham (which one may not be able to rebut) provide some grounds for doubting these and other affirmative moral claims. It just does not seem plausible to suppose that there are any logically indubitable moral beliefs, and so any version of moral foundationalism that would attempt to account for foundational beliefs in terms of this notion of indubitability is not plausible.

We arrive at a similar verdict if we weaken the notion of impossibility and construe the claim as saying that it is *nomologically impossible* for an individual to have certain moral beliefs and yet, at the same time, recognize grounds for doubting the truth of the moral propositions believed. Here, the idea would be that there is some sort of psychological law that guarantees the connection between having the belief and not recognizing grounds for doubt. But I can think of no reason to suppose that there are any such laws—at least with regard to any type of moral belief—and even if there were such laws, it is not clear how the fact that some moral belief is nomologically indubitable would confer justification on the belief.

A third possibility is to construe the notion of impossibility so that the claim is that it is *normatively impossible* for an individual to believe a moral proposition of a certain type and yet have good reasons to doubt the truth of the proposition. Here, the idea would be that were one to hold such and such moral belief and at the same time recognize grounds for doubting the truth of the proposition believed, then one would be in violation of some epistemic norm. In the simplest case, the epistemic norm in question would be something like:

> One ought not believe proposition p (of type M) if one recognizes grounds for doubting the truth of p.

One may need to tinker with the formulation of this norm to get it just right, but any refinements along these lines will not matter for our discussion because the main point I want to stress is that this notion of normative indubitability seems to come quite close in some ways to my characterization of contextually basic beliefs. According to my story, there are, or can be, moral beliefs that one holds that are (at least in the relevant context) not justified on the basis of other propositions one holds; in fact, they are not positively justified at all, but are nevertheless responsibly held moral beliefs. Non-justified, responsibly held moral beliefs are beliefs that one need have no positive grounds for accepting, though one is still responsible for holding them, at least in part because there are no obvious counterpossibilities (grounds for doubt) of which one is currently aware or of which one ought to be aware.

But this description of non-justified, responsibly held belief comes fairly close to the current description of a normatively indubitable belief. The foundationalist will prefer to use the term 'justified' in connection with such beliefs and then claim that they are prime candidates for non-inferentially justified moral beliefs that can serve as a foundation for inferentially justified moral beliefs. I am using the term 'justified' to refer only to those beliefs for which one has positive grounds or reasons for accepting—which does not rule out the possibility of there being non-inferentially justified beliefs. Some writers like to distinguish between *positively justified* and *negatively justified* beliefs, using the former to refer to what I am simply calling justified beliefs, and reserving the latter for what I prefer to call non-justified, responsibly held beliefs. How exactly one wants to use the terms 'justified' and 'non-justified' is not that important here. My claim is simply that if the foundationalist construes foundational moral beliefs in terms of normative indubitability, then, at bottom, there is not much difference between this brand of intuitionist foundationalism and my contextualism, at least in the accounts given about the epistemic status of basic moral beliefs.

However, there does remain one important difference between the views, namely, in my view, basic moral beliefs are context sensitive in a way that the foundationalist apparently denies. What sorts of counterpossibilities regarding one's moral beliefs one is responsible for checking depends on features of one's context in ways I have tried to indicate earlier in this chapter. So whether a moral belief is contextually basic depends on context, and what is basic in one context (e.g., an ordinary context of moral thought and deliberation) may not be basic in other contexts (e.g., skeptical contexts in which one's core moral beliefs are being challenged). I hope I have made a convincing case for the plausibility of this dimension of my view; if I have, then my contextualism is to be preferred to the sort of intuitionist foundationalism under consideration.

Basic Moral Beliefs as Self-Evident

I turn now to more modest versions of intuitionist foundationalism that appeal to the claims of *self-evidence* and, in some cases, to a fairly weak notion of non-inferential justification to account for the epistemic status of foundational moral beliefs.

To say that a proposition is self-evident (for someone at a specific time) is (roughly) to say that it is impossible for the person to believe that proposition and at the same time to fail to be justified in holding that belief. This formulation is perhaps too strong since it implies that merely holding some belief is enough for one to thereby be justified in holding it, but historically, philosophers have wanted to allow that a proposition could be self-evident without its being the case that mere belief implies justification. After all, one may believe some claim but fail to grasp its truth in the manner required for that claim's being self-evident. But we need to be clearer about this notion of self-evidence.

Robert Audi (1993a, 1996) has recently articulated and defended a modest form of intuitionism that involves the notion of self-evidence. In Audi's understanding of this notion, a self-evident proposition is:

> (roughly) a truth such that understanding it will meet two conditions: that understanding is (a) sufficient for one's being justified in believing it (i.e., for having justification for believing it, whether one in fact believes it or not)—this is why such a truth is evident *in itself*—and (b) sufficient for knowing the proposition provided one believes it on the *basis* of understanding it. (Audi, 1996: 114)

If we want to allow that foundational beliefs can be false, then we should perhaps replace this notion of self-evidence, which entails that self-evident propositions are true, with a notion of *self-justification*, which is like the notion of self-evidence, but lacking the truth implication. In any case, for both notions the crucial idea is that *adequate understanding* of the proposition yields non-inferential justification (and knowledge in the case of self-evident propositions) of the belief that has that proposition as it content (at least given that one's belief is based on one's understanding).

Following Ross, Audi thinks that propositions characterizing Rossian prima facie duties are prime candidates for being self-evident, though, as he points out, it may well be that for most ordinary people, being able to properly grasp the truth of a self-evident proposition may not be immediate, in the sense that merely understanding what such a proposition says is sufficient for grasping its truth. Rather, given the richness and complexity of, for example, the prima facie duty regarding the keeping of promises, grasping its truth through understanding may require some amount of reflection. Audi thus distinguishes between two classes of possible self-evident propositions: *immediately self-evident* and *mediately self-evident* propositions. Reflection is required for the sort of adequate understanding that provides the proper epistemic basis for having non-inferential justification of both types of self-evident propositions. However, the amount and type of reflection required for adequate understanding can differ: in the simplest cases — cases of immediate self-evidence — merely focusing on the proposition yields sufficient understanding, whereas in more complex cases (cases of mediate self-evidence) adequate understanding may require quite complicated and time-consuming reflection.[63]

This point about mediately self-evident moral propositions is important. On the one hand, it saves the intuitionist from the objection that since there are very few, if any, substantial moral propositions whose truth can be grasped immediately, there simply are not any self-evident moral propositions — or enough of them to provide an adequate foundation for arriving at an interesting set of justified non-foundational moral beliefs. But, on the other hand, it raises worries about the epistemology of ordinary moral belief. If one were to develop a version of moral intuitionism, according to which foundational moral beliefs satisfy the requirements of self-evidence, then, given the amount of serious reflection that seems required for adequately understanding a self-evident moral proposition in order to properly grasp its truth, one wonders whether very many ordinary folks would have any non-inferentially justified moral beliefs and hence any (or very many) justified moral beliefs at all. It all depends on what is needed for an *adequate* understanding of self-evident moral propositions. In one place, Audi notes that "in some cases one can see *what* a self-evident proposition says — and thus understand it — before seeing *that*, or how, it is true" (Audi, 1996: 115). Moreover, the prime candidates for self-evidence in ethics — general moral propositions that express prima facie duties — do seem (as already noted) to require some hard reflection to properly grasp their truth in a way that would yield non-inferential justification and possibly knowledge of them.

I suspect that most ordinary folks do not have the kind of adequate understanding required, and so Audi's notion of self-evidence will not help the intuitionist who is interested in the epistemology of ordinary moral belief and who wants her view to comport with the antiskeptical presumption. This does not mean, of course, that self-evident moral propositions have no role to play in moral epistemology; certainly, if there are such propositions, then they will have an important role to play in the epistemology of theory acceptance. But this is not our present concern.

Audi also allows that certain moral propositions — both particular and general — can be objects of intuition (a mode of non-inferential belief formation that typically yields non-inferentially justified moral beliefs). Thus, in Audi's view, there

---

63. Audi (1996: 112–13) usefully distinguishes what he calls *conclusions of reflection* from *conclusions of inference*. Conclusions of the former sort involve reflection on, for instance, particular cases and then, through such reflection, coming to properly understand and grasp some general proposition. But no inference from premises is involved in this process, and so the conclusion reached is not a conclusion of inference. This allows that certain kinds of reflection can yield what are, strictly speaking, non-inferentially justified beliefs.

can be non-inferentially prima facie justified moral beliefs of propositions that are not self-evident. Audi characterizes intuitions as beliefs or belief-like cognitive states whose objects are propositions and that are: (1) not arrived at by inference (they are genetically non-inferential), (2) firmly held, (3) relevantly pretheoretical, and (4) based on an adequate understanding of their subject matter. With regard to the epistemic status of intuitions Audi writes:

> [A]s I have characterized intuitions, they are not only justificationally defeasible, but need not even be prima facie justified. Still, insofar as they are like certain perceptual beliefs (e.g., in being noninferential, "natural," and pretheoretical)— and perhaps more important—insofar as they are based on an understanding of their propositional object, there is reason to consider them prima facie justified (*in part because in such cases one tends to find it at best difficult to see how the proposition might be false*). (Audi, 1996: 116, my emphasis)

If one does not impose heavy-duty requirements on what counts as an adequate understanding of propositions that are the objects of intuition, and one thinks of the positive epistemic status that they have in terms of the parenthetical remark about finding it hard to see how the proposition is false, then this view of non-inferentially justified moral belief seems to be quite similar to my story about contextually basic moral beliefs. Contextually basic moral beliefs are those for which one has no positive evidence or grounds, but that, in the relevant context, are responsibly held, partly because there are no counterpossibilities that one is responsible for checking. And this implies that one can think of no relevant reasons for seeing how the believed proposition might be false. The notion of non-inferential prima facie justification that Audi employs seems, then, to be quite minimal (not requiring positive evidence or grounds) and is, moreover, characterized negatively in much the same way as I have characterized contextually basic moral beliefs. The difference here seems to be a verbal one. Again, insofar as the intuitionist is proposing an epistemology of moral belief that is seriously at odds with my contextualism, then I suspect that the view is implausible. Modest intuitionism that comports with the antiskeptical presumption seems to be only verbally different, at least in its characterization of basic moral beliefs, from my contextualism. (Though, as I have already mentioned, I think the fact that my view explicitly allows that basic beliefs are context relative is an advantage over versions of intuitionism that do not allow for this feature.)

Given my brief survey of some important forms of moral intuitionism, I conclude that such views, insofar as they really differ from contextualism, are not as plausible as contextualism as views about the epistemology of moral belief.

Non-Intuitionist Versions of Moral Foundationalism

If one defines moral foundationalism as the view that there is a certain privileged class of moral beliefs such that moral beliefs outside this class owe their justification, at least in part, to one or more members of the privileged class, whereas the members of the privileged class do not owe their justification to any other moral beliefs, then we allow that foundational moral beliefs might be inferentially justified, so long as their justifiers are non-moral beliefs. In fact, the attempt by many moral philosophers to find some non-moral foundation for moral beliefs — some realm of non-moral belief that could be used to justify, prove, or demonstrate moral claims — has been a major preoccupation of many moral philosophers. (You may recall the discussion from §I.)

It might be argued that this sort of non-intuitionist foundationalism is hopeless because it requires that moral statements be deducible from factual statements, and thus that it is possible to bridge the is/ought gap. But this would be wrong for two reasons. First, even if 'ought' statements (and moral statements generally) cannot be logically deduced from factual statements, it may be possible to properly infer them in some non-deductive manner of inference. Second, even if 'ought' statements cannot be inferred either deductively or non-deductively from some set of factual statements, it may be possible to infer them from non-moral normative statements. For instance, one might attempt to infer moral 'oughts' from 'oughts' of rationality. So without some serious argumentation, I do not think non-intuitionist foundationalism can be dismissed.[64]

The point I wish to make about versions of this species of moral foundation-alism is that they are best interpreted as attempts to provide an epistemology of theory acceptance and not as attempts to provide an epistemology of moral belief. As already mentioned earlier in §I, if in order to justifiedly believe any moral proposition one must one first infer certain moral propositions from some non-moral basis and then use such justified propositions as an inferential basis for coming to have further moral beliefs, it will turn out that very few ordinary people have any justified moral beliefs. This is made especially clear if we consider the sorts of non-moral foundations that moral philosophers have proposed. Gewirth, for instance, thinks that what he calls the principle of generic consistency can be derived from morally neutral premises having to do with the 'normative structure' implicit in the notions of action and reason (1978: 25–26). This fundamental moral principle can then be used to derive (together with relevant factual premises) more specific moral requirements. Gauthier (1986) attempts to derive moral constraints from non-moral premises having to do with rational choice. These views do not purport to give us an epistemology of moral belief as I am conceiving of it; rather, they are attempts to develop and justify a moral theory from a set of non-moral premises.[65] To suppose that for anyone justifiedly to believe some moral proposi-tion requires that they base some of their moral beliefs on an argument that

---

64. For more in the way of defense of this claim, see Timmons, 1987.

65. This is especially clear if we bear in mind the fact that a moral theory can be construed as either a *decision procedure* (purporting to provide agents with a method for arriving at true or justified moral beliefs) or as providing, through its principles, a *criterion* of right and wrong action (specifying those features of an action that make it right or wrong). Of course, one could hope to provide both a decision procedure and a criterion. Brink (1989: ch. 8) exploits this distinction in arguing that an objective version of act utilitarianism is plausible when construed as a criterion of right action. Perhaps the supreme moral principles proposed by writers such as Gewirth and Gauthier are most charitably interpreted as only attempting to provide us with a criterion of right action and not as 'hands-on' moral decision procedures.

involves a set of non-moral premises of the sort featured in the writings of philosophers like Gewirth and Gauthier is surely to imply moral skepticism at the level of ordinary moral belief. Perhaps being able to do the sort of thing that Gewirth and Gauthier are trying to do is necessary for being able to answer certain skeptical challenges and, hence, is necessary for being justified in non-ordinary, skeptically framed contexts. Perhaps. But our epistemological interests here are much broader than special contexts that philosophers like to puzzle over.

I conclude, then, that non-intuitionist versions of moral foundationalism are not plausible as accounts of the epistemology of ordinary moral belief. My general conclusion about intuitionist versions of moral foundationalism was that, insofar as they involve epistemological requirements for justifiedly believing moral propositions that really differ from the requirements involved in my contextualist story, they are implausible.

Moral Coherentism

According to moral coherentism, there are no epistemically privileged moral beliefs like the sort featured in versions of foundationalism. Rather, (1) all justification (and knowledge) is based on inferential relations among beliefs and (2) there is no privileged set of moral propositions whose inferential justification is morally neutral in the sense of not ultimately resting on at least some other moral propositions. Clause 1 rules out intuitionist foundationalisms, and clause 2 rules out non-intuitionist foundationalisms. In recent years, a version of moral coherentism, namely, *wide reflective equilibrium*, has been the moral epistemology of choice among coherentists, and so I shall focus on it.[66]

The methodology of wide reflective equilibrium is supposed to be an improvement over narrow reflective equilibrium. According to the latter, justification of moral propositions results simply from bringing general moral claims into coherence with particular moral claims. The idea is that we begin with a battery of moral beliefs at all levels of generality. We then filter those beliefs to weed out any that seem thoroughly mistaken or at least dubious enough to justify withholding belief. The resulting set of beliefs (considered moral beliefs) then become the basis for attempting to work toward a set of beliefs—at all levels of generality—that cohere. Reaching a state in which one's moral beliefs at all levels of generality cohere with one another is for one's moral beliefs to be in narrow reflective equilibrium.

We apparently reach a more plausible version of moral coherentism if we expand the circle of beliefs to include, in addition to moral beliefs at all levels of generality, relevant non-moral beliefs—especially any beliefs that represent well-established assumptions from areas of empirical inquiry, most notably from biology, psychology, sociology, anthropology, and economics. As Mackie remarks,

---

66. But see Ebertz, 1993, who argues that the model of reflective equilibrium is best interpreted as a version of modest foundationalism.

"Moral principles and ethical theories do not stand alone: they affect and are affected by beliefs and assumptions which belong to other fields, and not least to psychology, metaphysics, and religion" (1977: 203). The proponent of wide reflective equilibrium recognizes this point and proposes that justification of moral belief emerges from the overall coherence of a battery of beliefs, both moral and non-moral. The main alleged advantage of wide over narrow reflective equilibrium is that a wider circle of coherent beliefs indicates a higher degree of reliability of those moral beliefs that are members of the coherent set and less chance that the general moral beliefs are merely rationalizations of some set of particular moral beliefs.[67]

The first thing to point out about wide reflective equilibrium is that, as originally proposed by Rawls (1951) and later refined by Daniels (1979), it is intended as an epistemology of theory acceptance in ethics and not as an epistemology of moral belief.[68] The main difference between this methodology and versions of non-intuitionist foundationalism (which, in contrast to intuitionist versions, might be called 'wide foundationalism') has to do with the justification of those non-moral beliefs and assumptions that presumably can play a role in the justification of moral beliefs. For the foundationalist, but not for the coherentist, such assumptions do not owe their justification to any moral beliefs or assumptions. Otherwise the views are similar. And so, the worries I have expressed about the plausibility of non-intuitionist foundationalism as an account of the epistemology of moral belief apply also to wide reflective equilibrium. In short, the requirements of wide reflective equilibrium are much too demanding of ordinary folks for them to be justified in holding many of the moral beliefs they hold.

I want to reinforce this verdict about the coherence theory by briefly considering Brink's articulation and defense of moral coherentism. Brink's work is particularly interesting for our purposes because he proposes coherentism as an account of the epistemology of moral belief and not just as an account of the epistemology of moral theory acceptance.

In defending moral coherentism, Brink's main strategy is to employ what he calls 'the epistemological requirement,' namely, that all justifying beliefs be justified, and then argue that from among competing epistemological theories (intuitionist foundationalism being the chief rival to coherentism), only coherentism adequately satisfies this requirement. His defense involves a distinction between what he calls *systematic* justification and *contextualist* justification.

> Systematic justification is absolute or complete justification and results from consistently applying the epistemological requirement that justifying beliefs be justified. Contextualist justification, by contrast, is partial or incomplete justification and results from refusing to apply the epistemological requirement consistently.
> ... We satisfy ourselves with some degree or other of contextualist justification, both because we believe our background beliefs can be justified, and because

---

67. See Daniels, 1979, for a discussion of the advantages of wide over narrow reflective equilibrium. But see Holmgren, 1989, for an opposing view.
68. See especially Daniels, 1979: 257, n. 1.

pursuit of systematic justification would prevent us from getting on with our inquiries. But the demand for systematic justification is an intelligible one that we must answer if we are to take skepticism seriously. (Brink, 1989: 123)

Coherentism, generally, and moral coherentism in particular, is understood by Brink to involve non-linear, holistic justification as primary in the justification of any particular belief. Linear inferential justification is what we might call 'belief-to-belief' justification, in which the inferential justification of any one belief is a matter of its being appropriately related to some other belief (or set of beliefs), the latter having some degree of justification that gets passed along to the inferentially justified belief. By contrast, holism about justification construes inferential justification in what we might call a 'system-to-belief' manner, in which the primary locus of justification is at the level of an entire system of an appropriately interconnected web of belief, in virtue of which the system enjoys the sort of systemic justification Brink has in mind. Individual beliefs are justified by being members of a coherent web of belief.[69] Having rejected foundationalism, Brink argues that only coherentism adequately meets the epistemological requirement.

[O]nce the epistemological requirement is enforced and the background beliefs of contextualist justification are brought into question, the systematic justification of any belief can only be explained as a function of its relation to the totality of other beliefs one does or might hold. Coherentism meets this demand for systematic justification by claiming that one's belief p is fully or systematically justified insofar as p is part of a maximally coherent system of beliefs and p's coherence at least partially explains why one holds p. (Brink, 1989: 124)

Leaving aside for a moment the question of whether coherentism generally, and moral coherentism in particular, represent adequate epistemologies, I want to argue that either Brink's moral coherentism, given its focus on systematic justification, is really not at odds with my moral contextualism or that, insofar as it is, it is implausible as an epistemological story. Let me begin with the first point.

As Brink makes clear, his moral coherentism is meant to give us an account of systematic justification; my focus has been on what he calls contextualist justification. I have argued that if we want an adequate epistemological story about the justification of moral beliefs held by ordinary people who are not typically engaged in the sort of systematic, dialectical process of arriving at some overall moral theory, then a contextualist epistemology is just what we want. Of course, I need not, and do not, deny that increasing the consistency, explanatory connectedness, and so forth that constitute coherence increases the level of epistemic justification among a set of beliefs. Both foundationalists and contextualists can and should allow that coherence considerations have epistemic value. I do reject, however, any claim to the effect that in order for an individual (in ordinary contexts especially) to be adequately justified in holding certain moral beliefs, those beliefs must be members of a maximally coherent set of beliefs. I reject, that is,

69. See BonJour, 1985: 89–93, for more detail on this sort of epistemic holism.

the claim that systematic justification is necessary for being adequately justified in many contexts.

Brink himself denies this claim when he remarks that "[b]ecause the process of reflective equilibrium is one we can (only) approximate to a greater or lesser extent," individuals can be adequately justified in their moral beliefs, short of having a maximally coherent belief set (Brink, 1989: 131). Indeed, he must allow that what he calls contextualist justification is adequate, given his response to the demand that certain moral beliefs be 'initially credible' well before we reach (or, more accurately, approximate) reflective equilibrium. He writes:

> Considered moral beliefs are initially credible; we have seen reason to regard the class of considered moral beliefs as generally, or at least significantly, reliable. Thus, although the systematic justification of any moral belief is reached only at the end point of coherentism, the reliability of considered moral beliefs can be contextually established before reflective equilibrium. (Brink, 1989: 135)[70]

So, for Brink's coherentism to work, he has to admit that contextualist justification is adequate for certain purposes. Exactly. Thus, a friendly response to Brink's moral coherentism is simply to point out that it is not really at odds with my contextualism since, for one thing, it does not purport to give an account of justification applicable to the sort of cases my story is intended to deal with, and for another, it must rely on a contextualist account of justification anyway.

I can think of two responses to these conciliatory remarks. First, one might want to claim that my contextualism is really inadequate because it implies that, even in skeptical contexts, certain beliefs are contextually basic, but that only systematic justification can satisfy the epistemic demands in such cases. My response is that talk of skeptical contexts is too vague here; it may be that in some skeptical contexts, in which certain of one's moral beliefs are under attack by a skeptic, one is permitted and hence responsible in making use of certain beliefs that, in the context, one need not have justifying reasons for holding. On the other hand, for extreme forms of skeptical challenge, by which one's whole corpus of belief is being challenged, there is reason for being pessimistic about the prospects of success.

A second possible response would be to argue that my version of contextualism is inadequate because, for any moral beliefs to be justified at all (even contextually), one must have relevant second-order non-moral beliefs about the reliability of one's first-order moral beliefs in order to have a stock of moral beliefs that can serve as justifiers for other moral beliefs. In other words, one might challenge my claim that moral beliefs can be contextually basic and serve as justifiers. The point takes us back to some ground already covered concerning what I called the thesis of epistemic adequacy, but it will help to go over that ground again in the context of the present discussion. The complaint in question might be developed as follows. The so-called epistemological requirement that all justifying beliefs be, them-

---

70. For more on the nature and role of considered moral beliefs in the coherentist's theory, see Timmons, 1990a.

selves, justified requires that our considered moral beliefs—those beliefs that are to serve as a (revisable) basis for coming to further justified beliefs—be, themselves, justified. According to Brink, the justification of such beliefs depends on having a stock of second-order non-moral beliefs about the reliability of our first-order considered moral beliefs. And, of course, applying the epistemological requirement again, these second-order beliefs must, themselves, be justified by further beliefs, and so on. Consequently, the sort of contextualism for which I have argued in this chapter cannot provide an adequate epistemological story about the justification of moral belief.

In response, I have two points to make. First, one suspects a confusion of levels in Brink's account of justification.[71] That is, one should distinguish between questions about the justification of a belief (or justifiedly believing some proposition) and questions about being justified in an epistemic claim about a belief—between *being justified* in holding some belief and *showing that one is justified*. To accomplish the latter requires that one have second-order beliefs about the reliability and, hence, epistemic status of first-order beliefs. But it is doubtful that one needs to have a second-order belief (of the sort in question) to be justified in holding a non-epistemic first-order belief.

But even if there is no confusion of levels in Brink's account, it still seems to impose epistemic burdens that most ordinary folks do not in fact satisfy. No doubt, individuals have some rough and intuitive sense for the sorts of conditions that affect the reliability of their beliefs, both moral and non-moral. But it is doubtful that they possess articulated beliefs about the reliability of their first-order considered moral beliefs that could serve as justifying premises for those beliefs. Furthermore, even if I am wrong about this, Brink's view requires that individuals have justifying beliefs for their second-order beliefs, which I really doubt most people in fact have. Compare Brink's account of the justification of considered moral beliefs with the sort of account I offer of contextually basic beliefs. As explained earlier, I favor what I called second-order conservatism about contextually basic belief, according to which one must at least be disposed to believe that one's first-order beliefs are epistemically sound if those beliefs are to be responsibly held. But note that this requirement is met if one simply would, upon some reflection, see no reason to doubt the reliability of the belief in question. Thus, my second-order conservatism is far less demanding than is Brink's coherentism, and therefore is much better able to accommodate the antiskeptical presumption.

Before closing, I want to add to my discussion of moral coherentism by pressing a bit harder on this view as an adequate epistemology for moral and non-moral belief. There is a problem for coherence theories stemming from the demands of naturalized epistemology. Here, I am going to summarize an argument by my colleague David Henderson (1994), who focuses on coherentism as an account of the justification of empirical belief. (Henderson's argument, by the way, supports the claim I made in the last paragraph that a thoroughgoing co-

---

71. For a discussion of level confusions in epistemology, see Alston, 1980. This worry about Brink's moral epistemology is raised by Copp (1991: 617).

herentism seems too demanding as an account of the justification of belief in requiring of individuals that they have an adequate battery of beliefs, including second-order beliefs, that can serve as justifiers of a certain class of first-order beliefs.) The basic idea is the following: the constraints imposed by the project of naturalizing epistemology on an adequate epistemology of belief tend to rule out a thoroughgoing coherentist account of justification.

Henderson focuses on the coherentist account of cognitively spontaneous perceptual beliefs offered by Laurence BonJour (1985). According to BonJour, the justification of such beliefs requires that the believer have a battery of other beliefs that are at least available to the believer as premises in a potential justificatory argument for the target perceptual belief. This battery of beliefs must include second-order beliefs about the reliability of the justificandum beliefs, as well as beliefs about the conditions in which the cognitively spontaneous beliefs were formed. Thus, on BonJour's view, in order for a cognitively spontaneous perceptual belief to be justifiedly held by an individual, she must possess the information necessary for justifying her cognitively spontaneous belief, and that information must be articulable by the agent for purposes of being able to produce the sort of argument that would serve to justify that belief. But, according to Henderson, the problem is that once we see that so-called connectionist models of mental processing are quite plausible in helping us to understand how human perceptual systems work,[72] and that such systems allow us to employ information in perceptual belief formation that is not articulable by the believer — either because the information stored in the weights of the connectionist system is not articulable by the believer or because the information is quite transitory in such a rapidly dynamic system — then it becomes clear that the information featured in the sorts of justifying arguments BonJour proposes for cognitively spontaneous beliefs is not, in general, available to the believer.

Summing up, Henderson writes:

> The upshot of all this is that emerging results of cognitive science strongly indicate that our actual perceptual competence is to be understood in generally connectionist terms. Because such connectionist competence may, and here very plausibly does, allow us, as a cognitive system, to employ information in appropriate, sensitive ways without being able to articulate it in a form that would make it accessible for the sort of argument entertained in the sophisticated coherentist model, a crucial problem arises for sophisticated coherentism: the dispositions that enable our generation of perceptual beliefs — our actual perceptual competence — are such that there will very commonly be cognitively spontaneous beliefs that (even individually) cannot be provided the sort of justificatory argumentation whose accessibility is demanded by coherentism. (Henderson, 1994: 645)

Henderson is making a stronger claim about coherentism than I have been making. I have been expressing doubts about ordinary believers truly having the sorts

---

72. These connectionist models have been recently proposed for understanding certain mental processing that does not seem to conform to the classical AI rule-based models. The details need not concern us here. For an introduction to connectionism, see Tienson, 1987.

of justifying beliefs featured in BonJour's account of the justification of perceptual beliefs and in Brink's account of considered moral beliefs. Henderson is arguing that, in general, believers will not even have access to some of the relevant information needed to provide a coherentist justification of such beliefs. Of course, I do not need this stronger claim to make my case against moral coherentism, but Henderson's argument does help to reinforce my doubts.

Incidently, another theme of Henderson's work is that the standard dismissal of contextualism — to the effect that contextualism simply describes actual epistemic practice, whereas other views such as foundationalism and coherentism provide appropriate epistemic norms for evaluating the epistemic status of beliefs — has things backwards. Once we take seriously the demands of naturalized epistemology, we see that contextualism, and not these other views, provides an adequate normative story about the epistemology of belief.

This conclusion is bolstered by some of Gilbert Harman's work in epistemology. Harman criticizes foundationalism as being overly demanding and hence unacceptable, in light of plausible naturalizing constraints on epistemological theorizing, and proposes what he calls a coherence theory of belief revision. He compares coherentism to foundationalism:

> The coherence theory is *conservative* in a way the foundations theory is not. The coherence theory supposes one's present beliefs are justified just as they are in the absence of special reasons to change them, where changes are allowed only to the extent that they yield sufficient increases in coherence. This is a striking difference from the foundations theory. The foundations theory says one is justified in continuing to believe something only if one has a special reason to continue to accept that belief, whereas the coherence theory says one is justified in continuing to believe something as long as one has no special reason to stop believing it. (Harman, 1986: 32)

What Harman calls coherentism — what some call 'negative' as opposed to 'positive' coherentism (the latter defended by BonJour and Brink) — is really quite close to my contextualism. Again, self-described coherentists who take seriously constraints on human cognition (and who respect the antiskeptical presumption) are quite naturally pulled in the direction of contextualism.

In closing, let me briefly summarize my rather extended discussion of moral foundationalism and moral coherentism. My conclusion about moral coherentism is similar to my conclusion about moral foundationalism. These views, insofar as they really compete with my view as an account of the epistemology of moral belief, are, at best, simply unrealistic and do not respect what I have called the antiskeptical presumption. I do not have to make a strong claim and argue that these views represent impossible epistemic ideals; I can happily allow that there can be adequate foundational beliefs (of a sort distinct from what I call non-justified responsible belief) for the inferential justification of other moral beliefs, and I can happily allow that bringing one's moral beliefs into a state of maximal coherence will significantly boost the level of epistemic justification he or she may now enjoy. My claim has been that neither moral foundationalism nor moral coherentism (insofar as these views involve standards that differ from contextualist standards) adequately accounts for the justification of ordinary moral belief; they tend to demand too much of ordinary agents.

External Accommodation

The project of external accommodation can be relatively brief. As explained above, there are two things involved here—one a metaphysical project, the other methodological. First, regarding the metaphysical dimension of external accommodation, we want our epistemological view to comport with any non-moral philosophical views that seem particularly well grounded. I am working from within a naturalistic metaphysics, and so this dimension of accommodation demands that our epistemology of moral belief not involve postulating any sort of cognitive capacity or mode of awareness whose operation cannot be thoroughly understood from a naturalistic perspective. Certainly, nothing about my epistemological contextualism violates this demand.

I should add that I am limiting what I need to do by way of external accommodation. As in the case with externally accommodating the sort of metaphysics and associated semantics of moral discourse, a full accommodation of epistemological discourse would require, first of all, that I accommodate any metaphysical assumptions of epistemic discourse that would be a part of a general meta-epistemological view about the metaphysics and associated semantics of epistemic discourse itself. So, for instance, were one to defend a version of epistemic realism, according to which there are objective epistemic facts and properties, then one would need to accommodate those facts and properties from within a naturalistic perspective. I have not taken a stance on metaphysical and associated semantic questions about epistemic discourse itself, and so I have not set for myself the sort of external accommodation task that would come with developing such a view.

The second, methodological dimension of external accommodation involves explaining how my epistemology of moral belief comports with various empirical views and assumptions from relevant areas of empirical research. Again, I think it is pretty clear that the sort of epistemological contextualism I have been defending meets this demand quite well. In fact, my characterization of a model epistemically responsible agent, on the basis of which I developed my view, was consistently informed by empirical results pertaining to limits on human cognitive capacities, including limits on memory. That is, my account of the epistemology of moral belief was conducted within the spirit of naturalized epistemology.

VIII. Moral Knowledge

Knowledge, unlike justification and epistemic responsibility, entails truth. The epistemology of moral belief that I have been defending is intended to be independent of my moral irrealism and the minimalism about moral truth that I defended in the previous chapter. So one could reject my irrealist moral metaphysics and associated semantics and still accept my contextualist moral epistemology. But given the connection between knowledge and truth, I have to say something about how moral knowledge is to be understood in my overall metaethical view.

As explained in the previous chapter, if one views things from a strictly metaphysical perspective (and takes for granted a broadly naturalistic worldview), then the proper thing to say about moral truth is that there is none. That is, from a strictly metaphysical perspective from which we are asking about what there really is, since there are no moral facts or properties, there is no moral truth (moral claims, from this perspective are neither correctly assertible nor correctly deniable). And so, if there is no moral truth, there cannot be moral knowledge, either. But, as explained in the previous chapter, this is not the whole story, nor is it even the most interesting part of the story about moral discourse. Things get interesting when we judge from within a moral outlook, a position from which genuine moral assertions and truth ascriptions to moral statements have a home, as it were. And it is from this morally engaged perspective that talk of moral knowledge becomes interesting and useful.

There are two very broad conceptions of knowledge. According to *externalist* conceptions, in order to have knowledge one need not have the sorts of evidential grounds (such as experiences or beliefs) for what one knows, or even be, in the relevant sense, epistemically responsible in one's belief-forming habits. Reliability accounts of knowledge have been the dominant version of this sort of view. So (speaking very roughly), on reliability versions of externalism, knowledge of some proposition is a matter of some belief in that proposition's having been reliably produced, period. *Internalist* conceptions of knowledge require that one base the belief of the known proposition on evidence one has (experiences or beliefs) so that one justifiedly believes — or perhaps warrantedly or just responsibly believes — the proposition in question. I do not propose to take a position on which of these two broad orientations toward knowledge is correct. Indeed, perhaps an appropriate epistemological view would have to somehow integrate both externalist and internalist ideas about knowledge. What I want to briefly indicate is how I view the issue of moral knowledge from each of these broad orientations. I will begin with the internalist conception of knowledge.

If we work with a notion of knowledge that requires, in addition to having a true belief, that one also at least justifiedly believe the proposition in question, then I think it is pretty obvious how the story about moral knowledge would go. There are two basic conceptions of justification, either one of which might be claimed to be necessary for knowledge. There are normative (deontological) conceptions, and there are truth-conduciveness conceptions.[73] Let us briefly address them in order.

According to normative conceptions of justified belief, justifiedly believing is a matter (roughly speaking) of conforming to a relevant set of epistemic norms that exonerate one from epistemic blame. My contextualist moral epistemology represents this sort of view. So if one takes knowledge to entail justification and construes justification (and responsible belief generally) normatively, what sort of

---

73. For a discussion of these conceptions, see Alston, 1985 and 1988.

story about moral knowledge can one tell, given my irrealist metaethical views? First, in thinking that someone knows one is judging from within a morally engaged perspective, one is, after all, tacitly agreeing with the content of the allegedly known proposition. But also, one is judging that the person justifiedly believes the moral proposition in question, and so, given a normative construal of justification, it must be true of the individual who knows that he is not in violation of any relevant epistemic norms. If my particular story is right, then one must not be in violation of ER* and other such norms. Thus, moral knowledge claims are correctly assertible (true) on this sort of view only if one has a justified true belief. (Further conditions having to do with Gettier's worries would presumably be needed in order to fill out the account.)

On the other hand, if one accepts a truth-conduciveness account of justified belief, according to which (roughly) a justified belief is one that is appropriately based on adequate grounds (including other justified beliefs or perhaps experiences), then again the implications for moral knowledge are pretty straightforward: one's knowledge ascription is correctly assertible (true) only if the belief that is known is adequately grounded.

Let us now consider how a story about moral knowledge would go if one were an externalist about knowledge. Again, we shall focus on third-person ascriptions of moral knowledge. First, in ascribing knowledge to someone (other than oneself), one is doing so from an engaged moral perspective, and thus one is tacitly agreeing with the moral proposition that one claims is known by the party in question. However, since there are no moral facts (MORAL FACTS, that is) one cannot tell a reliability story, according to which knowledge involves reliably tracking some objective moral facts. But there is a way, from within an irrealist moral metaethic, to adequately capture the basic idea of a reliabilist account of knowledge without having to invoke any kind of tracking story. The root idea of reliabilist views has to do with being intellectually virtuous, or, if talk of virtue implies a kind of habituation guided by conscious efforts on the part of the individual with regard to his belief-forming tendencies that one need not have gone through in order to be reliable in one's moral belief formation, then we can simply talk about an individual's having a moral sensibility that generates, as it were, a high proportion of true to false moral beliefs. Ascriptions of moral knowledge that are reliabilist in nature, then, are responsive to one's overall moral sensibility or faculty of moral judgment.

Of course, ascriptions of moral knowledge are made from the perspective of some moral outlook, but the significance of this fact should not be misunderstood. In judging, for example, that George knows that what Gertrude did was morally wrong, I am not just saying that—on this matter and a range of others—George agrees with me. Rather, what I am saying is that George is reliable about matters of moral concern (at least in his belief-forming tendencies) and that on this particular matter his moral opinion is true. My knowledge ascription to George is correctly assertible (true) if, and only if, George is reliable and the moral proposition about Gertrude is correctly assertible (true). Again, this basic story about third-person knowledge ascriptions seems directly applicable, mutatis mutandis, to the case of first-person ascriptions. Of course, there is an interesting story to be told about the correct assertibility of moral statements that I tried to elaborate and defend in the previous chapter. All I am attempting to do here is to show how I can make sense of moral knowledge from within my irrealist framework.

So, what I am suggesting about moral knowledge is that however it goes with the concept of knowledge, whether externalist or internalist (or some hybrid combination), one can make sense of the idea of ascriptions of moral knowledge in an irrealist metaethical view of the sort I have defended.

IX. Conclusion

Despite the length of this chapter, I have only been able to sketch an epistemology of moral belief, and my defense of this sort of view is far from complete. I hope I will be excused for not having done more in the way of elaboration and defense of my view since doing so would require a book-length treatment of matters of epistemology raised in this chapter. As I have already mentioned, I have tried to develop a moral epistemology about justification that is largely independent of my irrealist moral metaphysics and associated semantics, so that the plausibility of the epistemology does not depend on the metaphysics and semantics. I should also mention that, as far as I can see, my epistemological contextualism in ethics and its analog with regard to other domains of inquiry does not make very many assumptions about the metaphysics and associated semantics of epistemic discourse. Granted, one sort of contextualism in epistemology—what I have called 'normative contextualism'—does, indeed, seem to presuppose some brand of epistemic irrealism (at least, as it is typically construed), but I disavow this sort of contextualism. And granted, I have made use of Foley's schema for understanding the semantic workings of terms like 'rational' and 'justified' in the context of epistemic appraisal. But none of this commits one to any sort of epistemic irrealism with regard to the issue about the existence and nature of objective epistemic facts, and none of this commits one to descriptivist—as opposed to non-descriptivist—treatments of epistemic language.

Appendix

Some Remarks on Metaethical Rationalism

There is a metaethical option open to the irrealist that should be mentioned if not fully discussed—a version of metaethical rationalism. Metaethical rationalism is the view (roughly speaking) that morality has some sort of 'formal' foundation in reason; or perhaps in the very meanings of moral concepts in the sense that true, correct, or valid moral claims can be established on the basis of considerations having to do with the notions of rational choice and action; or perhaps on the basis of the very meanings (and the linguistic rules expressing those meanings) of moral concepts. Although most metaethical rationalists have been descriptivists, some have been non-descriptivists. Donagan (1977), Gewirth (1978), and Michael Smith (1994) are (or at least seem to be) descriptivists; Hare is, of course, a non-descriptivist.

For present purposes, I want to briefly consider attempts to establish moral norms on the basis of non-moral truths pertaining to what was called, in the 1950s, 'the logic of moral discourse.' The fundamental idea here is that the meaning of moral concepts, including any a priori formal constraints on correct moral reasoning, may be enough to establish some set of basic moral norms. The result would be that fundamental moral norms have a non-moral foundation in the semantic/formal norms that govern correct use of moral discourse. As I have said, this sort of view does not require any realm of objective moral facts; it is compatible with thoroughgoing moral irrealism. Hare (1981) for example, attempts to move from formal features of moral discourse (in particular, the features of prescriptivity and universalizability), together with a view about rational choice, to the result that proper moral thinking and reasoning (i.e., moral thinking and reasoning that is subject to constraints implicit in the formal features of moral language) yields a form of utilitarianism. I don't plan to engage in a critical evaluation of Hare's project—there is plenty of critical discussion already in the literature and I don't have anything novel to add. (I refer the reader to the papers in *Hare and Critics*, Seanor and Fotion [eds.], 1990.) Nor do I plan to discuss the views of all other major rationalist positions.[1] Rather, I shall simply raise a general worry about the rationalist's project.

Were an irrealist version of metaethical rationalism correct (at least of a sort that would attempt to reach substantive ethical results on the sole basis of so-called formal features of moral discourse and practice), then the dual project of accommodation would go smoothly. First, this metaethical position comports with philosophical naturalism since (1) ontologically, there are no moral facts or properties to be accommodated (but see the discussion of Michael Smith's view below) and (2) epistemologically, there is nothing suspicious about the manner through which we come to have knowledge of basic moral truths and then, together with morally relevant information, come to have knowledge of non-basic moral truths. Second, since on this view there is, as it were, a single 'true' or 'valid' set of moral norms, accommodating the possibility of genuine disagreement, and so forth, would be unproblematic. So, I take it that this form of moral irrealism is quite attractive.

However, as far as I can tell, all such views face a dilemma. On the one hand, if the semantic/formal norms governing rational moral thinking are indeed free from substantive moral content, then one suspects that such norms will not be strong enough to yield determinate moral truths. On the other hand, to get the desired determinacy, one needs to work with a morally loaded conception of the allegedly formal norms governing moral discourse, which would then compromise the project of the metaethical rationalist. Let me illustrate this seeming dilemma by first making some general remarks about rational constraints on moral inquiry and then focusing on the version of metaethical rationalism recently defended by Michael Smith.

First of all, my pessimism about rationalist irrealist views is reinforced by reflection on the sorts of systematic constraints on philosophical moral inquiry aimed at establishing some normative moral theory. One might suggest that a moral norm is 'true' or valid if, and only if, it is part of a system of moral norms established by an appeal to various non-moral constraints on moral inquiry. Consider, then, the following partial list of desiderata (expressible as meta-norms for evaluating first-order moral norms), often pressed into service in the evaluation (of the truth) of a normative moral system:

1. *Consistency*. In order for the members of a set of moral norms to be true, they must, taken singly, yield a consistent set of moral statements. But also, taken collectively, the moral norms constituting some system are expected to yield a set of consistent moral judgments. Inconsistency generated from a single norm refutes the truth of that moral norm; inconsistency generated from a system of norms refutes the truth of the system.

2. *Completeness*. A system of moral norms is to yield, in conjunction with relevant facts, the full range of true or correct moral judgments. So,

---

1. For some discussion of various versions of metaethical rationalism, see Arrington, 1989: ch. 3.

for example, normative systems that are rooted in self-interest tend to be incomplete, in the sense that the basic principles of the system are not powerful enough to generate moral requirements that pertain to matters beyond the horizon of one's self-interest.

3. *Explanatory power.* A normative system should properly explain the basis of various sorts of moral requirements. For example, one might argue that standard versions of contractarianism, because they place questions of fairness at moral center stage, cannot plausibly accommodate moral restrictions on cruelty to children or animals: the restriction on cruelty has moral force independent of that emerging from an agreement.[2]

The list of desiderata—I will call them *system-relevant desiderata*—can be extended, but the point I want to make (and I hope is fairly obvious) is that these sorts of formal constraints are too weak to yield any single determinate set of moral norms. To get determinacy, one needs to introduce a notion with some moral content, like impartiality. But even the notion of impartiality, which is arguably at the center of a moral outlook, requires interpretation. For instance, Griffin (1986: ch. 9) contrasts utilitarian with contractarian notions of equal respect/impartiality. A notion of impartiality fundamental to utilitarian thinking is encapsulated by Bentham's tenet, "Everyone to count for one, no one to count for more than one." But there is also a notion of impartiality, fundamental to contractarian thinking, represented, for example, by choice under a Rawlsian 'veil of ignorance.'[3] Griffin, after pointing out that the notion of impartiality for ethics involves the idea of *equal respect*, remarks:

> Every moral theory has the notion of equal respect at its heart: regarding each person as, in some sense, on an equal footing with every other one. Different moral theories parlay this vague notion into different conceptions. Ideas such as the Ideal Observer or the Ideal Contractor specify the notion a little further, but then they too are very vague and allow quite different moral theories to be got out of them. And the moral theories are not simply derivations from these vague notions, because the notions are too vague to allow anything as tight as a derivation. Too vague, but not totally empty; although the moral theories that we end up with put content into all these notions, the notions themselves also do something towards shaping the theories. (Griffin, 1986: 208; see also 231, 239)

So, mere appeal to what really are formal constraints on the proper use of moral language, together with any formal constraints on moral reasoning, simply will not yield (so I suspect) substantive moral results, and attempts to get somewhere with notions like impartiality and equal respect compromise the rationalist's project (or so it would seem).

---

2. Griffin (1986: 194) argues for this point.
3. Note that to take either one of these notions of impartiality (or some other) and to build it into the meaning of moral concepts simply will not work, as revealed by the Moral Twin Earth saga.

Since Kantians will no doubt disagree with this assessment of rationalism, let me reinforce these general remarks by briefly considering the sort of Kantian rationalism that Michael Smith defends in *The Moral Problem* (1994).

The backbone of Smith's view is the thesis of conceptual rationalism:

> CR If it is right for agents to do A in circumstances C, then there is a (normative) reason for those agents to do A in C.

Of course, a lot rides on the notion of a normative reason that Smith analyzes in terms of being fully rational. The concept of a fully rational agent is understood to involve these conditions: (1) the agent must have correct and full, relevant information, and (2) the agent must deliberate correctly where this involves reasoning in accordance with various principles of practical rationality (like the means-ends principle); using one's imagination in clearly and vividly representing the objects of one's desires and goals; being free of certain psychological maladies like compulsions and addictions; and coming to have a set of desires and attitudes that exhibit certain virtues like unity and explanatory connectedness that one has when one's set of beliefs and attitudes are in reflective equilibrium. So, for Smith, the notion of a normative reason is analyzed in terms of the hypothetical desires of fully rational agents—the desires one would have were one fully rational.

Furthermore, Smith argues for a Kantian, non-relativist conception of normative reasons (over a Humean, relativist conception), which requires that in order for one to have a normative reason to do A in C, it must be the case that *all* fully rational agents (human and non-human) would have the desire that anyone do A in C. More precisely, since Smith proposes to analyze moral rightness in terms of normative *reasons*, the idea is that "[t]he analysis tells us that the rightness of acts in certain circumstances C . . . is the feature that we would want acts to have in C if we were fully rational" (Smith, 1994: 185).

Since the class of moral requirements is a proper subset of the class of normative reasons for action, the special class of normative reasons in question is to be demarcated by their content. The idea is that there is a battery of platitudes concerning the content of morality (like 'right actions typically concern the promotion of human flourishing' and 'morally right acts are ones that express equal concern and respect'), and moral reasons are just reasons of the appropriately substantive kind.

Putting these ingredients together, Smith's analysis of moral rightness can be expressed this way:

> MR Our doing A in circumstances C is right if, and only if, we would desire that we do A in C, if we were fully rational, wherein doing A in C is an act of the appropriate substantive kind.

Smith's view is particularly intriguing in relation to the project of this book since he is a moral constructivist who is interested in accommodating the objective pretensions of moral discourse in a manner that is consistent with naturalism. Smith sums up his view this way:

> To say that performing an act of a certain sort in certain circumstances is right is, I have argued, to say *inter alia* that there is a normative reason to perform it.

And this, in turn, is simply to say that fully rational creatures would desire that such an act be performed in such circumstances, where such a desire is of the appropriate substantive kind. On this account, moral features like rightness thus simply are not 'entities or qualities or relations of a very strange sort'; no 'special faculty of moral perception or intuition' is required in order to gain knowledge of them. All that is required is the ability to think about what a more rational person would want. . . . [Mackie's] charge of strangeness is thus entirely misplaced. (Smith, 1994: 200)

However, despite the initial attractiveness of the view, I think it faces the sort of general problem with metaethical rationalism mentioned earlier.[4]

The problem with Smith's view stems from the very strong requirements placed on the concept of full rationality, and thus the very strong requirements that must be met in order for something to be a normative reason: *all* rational agents (both human and non-human) must converge in their hypothetical desires with regard to the feature that they would want some action A to have in circumstances C in order for there to be a normative reason to do A in C. But the Twin Earth scenario (presented in ch. 2) and the other so-called examples of moral symmetry (like the Putnam/Nozick disagreement over welfare spending in ch. 4) are cases in which it looks as if we have two groups or individuals who satisfy the requirements of being fully rational, yet do not converge in their hypothetical desires. In the Twin Earth scenario, you may recall, were Earthlings to engage in a process of reflective equilibrium, they would settle on a consequentialist moral theory, and so, in Smith's terms, they would, were they fully rational, desire that actions in circumstances calling for moral response instantiate consequentialist features. By contrast, the Twin Earthlings would desire that actions in circumstances calling for moral response would instantiate deontological features.

The same goes, mutatis mutandis, for the Putnam/Nozick dispute. The possibility of lack of convergence over what features of actions all rational agents would want to be instantiated yields the result that if we accept Smith's analysis of judgments of moral rightness in terms of the hypothetical desires of all fully rational agents, then we are driven to an error theory about moral requirements. That is, since there is reason to be very dubious that all fully rational agents would agree in their desires about what feature is to be brought about in cases calling for moral judgment, there are no normative reasons in those cases and, hence, no moral requirements.

The serious threat of an error theory results from what we might call a 'thin' conception of normative reason, a morally unloaded notion that is intended to be the basis of an illuminating and non-circular analysis of the concept of moral rightness — exactly what the metaethical rationalist wants. (In ch. 3, I described Smith as attempting to provide a weak reductive definition of moral rightness in terms of a morally unloaded notion of rationality.) But on such a conception the various constraints on being fully rational, and hence on there being normative

---

4. The following is a brief summary of the arguments against Smith's view to be found in Horgan and Timmons, 1996.

reasons, are simply not robust enough to yield determinacy among the hypothetical desires of all fully rational agents (as the symmetry scenarios strongly suggest).

There are, of course, 'thick' conceptions of rationality that are morally loaded. Putnam, for instance, remarks, "The question: *which is the rational conception of rationality itself* is difficult in *exactly* the way that the justification of an ethical system is difficult. There is no *neutral* conception of rationality to which to appeal" (1981: 136). He later goes on to say that "our standards of rational acceptability . . . rest on and presuppose our values. . . . [The] theory of rationality . . . presupposes our theory of the good" (215).

Recall again from chapter 3 that Putnam makes clear that in characterizing truth in terms of ideal rational acceptability, he is not taking epistemic concepts to be somehow prior to semantic concepts, and so he is not proposing to reduce truth to ideal rational acceptability. Rather, he thinks that these concepts are interdependent. Here, he is making the same sort of anti reductivist remark about the concepts of rationality and goodness. But, again, a morally loaded conception of basic moral concepts is of no use to the rationalist.

Fortunately, we aren't driven to an error theory since the thesis of conceptual rationalism does not require that we analyze moral rightness in terms of a thin conception of rationality (or so I would contend). Although (arguably) there is a conceptual connection between the concepts of moral rightness and normative reason, it does not involve the kind of conceptual priority needed by Smith and rationalists generally. Furthermore, I do not think that if we embrace an analysis of moral rightness in terms of a thick notion of rationality we are forced to some form of ethical relativism. Indeed, it seems to me that the sort of metaethical view that I have defended in this book avoids both error theories and relativism.

References

Alston, William. 1963. *Philosophy of Language*. Englewood Cliffs: Prentice-Hall.

———. 1971. "Varieties of Privileged Access." *American Philosophical Quarterly* 8: 223–41. Reprinted in Alston, 1989.

———. 1976a. "Has Foundationalism Been Refuted?" *Philosophical Studies* 29: 287–305. Reprinted in Alston, 1989.

———. 1976b. "Two Types of Foundationalism." *Journal of Philosophy* 73: 165–85. Reprinted in Alston, 1989.

———. 1980. "Level Confusions in Epistemology." *Midwest Studies in Philosophy* 5: 135–50. Reprinted in Alston, 1989.

———. 1985. "Concepts of Epistemic Justification." *The Monist* 68: 57–89. Reprinted in Alston, 1989.

———. 1988. "The Deontological Conception of Epistemic Justification." *Philosophical Perspectives* 2: 257–99. Reprinted in Alston, 1989.

———. 1989. *Epistemic Justification*. Ithaca, NY: Cornell University Press.

Annis, D. 1978. "A Contextualist Theory of Epistemic Justification." *American Philosophical Quarterly* 15: 213–19. Reprinted in Moser, 1986.

Armstrong, D. M. 1968. *A Materialist Theory of Mind*. London: Routledge & Kegan Paul.

———. 1973. *Belief, Truth and Knowledge*. Cambridge: Cambridge University Press.

Arrington, Robert L. 1989. *Rationalism, Realism, and Relativism*. Ithaca: Cornell University Press.

Audi, Robert. 1993a. "Ethical Reflectionism." *The Monist* 76: 295–315.

———. 1993b. *The Structure of Justification*. Cambridge: Cambridge University Press.

———. 1996. "Intuitionism, Pluralism, and the Foundations of Ethics." In Sinnott-Armstrong and Timmons, 1996.

Aune, B. 1967. *Knowledge, Mind and Nature*. New York: Random House.

Austin, J. L. 1961. *Philosophical Papers*. J. O. Urmson and G. J. Warnock (eds.). Oxford: Oxford University Press.

Ayer, A. J. 1946. *Language, Truth and Logic*. 2nd edition. New York: Dover.

Bellah, R. N., R. Madson, W. M. Sullivan, A. Swindler, and S. M. Tipton. 1985. *Habits of the Heart*. New York: Harper & Row.

Benacerraf, Paul. 1973. "Mathematical Truth." *Journal of Philosophy* 70: 661–79.

Blackburn, Simon. 1980. "Truth, Realism and the Regulation of Moral Theory." *Midwest Studies in Philosophy* 5: 353–71. Minneapolis: University of Minnesota Press. Reprinted in Blackburn, 1993.

———. 1981. "Rule Following and Moral Realism." In Steven Holtzman and Christopher M. Leitch (eds.), *Wittgenstein: To Follow a Rule*. London: Routledge & Kegan Paul.

———. 1984. *Spreading the Word*. New York: Oxford University Press.

———. 1985a. "Errors and the Phenomenology of Value." In T. Honderich (ed.), *Ethics and Objectivity*. London: Routledge & Kegan Paul, 1985. Reprinted in Blackburn, 1993.

———. 1985b. "Supervenience Revisited." In I. Hacking (ed.), *Exercises in Analysis: Essays by Students of Casimir Levy*. Cambridge: Cambridge University Press, 1985. Reprinted in Sayre-McCord, 1988, and in Blackburn, 1993.

———. 1988. "Attitudes and Contents." *Ethics* 98: 501–17. Reprinted in Blackburn, 1993.

———. 1993. *Essays in Quasi-Realism*. New York: Oxford University Press.

———. 1996. "Securing the Nots: Moral Epistemology for the Quasi-Realist." In Sinnott-Armstrong and Timmons, 1996.

Blanshard, B. 1949. "The New Subjectivism in Ethics." *Philosophy and Phenomenological Research* 9: 504–11.

Block, Ned (ed.). 1980. *Readings in Philosophy of Psychology*. Vol. 1. Cambridge, MA: Harvard University Press.

BonJour, Laurence. 1985. *The Structure of Empirical Knowledge*. Cambridge, MA: Harvard University Press.

Boyd, Richard. 1988. "How to Be a Moral Realist." In Geoffrey Sayre-McCord (ed.), *Essays on Moral Realism*. Ithaca: Cornell University Press, 1988.

Brandt, Richard. 1959. *Ethical Theory*. Englewood Cliffs, NJ: Prentice-Hall.

———. 1979. *A Theory of the Good and the Right*. New York: Oxford University Press.

Brink, David O. 1984. "Moral Realism and Skeptical Arguments from Disagreement and Queerness." *Australasian Journal of Philosophy* 62: 111–25.

———. 1989. *Moral Realism and the Foundations of Ethics*. Cambridge, MA: Cambridge University Press.

Broad, C. D. 1930. *Five Types of Ethical Theory*. London: Routledge & Kegan Paul.

———. 1942. "Certain Features in Moore's Ethical Doctrines." In P. A. Schlipp (ed.), *The Philosophy of G. E. Moore*. Vol. 1. La Salle, IL: Open Court Press, 1942.

———. 1945. "Some Reflections on Moral Sense Theories in Ethics." In D. Cheney (ed.), *Broad's Critical Essays in Moral Philosophy*. London: George Allen & Unwin, Ltd., 1971.

Brown, H. I. 1988. *Rationality*. London: Routledge.

Burge, Tyler. 1992. "Philosophy of Language and Mind: 1950–1990." *Philosophical Review* 101: 3–51.

Carson, Thomas. 1984. *The Status of Morality*. Dordrecht: D. Reidel Press.

Chalmers, David. 1996. *The Conscious Mind*. New York: Oxford University Press.

Cherniak, C. 1986. *Minimal Rationality*. Cambridge, MA: MIT Press.

Chisholm, R. 1981. *Foundations of Knowing*. Minneapolis: University of Minnesota Press.

Cohen, L. Jonathan. 1986. *The Dialectic of Reason*. Oxford: Oxford University Press.

Cohen, S. 1986. "Knowledge and Context." *Journal of Philosophy* 83: 574–83.

———. 1987. "Knowledge, Context and Social Standards." *Synthese* 73: 3–26.

Conee, Earl. 1987. "Critical Review of *Reason, Truth and History*." *Nous* 21: 91–95.

Copp, David. 1991. "Moral Realism: Facts and Norms." *Ethics* 101: 610–24.

———. Forthcoming. "Milk, Honey, and the Good Life on Moral Twin Earth."

Copp, David, and David Zimmerman (eds.). 1984. *Morality, Reason and Truth*. Totowa, NJ: Rowman & Littlefield.

Crisp, Roger. 1996. "Naturalism and Non-Naturalism in Ethics." In S. Lovibond and S. G. Williams (eds.), *Essays for David Wiggins: Identity, Truth and Value*. Oxford: Blackwell, 1996.

Dancy, Jonathan. 1993. *Moral Reasons*. Oxford: Blackwell.

Daniels, Norman. 1979. "Wide Reflective Equilibrium and Theory Acceptance in Ethics." *Journal of Philosophy* 76: 256–82.

Darwall, S., A. Gibbard, and P. Railton. 1992. "Toward *Fin de Siècle* Ethics: Some Trends." *Philosophical Review* 101: 115–89.

DePaul, Michael R. 1993. *Balance and Refinement: Beyond Coherentism in Moral Theory*. London: Routledge.

DeRose, Keith. 1991. "Epistemic Possibilities." *Philosophical Review* 100: 581–605.

———. 1992. "Contextualism and Knowledge Attributions." *Philosophy and Phenomenological Research* 52: 913–29.

Devitt, Michael. 1984. *Realism and Truth*. Princeton: Princeton University Press.

Donagan, A. 1977. *The Theory of Morality*. Chicago: University of Chicago Press.

Dreier, James. 1996. "Expressivist Embedding and Minimalist Truth." *Philosophical Studies* 83: 29–51.

Dreyfus, H. and S. Dreyfus. 1990. "What Is Morality? A Phenomenological Account of the Development of Ethics Expertise." In D. Rassmussen (ed.), *Universalism vs. Communitarianism*. Cambridge, MA: MIT Press, 1990.

Dummett, Michael. 1993. *Origins of Analytical Philosophy*. Cambridge, MA: Harvard University Press.

Ebertz, Roger. 1993. "Is Reflective Equilibrium a Coherentist Model?" *Canadian Journal of Philosophy* 23: 193–214.

Edwards, Paul. 1955. *The Logic of Moral Discourse*. New York: Free Press.

Ellis, Brian. 1990. *Truth and Objectivity*. Cambridge, MA: Blackwell.

Ewing, A. C. 1947. *The Definition of Good*. New York: Macmillan.

———. 1959. *Second Thoughts in Moral Philosophy*. New York: Macmillan.

Field, Hartry. 1972. "Tarski's Theory of Truth." *Journal of Philosophy* 69: 347–75.

Firth, R. 1952. "Ethical Absolutism and the Ideal Observer Theory." *Philosophy and Phenomenological Research* 12: 317–45.

Flanagan, Owen. 1991. *Varieties of Moral Personality*. Cambridge: Harvard University Press.

Fodor, J. A. 1974. "Special Sciences (or: The Disunity of Science as a Working Hypothesis)." *Synthese* 28: 97–115.

Foley, R. 1993. *Working without a Net*. Cambridge, MA: Harvard University Press.

Frankena, William. 1963. *Ethics*. Englewood Cliffs: Prentice-Hall.

———. 1965. " 'Cognitive' and 'Noncognitive.' " In P. Henle (ed.), *Language, Thought and Culture*. Ann Arbor: University of Michigan Press, 1965.

———. 1973. "Is Morality Logically Dependent on Religion?" In Gene Outka and John P. Reeder (eds.), *Religion and Morality: A Collection of Essays*. Garden City, NY: Doubleday. Reprinted in Paul Helm (ed.), *Divine Commands and Morality*. Oxford: Oxford University Press, 1981.

Gauthier, David. 1986. *Morals by Agreement*. Oxford: Oxford University Press.

Geach, Peter. 1960. "Ascriptivism." *Philosophical Review* 69: 221–25.

———. 1965. "Assertion." *Philosophical Review*. 74: 449–65.

Gettier, E. 1963. "Is Justified True Belief Knowledge?" *Analysis* 23: 121–23.

Gewirth, A. 1978. *Reason and Morality*. Chicago: University of Chicago Press.

Gibbard, Allan. 1990. *Wise Choices, Apt Feelings*. Cambridge, MA: Harvard University Press.

Gilligan, Carol. 1982. *In a Different Voice*. Cambridge: Harvard University Press.

———. 1988. "Remapping the Moral Domain: New Images of Self in Relationships." In Gilligan et al., 1988.

Gilligan, C., J. Ward, and J. Taylor. (eds.). 1988. *Mapping the Moral Domain*. Cambridge, MA: Harvard University Press.

Goldman, A. 1976. "Perceptual Knowledge and Discrimination." *Journal of Philosophy* 73: 771–91.

Goodman, Nelson. 1949. "On Likeness of Meaning." *Analysis* 10: 1–7.

Graham, G. and T. Horgan. 1994. "Southern Fundamentalism and the End of Philosophy." *Philosophical Issues* 5: 219–47.

Griffin, James. 1986. *Well-Being*. Oxford: Clarendon Press.

Griffiths, A. P. 1967. "Ultimate Moral Principles: Their Justification." *The Encyclopedia of Philosophy*. P. Edwards (ed.). New York: Macmillan, 1967.

Haack, Susan. 1993. *Evidence and Inquiry*. Oxford: Blackwell.

Hancock, Roger. 1974. *Twentieth Century Ethics*. New York: Columbia University Press.

Hare, R. M. 1952. *The Language of Morals*. Oxford: Oxford University Press.

———. 1963. *Freedom and Reason*. Oxford: Oxford University Press.

———. 1970. "Meaning and Speech Acts." *Philosophical Studies* 89: 3–24.

———. 1981. *Moral Thinking: Its Levels, Point and Method*. Oxford: Oxford University Press.

———. 1984. "Supervenience." *Proceedings of the Aristotelian Society* 58: 1–16. Supplementary volume. Reprinted in Hare, 1989.

———. 1985. "Ontology in Ethics." In Honderich, 1985. Reprinted in Hare, 1989.

———. 1989. *Essays in Ethical Theory*. Oxford: Oxford University Press.

Harman, G. 1977. *The Nature of Morality*. Oxford: Oxford University Press.

———. 1986. *Change in View*. Cambridge, MA: MIT Press.

Henderson, David. 1994. "Epistemic Competence and Contextualist Epistemology." *Journal of Philosophy* 91: 627–49.

Holmgren, M. 1989. "The Wide and Narrow of Reflective Equilibrium." *Canadian Journal of Philosophy* 19: 43–60.

———. 1990. "The Poverty of Naturalistic Moral Realism." In Timmons, 1990b.

Honderich, T. (ed.). 1985. *Morality and Objectivity: Essays in Memory of J. L. Mackie*. London: Routledge & Kegan Paul.

Horgan, T. 1986a. "Psychologism, Semantics, and Ontology." *Nous* 20: 21–31.

———. 1986b. "Truth and Ontology." *Philosophical Papers* 15: 1–21.

———. 1987. "Psychologistic Semantics and Moral Truth." *Philosophical Studies* 52: 357–70.

———. 1990. "Psychologistic Semantics, Robust Vagueness and the Philosophy of Language." In S. L. Tsohatzidis (ed.), *Meanings and Prototypes: Studies in Linguistic Categorization*. Cambridge: Routledge & Kegan Paul.

———. 1991. "Metaphysical Realism and Psychologistic Semantics." *Erkenntnis* 34: 297–322.

———. 1993. "From Supervenience to Superdupervenience: Meeting the Demands of a Material World." *Mind* 102: 555–86.

Horgan, T. and M. Timmons. 1991. "New Wave Moral Realism Meets Moral Twin Earth." *Journal of Philosophical Research* 16: 447–65. Reprinted in J. Heil (ed.), *Rationality, Morality, and Self-Interest*. New York: Rowman & Littlefield, 1993.

———. 1992a. "Troubles for New Wave Moral Semantics: The 'Open Question Argument' Revived." *Philosophical Papers* 21: 153–75.

———. 1992b. "Troubles on Moral Twin Earth: Moral Queerness Revived." *Synthese* 92: 221–60.

———. 1993. "Metaphysical Naturalism, Semantic Normativity, and Meta-Semantic Irrealism." *Philosophical Issues* 3: 180–204.

———. 1996a. "From Moral Realism to Moral Relativism in One Easy Step." *Critica* 28: 3–39.

———. 1996b. "Troubles for Michael Smith's Metaethical Rationalism." *Philosophical Papers* 25: 203–31.

———. Forthcoming a. "Copping Out on Moral Twin Earth."

———. Forthcoming b. "Cognitivist Non-Descriptivism."

Horwich, Paul. 1990. *Truth*. Oxford: Basil Blackwell.

———. 1994. "The Essence of Expressivism." *Analysis* 54: 19–20.

Hudson, W. D. 1970. *Modern Moral Philosophy*. Garden City, NY: Anchor.

Hume, David. 1739. *A Treatise of Human Nature*. Oxford: Oxford University Press.

———. 1777. *An Enquiry Concerning Human Nature*. In L. A. Selby-Bigge (ed.), *Hume's Enquiries*. 3rd edition. Oxford: Oxford University Press

Kant, Immanuel. 1785. *Groundwork of the Metaphysic of Morals*. H. J. Paton (trans.). London: Hutchinson, 1965.

Keeton, W. P., D. B. Dobbs, R. E. Keeton, and D. G. Owen. 1984. *Prosser and Keeton on the Law of Torts*. 5th edition. St. Paul, MN: West.

Kim, Jaegwon. 1988. "What Is Naturalized Epistemology?" In J. Tomberlin (ed.), *Philosophical Perspectives* 2: 381–405.

———. 1993. "Supervenience as a Philosophical Concept." In Kim, *Supervenience and Mind*. New York: Cambridge University Press, 1993.

Kitcher, Philip. 1992. "The Naturalists Return." *Philosophical Review* 101: 53–114.

Kohlberg, L. 1981. *Essays on Moral Development*. Vol 1. *The Philosophy of Moral Development*. New York: Harper & Row.

———. 1984. *Essays on Moral Development*. Vol. 2. *The Psychology of Moral Development*. New York: Harper & Row.

Kornblith, Hilary. 1980. "What Is Naturalized Epistemology?" In Kornblith (ed.), *Naturalized Epistemology*. Cambridge, MA: MIT Press, 1980.

———. 1983. "Justified Belief and Epistemically Responsible Action." *Philosophical Review* 92: 33–48.

———. 1994. "Naturalism: Both Metaphysical and Epistemological." *Midwest Studies in Philosophy* 19: 39–52.

Kraybill, Donald B. 1989. *The Riddle of the Amish Culture*. Baltimore: Johns Hopkins Press.

Kripke, S. 1972. *Naming and Necessity*. Cambridge, MA: Harvard University Press.

Kuhn, T. 1977. "Second Thoughts on Paradigms." In Kuhn, *The Essential Tension*. Chicago: University of Chicago Press, 1977.

Kvanvig, J. 1989. "Conservatism and Its Virtues." *Synthese* 79: 143–63.

———. 1992. *The Intellectual Virtues and the Life of the Mind*. Savage, MD: Rowman & Littlefield.

Ladd, John. 1957. *The Structure of a Moral Code*. Cambridge, MA: Harvard University Press.

Larmore, C. 1987. *Patterns of Moral Complexity*. Cambridge: Cambridge University Press.

Laudan, Larry. 1984. *Science and Values*. Berkeley: University of California Press.

Lewis, David. 1972. "Psychophysical and Theoretical Identifications." *Australasian Journal of Philosophy* 50: 249–58. Reprinted in Block, 1980.

———. 1985. Reprinted. "Scorekeeping in a Language Game." In Lewis, *Philosophical Papers*. New York: Oxford University Press, 1985. Originally published in *Journal of Philosophical Logic* 8: 339–59, 1979.

————. 1980. "Mad Pain and Martian Pain." In Block, 1980.

Mackie, J. L. 1946. "The Refutation of Morals." *Australasian Journal of Psychology and Philosophy* 24: 77–90.

————. 1977. *Ethics: Inventing Right and Wrong.* New York: Penguin.

————. 1982. *The Miracle of Theism.* Oxford: Oxford University Press.

McDowell, J. 1979. "Virtue and Reason." *The Monist* 63: 331–43.

————. 1985. "Values and Secondary Qualities." In Honderich, 1985.

McNaughton, David. 1988. *Moral Vision.* Oxford: Blackwell.

Mill, J. S. 1861. *Utilitarianism.* Indianapolis, IN: Hackett, 1979.

Moore, G. E. 1903. *Principia Ethica.* Cambridge: Cambridge University Press.

————. 1912. *Ethics.* New York: Oxford University Press.

————. 1942. "A Reply to My Critics." In P. A. Schilpp (ed.), *The Philosophy of G. E. Moore.* Vol. 2. La Salle, IL: Open Court Press, 1942.

Moser, P. (ed.). 1985. *Epistemic Justification.* Dordrecht: D. Reidel Press.

————. 1986. *Empirical Knowledge.* Totowa, NJ: Rowman & Littlefield.

Nagel, E. 1961. *The Structure of Science.* 2nd edition, 1979. Indianapolis: Hackett.

Nathanson, S. 1983. "Review of *Reason, Truth and History.*" *International Philosophical Quarterly* 23: 211–15.

Nowell-Smith, P. H. 1954. *Ethics.* New York: Philosophical Library.

Oppenheim, P. and H. Putnam. 1958. "Unity of Science as a Working Hypothesis." In H. Feigl, G. Maxwell, and M. Scriven (eds.), *Minnesota Studies in the Philosophy of Science* 2: 3–36. Minneapolis: University of Minnesota Press, 1958.

Paton, H. J. 1948. "The Emotive Theory of Ethics." *Aristotelian Society* 22: 107–26. Supplementary volume.

Plantinga, Alvin. 1993. *Warrant: The Current Debate.* New York: Oxford University Press.

Platts, Mark. 1979. *Ways of Meaning.* London: Routledge & Kegan Paul.

————. 1980. "Moral Reality and the Ends of Desire." In M. Platts (ed.), *Reference, Truth and Reality.* London: Routledge & Kegan Paul, 1985.

————. 1991. *Moral Realities.* London: Routledge.

Putnam, Hilary. 1970. "On Properties." In Putnam, 1975a.

————. 1975a. *Mathematics, Matter and Method.* Cambridge: Cambridge University Press.

————. 1975b. "The Meaning of 'Meaning.' " In Putnam, 1975c.

————. 1975c. *Mind, Language, and Reality.* Cambridge: Cambridge University Press.

————. 1978. *Meaning and the Moral Sciences.* London: Routledge & Kegan Paul.

————. 1981. *Reason, Truth and History.* Cambridge: Cambridge University Press.

————. 1983a. *Realism and Reason.* Cambridge: Cambridge University Press.

————. 1983b. "Two Dogmas Revisited." In Putnam, 1983a.

————. 1983c. "Why Reason Can't Be Naturalized." In Putnam, 1983a.

————. 1987. *The Many Faces of Realism.* LaSalle, IL: Open Court Press.

————. 1988. *Representation and Reality.* Cambridge, MA: The MIT Press.

————. 1990. *Realism with a Human Face.* Cambridge, MA: Harvard University Press.

————. 1991. "Replies and Comments." *Erkenntnis* 34: 401–24.

————. 1992. *Renewing Philosophy.* Cambridge, MA: Harvard University Press.

————. 1994. "The Dewey Lectures 1994." *Journal of Philosophy* 91: 445–517.

Quine, W. V. O. 1951. "Two Dogmas of Empiricism." *Philosophical Review* 60: 20–43.

Railton, Peter. 1984. "Alienation, Consequentialism, and the Demands of Morality." In S. Scheffler (ed.), *Consequentialism and Its Critics.* Oxford: Oxford University Press, 1984.

————. 1993. "Noncognitivism about Rationality: Benefits, Costs, and an Alternative." *Philosophical Issues* 4: 36–51.

Ramsey, F. P. 1931. *The Foundations of Mathematics, and Other Logical Essays*. London: Routledge.

Ramsey, William. 1992. "Prototypes and Conceptual Analysis." *Topoi* 11: 59–70.

Rawls, John. 1951. "Outline of a Decision Procedure in Ethics." *Philosophical Review* 60: 177–97.

———. 1971. *A Theory of Justice*. Cambridge, MA: Harvard University Press.

Rey, Georges. 1983. "Concepts and Stereotypes." *Cognition* 15: 237–62.

———. 1985. "Concepts and Conceptions: A Reply to Smith, Medin and Rips." *Cognition* 19: 297–303.

Rorty, Richard. 1967. *The Linguistic Turn*. Chicago: University of Chicago Press.

———. 1985. "Solidarity or Objectivity." In J. Rajchman and C. West (eds.), *Post-Analytic Philosophy*. New York: Columbia University Press, 1985.

Rosch, Eleanor. 1973. "On the Internal Structure of Perceptual and Semantic Categories." In T. E. Moore (ed.), *Cognitive Development and the Acquisition of Language*. New York: Academic Press, 1973.

———. 1975. "Cognitive Representation of Semantic Categories." *Journal of Experimental Psychology* 104: 192–233.

———. 1978. "Principles of Categorization." In E. Rosch and B. Lloyd (eds.), *Cognition and Categorization*. Hillsdale, NJ: Lawrence Earlbaum, 1978.

Ross, W. D. 1930. *The Right and the Good*. Oxford: Oxford University Press.

———. 1939. *The Foundations of Ethics*. Oxford: Oxford University Press.

Sayre-McCord, Geoffrey (ed.). 1988. *Essays on Moral Realism*. Ithaca, NY: Cornell University Press.

Schiffer, S. 1987. *Remnants of Meaning*. Cambridge, MA: MIT Press.

Seanor, D. and N. Fotion. (eds.). 1990. *Hare and Critics: Essays on Moral Thinking*. Oxford: Clarendon Press.

Searle, John. 1969. *Speech Acts*. Cambridge, MA: Cambridge University Press.

Sellars, Wilfrid. 1963. "Empiricism and the Philosophy of Mind." In Sellars, *Science, Perception and Reality*. London: Routledge & Kegan Paul, 1963.

Sidgwick, H. 1879. *Methods of Ethics*. New York, NY: Dover, 1966.

Singer, M. G. 1961. *Generalization in Ethics*. New York: Atheneum.

———. 1986. "The Ideal of a Rational Morality." *Proceedings and Addresses of the American Philosophical Association* 60: 15–38.

Sinnott-Armstrong, W. 1993. "Some Problems for Gibbard's Non-Expressivism." *Philosophical Studies* 69: 297–313.

———. 1996. "Limited Moral Skepticism." In Sinnott-Armstrong and Timmons, 1996.

Sinnott-Armstrong, W. and M. Timmons (eds.). 1996. *Moral Knowledge? New Readings in Moral Epistemology*. Oxford: Oxford University Press.

Slote, Michael. 1985. *Common-Sense Morality and Utilitarianism*. London: Routledge & Kegan Paul.

Smith, E. E. and D. L. Medin. 1981. *Categories and Concepts*. Cambridge, MA: Harvard University Press.

Smith, Michael. 1994. *The Moral Problem*. Oxford: Blackwell.

Snare, F. 1980. "The Diversity of Morals." *Mind* 89: 353–69.

Sober, E. 1982. "Realism and Independence." *Nous* 16: 369–85.

Sosa, Ernest. 1974. "How Do You Know?" *American Philosophical Quarterly* 11: 113–22. Reprinted in Sosa, 1991.

———. 1988. "Knowledge in Context, Skepticism in Doubt." *Philosophical Perspectives* 2: 139–57. Reprinted in Sosa, 1991.

———. 1991. *Knowledge in Perspective*. Cambridge: Cambridge University Press.

Spencer, Herbert. 1895. *The Principles of Ethics*. Vol. 1. New York: Appleton.

Stace, W. 1937. *The Concept of Morals*. New York: Macmillan.

Stevenson, C. L. 1937. "The Emotive Meaning of Ethical Terms." *Mind* 46: 21–25.

———. 1944. *Ethics and Language*. New Haven: Yale University Press.

———. 1948. "The Nature of Ethical Disagreement." In Stevenson, 1963.

———. 1963. *Facts and Values*. New Haven: Yale University Press.

———. 1966. "Ethical Fallibility." In Richard T. DeGeorge (ed.), *Ethics and Society*. Garden City, NY: Doubleday, 1966.

Stich, Stephen. 1992. "What Is a Theory of Mental Representation?" *Mind* 101: 243–61.

Stoljar, Daniel. 1993. "Emotivism and Truth Conditions." *Philosophical Studies* 70: 81–101.

Stout, J. 1993. "On Having a Morality in Common." In G. Outka and J. P. Reeder (eds.), *Prospects for a Common Morality*. Princeton: Princeton University Press, 1993.

Sturgeon, Nicholas. 1984. "Moral Explanations." In Copp and Zimmerman, 1984.

———. 1986. "What Difference Does It Make Whether Moral Realism Is True?" *Southern Journal of Philosophy* 24: 115–41. Supplementary volume on moral realism.

Throop, William. Unpublished. "Skepticism and Some Aims of Philosophy."

Throop, William and Katheryn Doran. 1991. "Putnam's Realism and Relativity: An Uneasy Balance." *Erkenntnis* 34: 357–69.

Tienson, John. 1987. "An Introduction to Connectionism." *Southern Journal of Philosophy* 26: 1–16.

———. 1989. "A Conception of Metaphysics." *American Philosophical Quarterly* 26: 63–71.

Timmons, Mark. 1987. "Foundationalism and the Structure of Justification in Ethics." *Ethics* 97: 595–609.

———. 1990a. "On the Epistemic Status of Considered Moral Judgments." In Timmons, 1990b: 97–129.

———. (ed.). 1990b. *Southern Journal of Philosophy* 29. Supplementary volume on moral epistemology.

———. 1991. "Putnam's Moral Objectivism." *Erkenntnis* 34: 371–99.

———. 1993a. "Irrealism and Error in Ethics." *Philosophia* 22: 373–406.

———. 1993b. "Moral Justification in Context." *The Monist* 76: 360–78.

———. 1996. "Outline of a Contextualist Moral Epistemology." In Sinnott-Armstrong and Timmons, 1996.

———. Forthcoming. "Logic and Ethics." *Routledge Encyclopedia of Philosophy*.

Tye, Michael. 1992. "Naturalism and the Mental." *Mind* 101: 421–41.

———. 1995. *The Ten Problems of Consciousness*. Cambridge, MA: MIT Press.

Unger, Peter. 1986. "The Cone Model of Knowledge." *Philosophical Topics* 14: 125–78.

———. 1995. "Contextual Analysis in Ethics." *Philosophy and Phenomenological Research* 55: 1–26.

Warnock, G. J. 1971. *The Object of Morality*. London: Methuen.

Wellman, C. 1971. *Challenge and Response: Justification in Ethics*. Carbondale, IL: Southern Illinois University Press.

Werner, Richard. 1983. "Ethical Realism." *Ethics* 93: 653–79.

White, Morton. 1950. "The Analytic and Synthetic: An Untenable Dualism." *John Dewey: Philosopher of Science and Freedom*. New York: Dial Press.

———. 1981. *What Is and What Ought to Be Done*. Oxford: Oxford University Press.

Williams, M. 1980. "Coherence, Truth and Justification." *Review of Metaphysics* 34: 243–72.

Wittgenstein, Ludwig. 1969. *On Certainty*. New York: Harper & Row.

Wong, David. 1984. *Moral Relativity*. Berkeley: University of California Press.

———. 1986. "On Moral Realism without Foundations." *Southern Journal of Philosophy* 24: 95–113.

Wright, Crispin. 1992. *Truth and Objectivity*. Cambridge, MA: Harvard University Press.

———. 1995. "Truth in Ethics." *Ratio* 8: 209–26.

Zangwill, Nick. 1997. "Explaining Supervenience: Moral and Mental." *Journal of Philosophical Research* 22: 509–18.

Index